The Atlantic Realists

THE ATLANTIC
REALISTS

*Empire and International Political Thought Between
Germany and the United States*

Matthew Specter

Stanford University Press
Stanford, California

STANFORD UNIVERSITY PRESS
Stanford, California

Printed in the United States of America on acid-free, archival-quality paper

Library of Congress Cataloging-in-Publication Data
Names: Specter, Matthew G. (Matthew Goodrich), 1968- author.
Title: The Atlantic realists : empire and international political thought between Germany and the United States / Matthew Specter.
Description: Stanford, California : Stanford University Press, 2022. | Includes bibliographical references and index.
Identifiers: LCCN 2021018692 | ISBN 9781503603127 (cloth) | ISBN 9781503629967 (paperback) | ISBN 9781503629974 (epub)
Subjects: LCSH: Political realism—History—20th century. | Balance of power—History—20th century. | Imperialism—History—20th century. | International relations—Philosophy. | Germany—Foreign relations—20th century. | United States—Foreign relations—20th century.
Classification: LCC JZ1307 .S64 2022 | DDC 327.101—dc23
LC record available at https://lccn.loc.gov/2021018692

Cover design: Rob Ehle

Cover image: Winslow Homer, *Northeaster* (1895; 1901), Metropolitan Museum of Art.

Typeset by Kevin Barrett Kane in Sabon LT Pro

For Marjan

Contents

Preface

We are living through a period of crisis in the transatlantic security relationship that has connected the United States to Germany since the end of World War II. It is not the first and will not be the last. But the peculiarities of this particular crisis are illuminated by the discussion of Atlantic realism I have undertaken in this book. When the Trump presidential campaign began to speak in 2016 of "America First," they were making a self-consciously historical gesture. They hearkened back to a time before the "globalists" and the "liberal internationalists" had won. The nativism and apologists for the Third Reich in the original America First movement did not trouble them; indeed, it added to the frisson of Trump the taboo-breaker. Under his administration, America's relations with all of its postwar allies were actively sabotaged or left to deteriorate. As Trump trash-talked NATO, it appeared that German chancellor Angela Merkel had a good claim to be the real leader of the so-called "free world." With her late and calculated decision to admit large numbers of refugees, she not only honored Germany's obligations under international law but affirmed that German citizenship was no longer based on blood. "Germanness" was attainable through naturalization. In the US, meanwhile, the Republican Party under Trump challenged constitutional guarantees of birthright citizenship that had long been taken for granted by both parties.

But the asymmetry between the current German and American political cultural moment is an illusion. In both countries, multiculturalism and liberal democracy are under siege from "identitarian" groups that insist on the impossible: the attainment of a homogenous nation, purged of "impurities." Minorities have been recast as foreign and parasitic. But in their quest for national purity the ascendant far-right groups are in fact able to build on old and new transnational linkages, many of which extend back decades. While liberals in the Euro-Atlantic world despair of the illiberal populism of Donald Trump and the crisis in transatlantic relations, far-right groups on both sides of the Atlantic are actively learning from one another. As right-wing mobs maraud through Charlottesville, Virginia, the German police are forced to confront far-right extremism in their own ranks. Underlying these developments, theorists of populism have detected the pursuit of "purity" with ethnic homogeneity and a closure of identity as its signature. Just as America Firsters, Tea Party patriots, and Border Wall builders concur that there is a pure American essence to be defended from demographic change, so do the newest iterations of the European far right bemoan the multicultural dissolution of both the national self and Western civilizational identity at large. To these rightists, the notion that our identities might already be hybrid or porous is a scandal. Debates, meanwhile, rage over whether Trump can be reasonably or profitably compared with Hitler, and more modestly, whether Trump's coziness with neo-Nazis and "white nationalists" signifies the emergence of fascism in an American key. All of these reversals—Good Americans, Bad Germans, Bad Americans, Good Germans—can make our Tarantino-filled heads spin.

One of this book's central themes suggests that the current crisis in the transatlantic relationship has a deeper meaning than merely the clash between neoliberal democracy and populist nationalism. As I argue, there is an elective affinity between a particular kind of national identity as the monologue of an ethnically homogenous majority (associated in the US with a waning sense of Anglo-Saxon whiteness) and the realist view that the national interest can be determined equally solipsistically. Americans often combine a paradoxical faith that their truths are universal and their provenance at the same time is exclusively national—the exceptional nation whose mission is universal. An investigation of the origins of this paradox can help us understand by contrast that there is no zero degree of American interest or American reflection on foreign policy. Instead, interest—just as identity—turns out to be the haphazard product of prodigious processes of borrowing. Much American reflection on its role on the world stage over the last century was the product of transatlantic intellectual exchange. While there are good reasons to emphasize the "special relationship" between the imperial democracies of the United States and Great Britain, and much attention has been paid to an "Anglo-American tradition" in foreign affairs, this book will empha- size the German-American tradition of international thought constructed by the thinkers I have named the Atlantic realists.

The ideas in this book have been gestating since I was a college stu- dent in the late 1980s. I was introduced to the realists and their ideas in a freshman seminar on ethics and foreign policy with Joseph Nye. One late night, I tapped into the keyboard of my first-generation Macintosh com- puter, "What is the national interest? Is it a kind of myth?" My skepticism about the totemic status of the idea of the national interest was amplified by my reading of Noam Chomsky's and Edward Herman's books, then a kind of *samizdat* literature. The shadow of nuclear apocalypse led me to the Nuclear Freeze protests in Central Park in 1982, and then to several years as a student critic and activist against Reagan's foreign policy in South Africa, Nicaragua, and El Salvador. Naming the United States as an empire broke the general taboos that existed in the academy and the political mainstream in the 1980s. I turned to French and German social theory for help in making sense of Reagan's Cold War America. These theoretical traditions inspired me to focus my undergraduate studies on intellectual history. As a doctoral student in European intellectual his- tory at Duke University, I experienced the national traumas of *Bush v. Gore* in 2000, the invasion of Iraq in 2003, and the excesses authorized by the War on Terror.

In previous work I have sought to reconstruct the legal, political, and social theory of Jürgen Habermas that underpins his liberal vision of a global order based on shared co-original commitments to democracy and human rights. This vision can be criticized as the last gasp of a Eurocen- tric conception of public reason or indeed the right-Hegelian ideology of American empire. But just as I spent the 2000s criticizing the "Schmit- tian" politics of George W. Bush and the neoconservatives of the Project for a New American Century, I simultaneously expressed my skepticism toward "left-Schmittian" critiques of Habermas's vision of peace, justice, and human rights under law. I, in any case, still prefer we deepen this unfinished project through immanent critique than reject it altogether.

This book is a work of historical reconstruction, but it is motivated by the normative aspiration to a world in which it is no longer common sense that the strong can do as they like and the weak do as they must. Whether this is a realistic utopia is beyond the ken of this book, but it is with these hopes in mind that it is written.

—Matthew Specter, March 2021

The Atlantic Realists

The Bildungsroman of Empire

> Throughout the history of the modern states system, there have been
> three competing traditions of thought: the Hobbesian or realist, which
> views international politics as a state of war; the Kantian or universalist,
> which sees at work in international politics a potential community
> of mankind; and the Grotian or internationalist, which views
> international politics as taking place within an international society.
> —Hedley Bull, 1977[1]

MANY DIFFERENT IDEAS have been labeled or claimed as "realist."
Like so many concepts in our political vocabulary, the term's meaning
is intensely contested. Who would not want to claim that theirs is a realistic view of politics? To shun realism in the commonsense meaning of
the term is to court the charge of idealism, naiveté, or utopianism. In the
field of international relations, however, the term "realist" (sometimes
rendered as "Realist") refers to a range of positions claimed by scholars
or intellectuals who self-identify, in whole or in part, along the spectrum
from "classical realism" to "neorealism."[2] The twentieth-century work
most responsible for consolidating "realism" as an identity for critics of
liberalism was E.H. Carr's withering polemic of 1939, *The Twenty Years'
Crisis*.[3] Contrary to its own name, the concept of classical realism was
only invented in Carr's wake, assembling a pantheon of ancestors from
ancients to moderns. The leading representatives of classical realism are
Hans Morgenthau, E.H. Carr, Reinhold Niebuhr, and Raymond Aron.

Stanley Hoffmann, the Harvard political scientist and connoisseur of
European politics, wrote in a brilliant 1977 essay on the evolution of international relations (subtitled "An American Social Science") that realist

scholars like himself were busy trying to ascertain whether growing global economic interdependence "shatters the 'realist' paradigm."[4] Two years later, Kenneth Waltz published his field-reshaping book, *The Theory of International Politics*, which is now regarded as the founding text of neorealism. Just as Hoffmann expressed a widely shared crisis of confidence among realists, Waltz set the wobbly paradigm on new foundations.[5]

In the decades since, fierce debates have occurred over whether Waltz's amendations of classical realism were much-needed refinements that strengthen it or a poor substitute for the original. Since the 1980s, critics have charged that realism is a "degenerating" research program that in patching holes in its own argument risks losing its identity in the process.[6] A profusion of modifiers—neorealist, structural realist, neoclassical realist—have subsequently been proposed to address the empirical critiques of its liberal institutionalist and constructivist rivals. Whether there is a coherent theoretical center to the tradition is a matter of ongoing controversy. As one of its finest historians, Nicolas Guilhot, has argued, "The realist project has three unresolvable, defining tensions: between realism and democracy, normative and descriptive, and power-maximizing vs. prudence."[7] Despite these profound constitutive tensions, realism has retained its prestige internationally as a major research program in political science and international relations. Given the cutting-edge trappings of this intradisciplinary debate, it is surprising to find that so many of the core concepts of realism—anarchy, tragedy, power politics, the national interest—have barely changed in over a century.

This book conducts a genealogy of the realist paradigm in North Atlantic international thought. By "international thought" I mean the political theory that explicitly or implicitly subtends the academic discipline of international relations, elite foreign policy discourse, and journalistic discourse on what constitutes "realism" in international affairs. How did intellectuals in these spheres come to believe that specific theories offered a privileged glimpse of international "reality"? Bringing the methods of the intellectual and cultural historian to the making of a realist tradition in the late nineteenth and twentieth centuries, this book argues that the entanglement of US and German historical experiences are the major tributaries of what I name the Atlantic realist tradition. Specifically, it focuses on how the German and American aspirations to empire and great power status—becoming a world power, in other words—were the crucible of the contemporary realist worldview. Realism was in this sense an ideological justification for empire. While it had ideological features, in the classical sociological sense of masking interests, it was also a set of mental habits and tools, what we may call a habitus. For much of the period covered by this book, from the 1880s to the 1980s, realism was not yet a formal academic theory. It was a sensibility and a discourse before it was formalized into the theories debated in the academy today. The predisciplinary development of realism is important beyond the academy, however. Despite its persistent normative and empirical weaknesses in the eyes of its critics, including this author, realism remains the default setting that prestructures most conversations about foreign policy and transatlantic relations in the United States. Why this is far less true in Germany today is another puzzle that this book seeks to solve.

Realism appears today to many US policymakers and "thought-leaders" as the only grand narrative remaining that can make sense of the world. As Guilhot observes,

> Interventions gone awry in the Middle East and a dangerous stand-off with Russia are today not condemned on the basis of anti-imperialist arguments or because they constitute breaches of international law. They are criticized because they ignore the basic precepts and wisdom of political realism.[8]

Nearly twenty years after the US invaded Iraq for the second time, neoconservatism is discredited.[9] The academic-cum-political revival of "realism" dates to the beginning of the Iraq War in 2003, when leading academic realists such as John Mearsheimer and Stephen Walt rightly opposed the war on the grounds that it was not in the US national interest.[10] When the Iraq war became an exhausting stalemate, policymakers began to give the "timeless wisdom" of classical realists like Hans Morgenthau a second look.[11] The rise of China and the new assertiveness of Russia under Putin since 2000 has further helped to bring an old notion back into fashion. Pundits increasingly describe a "return to great power competition" as the central motif of world politics. Geopolitics is also having a revival. As Robert Kaplan has argued, the end of history envisioned by Francis Fukuyama has yielded to "the revenge of geography."[12] While Putin indulges the Eurasian continentalist visions of the geopolitical intellectuals around him,[13] Trump and Biden are united in a worry about how to "contain" an expansionist China.[14] The frequent references to a "new cold war with China" reinforce the post–Iraq War consensus that the tradition of political thought in international affairs known as realism is having a renaissance. The Chinese have been reading the realists with interest too.[15]

After four years of incoherent and destructive policy-making under Donald Trump, many Atlantic security experts and policy practitioners wish to restore a less erratic form of American hegemony. The self-described classical realist IR scholar Patrick Porter criticizes those who view American empire as a "benign dispensation." He argues that the notion of a "rules-based liberal international order" is a myth that conceals the assumption of American primacy internationally. In contrast to those nostalgic for a restoration of the frayed liberal order, Porter counsels America to eschew its own myths of liberal order and pursue a power politics without illusions.[16]

Trump led a revolt against the "traditional" US role in the world, but the tradition of world "leadership" is only seventy years old. Trump's message resonated because of the exhaustion of large sections of the American public with twenty-five years of unipolarity and war. As historian and commentator retired Col. Andrew Bacevich observed, Trump's America First nationalism, which articulated frustration with elite-led globalization, created a rare opportunity for the United States to rethink its commitment to global military supremacy.[17]

Although leading US policymakers since World War II have often claimed the mantle of realism, the relationship of realism to US foreign policy in the Cold War is complex. While George Kennan, author of the "containment doctrine," considered himself, for example, part of the realist intellectual tradition, the precise meaning of realism in his thought remained "elusive" and was interpreted in highly divergent ways, often to Kennan's chagrin.[18] A similar pattern occurred with Morgenthau, whose great influence was matched by regret and eventually an effort to distance himself from the "Realism" he worked so tirelessly to create.[19] In their writings both Kennan and Morgenthau contributed to "realist" practices of the Cold War with which they personally dissented. The realists moved in and out of the driver seat and were often sidelined. The combined impact of Kennan, Morgenthau, and Henry Kissinger—who influenced every president from Eisenhower to Nixon and beyond—confirms the import of realism as a paradigm for Cold War and post–Cold War US policymaking. But major questions concerning the internal coherence of "realism" remain.[20]

Part of the complexity of determining the exact influence of the realists during the Cold War stems from the fact that many of the Cold Warriors were at once realists and liberals. By contrast, the academic tradition defines the two traditions as opposing poles. Already the leading classical realists of the twentieth century, E.H. Carr, Hans Morgenthau, Reinhold Niebuhr, Herbert Butterfield, and Arnold Wolfers described "liberalism" as their chief rival and opponent.[21] The first generation of classical realists, between 1939 and 1954, framed their arguments as a critique of Wilsonianism and a broader interwar "idealism" about the ability of the League of Nations and other international institutions to abolish war or mitigate serious conflicts. But this realism-liberalism dichotomy has made it hard to see the historical overlap between realism and liberalism before, during, and since the Cold War.

The anti-liberal, anti-idealist account of the interwar period was nonetheless central to the story the fledgling US field of international relations told itself beginning in the mid-1950s. With both feet firmly planted on realist ground the new discipline was said to have vanquished the idealists in a "great debate."[22] An important wave of revisionist historiography has since shown that many aspects of this realist origins story is incorrect. Interwar European, and especially British, thought was neither as idealistic and impractical as the realists depicted it, nor had a dialogic debate ever occurred.[23] Recent scholarship on Woodrow Wilson has similarly complicated this picture by pointing out that the realism-liberalism dichotomy obscured the extent to which Wilson was guided by his conception of the national interest, not universal principles.[24] National self-determination was not a blank check that any people could cash. A strict racial and civilizational hierarchy marked those who were fit to rule themselves. Wilson believed himself a realist when it came to race relations at home and abroad. As Beate Jahn has explained, realism is from this vantage point the disavowed shadow-side of liberalism. Realism ascribed a naivete and utopianism to liberalism, while liberals themselves had their own reasons for disavowing their will to power.[25]

From World War II until at least the early 1980s, writes Jahn, realism was "generally taken to be . . . the dominant theoretical and practical paradigm for International Relations."[26] Beginning in the 1950s, the realists also began to construct an intellectual pedigree for themselves. They anchored the "American Century" heralded by Henry Luce with the ballast of an invented tradition. As Guilhot writes, in the 1940s and 1950s, the realists "conscripted Thucydides, Machiavelli, Hobbes and Augustine into the role of precursors or pioneers of a realist tradition that soon became central to the disciplinary lore—even though some of these authors had never been considered 'realists' until then."[27] By the 1980s and 1990s, Robert Keohane, one of the leading neorealists of the time, articulated the assumption then widely shared in the field: there is a unitary realist tradition that connects Thucydides to Morgenthau.[28] The claim that realism's deep roots in Western thought disclose perennial truths seems to imply that the international realm has not changed much in twenty-five hundred years. Despite the shift from agrarian to industrial societies, the emergence of the modern state, the rise and globalization of capitalism, and the history of imperialism and decolonization, the international realm is said to have retained the fundamentally anarchic character that justifies realism's generally pessimistic conclusions about international cooperation.

In his 2001 volume *The Tragedy of Great Power Politics*, Mearsheimer emphasizes this pessimistic cyclical philosophy of history.

> The sad fact is that international politics has always been a ruthless and dangerous business, and it is likely to remain that way. Although the intensity of their competition waxes and wanes, great powers fear each other and always compete with each other for power. The overriding goal of each state is to maximize its share of world power,

which means gaining power at the expense of other states. But great powers do not merely strive to be the strongest of all the great powers, although that is a welcome outcome. Their ultimate aim is to be the hegemon—that is, the only great power in the system.[29]

In some respects, Mearsheimer's book merely recapitulates some of the fundamental motifs, tropes, and gestures of a century of realist thought. Often inadvertently, many of us utilize a vocabulary of international politics and foreign policy that depicts the international arena as anarchic and dangerously ungovernable, pregnant with danger and uncertainty, but ultimately knowable: a world where the weak do what they must and the strong do what they can, as Thucydides wrote.

International relations theory, obsessed as it is with paradigmatic truths, has paradoxically until recently lacked much interest in its own intellectual-historical roots. In the last twenty years, however, scholars of international history have become more interested in ideas, and intellectual history has been internationalized.[30] This has been described by leading practitioners as the "dawn of a historiographical trend" in international relations and the end of a "fifty years' rift" between international relations and history.[31] The writing of the history of international intellectual history, or the history of international thought, is now in full swing. One of the most impressive fruits of this historiography has been the revision of our understanding of both the liberal internationalist and realist traditions.[32]

Historians of "realism" in particular have in the process sought to dislodge Thucydides, Machiavelli, Hobbes, and other alleged precursors of twentieth-century realist thought from the Procrustean bed of a unified "Western tradition."[33] As others have remarked, realism seems to suffer from a broader failure of international relations theory to recognize its Eurocentrism.[34] Postcolonial critiques of international relations have begun to reconnect realism to its European roots. But the work of provincializing realism has really only begun.[35] This book joins this literature in articulating the ways in which the Atlantic realists mistook a Western tradition for a universal one. The IR realist tradition constructed in the United States over the last several decades considers great power politics the basso continuo of human history, turning an artifact of the post-Westphalian European-dominated globe into universal truth. This historiography of realism challenges the view of realism as a continuous tradition with deep roots in Western history and insights of permanent value for understanding international and global affairs.

Provincializing Realism: Historicizing the Midcentury Modern

The revisionist historians of international relations who have highlighted realism's midcentury moment of self-fashioning underscore the provincial nature of Western realism. We now know that the realism which shaped US conduct and conceptualization of the Cold War was, in large part, the work of German or German-speaking émigrés formed by particular European experiences. The émigrés of this generation, who formed the central players in the new discipline of international relations, most prominently, Hans Morgenthau (1905–1980), John Herz (1908–2005), and Arnold Wolfers (1892–1968), had been trained in law. They brought from Weimar Germany an obsession with its fragility, and as Martti Koskenniemi argued twenty years ago, projected these anxieties about Weimar law onto international law *in toto*.[36] Even before the United States entered WWII, American scholars began planning for the world they hoped would follow successful conclusion of the war. They argued for the necessity of a new "realism" about the role of power in international affairs. Guilhot has shown how the Rockefeller Foundation "excluded scholars associated with the study of international law and organizations. More importantly, it firmly located the interest in theory within a network of scholars and practitioners committed to the study of power politics."[37] From strongholds at Yale, Princeton, and the University of Chicago, and with the support of major foundations like the Rockefeller Foundation, the realists attempted to consolidate a discipline of international relations with realism as its guiding philosophy and raison d'être.[38] While they failed to stem the coming tide of the behavioral revolution, Morgenthau still was the discipline's leading public intellectual and "founding father."[39]

Alfons Söllner, Martti Koskenniemi, Nicolas Guilhot, Udi Greenberg, Jana Puglierin, Daniel Bessner, Felix Rösch, and Jeremy Suri have taught us that the midcentury modern version of classical realism was a response to a profoundly felt, but historically specific, crisis of liberal institutions and values.[40] Their emphasis on the force of the intellectual emigration from Germany to the US in the 1930s and 1940s has helped to draw attention to the way in which twentieth-century realists fashioned a self-narrative of their own discipline. But as I will argue in this book, by making the sea change of the American mind in the 1940s and 1950s the key moment of realism's consolidation, we risk replacing one myth with another: Realism derived much of its prestige in the last seventy years from a certain understanding of the tradition's origins. The cachet of the midcentury modern Atlantic realists derived, in part, from their status as émigrés from Nazi Germany. The realists' teachings were rightly said to reflect their experience as witnesses to the collapse of European liberalism in the 1930s. Their realism was its bitter fruit. Realism was the saving remnant of the greatest tragedy in modern history. The realists were the heroic protagonists of a redemptive narrative according to which liberalism would shed its illusions and emerge stronger.

The revisionists have brilliantly situated realism in its midcentury modern form. But this is not sufficient to prevent a new myth from taking hold. My book tells a different—complementary but also corrective—story that instead places realism's formative development earlier, in the 1880s and 1890s. The thinkers I examine there—Alfred Thayer Mahan, Friedrich Ratzel, Paul S. Reinsch, and Archibald Coolidge—are the first generation of the "Atlantic realist" tradition.[41] This was the period in which both Germany and the United States had achieved rapid industrialization and seeded ambitions to attain greater status through expanded naval power. The "competitive globalization" of late nineteenth-century nation-states was the main context in which the Atlantic realist tropes of great power competition as a Darwinian struggle first took shape. It was the era of imperialist globalization that gave realism its first stamp, not the crisis of liberalism in the 1930s. Stressing the imprint of fin de siècle concepts of *Lebensraum* and *Weltpolitik*, both cut from a Social Darwinian cloth, offers a different narrative than the alleged rediscovery of Bismarckian *Realpolitik* after disillusionment with Wilsonian idealism. Realism was thus in the first instance not the hard-won ideology of the victims of empire, nor the wisdom of those who had the courage to face the truths it disclosed. Instead, developing from the 1880s to the 1980s and beyond, this book tells the story of the relationships, both biographical and conceptual, between intellectuals in Germany and the US. The Atlantic realists presented themselves as objective diagnosticians of "great power politics," but reconstructing the German-American intellectual dialogue over the course of the century also highlights their role as expansionary ideologists of empire.

My decision to reconnect the 1930s to the 1890s is supported by the revisionist wave in the British historiography of international relations already mentioned. The leading historians of American international relations, Brian Schmidt and Robert Vitalis, have similarly redirected our gaze to the late nineteenth century, when the first course on world politics was offered in the US (at the University of Wisconsin in 1900) and the journal *Foreign Affairs* was still known by its Victorian-era title, *The Journal of Race Development*.[42] Charles Maier and Michael Geyer have redirected our attention to the 1860s and 1870s as the time when the modern nation-state first conquered the world. Maier has argued that the notion of a "short twentieth century" from 1914 to 1989 articulates the way "dramatic moments structure . . . our moral narratives," but urges us "to keep a different tempo and follow long-term processes."[43] The year 1945 was the beginning of the recivilization of the German people. But it was the 1890s that taught the Americans the practice of overseas empire as much as it had the Germans.[44]

It is true that the idea of raison d'état, or realism about "national interest," predates the 1890s in Europe and elsewhere.[45] Morgenthau often claimed that the American founders knew what subsequent generations of Americans forgot.[46] Mahan reached back to George Washington for his notion of an international order governed by natural law—the "nature of things" was the phrase Mahan borrowed from him. And both Mahan and Carl Schmitt looked to the 1823 Monroe Doctrine for a model of imperial hegemony applicable to the twentieth century. The importance of the Monroe Doctrine gives grounds for thinking that the roots of Atlantic realism are even earlier than the 1890s, but the periodization employed in this book has a clear rationale. As Charles Maier has argued, the history of the nation-state form—of "Leviathan 2.0"—spans from the

1870s to the 1970s. Other scholars of adjacent discourses have alighted on the same periodization. Koskenniemi's history of the rise and fall of international law traces an arc from 1870 to 1960. Robert Vitalis's history of the American discipline of international relations also begins in the 1880s and takes the story into the 1970s.

Conceptualizing realism as a predominantly transatlantic and German-American affair builds on the provincializing work of the revisionists but makes three fundamental innovations. First, the Germanization of the American mind that occurred in the middle of the twentieth century does not exhaust the transatlantic story. The flow of ideas went in both directions. To highlight two examples discussed in depth in the book, in the 1890s, German naval elites translated Mahan and learned much from him. Geographer Friedrich Ratzel formulated his influential theory of "*Lebensraum*" in 1900 after extensive travel in and study of the United States in its own "sphere of influence." Neither Wilhelm II's concept of an imperialism oriented to the sea, *Weltpolitik*, nor the interwar discourses on *Lebensraum* that fed into the Third Reich's official ideology, would have been possible without Ratzel, Mahan, and their experiences in America. Both the Foreign Office in the Third Reich, as well as legal theorists like Carl Schmitt and Wilhelm Grewe, devoted extensive commentary to the Monroe Doctrine; Hitler adopted the notion of a "Germanic Monroe Doctrine" as a way to describe German hegemony on the European continent. Realism's Atlantic crossings were a two-way street.

Second, realism is not the direct descendant of *Realpolitik*. As we know from excellent recent scholarship, *Realpolitik* was coined by Ludwig Rochau (1810–1873) in 1853.[47] It only became associated with Bismarck by later historians. In fact, as John Bew has argued, Bismarck never actually used the term.[48] While some American realists like Kissinger and Kennan found inspiration in Bismarck's practice of balancing Great Power competition, realism is not, in my account, really about balance. But my account departs from Bew's in major respects.[49] In contrast to the conventional view that realism is a form of *Realpolitik*, I argue that the first Atlantic realists were more influenced by the German term *Weltpolitik*, which developed in the 1890s as a counter-concept to the more conservative, status quo–oriented theory of *Realpolitik*. Realism in the fin-de-siècle Atlantic world was more informed by Social Darwinist ideas of dynamism, appetite, and mastery than Rochauian ideas of balance and equilibrium. This is the source of the view of human nature as a quest for dominance (*animus dominandi*) made axiomatic by Morgenthau. The leitmotif of all the Atlantic realists was a view of history as the struggle over power—not visions of balancing, prudential ethics, or a sense of the tragic.

Third, by reconnecting the discourses of the 1930s to those of the 1890s, I am able to tie the discussion of realism to the historiography of classical geopolitics.[50] While historians locate the origins of what is conventionally referred to as "classical geopolitics" between 1890 and 1910, they withhold the label "realist" until WWI.[51] The connection would seem to follow naturally from the hypothesis that American realism descended from German *Realpolitik*, but none of the intellectual biographies of Morgenthau or Herz trace the roots of their ideas to figures associated with geopolitics like the Briton Halford Mackinder, the Swede who coined the term, Rudolf Kjellén (1864–1922), or the doyen of Weimar geopolitics, Karl Haushofer (1869–1946). The self-image of realism was so distinct from geopolitics—and geopolitics so unfamiliar in the public sphere—that a veritable media panic erupted about geopolitics in America in 1942. Articles in *Life* and *Reader's Digest* obsessed about a geopolitical science that they imagined as a distinctly German "superweapon behind Hitler."[52] The implication that the US had never acted geopolitically was absurd. But the American denial that it shared a common Atlantic patrimony—that geopolitics was as much British and American as German—speaks volumes. The idea of realism in the US in the 1940s became a semantic refuge from a geopolitics tarnished by its association with the Nazi enemy.

Entangled Empires: A Transnational Intellectual History of Germany and the United States

The intellectuals, academic theories, and public discourses treated in this book provide a sharp lens on the development of an Atlantic realist tradition of international thought. The book argues that the two historiographies of foreign relations and intellectual history are illuminated better through the transnational lens than separately. Americans and Germans repeatedly denied the entangled nature of their thought, claiming the ideas as irreducibly German or American. This points to yet another paradox of realism. Over the course of a century, from 1848 to 1945, the German language developed a plethora of concepts to describe international politics: these included *Realpolitik, Machtpolitik, Weltpolitik, Großraum,* and *Lebensraum.* But none of these concepts was formulated in a national vacuum. Likewise, the history of "realism" in the American discipline of international relations and US foreign policy has been similarly sundered from its global roots. "Realism vs. idealism," "Anglo-American vs. continental," "American exceptionalism vs. German exceptionalism"—each of these framings has obscured the fact that this philosophy of the national interest was not national: it was a German-American coproduction.

This book focuses on moments when intellectuals in the US and Germany connected and produced thinking about the state and its international role that I call "Atlantic realism." Atlantic realism, in my transatlantic German-American sense, enables a focus on moments of connection and exchange between the two national experiences. These connections are not necessary for the work of comparative history, but they enable comparisons that are particularly meaningful. Not every aspect or chapter in the history of American and German empire in the twenYes, tieth century can be meaningfully compared; of course, the Holocaust has unique qualities in modern history that should not—and need not—be effaced by the study of comparative genocide. Nonetheless, and however one connects the experience of American and Nazi continental imperialism, the two modern nation-states have imperial histories that are not just kindred but entangled.[53] While at times uncomfortable to contemplate, the connection between the German and American empires in the twentieth century mitigates the temptation to treat either history as exceptionally virtuous or pathologically deviant from a purported liberal norm.[54]

In recent years, historians of US foreign relations have taught us to see the territorial dimensions of the US empire as an archipelago of islands and bases, or a "pointillist empire" not captured on the traditional continental map of the US. They have also shown us that foreign policy elites, many of German origin, were determined to insulate certain kinds of decision-making from too much democracy.[55] Military history has taught us how comparable and connected the naval ambitions of elites in Germany and the US were before WWI.[56] At the same time, historians of German empire (1870–1918), the Third Reich, and the Holocaust, but also other areas of German history, have made the transnational connection to the United States the fulcrum of their interpretations.[57] Since the mid-1990s, historians of German colonialism finally broke through the strictures of the *Sonderweg* narrative, arguing that the German colonial experience was as integral to the history of Germany as their respective colonial empires were to metropolitan Britain and France. Today, one of the field's leading scholars, Geoff Eley, argues that the links between "colonialism overseas and twentieth century expansionism inside Europe itself are too clear to ignore": they have become "noncontroversial."[58] German imperialists of the late nineteenth century considered America the model empire.[59] Eley's most recent programmatic guidance for the field concludes: "In recovering the genealogies of Nazism, it is to the connective dynamics of the period between the 1890s and the 1930s that we should look."[60] The writings of these scholars convinced me that the Nazi spatial imaginary was rooted in the "German Atlantic" of the 1880s and 1890s.[61] In the process my attention was directed away from the 1930s and 1940s and instead back to an earlier period in search of realism's deeper roots.

The Atlantic realists worked within, and across, a range of fields of international thought including geopolitics, naval theory, geography, law, diplomacy, and political science. The first generation of Atlantic realists considered the American and German empires highly comparable: both were poised to attain the rank of a "world power," and both deserved this elevated status. The Atlantic realists engaged in practices of comparison that had tangible effects. These intellectual practices accentuated national rivalries but also created a seemingly objective criterion by which to determine "reasonable" behavior in international politics.[62] However, something about the practice of ranking nations and the practice of comparison caused a mutation in thought. Realism was this mutation. It was founded on a practice of comparing that took the globe as a fully knowable space in which rank could be clearly established.

Realism was the linguistic shorthand that developed to capture this *savoir-faire*, the "knowing how" to act like a world power. In principle this knowledge was open to all. Only later did realist motifs become combined with narratives that insisted on the exceptional character of American or German nationhood and empire. The sympathy of American writers at the turn of the century such as Mahan, Reinsch, and Coolidge for the Germans' appetite for empire is a jarring revelation. Together, they disputed the Anglo-American alliance, forming a new "special relationship" instead. There was temporal synchronicity in the two countries' world-historical position that led them to recognize the other as a peer. Realism resulted from this practice of comparison and reflection on the national self.

The first Atlantic realists authored the *Bildungsroman* of German and American empire. Begun as an intra-Atlantic project of imperial comparison, realism dates to a moment when the world began to feel to many observers as if it had lost its frontier zones. Just as the world became knowable in its totality, a closed space, intellectuals and statesmen and citizens wanted tools with which to grasp this world whole and make sense of it. Over the course of a century, from 1880 to 1980, this realism evolved and transformed under the pressure of WWI and the interwar crisis, WWII and the Holocaust, the Cold War and détente. The "science" of geopolitics, discussed in chapters 2 and 5, was one such tool. The realist language of international politics, discussed in chapters 3, 4, 6, and 7, was another. The synchronicity of the two countries' historical positions at the turn of the century was upended by two world wars. A wholly asymmetrical relation of power took its place. After 1945, the American empire championed discourses of realism and geopolitics that were regarded with deep suspicion by Germans. By the early 1970s, Atlantic realists in Germany began to protest that Germany could and should relearn power politics. If it could not be a world power of the first rank, it should at least outgrow the progressive-liberal illusions that had become fashionable during the heyday of Social Democracy and détente-oriented "peace research."

Max Weber, Carl Schmitt, and Hans Morgenthau are the most familiar figures from the canon of international political thought treated here.

Scholars have studied the Weimar roots of Morgenthau's ideas, emphasizing his relation to Nietzsche and Freud but also Weber and Schmitt. But these figures of the canon are too often abstracted from the transnational Atlantic intellectual and political contexts I reconstruct and analyze here. My work builds on the voluminous German- and English-language literature on Schmitt and Morgenthau, and offers a new interpretation of the Schmitt-Morgenthau relationship. I examine thinkers from a wide range of disciplinary and institutional locations where intellectuals created conceptions of international politics. The major protagonists of the chronologically ordered chapters that follow, in the order of appearance, are: Friedrich Ratzel, Max Weber, Paul Reinsch, Archibald Coolidge, and Alfred Mahan (chapter 1); Karl Haushofer, Isaiah Bowman, and Ellen Semple (chapter 2); Carl Schmitt (chapter 3); Wilhelm Grewe (chapter 4); Haushofer and Bowman (once more), Edmund J. Walsh, and Nicholas Spykman (chapter 5); Hans Morgenthau (chapter 6); Morgenthau and Grewe (once more), Ernst-Otto Czempiel, and Hans-Peter Schwarz (chapter 7).

Why does the book describe the United States and Germany as the major representatives of a realist tradition conceived as "Atlantic"? Comparable studies could be written for Britain and France and other European countries. There are significant British and French figures, like E.H. Carr and Raymond Aron, who would enrich a study of realism's Atlantic crossings. But the particularly intense dialogue between US and German thinkers was not replicated by Anglo-American, British-French, or French-German exchanges. While there are major French realists, like Raymond Aron, Morgenthau's relationship with Aron was superficial and left no mark on his work.[63] Moreover, the Anglo-American dialogue has already been well researched.[64] The US-German story does not preclude other mappings of the flow of ideas in the North Atlantic. Nonetheless, recognizing the cultural specificity of the American-German synthesis is, I hope to show, one major step toward the provincialization of a major tradition in Western intellectual history, a task in service of a more pluralistic and cosmopolitan perspective on global problems.

This book addresses the questions that are addressed under the rubrics of "great power politics" and "geopolitics," but it differs from others by inquiring how these categories came to be in the first place.

Reconstructing the genesis and itinerary of the concepts associated with realism—in the academic discipline of IR and in the public sphere—this is a study of the intellectual history of political ideas about the international realm.[65] My approach is genealogical. It looks for the origins, development, and transformation of ideas that were self-consciously labeled "realist" or cognates like "realistic" by politicians, intellectuals, the military, and civilian bureaucracies in the US and Germany, over the course of a century. The story it tells is filled with ironies and reversals, borrowings and forgettings, recognition of affinities and denial. It offers an account of how realism, a public philosophy of power and its exercise, achieved a dominant place in the political imagination of the North Atlantic democracies, and global resonance beyond.

Realism is an intellectual tradition of global importance, but not for the reasons that are usually given. It is not a storehouse of accumulated historical "wisdom," but rather a historical artifact—and one that has, tragically, exerted too much power over world politics. This book reconstructs the mental universe of the realists in order to loosen their spell. Atlantic realists succeeded beyond their wildest dreams in turning a local history into a universal one. They turned realism from a European varietal of empire-talk into the global common sense of the international realm. Historicizing this common sense, and subjecting it to rigorous normative and contextual critique, can help to emancipate ourselves from realism's tyranny over the political imagination.

Seeing like a World Power

The German-American Synthesis

BETWEEN 1895 AND 1898, German and American conceptions of world politics changed fundamentally. The decision in 1896 by the German chancellor to launch *Weltpolitik*, a politics oriented to the global projection of power, capped one decade of German-American rivalry and inaugurated a second. Meanwhile, American renegotiation of its relationship with Great Britain after 1895 and its victory in the Spanish-American War in 1898 led many US observers to announce a new epoch in US history. The United States had finally emerged as a "world power," a power of the first "rank" on the "world stage." These dramatic announcements concealed the emptiness of the signifier "world power." Intellectuals rushed in to articulate the requirements of national "greatness" in an era of "world politics." The discourse on world power and world politics was part of what Geoff Eley has called the "empire talk" of the 1890s, and what Sönke Neitzel and Dirk Bönker have discussed as the *Weltreichslehre.*[1] Faced with uncertainty and anxiety about the demands of this new global epoch, German and American intellectuals turned toward each other. They were, after all, both "rising" powers in comparison with Great Britain. In a complex dialectic of recognition and denial of their comparability, American and German thinkers became a team of rivals. For Germans and Americans interested in competing with one another and with Great Britain, a transatlantic practice of comparison helped intellectuals envision what it meant to be a power of the first rank.

A transatlantic exchange of ideas among four thinkers helped this practice of imperial comparison to develop. Together, the Germans, Max Weber and Friedrich Ratzel, and the Americans, Paul Reinsch and Alfred Mahan, created a language of *Weltpolitik*. They concurred that for a nation to be a "great power," it also had to be a sea power of the first rank. Friedrich Ratzel argued that due to an epochal shift in the 1890s the Germans needed a "truer *Realpolitik*" more adequate to the times. The first Atlantic realism resulted from this perceived need for a new language of international politics. German discourses on *Weltpolitik* and *Lebensraum* were nourished by American sources and experiences, and ultimately Americanized, as discourses on "world power" and the "nature" of international relations. The writings of Alfred Mahan between 1890 and 1912 are one of the key sites where a German discourse on *Lebensraum*, namely, Ratzel's Darwinian notion of a perennial struggle for space, fused with notions of the global scale of imperial competition drawn from *Weltpolitik*. The synthesis, worked out through reflection on the evolutionary character of the Monroe Doctrine, was a discourse on international relations as an aspect of "nature." Realism did not descend from *Realpolitik* but from its competitor, *Weltpolitik*. This genealogy helps us to appreciate the change in the scale of thought from continental to global. Realism was a tool for acting on the "world stage."

German Empire by Land or by Sea: *Weltpolitik or Lebensraum?*

"Empire talk," specifically discussions of how and why to aspire to the status of a "great world empire," dominated intellectual discussion in the German public sphere from the mid-1880s to the outbreak of World War I. In this German *Weltreichslehre*, or discourse on the "world empires," Great Britain, Russia, and the United States were always ranked among the top three empires. France was sometimes included as the fourth, but Germany usually took its place.[2] *Weltreichslehre* dictated a stark choice: attain parity with the US, Britain, and Russia, or face rapid decline and ruin. For the *Kaiserreich*, the major strategic foreign policy question was whether "greatness" would be attained overseas via colonies, through the expansion of trade, or within Europe, through territorial expansion of a German-dominated trading region (*Zollverein*). The Kaiser's 1896 speech on the twenty-fifth anniversary of the founding of the Reich, announcing Germany's arrival as a "world power," was a turning point in modern German history. "Germany's future lies on the sea!" he said. *Weltpolitik* dominated from 1896 to 1911 but never fully displaced German objectives to achieve dominance on the continent. The projects of empire by land or empire by sea competed for primacy but were not mutually exclusive. While the battle lines hardened around 1904/5, it was not until 1911 that the government reverted to the more orthodox vision of an armaments-based policy, after the navy's long dominance.[3] The ideology of the Pan-German League, which scholars have long associated with the rejection of capitalist *Weltpolitik* in favor of continental objectives, did not refuse overseas colonies as much as an earlier generation of scholars thought.[4] The partisans of empire by land or by sea did not fall into neat camps.[5] Still, in the 1890s, there was a pronounced paradigm shift from land to sea power as the way of the future. Intellectuals in both countries set to work defining what *Weltpolitik* entailed for national and international politics.

Weltpolitik and *Lebensraum* are the two most important concepts in the first Atlantic realist synthesis of the fin de siècle. Both concepts have a transatlantic pedigree. Friedrich Ratzel's thought promiscuously partook of both. By doing so, he catalyzed the demand for a new political language that could encompass both ideas. The various projects for a globalized Greater Germany, reflected in the terms *Weltpolitik* and *Lebensraum*, made Rochau's *Realpolitik*, a continent-focused term, seem inadequate. Only a "truer *Realpolitik*," to employ Ratzel's phrase, could do justice to the dynamism of the modern world. They argued that *Realpolitik*, with its emphasis on balance over struggle, the continent versus the globe, seemed outdated.

Realpolitik vs. *Weltpolitik*: A Generational Struggle?

In 1897, Friedrich Ratzel wrote an essay on the so-called "Fleet Question," which posited the dichotomy between "continental" and "world powers" as the driving force of discussions that culminated in realism:

> There will be peoples who rule and peoples who serve . . . Whether they [i.e., we Germans] become one or the other depends on their recognizing the demands which the world situation presents . . . Prussia's task in the 18th—to win for itself a position as a major power in the middle of the European continental powers—was different from that of Germany in the 19th century: to win a place among the world powers. This task can no longer be solved in Europe alone;

it is only as a world [i.e., global] power that Germany can hope to secure for its people the land which it needs for its growth.[6]

He explained how the turn to *Weltpolitik* represented a break with *Realpolitik*—a turn to a "truer *Realpolitik*":

The policy that recognizes the more distant goals towards which the state strives, and for this reason secures for the growing nation (*Volk*) the necessary land for its future, is a truer *Realpolitik* than that which bears this name because it accomplishes only that which is immediately tangible, for the sake of the present day alone.

To understand how *Realpolitik* became associated with Bismarck and continental balance deserves some brief attention. August Rochau coined the concept of "Realpolitik" in his 1853 work, *Foundations of Realpolitik: Applied to the Current State of Germany*.[7] Rochau was a German liberal disillusioned with the failure of the March 1848 revolution.[8] At the time he wrote *Foundations*, Rochau was part of the Progressive Party, an umbrella group for liberal and radical opponents of the monarchy, and a critic of Bismarck. By the time he published the second volume in 1868, the Progressive Party split, and Rochau became a founding member of the National Liberals, the faction that supported Bismarck.[9] Even before his death, Rochau's liberalism was forgotten and the concept came to be chiefly associated with the right (68). After the achievement of unification, Bismarck's priority was to maintain balance and equilibrium in Europe. Bismarck's sudden decision to acquire colonies in the period April 1884 to February 1885 was half-hearted; he believed in an overseas presence for raw materials, markets, trading posts, and investment, but generally shunned colonies as unprofitable.

The great German sociologist Max Weber (1864–1920), often identified as a representative of political realism in twentieth-century thought, shunned the *Realpolitik* he associated with Bismarck. According to the classic study by Wolfgang Mommsen, "[the] young Weber recognized the unfortunate side of naïve 'Bismarckism'; the uncritical admiration of mere power and purposeless Realpolitik."[10] Weber had his own understanding of a truly effective "*Realpolitik*." He was scathing toward what he called the "so-called modern German '*Realpolitiker*,'" or "today's ignorant philistines of *Realpolitik*."[11] In an 1887 letter regarding the historian Heinrich von Treitschke (1834–1896), Weber wrote: "If my generation did not already worship militarism and other monstrosities, the culture of so-called 'realism' . . . a predilection for what is now called *Realpolitik* that has arisen under the compelling impact of success would not be the only things they take with them from Treitschke's classes."[12]

Weber's famous Freiburg Inaugural Address of 1895, "Nation-State and Economic Policy," anticipated Ratzel's opposition to an older continent-focused *Realpolitik* and shift to a newer, globe-facing *Weltpolitik*. In 1898, Weber described the founding of the Reich as the "first step . . . on the path to a world power position."[13] Weber believed that national power depended on mature leadership capable of grasping the requirements of modern politics, such as overseas imperialism. Weber criticized the unification of Germany in 1871 as a "youthful prank carried out by the nation in its old age," and added, "[better] undone if it was to be the beginning rather than the end of the nation's involvement in world politics."[14] Overseas expansion was a "positive political task," shunned only by ignorant "philistines" (25).

In his Freiburg address, Weber clearly drew from both Darwinism and Nietzsche. "We do not have peace and human happiness to hand down to our descendants, but rather the eternal struggle to preserve and raise the quality of our national species . . . Our successors will hold us answerable to history not primarily for the kind of economic organization we hand down to them, but for the amount of elbow-room in the world which we conquer and bequeath to them" (16–17). By rejecting *Realpolitik* and Bismarck alike in his 1895 essay, Weber subverted a whole tradition associated with Rochau and landed continental power, in favor of sea power and *Weltpolitik*. While Weber found certain aspects of Treitschke distasteful, in matters of empire he agreed with Treitschke that Britain's naval supremacy must yield to what Treitschke called "a fairer and therefore more 'moral' distribution of power relationships" in the world.[15]

Treitschke's concept of *Weltpolitik* signified a break with a foreign policy exclusively oriented to the continent. With his demands for a fleet capable of conquering England in the 1870s, Treitschke was an outlier;

by the 1890s, however, his one-time student Tirpitz was in a position to advance the theory to practice. In 1876, Treitschke advanced the very un-Bismarckian notion "[that] only the sea-faring nations and the rulers of overseas territories could be counted among the 'great powers of the earth.'"[16] Treitschke closely linked maritime power, world power, and national greatness, emphasizing that "possession of overseas lands and maritime greatness, without which a truly great power would not exist nowadays, will remain out of the reach even of united Germany for a long time" (159).[17] According to one colonial activist who had attended Treitschke's lectures, Treitschke contrasted the "higher aims of a world power" with the "narrow-minded policy of a continental great power" (164).[18] The dichotomies that underlie the influential writings of Weber and Ratzel from the 1890s were pioneered by Treitschke in the 1870s. This genealogy helps us understand why *Weltpolitik*, an insurgent counter-concept to *Realpolitik*, was at times confused with it. Its partisans would have to fight their way free of the older concept.

Treitschke was a major influence on leading figures in the Wilhelmine military and diplomatic establishment, including Johannes von Moltke, chief of the General Staff in 1914; Bernhard von Bülow; Heinrich Class, president of the Pan-German League in 1908; and Alfred von Tirpitz (155). When the Russian-German Reinsurance Treaty lapsed in 1890, the partisans of *Weltpolitik* had their chance. The *Weltpolitiker*, a dissenting minority allied with Germany's industrial and commercial sector, were not strictly annexationist. But *Weltpolitik* did not dispatch *Realpolitik* in one fell swoop.[19] The blurriness of these lines heightened the need for theoretical differentiation. The abstraction "*Weltpolitik*" gained concrete meaning in the hands of Admiral Tirpitz.[20] *Weltpolitik* encompassed both Treitschkean animus toward Britain and a more pragmatic strategy to accommodate it (72). Initially, the *Weltpolitiker* believed that Germany and Britain shared an interest in protecting themselves from the economic power generated by two "continental powers"—the US and Russia. The main goal of German naval power after the turn to *Weltpolitik* was to be an "equal among others." This meant being able to deter the British from attacking and convincing the British and other *Weltmächte* to accept its aspirations.[21] By 1900, Admiral Tirpitz was writing that Germans would be choked to death in their own country "without the expansion and strengthening of our maritime interests" (26–27). The leading scholar of German naval theory and practice in this period, Dirk Bönker, concluded that the navalists "kept a considerable distance from visions of a German continental empire in the Eurasian realm as the primary destiny for the German empire in the 20th century" (32). In the hands of Tirpitz and the navalists, the boundaries between the concepts of *Lebensraum* and *Weltpolitik,* often blurred in the writings of politicians or publicists of the Pan-German League, were reinforced. Above all, an expansionist capitalist world policy required sea power.

Germany's ambition to become a *Weltmacht* by sea in the 1890s was deeply informed by both American theory and practice. The basis of the German navalists' identification with the Americans was the fact that they both significantly lagged Great Britain. Alfred Mahan's *The Influence of Sea Power on History*, published in 1890, had a major impact on the German emperor and navy alike. By 1893, at the prodding of Admiral Tirpitz, the German Naval High Command urged all officers to study "the works of Captain Mahan" (256). Emperor Wilhelm II claimed in 1894 that he was "not reading but devouring" Mahan's first book, *The Influence of Sea Power.* While there were other intellectual influences on German naval science, Mahan's was preeminent (257–58). The special appeal of Mahan was that he offered the imprimatur of science: "The navalists' science of sea power fused military strategy, naval history and imperial ideology into a self-contained whole" (252–53). Admiral Fiske stated in 1911 that "Mahan . . . proved that sea power has been necessary for commercial success in peace and military success in war." Mahan's histories enabled one "to draw from the lessons of history inferences applicable to one's own country and service." Ludwig Borckenhagen, a teacher of naval history at the German *Marineakademie*, too, credited Mahan with discovery of a "new law" of the utmost practical influence (256).

Friedrich Ratzel's Journey from American *Lebensraum* to German *Weltpolitik*

German theorists of navalism and *Weltpolitik* at the turn of the century found much to admire in Mahan's worldview. German liberals of the same period looked to the American continent for other models that Germany's colonial ventures might emulate. According to the important study by historian Jens-Uwe Guettel, in the first decade of the twentieth century, the United States was an "omnipresent" fixture in German colonial discourse: colonialists attempted to import American cotton cultivation methods and modeled race decrees in German South West Africa, East Africa, and German Samoa on American precedents.[22] "By 1914," writes Guettel, "many Germans were familiar with representations of America as a nation destined to grow and in doing so to educate, dominate, and sometimes exterminate other races" (81). This was the broad context in which Ratzel, who traveled to the United States and developed intellectual ties there, became a significant figure in the intellectual history of empire.

Ratzel's conceptions of space and race were deeply influenced by his travels in the US in the 1870s. Ratzel was Germany's leading geographer from the 1880s until his death in 1904, and the man most responsible for the dissemination of the term *"Lebensraum"* in modern European thought. The term originated with Oscar Peschel (1826–1875), occupant of the first chair (*Lehrstuhl*) in geography at Leipzig from 1871–75. Ratzel's elaboration of the concept in 1901 was the most sustained and influential. Ratzel's first mention of *Lebensraum* dates to 1897.[23] Ratzel was a cultural and political geographer, a polymath nineteenth-century thinker trained by geographers and zoographers in the German Darwinian tradition.[24] Although Ratzel was an activist public intellectual committed to the cause of German national power, especially through the attainment of overseas colonies, he was no less significant for the development of academic geography on both sides of the Atlantic. By his death in 1904, Ratzel had influenced a wide range of intellectuals in the US, from the historian Frederick Jackson Turner to leading geographers like Nathaniel Shaler.[25]

Ratzel had long pressed for German *Lebensraum*, finding inspiration in the great spaces of America. In 1882, he was a founding member of the *Kolonialgesellschaft* and, later, the *Kolonialverein*, groups that advocated for the acquisition of colonies for the sake of emigration. In his 1884 work, he argued that Germany needed to prioritize the attainment of overseas colonies to counter the depleting effects of migration overseas, especially to America.[26] Ratzel believed colonies could provide space for small farmers, traders, and artisans besieged by German industrialization. He led the National-Liberals to the party's colonialist position in the mid-1880s (59). In the early 1890s, he joined the Pan-German League and became one of the so-called "fleet professors" for whom *Weltpolitik* represented the solution to the problem of Germany's lack of *Lebensraum*. Through his advocacy of sea power, Ratzel lent the authority of geographic science to Germany's national struggle to compete. Between 1897 and 1901, Ratzel combined the discourses of *Lebensraum* and *Weltpolitik* in a particularly explosive way, creating a spark that ignited the first Atlantic realist synthesis.

Ratzel defined *Lebensraum* as "the geographical surface area required to support a living species at its current population size and mode of existence."[27] Ratzel spatialized Darwin's concept of struggle (*Kampf*).[28] As Ratzel put it: "The struggle for life (*Kampf um Dasein*) . . . primarily means nothing more than a struggle for space (*Kampf um Raum*)."[29] "Space is the very first condition for life," Ratzel wrote in 1901. As two leading scholars explain, the *Lebensraum* essay "takes off from an understanding of the human as part of the natural world. . . . Life, he is never tired of repeating, is 'earthbound.'"[30]

Ratzel can be characterized as an Atlantic realist because of the influence his travels to the US had on his work.[31] Already in his 1878 book on the United States, Ratzel's language anticipated his mature *Lebensraum* concept. For him, the United States illustrated a "general truth of political geography—that states are living essences that are never fixed, always growing or in retreat."[32] Ratzel was an innovator of the lexicon of realism, utilizing the concepts of "*Weltmacht*" and "*Großraum*," the latter an important one for Carl Schmitt. "In comparison with other continental states, [the United States] belongs to the group of the world-powers (*Weltmächte*) as indicated by size. These are the true great powers (*Großmächte*), that take up nearly three-fifths of the earth's four continents; one can name them 'continental powers'" (85). In a peculiar inversion of Treitschkean anxieties about British naval power as the gold standard of *Weltpolitik*, Ratzel wrote: "The British empire with its possessions strewn across the world can least of all be compared with the compact power of the United States" (87). It was the size of the US that impressed Ratzel most.

While Europe was overpopulated, America was only lightly inhabited. "The Americans seem to be greatly influenced in their process of development by the mobility which the consciousness of free space (*Spielraum*) and the necessity of conquering this space brings out in each individual."[33] European states would have to attain their *Großraum* through territorial acquisition of "empty land in the non-European world, that is, through imperialist expansion."[34] He argued that the "squeezed-in" (*eingezwängte*) peoples of Europe needed a "safety valve."[35] Ratzel's theory of *Lebensraum* built on lessons about empire that he believed he had learned from his studies in and of the United States.

Ratzel was not a typical ethnonationalist or *völkisch* thinker of the fin de siècle.[36] Nonetheless, Ratzel did believe in a kind of neo-racism centered on culture: some cultures were more "equipped" to deal with space.[37] Ratzel believed it was their superior "political sense of space" that had yielded to the Anglo-Celtic peoples "the best and biggest countries in the Old and the New World."[38] In "*Lebensraum*," Ratzel argued that the mastery of space is a tendency of all species and is not the exclusive trait of *Homo sapiens*:

> Relationships to space vary greatly between an amoeba, a coral, a pelagic jellyfish, a land snail . . . A small Indian tribe in the South American forest has needs and expectations regarding space that are very different from those of a European for whom the well-being of his people can only lie in grasping the whole world (*Weltumfassung*).

While some peoples required a bounded space, he posited, others needed larger spaces, even global ones—as Ratzel's term *Weltumfassung* implies.[39]

Ratzel's Art of Seeing

To grasp the world whole required a novel way of seeing. As Ratzel's admirers believed, Ratzel's geographic science was the foundation for an "art" of political judgment that eluded formal systematization. If Ratzel's writings on geographic nature were introduced to the educational habitus of German statesmen, his teachings would become the statesman's "second nature." In 1903, Ratzel devoted a lengthy two-part essay to this question of the geographic foundations of political power entitled "The North Atlantic Powers."[40] The scope of the essay reveals the growing self-consciousness of this generation of thinkers about the Atlantic dimensions of the problems they theorized: "Seldom do we encounter the summary expression, '*Atlantische Mächte*' (Atlantic powers), while the term 'Mediterranean powers' is commonplace." But current events, he felt, justified his focus: "In a time when Atlantic commerce is the greatest and is with each year still growing, where the greatest and most active states and peoples, and especially the greatest sea powers attempt to strengthen their mastery of this ocean, can one consider necessary a summarizing and comparative reflection on the Atlantic powers" (914). The essay illustrates how Ratzel advanced the first Atlantic realist moment through a practice of intra-Atlantic national comparison.

In important passages, Ratzel insisted that recent US history illustrated a major shift from continental to maritime power, one that offered lessons for Germany: "Germany is no Atlantic Power in the sense of its geographical situation" (933). But, he continued, "North America and Europe together form the largest economic area on earth, Europe is the best customer of the United States" (1055). Ratzel hoped that instead of a future of sharpened conflicts between the Atlantic powers "we may rather speak of the north-Atlantic family" (1062). Germany had much to learn from the recent experience of the United States, asserted Ratzel. The conquest of Puerto Rico, the Philippines and the Marianas, Hawaii, Samoa, and through the Platt Amendment in Cuba, showed that "the US has become a colonial power (*Kolonialmacht*)."[41] Furthermore, an interoceanic canal was now on the agenda. "What is not sufficiently appreciated in Europe, is the effect of this expansion on the inner life of the Union"—it has tied "Pacific North America more closely to the Atlantic," and strengthened the US internally (1054). "The consciousness of a great *Lebensraum* makes [the Americans] lovely, industrious, optimistic . . . Even in foreign policy, they work with greater ideas of space (*Raumvorstellungen*) than the Europeans" (1058).

The implication Ratzel drew from the US expansion into the Pacific was that Atlantic powers must now operate on a global scale. "Germany was until 1870 a nearly pure land power, and solely as it began to explore the sea, did it begin to protect its longstanding sea trade, to compete for colonies and to practice *Weltpolitik*" (935). The consequences were clear: "Where [today] each country strives to increase its chief trading areas in order to shorten and to cheapen the distances it must travel . . . [so does] it appear superfluous to speak today of a Central European customs union or of comparable projects, as [some of our] statesman have spoken of a necessary return to forming a continental power base in Europe" (1062). Both with regard to its continental reach and its post-1898 scale of influence, Ratzel saw America as the great model and necessary point of comparison.

In 1900, Ratzel published *The Ocean as the Source of National Greatness*. The text helps us see that like many of his German imperialist contemporaries, Ratzel saw no contradiction between naval *Weltpolitik* and *Lebensraum*. Echoing Max Weber, he wrote in the preface, "my foundational belief is that Germany must also be strong on the seas in order to fulfill its global vocation (*Weltberuf*)."[42] In it, he argued that more sea power would determine the difference between "strong" and "weak peoples":

> The age-old contrast of sea peoples and land peoples, sea powers and land powers, is dissolving . . . Every great people (*Großvolk*) and every powerful state (*mächtiger Staat*) strives towards and on the sea . . . This movement will reshape the political face of Europe. Since a great state (*Großstaat*) without worldwide economic interests has become unthinkable, it is also no longer possible to conceive of a true *Großstaat* without seapower. Fleets will become as necessary as armies.[43]

The proliferation of "greats" and "greatness" is a key part of the fin de siècle discourse on world power.

Greatness could also be taught. It was considered an "excellent foundation for the professional education of naval officers."[44] One influential admirer of Ratzel's was Rear-Admiral Curt Maltzahn (1849–1930). Maltzahn taught naval history and strategy at the *Marineakademie* and served as its director between 1900 and 1903. He had a lasting influence on naval strategy during and after World War I.[45] The commemoration he wrote in the navy's house journal, the *Marine-Rundschau*, on the occasion of Ratzel's death was glowing. Commending Ratzel's writings to every naval officer, he reached lofty heights: "His works are valuable for every sea officer who aspires to meet the high goals of his beautiful vocation"; the work "brings states and people into relationship to the historical-geographical foundation which runs through their life."[46] Maltzahn recommended Ratzel's work as a tool of enlightenment of the German people and the naval officer in particular. *Ocean* "provides a rich source of education: through the intellectual portrayal of the distinctiveness of the sea, it can serve as a foundation of his thought and even be relevant to tactical questions" (219). Ratzel wanted to help "develop the geographical sense" in naval officers necessary to clarify problems and identify solutions (218). Maltzahn's discourse on the geographical "sense" anticipates how Karl Haushofer, the major figure in Weimar geopolitical discourse, articulated the "artistic" dimensions of realistic judgment.

Maltzahn's tribute illustrates the charismatic appeal of Ratzel's ideas in certain German circles at the turn of the century.[47] Ratzel was the "rare encyclopedic" thinker who worked across many disciplinary boundaries and "who conceives of geography as bringing all realms of human knowledge and life together" (218). In this time of "scientific specialization," science connected to the "practical side of life" was rare, and welcome. Maltzahn encouraged readers to view Ratzel as an artist "who combines richness of thought with graphic description (*plastische Schilderung*) and the power to create aesthetic form (*ästhetische Gestaltungskraft*)." Maltzahn's words help us conceptualize Ratzel as a founder of a realist habitus—a way of seeing the world that required training and cultivation. As he put it in the introduction to his *Political Geography*, Ratzel wanted the "geographic sense" and the "habit of viewing things spatially" to "become second nature," or literally "to get into the blood (*ins Blut übergehen*)" (218). Political instincts themselves could be taught: "Practical statesman have never lacked geographical sense," and where "one speaks of political instinct, there one mostly means the correct estimate of the geographic foundations of political power." This gave Maltzahn "the hope that this book will not be of interest merely to geographers" (218). His hopes were not disappointed. Like Mahan, Ratzel became an important reference point for German naval officers trying to flesh out the implications of a politics on a world scale.

The Peculiar Prominence of Germany in the American Discourse on World Power

In 1909, Harvard professor and historian Archibald Cary Coolidge published *The United States as a World Power*.[48] The book captures the novelty of the very term "world power" in English. "Twenty years ago, the expression 'world power' was unknown in most languages; today it is a political commonplace, bandied about in wide discussion" (1). In reference to the scramble for colonies in the last third of the nineteenth century, Coolidge explained, "political writers . . . began to employ an expression, which has now passed into common use—'world powers,' that is to say, powers which are directly interested in all parts of the world and whose voices must be listened to everywhere" (7). Coolidge went on to say that the United States was already great, but "greatness" had attained new dimensions and import. "In 1897 [the Americans] had already long been imbued with the feeling, not since diminished, that the history of their country had been one of tremendous achievement. In a little over a century it had grown to be, without question, one of the greatest—in their opinion—the greatest—in the world" (82). But 1898—the year of the Spanish-American War—marked an epochal change: It is a "truth, now generally accepted, that the war of 1898 was a turning-point in the history of the American republic. The reason therefor (*sic*) is usually summed up in the phrase that since that date the United States has been a world power" (121). Before that, "in the great game of international politics they took little part. European statesmen could usually leave them out of their reckonings" (131). The US was widely known to be "a power of great resources . . . [but] if one . . . kept clear of the Monroe Doctrine, in which most of Europe had small interest, then in practice the US need not often be taken into consideration. It belonged, so to speak, to a different world" (131).

Coolidge's essay is just one of many contemporary American texts that illustrate that the United States had its own version of Germany's *Weltreichslehre* in the 1890s. The notion that the US post-1898 was now a "world power" representing a new dimension of American national "greatness" was widely shared by elite US commentators. Historian John Thompson has described this discourse as part of the paradigm-shifting new "sense of power" that widened US ambitions more than any material force. Numerous books appeared in the years immediately before and after 1898 with the words "world politics" in the title.[49] Figures like Henry Cabot Lodge and Theodore Roosevelt frequently used these terms in speeches and letters from 1895–1900. Cabot Lodge, in advocating for the annexation of Hawaii, said: "The great nations are rapidly absorbing for their future expansion and their present defense all the waste places of the earth . . . As one of the great nations of the world, the US must not fall out of the line of march" (31). Lodge did not have a specific territorial goal in mind—as he repeatedly said, the US should take "rank where we belong, as one of the greatest of the great world powers" (26). Because the territorial perquisites of "greatness" were only vaguely formulated, the category was an empty signifier. Only by referring to an imagined Atlantic community of peer nations could the rank of the "great" be established. National "greatness" was an artifact of a practice of comparison.

The discourses of national greatness and world power status were sometimes couched in gendered terms. Turning "outwards" to the international involved a turning away from the "domestic" sphere of continental politics to a broader world-political orientation. Greatness entailed a rejection of "isolation." As Lodge put it in 1895: "We cannot avoid our destiny. We are too great to be any longer an isolated power." In the same vein, Woodrow Wilson understood the war of 1898 as a turning point in US development: "We cannot return to the point whence we set out. We have left the continent which has hitherto been our only field of action and have gone out upon the seas, where the nations are rivals and we cannot live or act apart." The turn from "isolation" to "intercourse" with other nations was also presented as an evolution of the nation from solipsistic youth to manhood. As a professor at Princeton, Wilson wrote in 1901 that a nation once devoted to its "domestic development now finds its first task roughly finished and turns about to look curiously into the tasks of the great world at large, seeking its special part and place of power" (51).

The American discourse on "world power" closely resembles German discourses of *Weltpolitik*. One major conduit for the transmission and reception of *Weltpolitik* in the US was the German-educated US political scientist, Paul S. Reinsch (1869–1923). Although a major figure in the profession at the turn of the century, he is little known today. Reinsch is, however, an important missing link in the story of Atlantic realism.

In 1900, at the University of Wisconsin, Reinsch became the first professor to offer a course on "world politics" in the United States.[50] His first book, *World Politics at the End of the 19th Century, as Influenced by the Oriental Situation*, has been described by two leading historians as "the first glimmerings of international relations as a discipline."[51] Lodge, Roosevelt, Mahan, and Wilson often described the Spanish-American War of 1898 as a watershed in American development; a new stage of "maturity" reflected in an outer-directedness. "That the US is to play a leading part in international affairs,—that she is to be one of the five leading world powers,—has been irrevocably decided by the events of the recent past. A nation of our power and resources would be untrue to its vocation if it did not sooner or later realize its duty in this important position to which it has attained."[52] Reinsch's work was part of a cluster of works on imperialism and colonial administration that emerged in response to the Spanish-American War.[53] Reinsch partook in this broader excitement about the irreversible direction of US and world history.

The son of German immigrants, Reinsch graduated from the University of Wisconsin in 1892, and returned in 1895 as a PhD student to work with Frederick Turner in the School of Economics, Political Science and History.[54] Reinsch helped establish the American Political Science Association in 1903, eventually became its president, and served on the editorial board of the *American Political Science Review*.[55] Reinsch ended his career as the US ambassador to China from 1913–19. While *World Politics* centered on the question of the Open Door in China, it also contained extensive discussion of US and German imperialism and showed his familiarity with German sources. During his visit to Berlin in 1898, Reinsch surely would have found many still debating the discourse on *Weltpolitik* that was stimulated too by Max Weber's inaugural lecture at the University of Freiburg in 1895.

Weber was preoccupied with the question of what makes a nation "great": "The reverberations of a position of world power [in England and France] . . . constantly confron[t] the state with great power-political tasks and expos[e] the individual to 'chronic' political schooling." In Germany, by contrast, such "training" occurs only when borders are threatened. "The question of whether politics on the grand scale can make us aware once more of the significance of the great political issues of power is also decisive for *our* development."[56] Weber's investment in the nation-state's competitive struggle for economic position concerned more than material riches. It concerns "what kind of people [the Germans] will be" (15). Echoing Friedrich Nietzsche, Weber wrote, "We do not want to breed well-being in people, but rather those characteristics which we think of as constituting human greatness and nobility of our nature . . . Through our work we want to be the forerunner of that future race" (15). Where an individual's youth depends on whether he "is able to feel the *great* passions nature has implanted in us," nations face an analogous challenge: a nation "will remain young as long as it has the capacity and courage to keep faith with itself and with the great instincts it has been given, and if its leading strata are able to raise themselves into the hard clear air in which the sober work of German politics flourishes, an atmosphere which, however, is also filled with the earnest grandeur of national sentiment" (28). Neither man questioned the mysterious, fetishistic aura surrounding the category of "greatness." Echoing Ratzel and Weber, Reinsch concluded that the United States had a vocation for "great politics." Perhaps the concept's charisma depended on its lack of clear definition.

At first glance, Reinsch's repetition of the term "great" in diverse contexts in *World Politics* seems to be as compulsive and vague as Weber's. Examples abound: "The fleet law of 1898 marks a great change in German politics"; "the people of the empire realized that the great struggles of the future would be fought on the seas"; "the great give-and-take of the world's politics"; "the great work of civilizing and developing the world."[57] But Reinsch expressed ambivalence about the new prospects for greatness that had opened for the United States. Reinsch worried that greatness on the world stage could takes a toll at home: "Before all, and above all, we should guard the purity of domestic politics, lest, while we are gaining great influence in the affairs of the world, our national life at home weaken and deteriorate."[58]

This self-reflexivity about the potential costs of "great politics" made Reinsch a different kind of Atlantic realist, one who set the template for another Progressive who taught at the University of Wisconsin, Charles Beard. Reinsch worried that the price of world-political status might be too high: "Though we have entered upon an active share in international politics, it does not follow that we must . . . become the docile imitators of other nations." The notion of imitation as docility always shadowed the intellectual work of comparison—a sign of nagging doubt. Yet, in a vitalistic idiom that reminds us of the organicist thinking of Ratzel or Turner, Reinsch conveyed ambivalence about the American debut as a world power in the language of "life," "vitality," and "health." "Happily, a nation is rarely in this condition of overpowering enthusiasm," wrote Reinsch of the mood after victory in the war of 1898. "And yet, if its vitality has not been exhausted, it must have these periodical outbreaks, which are indeed, to that extent a sign of health" (310). Here, fin de siècle German anxieties about cultural decadence found their American counterpart.

Although his intellectual history is idiosyncratic, his *World Politics* offers a fascinating interpretation of the mood of the fin de siècle. "There has been a complete change of ideals during the past hundred years," Reinsch wrote (7). The "broad humanitarianism" and "rationalistic optimism" of the generations of Jefferson, Kant, the Humboldts, and Rousseau "was followed by what may be called the age of force." 1848 was the turning point. "When the philosophic optimism of Rousseau and Hegel had passed for the first time, realism and a realistic policy (*Realpolitik*) came into favor. Such ideas as that of world peace, of justice to a hostile nation, of development of civilization by the united efforts of humanity, were looked upon as mirages of optimism." An age of pessimism followed for which Schopenhauer was representative. Echoing the vitalist, organicist description of states common to both Ratzel and Mahan, Reinsch's texts synthesized Ratzel's discourse on *Lebensraum* with the transatlantic discourse on world-power status. Only within the "last decade"—the 1890s, that is—has "this pessimism [been] in turn replaced by a new optimism, the optimism of force, which sees in triumphant energy the sole condition of happy existence. Of this tendency Nietzsche is the main exponent" (7). Drawing on literary and philosophical texts, Reinsch's account illustrates his effort to support an intellectual transition from *Realpolitik* to *Weltpolitik*.

The key to the shift was captured in the contrasting images of a balanced equilibrium versus a life and death struggle. In this new age of national imperialism, Reinsch wrote, "the idea of a serene equilibrium maintained unchangeably, a balance of power, under which everybody can live in ease and peace, has given place to the conception of a great struggle among warring forces" (16). Now countries want more than "mere security . . . and a moderately wealthy national existence. Only in exercising its powers to the utmost, in 'living itself out,' does a nation find satisfaction. Like the modern man of Ibsen's dramas." Reinsch's description of *Realpolitik* as a "pessimistic" worldview recalls Ratzel's call, a few years earlier, to develop a "*Realpolitik* worthy of the name." Reinsch's "struggle," in the name of life and will and force, echoed Weber's. They both conceived of "struggle" as an alternative to the old policies of balance and equilibrium thematized by Rochau in the 1850s and 1860s and practiced by Bismarck in the 1870s. Reinsch traced the transition of Germany from "a great land power" to "world power." Strikingly, Reinsch chose a comparative strategy that eschewed national exceptionalism: "The US, by its avowed intention to play a leading part in Asiatic affairs and to foster actively its present and prospective interests in the region, has left the sphere which the policy of the Monroe Doctrine seemed to have assigned to it" (284). Therefore, the European powers were right to eschew "merely sentimental ideal affinities," recognizing instead that "any country . . . which has material, actual interests in South America, has . . . a right to interfere." *World Politics* demonstrates intimate familiarity with German sources, both scholarly and popular ones. By 1890, Reinsch wrote, it became clear that Germany's "expansionist tendencies" in Africa and South America represented a break with the purely commercial imperialism championed by Bismarck. The comparability of the German and American empires led Reinsch to defend Germany's desire to protect "the rights of her colonists" abroad (284). "The advance of German enterprises

has undoubtedly been exaggerated by interested writers, whose purpose has been to add fuel to existing international hostilities" (281).
Reinsch explained that Germany must be counted among the leading
"world powers." But that "the world in general . . . [should] for a long
time to come remain an open field for the free and equal exploitation
by all nations that possess great industrial power" (286). Germany's
rise should be accommodated, not resisted: "[Germany] has acted as
its interests at any given time have dictated, fostering friendly relations
with all great powers, but yielding to none in matters of vital national
interest" (289). Reinsch's writing reveals an Atlantic realism before the
carapace of American exceptionalism was fastened to it.

Coolidge's 1908 book, *The United States as a World Power*, echoed
Reinsch's exhortation that the United States need not overreact to German power. Recognizing that Germany was a competitor and adversary
of the US, his narrative nonetheless engendered sympathy for its rival.
Coolidge reminded his readers that Americans once "admired the genius
of Bismarck, the triumphs of the German army, and the splendid energy of the whole nation in every department of human activity" (197).
Coolidge downplayed the fact that Germany had expressed its support
for Spain, deployed its navy in support, and purchased the Caroline and
Landrone Islands, writing that "many Americans were firmly convinced
that Germany was not only a covetous, greedy power, but also one that,
from jealousy, was willing to do the US an ill-turn if she could" (200).
Developments in China from 1897–1901 fueled a "growing alienation
between two states long on amicable terms grieved and alarmed well-
wishers in both" (201). Although Germany was not the only power in
1902 that sought to collect debts in Venezuela (England and Italy did
too), "all the vials of wrath were poured on Germany" (203). Coolidge
suggested that the rapprochement between England and the US after the
Venezuela crisis of 1895–86, and English efforts to "blacken the reputation" of the Germans during the Boer War (1899–1902), had led Americans to a distorted view of the Germans: "Since then passions have had
time to cool down . . . the relations between the two countries are again
good. Before deciding whether they are likely to continue so, we must
first understand why their interests clash, and this without the fault of

anyone" (203). Coolidge thus counseled a nonemotional approach to the adjudication of interests.

Coolidge argued that beneath the surface confrontations lay a deeper German-US kinship: "England and France appear to us like two rich, long-established and somewhat old-fashioned commercial houses . . . Compared with them, Germany and the US are like two young pushing firms who have yet their way to make. Already their achievements have excited the alarm of their staid rivals, and they might look forward joyously to more brilliant triumphs in the future, if each were not worried by the presence of the other" (203). Coolidge's celebratory tone extended to the prospects for German colonialism in South America: "Here then would seem to be a splendid opening for German enterprise, a unique chance for the nation to control permanently a territory comparable to that held by the Anglo-Saxon and the Slav" (206). The dynamics of German-American competition were a subset of the larger logic of world empire: "Wherever on the globe there is a good opening for trade, there we may expect to find the Germans and the Americans striving in ardent rivalry" (204). Like Reinsch, Coolidge suggested that German ambitions in South America were no cause for alarm: "What they have done is to entertain the hope that sooner or later, *in the nature of things*, by peaceable attraction or as a result of collision provoked by misgovernment, some of the Latin American republics would fall into the hands of the superior race. This dream may appear fantastic to many people, even in Germany itself, but we need not wonder at its existence or to deny to it a measure of reasonableness" (207; emphasis added). Reinsch's phrase "in the nature of things" is significant, since it echoes the phrase used by Mahan in a 1902 essay. It also recalls Maltzahn's theme that geography should become the statesman's "second nature." Like Coolidge, Mahan placed significant weight on the German-American rivalry and Central and South America as a theater of strategic significance. In the next and final section, I argue that in his writings, Alfred Mahan gave the American idiom of realism its enduring signature.

The first Atlantic realists emphasized the comparability of the American and German empires at the turn of the century. The practice of comparison could accentuate rivalry but could also furnish a measure for what constituted "reasonable" behavior. In later chapters, I examine the melding of realist motifs with American exceptionalism and German exceptionalism. This chapter returns us to a realist moment before these exceptionalisms took hold. There was a temporal synchronicity in the two countries' world-historical position: for both it was a period of exploration and growth. "Realism" was a product of this coincidence in time, the co-authored *Bildungsroman* of German and American empire.

Mahan, the Monroe Doctrine, and the "Nature of Things": 1890–1912

In Charles Beard's critical writings on American navalism of the 1930s, the name Mahan would stand for everything he rejected. Mahan was the tribune of *Weltpolitik, Realpolitik*, and *Machtpolitik*, wrote Beard, indiscriminately stirring distinct German concepts together.[59] Mahan's 1890 book on sea power made him one of the most celebrated international writers of the decade. In 1893, he was invited to audiences with Queen Victoria and Kaiser Wilhelm II. His influence on Tirpitz and German *Weltpolitik* was profound. Mahan has been contextualized within American history mostly by scholars who emphasize his influence on Theodore Roosevelt's career as assistant secretary of the navy (1897–98) and as president (1901–9). Mahan has been described as a realist or "proto-realist" for his emphasis on national self-interest and his allergy to abstractions and free-floating moral norms.[60]

Much has been missed in these accounts of Mahan as proto-realist. First is the extent to which Mahan's reflections were seminal experiments in writing—rehearsals of phrases that would become sedimented in American realist discourse. Although their authorship and context would be erased over time, Mahan is one of the most important craftsmen of the Atlantic realist sensibility. Moreover, the thinker with the reputation for a "hard-headed" materialism was, in fact, enchanted by highly value-laden abstract ideals concerning race, culture, and a coming clash of civilizations between Europe and America, on the one hand, and Asia, on the other. These ideals subtended his notions of the "real" and the "natural" in international relations. Mahan's writings were an important thread connecting the emergence of German

Weltpolitik to the American discovery of itself as a world power that I have discussed above. In his writings of the 1890s, Mahan exhorted US leaders to confront a shrinking globe by embracing a more assertive foreign policy. "The outlook—the signs of the times, what are they?" One sign was "the general outward impulse of all the civilized nations of the first order of greatness—except our own."[61] This phrase—"first order of greatness"—was key: Mahan wanted to teach his readers how to see the world, not only as it was, but also as it should be. And that world was one in which the US ranked among the "great."

In December 1890, just six months after the *Influence of Sea Power*, Mahan published an article, "The US Looks Outwards." The title established the trope of American extroversion that Lodge and Wilson adopted, exhorting America to recognize that it had "reached its maturity."[62] Once a "continental power," now the US was discovering its vocation on the seas. "The sea, now . . . is traversed with a rapidity and a certainty that have minimized distances . . . The world has grown smaller" (148). Globalization has made "proximity the characteristic of the age," and proximity means that the US has vital interests everywhere: "Positions formerly distant have become to us of vital importance from their nearness." A navy is, for the US, "the indispensable instrument by which, when emergencies arise, the nation can project its power beyond its own shore-line" (149). The identification of "vital interests" was a building block in a realist vocabulary that imagined the globe in terms of openings and closings, use-value, and the not-yet-used.

Mahan pioneered key tropes of the realist discourse: "To look with clear, dispassionate, but resolute eyes" at the fact that "the face of the world has changed, economically and politically."[63] But this unobjectionable insistence on "seeing" concealed deep notions of racial and civilizational hierarchy: "It is essential to our own good, it is yet more essential as part of our duty to the commonwealth of peoples to which we racially belong that we look with clear, dispassionate, but resolute eyes upon the fact that civilizations on different planes of material prosperity and progress, with different spiritual ideals, and with very different political capacities, are fast closing together" (263). Like Ratzel, Mahan emphasized the superiority of the European races.

Although his writings predated Ratzel's formulation of the concept, Mahan aimed at what Ratzel would eventually call *Lebensraum*. Mahan shared the Social Darwinian influence: "All around us now is strife: 'the struggle of life,' 'the race of life,' are phrases so familiar that we do not feel their significance till we stop to think about them."[64] In 1895, he wrote: "More and more civilized man is needing and seeking ground to expand and in which to live. Like all natural forces, the impulse takes the direction of least resistance, but when in its course it comes upon some region rich in possibilities, but unfruitful through the incapacity or negligence of those who dwell therein, the incompetent race or system will go down, as the inferior race ever has fallen back and disappeared before the persistent impact of the superior."[65] The incapacity of "the savage" to develop the territory they occupy invites the Europeans who "are finding lack of openings and scantiness of livelihood at home" (168). Optimizing the "use" of the Earth was the world-historical duty of the "superior races." To meet the challenge of a world grown smaller, Mahan exhorted his readers to defend European-American "civilization." Mahan's United States—what he calls "America"—was an "offshoot" of Europe; Americans were members of the "European family" (161). Not just America's interests, but also "the welfare of mankind . . . [is] bound up, so far as we can see, in the security and strength of that civilization which is identified with Europe and its offshoots in America. For what, after all, is our not unjustly vaunted European and American civilization? An oasis set in the midst of a desert of barbarism."[66]

Who were the barbarians in this scenario? Mahan was preoccupied with the expansion of the Russian empire in Asia: "Our Pacific slope, and the Pacific colonies of Great Britain, with an instinctive shudder have felt the threat, which able Europeans have seen in the teeming multitudes of central and northern Asia" (123). The United States must look outward, across the Atlantic to Europe, in a common struggle: "Whereas once to avoid European entanglement was essential to the development of her individuality, now to take her share of the travail of Europe is but to assume an inevitable task, an appointed lot, in the work of upholding the common interests of our civilization" (123). Mahan's definition of the American national interest was not strictly circumscribed by the nation's political territory, but extended globally. Mahan's United States was a Christian, "European" nation with an international vocation to preserve civilizational hierarchy.

To what subsection of European civilization did Mahan believe the United States owed allegiance? Mahan's Anglophilia vied with his pro-Teutonism. Throughout the 1890s, the US navy considered Germany a threat to the Western Hemisphere and featured it prominently in its war-planning scenarios. Mahan helped contribute to this posture as a member of the navy's War Planning Board. "All over the world German commercial and colonial push is coming into collision with other nations," he wrote in 1890.[67] The United States, he asserted, was "woefully unready, not only in fact but in purpose, to assert in the Caribbean and Central America a weight of influence proportioned to the extent of her interests" (13). But he rarely let his Anglophilia outweigh his sympathetic view of German power. In 1902, Mahan wrote that the "bitter temper" shown by the Germans toward the British in the Boer War would not "prevent a co-operation among the three Teutonic states which all need, but Germany most of all."[68] At other times he cleaved closer to the traditional Anglo-American alliance.[69] In "Possibilities of an Anglo-American Reunion" (1894), Mahan emphasized a common interest in sea power as a source of national prosperity. Buoyed by Britain's recent capitulation to the US in the Venezuela crisis, Mahan wrote in 1897 that in "unity of heart among the English-speaking races lies the best hope of humanity in the doubtful days ahead."[70]

Between 1895 and 1903, Mahan returned constantly to the Monroe Doctrine, a topic around which he developed some of his most enduring phrases, becoming part of a shared Atlantic realist habitus. The Monroe Doctrine forms the master-key to his work for three reasons. The first is the overarching strategic significance he attributed to the Caribbean—"one of the greatest nerve centres of European civilization" (261). The "fundamental meaning" of the isthmus that separated the Atlantic and Pacific oceans transcended the pragmatic benefits to US shipping: "it advances by thousands of miles the frontiers of European civilization in general, and of the US in particular" (260–61). Mahan hoped it would bind "the exposed pioneers of European civilization [on the Pacific Coast] more closely to the main body and to protect, by due foresight over the approach to them from either side" (260). The importance of sea power for US history could not be grasped without attention to the specificities of the hemisphere. Second, by inaugurating the US hemispheric interest, the Monroe Doctrine marked an epochal break with the US's "continental" phase, as Mahan defined it. Mahan's argument resembles Ratzel's argument of the late 1890s that *Weltpolitik* would mark the necessary break with Bismarckian *Realpolitik* (378). As Mahan explained, the Monroe Doctrine broke with the Jeffersonian school of foreign policy, which "strictly confined national expansion" to the continent (378).

Third, the Monroe Doctrine became much more prominent in the national conversation between 1895 and 1905 than it had been in the previous century. Debated, amended, and stretched interpretively by American and foreign diplomats, the Monroe Doctrine never seemed to break. It thus came to symbolize the resilience of the US itself. Mahan reached for metaphors of organic nature, spirit, and principle to describe the dramatic evolution of the Monroe Doctrine from the Olney Note (1895) to the Roosevelt Corollary (1904). These metaphors rationalized the "growth" of American empire in the Western Hemisphere. But Mahan's organicist language evoked Ratzel's notion of *Lebensraum* and related fin de siècle visions of nature. In reflecting on the specificities of the Monroe Doctrine, Mahan arrived at broader generalizations on the "nature of things" in international relations, a phrase with both organicist and vitalist connotations.

Mahan also prided himself on not being *doctrinaire*. "The French word doctrinaire, fully adopted into English, gives warning of the danger that attends doctrine. . . . of exaggerating the letter instead of the spirit, of becoming mechanical rather than discriminating."[71] Since its spirit seemed to transcend the letter, the Monroe Doctrine was the perfect object with which to think: "The virtue of the Monroe Doctrine, without which it would die deservedly, is that, through its correspondence with the national necessities of the US, it possesses an inherent principle of life, which adapts itself with the flexibility of a growing plant to the successive conditions it encounters. One of these conditions of course is the growing strength of the nation itself."[72] But in so doing, Mahan offered a quasi-Hegelian history of the spirit of the Monroe Doctrine's realization in the world: "It is more instructive . . . to consider its development by successive exhibitions of the past than to strive to cage its free spirit within the bars of a definition attempted at any moment" (377).

The Monroe Doctrine evolved dramatically in the decade from 1895 to 1904, and some summary of context is necessary to situate Mahan's writings. In 1895, President Cleveland directed his secretary of state, Richard Olney, to invoke the Monroe Doctrine in a border dispute between British Guiana and Venezuela. On July 20, Olney wrote, "Today the US is practically sovereign on [the American] continent and its fiat is law."[73] Cleveland's intention was to send a message to the Germans and the British about Central America and undercut the Republicans who were agitating for a more expansionist foreign policy. Cleveland and Olney sought to restrict the doctrine's meaning by "dissociating it from protectorates and intervention in Latin America" (209–10). But Britain's acceptance of the Olney Note did not slow the evolution of the Monroe Doctrine from a defensive to an offensive one. The US dispute with Britain over Venezuela's boundaries in 1895–96 gave new weight to the Monroe Doctrine.[74] Although arbitrators awarded a larger part of disputed Venezuelan territory to Great Britain, the outcome brought the Monroe Doctrine to the attention of the world.[75] At the close of the first Hague Peace Conference in 1899, the US delegation signed the Convention on Land Warfare but added a key reservation: nothing in the document could be construed to require the "relinquishment of [the United States'] traditional attitude towards American questions" (105). The Democratic platform of 1900 declared the Monroe Doctrine as interpreted by successive presidents a "permanent part of the foreign policy of the US" (105). The 1901 Hay-Pauncefote Treaty clarified the right of the United States to construct, manage, and regulate a canal through the Isthmus, putting an end to fifty years of shared British-US control of the Panamanian territory. The Platt Amendment of 1901 circumscribed Cuban sovereignty.

Mahan's idealistic reading of the recent history of US diplomacy in the region omitted the opportunism shown by Democrats and Republicans, and the challenge posed by the Argentine foreign affairs minister Luis Marìa Drago and other Pan-American interpreters of the Monroe

Doctrine as a doctrine of comprehensive nonintervention.[76] As one scholar explains, Roosevelt's Corollary "explicitly transformed the negatively framed and noninterventionist message of 1823 into a proactive call for intervention."[77] Reflecting in 1908 on the Monroe Doctrine once more, Mahan wrote that its flexibility was no sign of inconsistency, but rather a "turn in a river, or a divergence, resembling that of a new branch put forth by a tree."[78] As he concluded sanguinely, "That a policy framed to assure the independence of certain states should lead irresistibly to interference in functions attendant upon independence is something of a paradox . . . To state the qualities of an apple and of an apple tree is to formulate a series of paradoxes; but all the same the apple is the fruit of the tree" (409). Mahan's use of organic metaphors served his purpose of naturalizing the prerogatives of empire well.

From 1897–1903, the US navy considered Germany the major threat to the US sphere of influence in the Caribbean and Latin America. But at no time during this period did Mahan succumb to the anti-German rhetoric that dominated the American press after confrontations with the German navy in Manila in 1898, during the presidential election of 1900, or after Germany shelled Venezuela at the conclusion of its blockade of Venezuela in 1902–3.[79] Like Coolidge and Reinsch, Mahan consistently held a sympathetic view of German expansion via formal or informal empire. As Germany became more and more isolated within Europe, by the Anglo-French entente (1904), the Algeciras crisis of 1906, and the Anglo-Russian agreement (1907), Mahan retained his sympathetic view of German power. "Germany has never recognized the Monroe Doctrine as publicly as Great Britain," he wrote in 1911, but "the official attitude of Germany towards the Monroe Doctrine leaves nothing to be desired by the Americans."[80] In fact, Mahan suggested that the Monroe Doctrine could one day serve as a model for the Germans, since Germany has parallel interests, equally insusceptible to arbitration by tribunal or codification in international law: "In questions of policy, like the Monroe Doctrine, or the fortification of the Panama Canal before the Zone became US territory, or the position of the British in Egypt, or of Japan in Manchuria, determination does not concern lawyers as such, but men of affairs, because therefore being no law applicable, what is a needed is a workable arrangement based on recognized conditions" (32). Deploying the comparative method, he showed a remarkable sangfroid toward Germany at a moment of intense Anglo-German naval rivalry, and in spite of his own Anglophilia. Military force was essential to the "extension" of national power in the "sphere of German interests in the outside world, and therefore legitimate policy. Locked up in a territory narrow for its inhabitants, Germany must have an outlet for her industries secured by her own power, the only certain dependence. Her claims for such opportunity do not derive from law, and therefore like many other questions, cannot in ultimate resort be settled by legal tribunals" (32–33). As Mahan put it, in what could serve as his epitaph: "Whether named or not, vital interests remain. That is a quality necessarily inherent in vitality; and a nation may refuse to arbitrate them even if it abandons the phrase in a treaty."[81] The notion that there is a shadow world of rights, of natural rights that exist before and outside to law, is a key to the emerging realist vocabulary. As he explained in 1890, there was a sphere of "equally real rights which, though not conferred by the law, depend upon a clear preponderance of interest, upon obviously necessary policy, upon self-preservation, either total or partial."[82] Historians of foreign policy justifications in terms of national interests or "vital interests" should not overlook Mahan's seminal contributions to the language.

Although Mahan sometimes implied that this hidden realm of the "real" can be ascertained by an empirical process of weighing and measuring influence "proportionate" to interest, he also suggested that there was something ethereal about the process of judgment: the Monroe Doctrine was "the expression of an intuitive national sensitiveness to occurrences of various kinds in regions beyond the sea."[83] His idealism also comes through in his critique of Norman Angell's widely read book *The Great Illusion* (1911). Angell claimed that armament was motivated by an illusory belief in the economic advantage obtained by war. Mahan argued that the problem was not that nations were under such illusions about their interests, but that nations were motivated by forces other than self-interest. Moral reasons, like the preservation of honor, for example, were more frequently the cause.[84] In the recent struggle for influence in Morocco in 1911, the French and Germans persisted in unsuccessful courses of action because they were driven by a deeper drive: "the ambition to bear a racial and national share in the shaping of the world's advance" (141).

"Sentiment" too plays an important role in Mahan's constitution of "the real." In a striking juxtaposition of quotations from the chancellor of Germany and Winston Churchill, then head of the British Admiralty, Mahan noted the similarity of sentiments expressed by them. Whereas the German spoke of widespread "feeling," "passion," and "determination to make its strength and capability prevail in the world," Churchill invoked the "power to put our own characteristic and distinctive mark upon the unfolding of the civilization of mankind" (139). Of these two utterances, Mahan observed that it would be impossible to deny "that something more and higher than mere pecuniary profit, which is the exponent of material self-interest, enters into the recognized motives of the nations," engaged in "exploiting the as yet unimproved regions of the world" (139). From the practice of comparing imperial sentiment, Mahan arrived at the conclusion that great European empires seek a "fair share of the world's activities . . . a suitable entrance to play the part to which she is equal." Mahan's recourse to metaphors drawn from the theater—"role," "part," and "stage"—suggests a growing consciousness among political thinkers of the fin de siècle of a world-stage. But if Mahan has rightly identified the role of amour-propre, honor, and sentiment in national self-assertion, he has no critical distance from it. Scripting the role of the "great" national actor on the imperialist world-stage, Mahan the author disappears, making the principles of life and nature direct the action.

Mahan's essays from 1890 to 1912 function like a laboratory in which concepts like "vital interests," "prestige," "position," "national honor," and great-power status are measured and weighed, their proportions examined. "Vital interests," in particular, is a forerunner of one of the central concepts of mid-twentieth-century realism, "the national interest." Referring to a statement from Lloyd George dated July 24, 1911, Mahan noted, "The phrases 'vital interests' and 'national honor' carefully excluded from the recent treaties of general arbitration—the exclusion of which was indeed a chief object of the treaties—appear here again in terms and in full force" (89). Mahan quoted the chancellor of the German

Empire as additional illustration of the general truth: "Let there arise between the two nations antagonisms which touch their vital interests, then
I would like to see the arbitration treaty that does not burn like tinder"
(96). Essential to great-power status, and the related concepts of prestige,
position, and national honor, implied Mahan, is the ability of national
elites to recognize the demands of "vital interests." Mahan's discourse on
vital interests descended from a branch of turn-of-the century *Lebensphilosophie*, sharing patrimony with the life-force (*Lebenskraft*) animating
Ratzel's political geography.

The authority-conferring power of nature is a recurrent theme in Mahan's writings, linking an Enlightenment-era language of natural rights
to fin de siècle geopolitics. A realm of natural rights trumps legal rights.
As he wrote in 1911, "The Monroe Doctrine is . . . the reflex, as against
distant outsiders, of the instinctive impulse toward self-preservation, and
as such represents natural right—which is moral right—as opposed to
legal."[85] The Monroe Doctrine "must rest upon diplomacy, and its instrument, armament; not upon law" (81). Turning his gaze from the Americas
to the Persian Gulf, Mahan developed similar arguments about nature
as the sole valid tribunal. He insisted that British, Russian, and German
imperial competition must reflect on nature as criterion of right. "How
far are they guided by the natural tendency of things? How far are they
seeking to interject artificial arrangements, forced ambitions?"[86] Mahan
borrowed the phrase from the "wisdom" of an American, George Washington, who liked to advise, "Consulting the natural course of things,
forcing nothing" (214). The contrast of the "natural" with the "artificial"
is a deep structure in the text.

Mahan applied the nature/artifice dichotomy to the two states with
the greatest legitimate concerns in the political and military security of
the Gulf, based on "the fact of propinquity, of geographic nearness, or
of direct political interest" (222)—Britain and Russia. The northern part
of Persian trade, by land, was with Russia; the southern was by sea with
Great Britain. "By the disposition of all living things to grow, the two
tend continually to approach" (228). But "as a matter of fact, founded
on present territorial positions, there is in the nature of things no real, no
enduring antagonism concerning the Persian Gulf, except between Great

Britain and Russia. It is not to the interest of any third state to . . . disturb . . . the local balance of power." There is an "equilibrium" between the land power of the one and the sea power of the other (240). "The two systems are not dead, but living; not machines, but organisms; not merely founded, but rooted, in past history and present conditions" (241). What seems so odd about Mahan's references to "the nature of things" is that empire is rendered as a "living thing," a part of the natural world. But empires are not "things" and not governed by laws of nature. Mahan's confident pronouncements on the nature of things occluded normative questions about hierarchy and inequality, about whose rights to life and space matter most.

Ratzel and Mahan were both charismatic thinkers who helped create the perception that new intellectual tools were necessary to make sense of an interconnected world of imperial and capitalist competition. Sea power had changed the game of international politics and rendered the old continental *Realpolitik* passé. The concepts of *Lebensraum* and *Weltpolitik* met the demand for new concepts of national power and imperial strategy. Americans and Germans spent the 1890s glancing back and forth across the Atlantic Ocean at a rival they admired and feared. While Ratzel imagined an Atlantic "family" of nations, Mahan sought to mediate his sympathies for both England and Germany. The sympathetic view of German imperial ambitions shared by Reinsch, Coolidge, and Mahan at the turn of the century evaporated in 1914. Mahan's vitalistic and organic view of international relations emerged from his rationalizing reflections on the elasticity of the Monroe Doctrine over time. Through intellectual practices of comparison, intellectuals cultivated habits of mind and introduced turns of phrase that long outlived their authors. Though none of the actors in this drama called themselves "realists," many of their most characteristic gestures were developed in the years 1890–1910. Atlantic realism took shape in a competitive, mimetic process, furnishing a kind of mirror in which Germany's and the United States' international personae were constituted. This was the first Atlantic realist moment.

CHAPTER 2

Realism before "Realism"

Geopolitics in the Interwar Atlantic

THE FIRST ATLANTIC REALIST MOMENT stretched from the 1890s through the 1910s. Historians of geopolitics and international thought have described figures of this period like Alfred Mahan as a kind of proto-realist.[1] But it was not until Hans Morgenthau's field- and paradigm-defining works, written from 1946 to 1954, that realism attained its midcentury modern contours.[2] While the realists of the late 1940s and early 1950s generally characterized their interwar American predecessors as Wilsonians, this self-serving narrative occluded the fact that "realism" had already emerged as an intellectual motif in the fields of theology, law, and political science in the early 1930s.[3] One prominent convert to realism, William T.R. Fox of Columbia University, half-admitted as much in an essay in 1949. American research on international relations in the interwar period was largely sterile but punctuated already in the 1930s with examples of a "new realism."[4]

> Whether from Marx or from Machiavelli, from European geopolitics or American war debunking, from German sociology or Columbia historians, or from a change in the intellectual climate of American social science, generally, a new realism and a new interest in group interests—national, transnational, and subnational—was increasingly felt. Studies which interrelated the domestic and international political process became more frequent. (77)

Tracing the connections from the 1910s to the 1930s is an important challenge. Robert Vitalis rightly insists on "the protean nature of mid-1930s American realist discourse," and cautions against reading the 1930s backwards from the perspective of the late 1940s.[5]

The careers of the geographers Isaiah Bowman (1878–1950) and Karl Haushofer (1869–1946) shed light on a missing chapter in international thought: realism before it became "realism" in the paradigmatic IR sense. Bowman, an American geographer and advisor to Presidents Wilson and Franklin Roosevelt, and Karl Haushofer (1869–1946), Weimar Germany's most famous geopolitician and tutor to Adolf Hitler, may seem an unlikely pair. But the two led parallel and convergent lives in the interwar Atlantic.

Haushofer was a military man. The son of a professor in Munich, Haushofer often accompanied his father on walks with his colleague, the geographer Friedrich Ratzel. He enlisted in the Bavarian army at 18, taught at the Bavarian War Academy in 1903, and was stationed in Tokyo in 1909–10. As a member of the German East Asiatic Society (*Deutsche Gesellschaft für Natur- und Volkerkunde Ostasiens*), he mixed with other scholars and diplomats, and wrote over two dozen reports on Japan's lessons for the German army. Between 1910 and 1913, he turned these reports into a celebrated dissertation, *Greater Japan's Military Strength, World Position and Future.*[6] In World War I, he commanded regiments of up to three thousand soldiers at the battles of Jaroslaw, Dachnow, Rava-Ruska, and Lemberg (Lwow). Haushofer was named honorary professor in Munich in 1919. He eventually founded the *Zeitschrift für Geopolitik* (*Journal of Geopolitics*) in late 1923 with three other political geographers and became its sole editor in 1931.[7]

Before 1933, geopolitics in Germany flourished. As historian David T. Murphy writes, "geopolitical ideas, despite their frequent pseudoscientific vulgarity and theoretical inconsistency, attracted thinkers from across the political spectrum" (23). The discourse of geopolitics in Germany popularized the notion of Germany as a "people without space" (*Volk ohne Raum*), as a famous novel of the period was titled.[8] But Weimar geopoliticians did not share a consensus on Germany's demographic challenge: Was it overpopulated and therefore in need of more space, or declining in population, a "*Raum ohne Volk*"? (35) The *Zeitschrift* was the leading forum for the intellectually creative and ideologically diverse field of Weimar geopolitics. Aimed at a readership of academics, politicians, journalists, and teachers, the compact journal (never more than fifty pages), which was sold at newsstands across the country, appeared monthly from 1924 to 1944. Although it was "conservative and anti-Weimar in its general tone, it was nevertheless an often eccentric collection."[9] Despite pressure from his publisher, Kurt Vowinckel, who aligned with the Nazis in 1928, Haushofer published republicans like Eckart Kehr and Adolf Grabowsky, the liberal Jewish historian Hans Kohn, and even Communists like Institute for Social Research member Karl Wittfogel as late as 1932.[10] In dozens of books and hundreds of articles, Haushofer popularized the concept he drew from Ratzel of an expanded German "living space" (*Lebensraum*) in Central Europe. Not only parties on the Weimar Right but also the DDP and SPD Zentrum shared the goal of undoing the territorial losses imposed at Versailles. The *Zeitschrift* amplified these resentments about the amputation of German empire. It preached a fairer "distribution" of the earth's territory befitting a "great" European nation. The *Zeitschrift* had an international profile and readership; fully one quarter of its subscribers were foreign. It gave a platform to the anti-Wilsonian isolationist and Idaho senator William Borah (1865–1940), whom the editors dubbed the "steady champion of fair play in international relations."[11] With its short articles (no more than eight pages), the accessible journal had greater overseas sales than any other German journal by 1939.[12]

In his 1945 apologia Haushofer claimed, "All that was written and printed after 1933 was 'under pressure'."[13] While at times in real tension with the regime, Haushofer was nonetheless an opportunist who was willing to adapt his ideas in order to maintain his relevance until at least Barbarossa. But as early as 1931 he had made room in the journal for articles by Nazi Party members from the Working Group for Geopolitics.[14] At a meeting of geopoliticians called by the Central Institute for Education in 1935, he reassured the party representatives that "racial thinking" (*Rassedenken*) would be as central to geopolitical education as "spatial thinking" (*Raumdenken*) (126).[15] While his half-Jewish wife Martha represented a liability for him, Haushofer nevertheless ascended to top positions in the academic echelons of the Reich. Haushofer served as president of the German Academy from 1933 to 1937; as professor of geography at the University of Munich from 1933; as a member of the editorial board of the publishing company that controlled six of

Germany's largest circulation newspapers; and on the Reichsreform commission, which was charged with changing the regional divisions (*Gaue*) within Germany.[16]

Haushofer's ties to the Nazi Party extended to Hitler himself. After the failed "Beer Hall putsch" in Munich in 1923, Hitler was sentenced to Landsberg prison near Munich. Before Hitler went to prison, the concept of *Lebensraum* was not a prominent part of National Socialist discourse. Karl Haushofer helped change that. Rudolf Hess, the future deputy Führer of the Third Reich, brought Haushofer to visit Hitler in prison at least eight times in 1924.[17] Hess had fought under Haushofer in WWI and became his close friend, student, and research assistant. Hess became personal secretary to Hitler, and recorder of the first, dictated draft of *Mein Kampf*. With Hess's mediation, Haushofer visited repeatedly, tutoring Hitler on Clausewitz, Ratzel's *Political Geography* (1897), and the first issues of the *Zeitschrift*.[18] In 1940, Haushofer romanticized these meetings, recalling, in Herwig's words, "that a 'well-thumbed' copy of *Politische Geographie* had been among the 'most effective, most worked–through' volumes at Landsberg," a book that Hess and Hitler had "read with the sacred fire of passion."[19] Most historians agree that Haushofer had some direct influence on Hitler. Historian Hans-Adolf Jacobsen, for example, insists that the "similarities between Ratzel, Haushofer and Hitler on 'Geopolitik' are too serious to ignore."[20] But Haushofer's real significance in the 1920s was that he helped prepare German public opinion to accept the legitimacy of German empire-building, not his personal links to Hitler.[21] Haushofer and the *Zeitschrift* "generated intellectual arguments and linguistic formulations that buttressed the general legitimacy of a revanchist Nazi foreign policy, the full dimensions of which Haushofer could neither control, nor increasingly even influence."[22] Space, not race, was the defining orientation of German geopolitics before 1933, and the cause of its ultimate marginalization by the Nazi regime.[23]

Bowman was, like Haushofer, a prolific academic geographer in close proximity to the political class. But where Haushofer ultimately failed to achieve his geopolitical objectives for Germany, Bowman was more successful in shaping the US posture during and after World War II. Bowman was a WASP figure of the Eastern establishment, the president of the

American Geographical Society from 1915–35, and played a key role as advisor to Wilson at Versailles. He was a fixture of elite institutions like the Council on Foreign Relations and the Social Science Research Council. A professor of geography at Johns Hopkins, he became its president in 1935 and remained until 1948. After *Kristallnacht*, November 9, 1938, President Roosevelt formed an Advisory Committee on Political Refugees, asking Bowman to join it. The two men had known each other since 1921, both through the New York–based Council on Foreign Relations and the American Association of Geographers (CFR and AAG hereafter). Roosevelt endorsed the "M Project," one "conceived by Bowman as an updated and more focused [version of the wartime] Inquiry." Its mandate was to envision a postwar peace that would resettle refugees while thinking globally about population growth and possibilities of economic development in Europe's colonies.[24] By early November 1942, Bowman knew that the genocide of the Jews was occurring. In the seven years he was involved in resettlement planning, Bowman never expressed urgency about the extermination of European Jewry. According to the geographer Owen Lattimore, who worked with him at the M Project, Bowman "was profoundly anti-Semitic."[25] Bowman dissuaded President Roosevelt from supporting a Jewish homeland in Palestine. Bowman's concept of race played a key role in his scientific recommendations. "He was emphatic that white (including Jewish) settlement is differentially restricted by climate and just as emphatic that different peoples, defined by nationality, race or ethnicity, carried different cultures that made them more or less suitable for settlement in any given environment." For these reasons, Bowman supported restrictions on immigration to the United States, including quotas for Jews (308–9). At the end of 1939, Bowman was hired by the council to write a series of secret intelligence reports entitled "War and Peace Studies," to advise the State Department (325). At a meeting with the editor of *Foreign Affairs* and the CFR's executive director, Bowman told them the war offered a "grand opportunity" for the US to emerge as "the premier power in the world."[26] When it ended in February 1942, the War and Peace Studies project had "established a vital foundation for State Department postwar planning" (331). Bowman was an important architect of the US's postwar global role.

Haushofer was in some ways his direct antipode. He despised America, and spent the entire interwar period constructing a discipline, *Geopolitik* (geopolitics), the raison d'être of which was to right the territorial wrongs inflicted at Versailles. But like Haushofer, Bowman too was a serious student of Ratzel and Mackinder. Bowman followed Haushofer's career closely and knew of his ties to the Nazi Party. At the height of the Third Reich's military successes, in 1942, a panic broke out across leading American media: What was to be done about Haushofer, the genius who had manufactured Nazi Germany's mysterious superweapon, geopolitics? Soon, Bowman's previous associations with German geography earned him a moniker in the press that he hated: "America's Haushofer." That prompted Bowman to write an essay in which he drew a clear red line between his version of political geography and Haushofer's geopolitics: The "recent 'science' of geopolitics which assumes that political events depend upon the soil" puts forth "doctrines that are separated from democracy by an abyss so wide that today only war can bridge it."[27] Bowman struggled against the conflation of his thought with Haushofer's.

Bowman ultimately succeeded too well in disavowing any connection between German *Geopolitik* and American political geography. His narration, and others like it, reinforced a folk wisdom that remains nearly intact today: Wilsonians like Bowman were innocent of geopolitics. They were "idealists." The insurgent realists of the 1930s and 1940s exaggerated the need for their "old world" truths about power politics. Some of the Wilsonians, Quincy Wright, Frederick Schuman, and Denna Fleming, already had views that overlapped with those of the later realists.[28] The authors of the 1940s who exaggerated the differences between the "new" realism and the old American diplomacy made it difficult to recognize these continuities in the management of American empire. The Haushofer-Bowman dialogue, conducted through their writings, undercuts the force of exceptionalist narratives that treat American or German empire as unique. Despite national variations of emphasis, British, American, and German geopolitical thinkers of the interwar years shared a common vocabulary and carried on a common conversation. The Germans Ratzel and Haushofer, the Swede Kjellén, the Briton Mackinder, and the Americans Bowman and Semple read each other's work and found their national experiences to be comparable and relevant. Given the distortions of the 1940s, when geopolitics was imagined as an *urdeutsch* specialty, returning to Haushofer's writings before 1933 is revelatory: for him, British and American thinkers were the world leaders in geopolitics. Though they lacked the word, they pioneered the substance, Haushofer argued. The Americans forgot or denied their geopolitical past; Haushofer remembered.

Isaiah Bowman, Archibald Coolidge, and Elihu Root: Interwar International Thought in the US

An extensive historiography of British international thought has sought to correct the misleading impression generated by E.H. Carr's work that the interwar years were dominated by unworldly idealism, utopianism, and sentimentalism about international law.[29] Realists like Carr constructed an image of liberalism in international thought that bordered on caricature.[30] The tenor of the spaces in which the elite American policymakers Bowman, Archibald Coolidge, and Elihu Root overlapped, shifts our picture of the Wilsonian elite. Looking back in the 1990s, Anne-Marie Slaughter described Root as a forerunner of her own "liberal internationalism."[31] But as Samuel Moyn has noted, liberal internationalists of the 1990s were neither consistently liberal nor internationalist.[32] "Liberal internationalist" is an even more dubious descriptor of elite foreign policy opinion in the 1920s. Coolidge and Root opposed Wilson's plans to commit the US to the League of Nations.[33] Under Bowman's tenure, the American Geographical Society became a major resource for US diplomats and politicians who came to consult its maps and books. Famous geographers like Halford Mackinder and Paul Vidal de la Blache lectured there. Bowman built a team of researchers that he referred to as a sort of "faculty."[34] In 1917, Bowman was tapped to lead "the Inquiry," a prodigiously productive outfit that prepared Wilson with geographical research relevant to the postwar settlement, included as many as 150 members, and generated 2,000 reports and 1,200 maps. It has been called the first foreign policy "think tank." After the war's conclusion, President Wilson appointed Bowman chief territorial specialist of the US delegation to the Versailles Peace Conference. Drawing upon the research conducted at the

Inquiry, Bowman wrote *The New World: Problems in Political Geography*, a major work distributed to US consular offices around the world and used by the army as its standard global geography text through the end of WWII.[35]

Elihu Root was secretary of war under Presidents McKinley and Roosevelt 1899–1904; main architect of the Platt Amendment (1901), which reserved to the US the right to intervene in Cuba; secretary of state (1905–9) under Theodore Roosevelt; and senator from New York (1909–13). Root founded the Council on Foreign Relations in 1918.[36] *The New World* (1921) brought Bowman into Root's circle. In 1921, Root asked Bowman to join the council. In 1922, the council purchased the *Journal of International Relations* (formerly the *Journal of Race Development*), renamed it *Foreign Affairs*, and invited Bowman onto its editorial board.[37] In a private letter Bowman described the journal as "a plea for a forward foreign policy, interested in exploiting the world's natural resources and putting affairs in Washington in the hands of dispassionate experts who, unlike the public at large, know what they are doing."[38] The council evolved into an institution associated with Wilsonian ideas often described as "liberal internationalist."[39] But at the outset, liberalism and internationalism were highly circumscribed.

Beneath the genteel facade of *Foreign Affairs* lay the explicit racism of Social Darwinists like Madison Grant and Lothrop Stoddard. Archibald Coolidge, a professor of Russian history at Harvard, was appointed the journal's first editor. A year before, T. Lothrop Stoddard had published *The Rising Tide of Color: The Threat against White World Supremacy* (1920), a book "which made him the leading apostle of Nordic racial supremacy in the United States" (62). Stoddard was commonly known at the time as the protégé of Madison Grant, author of the best-selling *Passing of the Great Race* (1916), who wrote the introduction to *Rising Tide*. "No one now bothers to note," Robert Vitalis has written, "that Stoddard had been the protégé first of Archibald Cary Coolidge." Coolidge had supervised Stoddard's PhD thesis at Harvard.[40] Vitalis has shown in his revolutionary interpretation of American international relations thought that the maintenance of global racial hierarchy was the central rationale of the early American study of international relations.

Beneath the genteel facade of *Foreign Affairs* lay the explicit racism of Social Darwinists like Grant and Stoddard (64). As the fiery Stoddard "lectured widely and testified before Congress on the necessity of closing the country's borders," the staid articles in *Foreign Affairs* in the 1920s advanced the same global hierarchy of races and civilizations. In 1927, for example, Isaiah Bowman published an article in *Foreign Affairs* entitled "The Pioneer Fringe," which outlined "a science of settlement in aid of white peoples' expansion in northwest Canada, Rhodesia, western Australia and elsewhere."[41] His biographer writes, "With the Ratzelian influence on his geography increasingly applied to social concerns, a thread of Social Darwinism mixed with American racial prejudice continues in *The New World*" (190). The nexus of Bowman, Coolidge, and Root illustrates the need for a revised account of international thought in the interwar United States. Given these overlapping contexts and relationships between racist thought and elite liberal foreign policy-making, the common characterization of *Foreign Affairs*, or the council, as a vehicle of "liberal internationalism" is inadequate.

The notion of a clear division between liberal "idealists" and nonliberal "realists" in the interwar years is a tenacious myth. Root, Scott, and Hughes were the first three presidents of the American Society for International Law. Historian Pablo Scarfi writes, "All three epitomized the liberal internationalist mindset of the US political and foreign policy establishment, particularly of the Republican Party." Although Root and Scott could be seen to some extent as products of a "Wilsonian moment," they sought to distinguish themselves from Wilson's approach to world order, which was based on the enforcement of peace through alliances of power and collective security rather than legal diplomacy. They consistently opposed Wilson's initiative for international organization."[42] "Legalist imperialism" better captures the hegemonic ambitions of the American Society for International Law and *Foreign Affairs*.[43] Bowman, Coolidge, and Root were rooted in the Roosevelt-Mahan era and do not represent a break with it.[44] The transatlantic *Weltpolitik* of the fin de siècle linked Coolidge and Reinsch to Weber and Ratzel. Historian John Bew has shown that at least for a short time, the liberals at the *New Republic* also shared the commitment to the geopolitical thinking of

Theodore Roosevelt and Mahan.[45] Bowman's Wilsonianism was rooted in the Victorian-era debates shaped by Darwin, Ratzel, Turner, and Mackinder that emphasized the challenges posed by the "closing space" of the world carved by rival empires.[46] Haushofer and Bowman agreed with Mackinder: the twentieth century inaugurated an epochal break, a "post-Columbian age," in which there was no space left to discover.[47]

Haushofer's Synthesis: Ratzel, Kjellén, Mackinder

More than any other European or American figure, Haushofer institutionalized geopolitics as an academic field and made its concepts visible on a global scale. Institutes and journals around the world, from Italy to Japan, utilized Haushofer and German *Geopolitik* as their model.[48] While it was often misrepresented as an essentially German specialty, geopolitics was a multinational enterprise from its inception. Of the five scholars typically described as the founders and exemplars of "classical geopolitics"—Mahan, Ratzel, Kjellén, Mackinder, and Haushofer— only two are German.[49] Haushofer edited an edition of Ratzel's writings, praising Ratzel as "the far-seeing educator of his people, teaching [the Germans] a view of the world as consisting of great spaces"; he was, moreover, the prophet of "the Third Reich's requirement of growth."[50] Ratzel coined the term *Lebensraum*. But the term "*Geopolitik*," a neologism for which there was no Swedish equivalent, had been invented two decades earlier by the political scientist Rudolf Kjellén in 1899.[51] In the fall of 1917, at Péronne near the Somme River, Haushofer read Kjellén's book, *Contemporary Great Powers* (1914), and was delighted to see his own work cited as authoritative.[52] The discourse on "great powers" is a leitmotif of this study. In his 1915 work, Kjellén identified four powers of the first rank, and four just below it. Kjellén thus updated the *Weltreichslehre* of the 1890s. Britain, Germany, Russia, and the United States alone were "world powers." Austria-Hungary, France, Italy, and Japan counted as "great powers"—slightly below the world powers. Kjellén's language recalls the Atlantic discourse of vitalism and *Weltpolitik* in the 1890s: "Vigorous, vital states with limited space were held together by neither laws nor constitutions [but rather by] the categorical imperative of expanding their space by colonization, amalgamation, or conquest."[53]

Haushofer built bridges from the 1890s to the 1930s. In a 1931 radio address, Haushofer said, "[Standing on] the shoulders of Ratzel," and through his "research into the present-day Great Powers (*Großmächte*) . . . Kjellén was the first to identify the geopolitical path."[54] The Swede Kjellén was a friend who saw clearly that "the Germanic race" was now compelled to engage in a "decisive struggle for breathing space and living space" (544). From the early 1920s, Haushofer and his colleagues believed that this *Lebensraum* lay to the East, in the "undersettled spaces of Eurasia" (544).

Throughout the 1920s and 1930s, Haushofer argued that Germany needed to think beyond the nation-state and build a continental "Indo-European block" to "counterbalance" the sea power of Great Britain. Haushofer was deeply impressed by the (now classic) 1904 essay of Mackinder, "The Geographic Pivot of History." Haushofer followed Mackinder's description of the Eurasian continent as the "heartland." "He who controls the heartland, controls the Earth," Mackinder believed. Mackinder argued that the peoples of the "rimland"—the English, the Americans, and the Japanese—could only thrive if the Eurasian continent remained divided. Haushofer agreed with the diagnosis but flipped the value signs. In the decades-long debate over whether Germany's path to the status of a world power was better accomplished by land or sea, Haushofer was firmly in the Heartland (*Festland*) camp. The task of geopolitics, he wrote in *World Politics Today* (1932), was to overcome the division of Europe imposed at Versailles into "colony-possessing powers in the West, space-possessing powers in the East, and strangulated states in the Center."[55] Haushofer and Bowman, the architect and the foe of Versailles, were on a collision course.

Haushofer was ecstatic over the Munich Accord. He described the conference as "a happy day in the history of geopolitics" that had "severed the bonds of Versailles." After *Kristallnacht*, Haushofer appealed to Hess on behalf of Karl's half-Jewish wife, Martha for a letter of protection for his wife and two sons. Hess issued a "certificate of Aryan purity" on November 14. In a private letter to Ilse Hess from April 1939, he wrote that Hitler was like no other statesman since Bismarck. With the *Anschluss* and annexation of Bohemia and Moravia Hitler had "seized the hem of the gown of God." What Haushofer termed the "rejuvenating powers" (Germany, Italy, and Japan) were thwarting the "persisting powers" (Britain, France, and the United States).[56] The Molotov-Ribbentrop Pact signed the following August, was the fulfillment of his decades-long dream. Operation Barbarossa, the invasion of the Soviet Union launched two years later, erased all that he had helped accomplish.

The German Connection in American Geography

In the same year that Bowman joined the CFR, fellow geographer Ellen Semple (1863–1932) was elected president of the AAG.[57] She and Bowman shared a deep connection to Germany. Both were devoted readers of the German geographer Friedrich Ratzel. At Harvard University in the 1890s, Bowman had studied under William Morris Davis (1850–1934) and Nathaniel Shaler (1841–1906), both of whom were deeply influenced by Ratzel and turn-of-the-century race thinking.[58] Semple went straight to the source.

After Vassar, she went to Leipzig to study with Ratzel from 1891–92, returning to work with him in 1895.[59] She reviewed many of Ratzel's works for American journals in the 1890s.[60] In 1903 she published *American History and Its Geographic Conditions*, a book which responded to the anxieties generated by Turner's thesis that the frontier was at an end. Semple argued that geographical "laws" of expansion indicated that there was no limit to potential American growth.[61] Invoking Ratzel's authority, Semple declared that the "commercial strength of the American Republic was bound sooner or later to find a political expression in that international struggle for existence, which is a struggle for space."[62] Turner invited her to join a prominent panel on the relationship of geography and history at the American Historical Association's annual conference in 1907.[63] Semple's *Influences of Geographic Environment: On the Basis of Ratzel's System of Anthropo-Geography* is dedicated "to the memory of Friedrich Ratzel . . . the great master who was my teacher and friend during his life, and after his death my inspiration."[64] Semple was an influential popularizer of Ratzel's environmental determinist view of geography.[65]

Given their own self-conscious debts to Ratzel, it is not surprising that both Bowman and Semple carefully followed developments in German political geography and geopolitics. In a 1924 review of another author from the Haushofer circle, Alexander Supan,[66] Semple wrote, "It is characteristic of the German school of political geography that its logic so often rests upon mere classification, and the descent is not far from this to *obiter dicta* and the worship of ritual and mummery" (665). In 1927, Bowman unfavorably reviewed books by three authors in the Haushofer circle, Otto Maull, Walther Vogel, and Rudolf Reinhard. There, Bowman distinguished between an allegedly rational American political geography and a German geopolitics "intoxicated" with the state.[67] Yet in that year, apparently, Bowman's concerns about the deterioration of intellectual standards took a back seat to his international scientific diplomacy. With the Germans excluded from the International Geographic Union (IGU) since the end of the war, the British, French, and Italians dominated. As a result, "US geographers begrudged the exclusion of German geographers with whom they had such close ties" (279). In 1927, the Germans were invited to join the League of Nations, and also to the next IGU congress. In 1931, Bowman accepted the presidency of the IGU with the express goal of steering both the Germans and the Americans back into the union. Although Bowman had the support of several German geographers, "Nazi geographers bullied their colleagues into officially boycotting the 1931 Paris congress, where Bowman took over the Presidency" (280). This was understandable, since Bowman had long been a hero to Polish nationalists. He was "internationally identified" with his role in 1919 "in establishing a western Polish boundary that cut deep into prewar German territory" as well as the Danzig corridor that split East Prussia from the rest of Germany (280). Because his *New World* represented a "winner's eye global vision" to German and Austrian geographers, he "became the principal academic nemesis against which theories and ideas of German geopolitics were fashioned" (281). Bowman failed to bring the Germans into the IGU. Though he "devoured every text on [geopolitics] coming out of Germany," he "published nothing on geopolitics throughout the 1930s," a "puzzling" silence (283). Smith surmises that Bowman "sensed he could not lead the public critique of

German geopolitics in the US, simultaneously lead the effort to pull German geographers into the IGU and champion the discipline of geography at home" (284). Once World War II started, Bowman's close ties to the Germans would become a liability.[68]

Catching Up with the Americans: Belatedness and Comparison in Haushofer's *Geopolitik*

In his writings of the 1920s and up to Hitler's accession to power, Haushofer depicted German geopolitics as a belated science. German thinkers needed to catch up with the more advanced Anglo-American theorists of geopolitics. Haushofer's debts to the British geographer Mackinder are debated but at least discussed in the secondary literature.[69] The praise he reserved for the Americans he considered his peer geopoliticians, Mahan, Semple, and Reinsch, illustrates the existence of an Atlantic realist tradition that stretches from the 1890s to the 1930s. It is also astonishing in light of his visceral dislike of America in general. In a private letter of 1918, the 49-year-old artillery commander Haushofer wrote, "The Americans are truly the only people on earth towards whom I feel a deep instinctive hatred."[70] But in 1925, Haushofer published a major book on the "building blocks" of the discipline to which he had devoted his life.[71] "Why has the intellectual leadership of the field been so conspicuously dominated by the Anglo-Saxon countries (Mackinder, Curzon, Semple, P.M. Roxby, A. Mahan, Brooks, Bowman and other Americans)?"[72] France, England, Japan, the USSR, and the US all had institutions designed to advise politicians on geopolitics and foreign policy, he noted. In the US in particular, Haushofer argued, professors like Woodrow Wilson and Paul Reinsch had exercised real influence on foreign affairs (64). Haushofer asserted that Americans and British were geopoliticians in all but name (59).[73] "British imperial phraseology," he wrote, "seldom uses the word '*Geopolitik*' . . . but it makes the case for it much more forcefully than the continental Europeans under the name 'political and commercial geography.'"[74] Haushofer was right. The author James Fairgrieve, for example, with his *Geography and World Power* (1915), contributed "a very valuable textbook of geopolitics in the British imperial view, though the word does not appear therein at all" (272).[75] Karl's wife,

Martha translated the entire volume into German in 1925.[76] In his lau-
datory introduction, Haushofer wrote, "It does not seem unjustified for
a German publisher which seeks to foster geopolitics as a mission that it
adopt for its own a handbook (*Handbuch*) based on the practice of the
most successful empire-builders of our time—the Anglo-Saxons!" (8).
The Haushofers' Fairgrieve translation illustrates how relevant they found
Anglo-American models for German geopolitics. It also attests to an Atlantic space of geopolitics constituted by translation and conceptual flow.

The sense of belatedness also drove his 1931 radio address, "On Geopolitics." Haushofer wrote that the development of geopolitics in Germany
represented a response to global trends evident since the late nineteenth
century: the "rapidly advancing trend of creating universities and profes-
sorships in political science," in France, the US, England, and Japan.[77]
"Some of the best geopolitical works of our time could be found in the
tough representatives of world capitalism in the Anglo-Saxon lands" (545).
The death of Ratzel at age 59 slowed the progress of the "people in the
world best educated in geography" (543). But Ratzel was not his own
best popularizer, Haushofer admitted. "In the Anglo-Saxon countries, in
France, Russia and Japan, one took up the stimulating notions of Ratzel,
made them more accessible than they were in his somewhat difficult, dark
and aphoristic style, and utilized them for practical politics . . . as Mackinder and Fairgrieve in England [and] Mahan and Roosevelt did in the US"
(543). We see with "all the great powers of our the day, not only with their
armament preparations but also in the influence of their national culture,
their economic links . . . wide outside of their own borders." Haushofer
foregrounded the concept of "vital interests" as useful. That concept had
emerged from the vitalism of *Lebensphilosophie*, and was developed by
Ratzel, Mahan, and Reinsch. "Wholly unabashedly . . . the English speak
of their vital interests (*lebenswichtige Interessen*) in Japan," while insisting on defending the Belgian and Dutch border vis Germany (550). By
describing the "great powers" as having set a challenging "tempo" (549),
Haushofer admonished Germany to catch up.

Haushofer therefore imagined geopolitics as the motor that could
speed Germany's historical tempo. Haushofer attributed Germany's back-
wardness in geopolitics to the dominance of its educational system by legal

training. For geopolitics to make a difference in Germany's fate therefore required a new type of academic learning: "Despite all the refinement of the juristic education of our statesmen, the natural scientific methods for the determination of political-geographic processes remain alien to [us]." Haushofer disparaged this "nation of lawyers," focused as they were on dead history and the *lex lata*: "We looked back rather than ahead. In this manner we lost contact with the future."[78] He argued that law was too static to respond to the dynamics of change in the relative power of states. But this insight concealed its own blind spot: geopolitics froze history in its own way too.

His focus on the Anglo-Saxons in these essays slights the Japanese geopolitical thinkers with whom he had significant exchanges.[79] Haushofer's area of expertise was East Asia and the Pacific, not England, America or northern Europe. Between 1927 and 1941, Haushofer published ten books in the German East Asia Society series.[80] Haushofer was more personally invested in the politics of the Pacific world. But his claims about the Anglo-American orientation of German *Geopolitik* still are highly valuable for remapping the history of realism in the North Atlantic before 1930. They show that the Anglo-Saxon and American empires were important to the German's comparative imagination of the prerequisites of world power. There is, as Christian Spang has shown, also a very strong German-Japanese connection, stretching from the Meiji period forward. But these particular texts demonstrate that realism was constituted through practices of comparison that were, in this instance, transatlantic. Haushofer's testimony is corroborated by many texts in which he, or members of his circle, were preoccupied with the unmatched "success" of Anglo-Saxon imperialists. Throughout the 1920s and early 1930s, Haushofer offered a narrative of geopolitics that depicted Germany as a laggard compared with other nations. France, Soviet Russia, Japan, but preeminently the "Anglo-Saxon" countries of Great Britain and the US, were the leaders in the field.

Haushofer looked to Britain because the tasks British scientific geography set for itself at the turn of the century matched what he was looking for. Scientific geography would be an "aid to statecraft by identifying the major foreign policy dilemmas facing the British and by training children to become fierce imperial citizens."[81] Haushofer had a similar goal for German *Geopolitik*. But in Haushofer's hands, geopolitics pursued contradictory strategies of intellectual legitimation. The geopoliticians struggled to attain theoretical consistency, expending enormous energy on hair-splitting distinctions between *politische Geographie* and *Geopolitik*, on the exact contributions of Ratzel or Kjellén to the state of the art.[82] Perhaps that is why Haushofer and the others often retreated to definitions of their enterprise as an artistic teaching, a *"Kunstlehre"* or aid to the "art of politics" (*Kunst der Politik*). In many passages of his writings, Haushofer described geopolitics as an "art" (*Kunst*).[83] In a letter to his wife in 1917, Haushofer describes his experience of reading Kjellén for the first time as an epiphany: *Geopolitik* was a posture of the soul (*Seelen-Haltung*)! Later, in 1931, Haushofer described Kjellén in similar language as a *"Volksseelenkenner"*—a knower of the people's soul.[84] The language points to the paradox that geopolitics legitimated itself through a combination of romantic idealism and deterministic positivism. Haushofer articulated this strange amalgam when he averred that geopolitics was "not only scholarship, [but] rather an applied discipline, a doctrine of an art (*Kunstlehre*), without which the statesman and . . . the whole people risks danger . . . or error."[85] Geopolitics, he continued, is the "most faithful preparation for the art of political action of politically formative and creative men."[86] In a private letter to Haushofer from 1941, his publisher Vowinckel wrote worriedly that Haushofer's unique combination of outstanding knowledge and the artistic capacity (*künstlerische Fähigkeit*) to shape it in the service of politics could not be easily institutionalized. "I ask: we have called ourselves a *Kunstlehre*. How shall a *Kunstlehre* be institutionalized in the university?"[87] The midcentury American realists would soon face a similar set of dilemmas.

Haushofer and his circle built on the Rankean notion of seeing the world as it actually is. This is an epistemological claim described in a visual register: "*Geopolitik* . . . will present our statesmen with the scientific equipment of concrete facts and proven laws to help them see political situations as they really are."[88] The description of *Geopolitik* as a type of "equipment" suggests what social theorists mean by a habitus. Education, socialization, and training would give the geopolitician a privileged tool for *seeing things as they really are.* "Only a nation as ungifted in geopolitics as Germany," he wrote, "could produce a work like *The World as Will and Representation* without any effort to situate human beings within the specific environment (*Lebensraum*) which shapes their being" (65).[89] These stereotypes illustrate the lack of rigor in the geopoliticians' thinking. A nation "ungifted" in geopolitics would have to be taught it as science. Paradoxically, this work would be taught by elites governed by their intuition.

Haushofer and his circle offered an answer to a Weberian question: "How shall we routinize the charisma of the statesman?" The notion of geopolitics as a *Kunstlehre* anticipates the solution the next generation of Atlantic realists found to this dilemma in the 1940s and 1950s. Many of the German émigrés who later described themselves as realists also commonly spoke of the "art of politics" as a way of describing its ineffable qualities.[90] Haushofer's musings on the *Kunstlehre* of geopolitics also recall Maltzahn's advice to his fellow German naval officers at the turn of the century to read Ratzel and allow it to sharpen their faculties of perception and judgment. Geopolitics was an important component of the interwar Atlantic realist tradition.

CHAPTER 3

Carl Schmitt's Practice of Imperial Comparison in the 1930s and 1940s

POLITICAL THEORISTS, legal theorists, and historians in the last fifteen years, especially those who identify as politically Left, have found much to admire in Schmitt's writings on empire and international relations from the Weimar Republic, Third Reich, and postwar era. These scholars do not deny that Schmitt's career is marred by personal opportunism and his work by a deep-seated antisemitism. They recognize that his work expresses strongly authoritarian preferences, and often functioned as propaganda which rationalized and legitimate Nazi state-building, empire-building, and even the Holocaust. They tend to condemn the man, or at least many of his "choices," but excuse the work. They assert that he is an intellectual of the first rank, a "classic" whose significance transcends the contingencies of the life and its original historical contexts.

Schmitt's 1950 *The Nomos of the Earth*, a book nearly complete in 1945 and therefore a "wartime book," is illustrative of this canonizing trend. It has had a surprisingly galvanizing impact on left theorists of international relations in the last fifteen years. Scholars such as Anthony Anghie, Andreas Kalyvas, William Rasch, and Chantal Mouffe have made the case that even Schmitt's wartime writings contain a profound and relevant critique of imperialism and thus prefigure postcolonial critiques of international law and Eurocentric world order. In the early 2000s, Chantal Mouffe argued that Schmitt's juxtaposition of legitimate *Großräume* to abstract universalisms offered a fitting template for resisting US unipolarity. A multipolar "pluriverse" of competing great powers in balance was preferable to a US. unchecked by any rival.[1] However, the appropriation of *Großraum* risks importing more assumptions about the international political realm than are prudent for a progressive Left to do. Contra Mouffe, and others, Schmitt's writings require such deep theoretical reconstruction in order to be useful that they would cease to be recognizably Schmittian. But neither is the critical task to erect a cordon sanitaire around Schmitt. A much more promising strategy is to open Schmitt's texts to the transatlantic contexts that formed and informed them, to see how they participated in a multipolar conversation among empires about the sources and methods of global power.

The conceptual history of the term *Großraum* in Schmitt's wartime writings illustrates one way we might advance beyond the current impasse of reading Schmitt's wartime writings either too concretely (as a direct articulation of the Third Reich's policy goals and rationales) or too abstractly (as a theorist of the contemporary postcolonial moment). One can read this concept concretely, as he urged us to treat concepts in general; indeed, his own theory of concepts requires us to turn the contextual gaze on him as well. As he wrote in *The Concept of the Political* and elsewhere, concepts obtain their meaning from "concrete" contexts, and mean nothing outside them.[2] But instead of situating Schmitt deeper and deeper in the German context, and making him, in some ways, irredeemably alien, one can contextualize him anew. A genealogy of the conceptual pair *Großraum/Lebensraum* begins with the German national frame but opens onto a broader comparative and transnational context: an Atlantic intellectual context of geopolitical theorizing that stretches back to the 1890s and forward through the Cold War. At Nuremberg, Haushofer pleaded, "What about Mackinder?", referring to his intellectual debts to the British geopolitician Halford Mackinder. Haushofer was arguing that if geopolitics was a shared Atlantic intellectual project, it was unjust to single him out for calumny.[3] Resituating Schmitt in the *moyen durée* (1890–1945) of Atlantic debate about empire can help us to better appreciate the ways in which neither American nor British nor German history is exceptional. The relationship of race and space, geopolitics and biopolitics, is an artifact of a transnational history from which no imperial nation-state was exempt. Schmitt would become less the exceptionally "dangerous mind," whom we alternately taboo and fetishize, but a more pedestrian site of investigation, an important node in the making of spatial and racial imaginaries, a creative thinker in the competitive struggles between the German empire and its rivals, particularly the United States.

This alternative contextualization would not preclude the kinds of theoretical appropriation of his theory we have seen heretofore, but neither would they permit us to exaggerate Schmitt's originality, benignity, or exceptional status as "classic."

In this chapter, I offer the term *Großraum* as a test case for the assertion that Schmitt's salience as a political theorist of empire transcends his own imbrication with the Nazi imperial project of the 1940s. I argue that Schmitt's concept of *Großraum* does not fully overlap with the Nazi pursuit of *Lebensraum* in which it eventually culminated, but it cannot be neatly removed from it either. I reconstruct the discourse on *Großraum* on the basis of surviving evidence. On the basis of this constructive and reconstructive work, I argue that a genealogy of Schmitt's "realist" geopolitics takes one deep into the heart of Nazi biopolitics, and that any genealogy of realism in the twentieth century must contend with this important chapter.

Beginning in the late 1880s and early 1890s, Germany wrestled with the question of whether it should aim chiefly at the goal of becoming the most important continental power in Europe, or at an expanded overseas presence of colonies backed by sea power.[4] The question of empire by land or by sea generated a kind of essentialist ontology of power: a nation was fundamentally either a land power or a sea power. Carl Schmitt's notion of *Großraum* was influenced by Ratzel's concept of *Lebensraum*, his reading of the Monroe Doctrine, and the writings of Haushofer and Mackinder, both telluric (land-centered) thinkers. Schmitt's writings on *Großraum* modernized and transmitted to the twentieth century the most influential theories of political geography and geopolitics developed in the years 1890–1910 by the Anglo-American and German thinkers Friedrich Ratzel, Karl Haushofer, Halford Mackinder, and Alfred Thayer Mahan.

Schmitt cited Ratzel, Haushofer, and Mackinder as influences on his thought. In Schmitt's 1939 essay, he acknowledged Ratzel as "the founder of a new science of space," who argued that "coming to terms with space [is] the defining trait of all life."[5] Schmitt also referred to Haushofer as "the master of geopolitical scholarship."[6] Schmitt acknowledged Mackinder in the preface to *Nomos of the Earth* (1950): "I am much endebted to geographers, most of all to Mackinder. Nevertheless, a juridical way of thinking is far different from geography."[7] One leading interpretation of the tradition of German geopolitics lends support to Schmitt's claim that *Großraum* should not be conflated with *Lebensraum*. Indeed, Schmitt's writings on *Großraum* were criticized by some of his critics in the regime for being insufficiently "*völkisch*."[8] In their important works, Mark Bassin and David Murphy argue that space, not race, was the guiding framework of geopolitical thought, and that this framework led to the marginalization of the discipline in the Third Reich.[9] Bassin and Murphy raise doubts as to whether and how German geopolitics can be mapped onto German wartime biopolitics. While this is a convincing argument for Weimar geopolitics, the boundaries between "spatial" and "racial" thought broke down quickly after 1933.

Although by the time he wrote *Nomos*, Schmitt had become skeptical of the dichotomy of land power and sea power, there is a great deal of evidence in the texts from 1939–42 that Schmitt emphasized the telluric pole of this dichotomy. Dan Diner has written of the centrality of the land-sea distinction in Haushofer, and the influence of Halford Mackinder on Haushofer.[10] Schmitt's commitment to this distinction is a foundational one, visible not only in the 1939/41 essay, but in his *Land und Meer* (1942). While the original Monroe Doctrine obtained its legitimacy from the integrity of the continental space it describes, Schmitt explains, the British fail to ground its "political idea" in a correspondingly discrete territorial space:

> [The] Monroe Doctrine and British sea-lane doctrine are often spoken of as parallel but they are more like opposites . . . The one had a cohesive spatial dimension [*zuhammenhängenden Raum*], the American continent, in view. The British by contrast have no cohesive continent [*zuhammenhängender Kontinent*], but rather the most dispersed locations . . . The Mediterranean for England is only one path (*Strasse*) among many, indeed only a shortcut and a canal, while for Italy it represents *Lebensraum*. The contrast between path and *Lebensraum* is in the entirety of its depth visible. (34–35)

Schmitt's commitment to extending the Ratzelian-Haushoferian geo-imaginary is also evident in his dichotomized understanding of world powers: the terrestrial German Reich, "in the middle of Europe," must defend itself on two "fronts" against the "universalism" of the liberal-democratic West and the "universalism" of the Bolshevik world revolutionary East (51). In his characterization of the Soviet Union as the embodiment of a space-transcending—and therefore illegitimate—"universalism," Schmitt gave us an account consistent with the general Nazi figuration of a two-front war against Judeo-Bolshevism. But Schmitt equivocated on the question of whether the Soviet Union deserved its own *Großraum*. At times the Soviet Union is viewed through the Ratzelian/Haushoferian lens of a "land power" commanding respect; at other times, it is an embodiment of a fissiparous land-disregarding universalism—a "spaceless political idea," par excellence.

There is some evidence in his writings of 1941–42 that Schmitt viewed the decision to invade the Soviet Union as a major strategic mistake. So testified his contemporaries, Nicholas Sombart and Julien Freund, decades later.[11] This view—if it is credible—may have reflected his preference for a German-Russian alliance of land powers—also Haushofer's dearest hope and greatest disappointment. Scholars of Schmitt have noted that the fourth edition of *Völkerrechtliche Großraumordnung* appeared with a new, signed preface dated July 28, 1941—several weeks after Operation Barbarossa had begun. By retaining a passage that appeared to reaffirm the validity of the German-Soviet Boundary and Friendship Treaty of September 28, 1939—a supplement to the nonaggression pact signed by Molotov and Von Ribbentrop in August—he implied that he viewed the invasion of the Soviet Union as an international crime. Requiring very close reading between the lines—the treaty offers a precedent for the concept of Reich more broadly—Schmitt's decision to reference the treaty can in no way be construed as a heroic act of defiance, as Sombart and Freund imply in their apologetic accounts. Regardless of his exact intent, by doing so Schmitt gave himself a building block of the defense he would use at Nuremberg four years later: his opposition to the invasion underscored his status as a nonpolitical scholar—a theorist of *Großraum* not *Lebensraum*. His defense of German *Großraum* in Central Europe could be neatly sundered from the war of extermination in the East.[12]

An alternative path of contextualization is to open Schmitt's texts to the transatlantic discussion that begins with the Monroe Doctrine and reaches its first crest of intensity in the 1890s. Already in Ratzel's 1878 book on the United States, we hear prefigurations of Ratzel's mature *Lebensraum* concept, echoes of Mahan, and anticipations of Carl Schmitt. He explains that the US illustrates a "general truth of political geography—that states are living essences that are never fixed, always growing or in retreat." Echoing Mahan's reflections on the naval competition between Great Britain and the US: "In comparison with other continental states, [the US] belongs to the group of the world-powers [*Weltmächte*] as indicated by size. These are the true great-powers [*Großmächte*], that take up nearly 3/5 of the earth's four continents; one can name them 'continental powers.'"[13] Anticipating Carl Schmitt's contrast of the British Empire with the United States, Ratzel wrote, "The British empire with its possessions strewn across the world can least of all be compared with the compact power of the United States" (87).

In his essay for a *Festschrift* for Carl Schmitt, the influential conservative jurist Joseph Kaiser (1921–1998) described *Großraum* as a concept that has "stood the test of time." NATO, COMECON, the Warsaw Pact, and the Latin American Free Trade Zone are all examples of *Großräume*. Even the treaties of Paris and Rome contain language describing the "same binding of political, economic and legal organization" that Schmitt pioneered with his concept in 1939. "In reality," he writes, "this was a scientific diagnosis . . . nothing other than a *völkerrechtliche* [international-legal] construction." The analytical adequacy of the concept is taken as proof of its historical innocence and essential normality: "This reality was worldwide. It was also not a wholly new category."[14] Kaiser also points to the vigorous National Socialist critique of Schmitt, indeed, its supposed "vehemence" (544). Gruchmann and others are wrong to see in Schmitt the Nazi project, Kaiser argues, because of the "deep irreconcilability of biological-racial Lebensraum and the rationally constructed *Großraum* concept" (545).

On April 1, 1939, at the Kiel Institute for Politics and International Law, Carl Schmitt, then a professor at the University of Berlin, delivered the lecture "*Völkerrechtliche Großraumordnung* with a Ban on

Intervention for Spatially Foreign Powers: A Contribution to the Concept of Empire in *Völkerrecht*." The concept of *Großraum* articulated the notion of a hegemonic Reich that shapes the borders, sovereignty, and identity of a territory or region. There, Schmitt made the case for the Monroe Doctrine as a "precedent case," "the first and until now most successful example of an international-legal *Großraumsprinzip*." He argued that "the core, the idea of a *Völkerrechtliche Großraumordnung*, can be transferred to other spaces [*Räume*], other historical situations, and other friend-foe groupings" (22). Schmitt explained that from the international-legal perspective, "space" and "political ideas" cannot be separated: "For us there are neither space-less political ideas, nor the obverse, spaces or principles of space without ideas" (29). Indeed, the spatial referent of the concept itself shifted between and within the four different editions printed between April 1939 and the fall of 1941. As Peter Stirk noted, a comparison of editions reveals that Schmitt was "rather imprecise, referring at times to 'East European space' or 'Central and Eastern European space', and at others to 'Middle and Eastern European space.'"[15] Widely reported in the foreign press,[16] the original lecture suggested to some observers that Schmitt was the most influential theorist of Hitler's expansive foreign policy, whereas, in fact, Schmitt was less powerful than he had been from 1933 to 1936.

Can Schmitt's concept of *Großraum* can be disentangled from the broader Nazi discourse on Lebensraum in this period? When the prosecutor Robert Kempner at Nuremberg charged Schmitt with being the architect of the policy of conquering *Lebensraum*, Schmitt replied that when he spoke of *Großraum*, he was speaking the language of "scholarship" (*Wissenschaft*) and not politics, of space and not race. Schmitt asserted that there was no connection between his internationally recognized and legitimate scholarly work, and the racist language of *Lebensraum* promoted by the SS. He attempted to distinguish sharply between "the intention to promote scholarly research and knowledge," on the one hand, and the intention "to promote practical goals and practical results," on the other.[17] When Kempner shifted tack, reminding Schmitt that Hitler used the term *Großraum* too, Schmitt parried by asserting that it was also used by representatives of other states.[18] His point is not without merit: the concept belongs to a larger universe of geopolitical concepts which were, if not the common property of mankind, at least that of the Atlantic great powers. However, it is belied by the fact that in Schmitt's own work he at times uses the terms interchangeably.[19]

In one of the most convincing readings of the text, Stirk writes that judgments of this period of Schmitt's work "range from qualified exoneration, through assertions that his ideas, though deplorable, were vague and irrelevant to the practice of the Nazi New Order, to condemnation for legitimating the worst excesses of the regime."[20] Indeed, scholars diverge widely on the question of the extent to which Schmitt, who indisputably served the Reich between 1933 and 1936, was equally complicit—between 1939 and 1942—with Nazi empire-building and the genocide of Jews, Slavs, and Poles that accompanied it. Diemut Majer pointedly designates the demographic reordering project *Plan Ost* ("Plan East"), the "highpoint of Nazi *Großraum* thought (*Großraumdenken*)."[21] Günther Maschke, one of Schmitt's most dedicated defenders, "dismisses Majer out of hand."[22] But as Stirk writes, even a biographer as sympathetic as Bendersky finds Schmitt's defense at Nuremberg unconvincing: "Schmitt had taken pride in the combative stance of his works . . . his contemporaries were in no doubt about this aspect of his thought." Stirk concludes judiciously, "Despite the blatant anti-Semitism of [*Völkerrechtliche Großraumordnung*] and approval of ethnic cleansing, racial principles played little direct role in Schmitt's elusive comments on the internal structure of the *Großraum*." Not explicitly racist in intent, the concept of a *Großraumordnung* was easily instrumentalized; "precisely because of its lacunae, [it] created the intellectual space which others, including consistent racists, could fill in."[23]

Stirk's conclusion dovetails with that of legal historian Michael Stolleis, who argues that scholars "competed to provide the slogans and catchwords" for a fast-changing relationship of the Reich to the states it conquered and occupied.[24] Stirk too explains that the concept "*Großraum*" was designed to solve a concrete problem: how to "reconcile German hegemony with something short of direct annexation and radical Germanization."[25] In other words, at this stage in the war, the Third Reich was attempting to figure out "how to generate sufficient political homogeneity to be able to dispense with the cruder forms of occupation and repression" (373). Schmitt invented new language for this colonial relationship with the neologism "*bündische Zusammenfassung*," which might be translated as "associated amalgamation."

The boundaries of the Third Reich's *Großraum* expanded with each new conquest. But this conditioning by wartime did not resolve the question: To which historical time did *Großraum* belong? Schmitt offered a contradictory account. He asserted that Germany's 1939 claim to hegemony in Central Europe had a clear historical precedent. The current conception of *Großraum* finds its "precedent" and precursor in the Monroe Declaration—it is "the first in the history of modern international law to speak of a *Großraum*."[26] But he also insisted that the concept's meaning was without precedent. As such, Schmitt flirted with paradox: "The transformation of the spatial concept is today powerfully underway in all realms of human thought and action . . . The word *Großraum* will serve to bring this change to scientific self-awareness" (74). Deriving from a precedent set a century before, it is also supposed to embody an epistemic break with all concepts of space preceding it (11).

Schmitt correctly noted that the concept appeared first in the technical-industrial realm, not the juristic or political sphere. "The word *Großraum* however obtained its first concrete realization, decisive for its concept-formation, after the first World War and then only in the conjunction *Großraumwirtschaft*" (22). Still, economic historians of Germany have given us some evidence that the discourse on *Großraumwirtschaft*, on which Schmitt draws, long predates the Third Reich, and is more indicative of the presence of "informal" empire of economic penetration than direct occupation or "formal" empire.[27]

But *Großraum* was a work-in-progress. Schmitt ingratiatingly credited the "practical work and publications" of various Nazi ministers whose work has helped "*Großraum*"-thought to develop. Stirk explains that "the emphasis on *Großraum* as a 'realm of achievement' (*Leistungsraum*) in the later editions of *VRGO* is difficult to separate from the efforts of the Third Reich to mobilize the industrial potential of the conquered states."[28] The discourse of *Großraum* in the 1930s pointed toward the United States in economic terms, not just in terms of the Monroe Doctrine. As Carl Duisburg of the IG Farben chemicals trust wrote in March 1931: "[The] strong industrial states and the agrarian states looking for new markets push toward greater international economic spaces . . . This tendency was started by the United States . . . [but] also in Europe this aim of the regional economic space seems to be gradually taking shape."[29] Intellectuals affiliated with research institutes, whom Berghahn refers to as "*Großraum* theoreticians," shared "the belief that the world was evolving in terms of *Großraum* blocs," a belief "no less axiomatic than elsewhere in government and industry."[30] Berghahn identifies a more "probusiness" camp that included Walter Funk's economics ministry, in which State Secretary Schlotterer was the key figure. Schlotterer and others urged the *Reichsgruppe Industrie* to develop more concrete proposals: for example, Werner Daitz (a name Schmitt mentioned too)[31] and some of the big corporations advocated a degree of economic development among the conquered, though not so much that they would move beyond purveyors of raw materials and handicrafts. The agrarian wing in the Nazi movement and the SS with its resettlement plans, by contrast, were united that Europe's organization should not be left to private industry. The models envisioned by *Großraum* theory

> were almost benign by comparison with those of the Ludendorffians who . . . more than ever before . . . aimed for formal empire, complete autarky and the underdevelopment of the East through criminal exploitation . . . The more the conquered territories were given over in 1941–42 to these forces as an experimental field for their racist New Order recipes, the more the balance of power tilted away from Schlotterer, the *Reichsgruppe* and big business. Reckless exploitation and Germanization slowly replaced the more indirect approaches of industrial cooperation of 1940. Purely biological visions began to outflank the proposals of the *Reichsgruppe*, which arguably, until that time, still contained some measure of rational calculation.[32]

Berghahn's analysis is important here because it supports the contrasts advocated by Maschke, Kaiser, and Schmitt himself: *Großraum* was not inherently tied to "racial" considerations.

The analyses of the fields of international law by two leading historians, Ulrich Herbert and Michael Stolleis, also support this dichotomy of racial and spatial thought. Before showing how this dichotomy collapses in the texts in question, let us first set out the case for their separateness, a case in which the prize evidence is the critiques of Schmitt by the *völkisch* Right and the SS. It is true that Schmitt was criticized by numerous scholars of international law active in the Third Reich, as Joseph Kaiser and others have noted. Schmitt has adduced this as evidence of his fundamental innocence of complicity with the regime. But where he fits in the "intellectual field" of international law is a complex question, one made no easier by the way in which Schmitt's texts probe the national and disciplinary boundaries of the field. Stolleis has given the best account of how a separate "National Socialist-*völkisch*" conception of international law emerged "only slowly."[33] "In the phase of immediate war preparations, the proponents of traditional international law found themselves on the defensive . . . As the SS gained in importance, the subordination of international law to *völkisch* concerns became increasingly a semantic identification mark" (416). On the one hand, Stolleis describes Schmitt's "National Socialism and *Völkerrecht*" (1934) as "the first sketch of an international law unique to National Socialism, in Schmitt's words, not an abstract order of all nations, but a 'concrete order of certain states and peoples recognized for their concrete characteristics.'" Further, Stolleis asserts that beginning around 1938, the term "Reich" came to fill a gap left behind by the state (*Staat*) for traditional-minded authors. "But this kind of thinking was also pervaded by racist considerations . . . These chains of concepts, which were open with respect to their actual content, were thus relatively simple to manipulate" (412). On the other hand, Stolleis implies that Schmitt's 1939 articulation of the concept of *Großraum* was more of a traditional National Conservative view than a Nazi idea (417).[34]

Ulrich Herbert's biography of Werner Best, one of Schmitt's critics, also establishes some distance between Schmitt and the SS: In fall 1939, a circle of SS leaders around Best, Höhn, and Stuckart formed to discuss questions of how to organize German *Herrschaft* in Europe along *völkisch* principles.[35] Werner Best was director of Office I (Administration and Law) of the Main Bureau of the Security Police in the Reich's Inner Ministry as well as chairman of the Committee on Police

Law in the Academy for German Law. Herbert explains that the Best-Höhn-Stuckart circle within the SS shared a different ideological agenda than two other groups in the regime—namely, what he refers to as "the conservative *Großmachtpolitiker* of the old style, still dominant in the economy, administration and military, and of which Schmitt in a certain way is representative . . . and against *Gauleiter* in the circle around Goebbels, Göring and Ley in the tradition of the SA" (279). Therefore, we can conclude that both Stolleis and Herbert concur that there is some distance between Schmitt and the SS, and that this difference is a measurable proxy for the distance between "*völkisch*" or racial thinking, and the more generic, spatial theory of the functioning of great powers or empires. According to Herbert, Schmitt's lack of a transcendental, *weltanschaulich*, or teleological perspective represented a provocation for "the guardians of the pure teaching of National Socialism in the SD and SS."[36] Much has been made of the SS "critique" of Schmitt both in 1936 and in 1939–41; the figure most responsible for Schmitt's fall from grace in 1936, Reinhard Höhn, was one of the most voluble critics of Schmitt's 1939 text. To adjudicate the debate over the place of Schmitt's concept of a *Völkerrechtliche Großraumordnung*, I reconstruct the debate over his work in the pages of National Socialist journals, including the SS journal edited by Höhn, Stuckart, and Best, *Reich, Volksordnung, Lebensraum*, published between 1941 and 1944.[37]

While Stolleis, Herbert, and Berghahn provide grounds for reservations, too much has been made of the split between Schmitt and *völkisch* thought, of spatial from racial thought in this period. At Nuremberg, Schmitt discussed his critical reception by the SS, by Best and Höhn, in detail.[38] A reading of the actual "critiques" of Schmitt, however, reveals more commonalities than differences in content; and discursively, how proximate the concepts of *Lebensraum* and the concept of *Großraum* were—often appearing in the same sentence as if they were synonyms. Although the two concepts may be separated analytically—each seems to refer to a different discursive and institutional space—their actual conceptual history is intertwined. The critiques are also illuminating in their own right as windows on the grotesque efflorescence of analytical, legal reasoning in the service of the Third Reich's *Unrechtsstaat*.

Interpreting Objections to Schmitt's
Großraum Theory from the Right

One of the most common objections to Schmitt's text was that the concept of a *Großraumordnung* was too empty of "concrete" content to serve the particular needs of the *Volksgemeinschaft* (national community) that the Reich had so successfully raised to consciousness of its *völkisch* identity. It was, in short, too "abstract." This critique must have been particularly unwelcome to Schmitt, since the dichotomy of abstract and concrete— and the claim to superior concreteness of Schmitt's own views—was centrally constitutive of his own text. Schmitt was eager to convince that the "*Großraum*" concept was concrete in a way that earlier conceptions of "*Raum*" were abstract. "Whereas '*Raum*' alongside the various specific meanings retains a general, neutral, mathematical-physical significance, '*Großraum*' is for us a concrete, historical-political concept of the present."[39] This opposition relies on a dichotomy of historicism and rationalism, where, as in other parts of Schmitt's oeuvre, rationalism is coded Jewish.[40] "Authentic" German thinkers like Ratzel and Heidegger were deployed against Enlightenment rationalists (like Kant, for example) and Jews. Schmitt asserted that Jewish authors bear a special responsibility for their contribution to the development of the notion of "empty space." This is a function of the "peculiar incongruity of the Jewish people with everything that concerns land, country and region."[41] The "founder of a new science of space, [Friedrich] Ratzel, has already recognized that coming to terms with space is the characteristic of all life" (79).[42] "The a priorism of Kantian philosophy where space is an a priori form of knowledge" is adduced as an example of a natural-scientific worldview inadequate to the most advanced thinking in phenomenology, quantum physics, and biology alike.[43] Biologist Viktor von Weizsäcker, wrote Schmitt, understands that "the world is not in space, but rather space is in and of the world."[44] The concept of *Großraum* breaks the monopoly position of a century of spatial thought, substituting something allegedly full for something empty, the concrete for the abstract.

It is ironic therefore that Höhn claims that "abstraction" is the real Achilles' heel of Schmitt's theory of *Großraum*. Because space and political ideas are intertwined, and the distinction of friend and enemy underpins the political, Höhn reasoned, in Schmitt's work, "all political and historically entangled problems are subordinated to a simple astonishing formula."[45] Höhn claimed that the concept of the political as friend-foe polarity "no longer grasps the essential," for the astonishing reason that "the stronger the people grows into a *Volksgemeinschaft*, so much more must the concept of the political as expression of the friend-foe grouping be experienced as *lebensfremd* [alien to life] . . . The concept of the political as friend-foe grouping lost all general validity that it had as a situation-bound concept, whose one-sided sharpness no longer grasps the essential" (270).[46] Schmitt missed the "total ethos" (*Gesamtethos*), and "the contents, which we associate with the idea of *Großraum* today." The concept of *Großraum* thereby "fell into the danger of becoming a mere construction. It is neither good nor bad, in content value-free and simultaneously open to any valuation." Werner Best was right therefore, Höhn wrote, to criticize it on the grounds that a *Großraum* (should) be seen as "the expression of a deep, *lebensgesetzlich* [natural law-like] certainty" (276). Mere "boundary-setting" is not adequate. We must guard against a "substanceless concept of *Großraum* and the Reich as the concept of the state once was." This is how it appeared to at least one contemporary observer of the Schmitt-Höhn debate as well. In a review of an article by Suthoff-Gross, Mallmann characterized the conflict thusly: Schmitt and his "general concept," versus Höhn, who "grasped the concretely present European *Großraum* from within and filled it with richly living (*lebensvoll*) content."[47] While Schmitt was sometimes criticized in the pages of *Reich, Volksordnung, Lebensraum*, writers in other Nazi journals criticized the SS-edited volumes on different grounds in turn. This evidence of a certain degree of ideological "polycracy" within the regime should caution us against defining the SS as the exclusive bearer of core-Nazi ideology.

Höhn, Best, Spanner, Huber, and Jahrreiss all dedicated full articles in scholarly journals to their *Auseinandersetzung* with Schmitt. Besides the related charges of emptiness or abstraction, the authors also levied critiques of Schmitt, citing a lack of specificity about the relations between *Großräume*; insufficient respect for German particularity;

anachronism—and paradoxically, trendiness. As Höhn wrote, the non-intervention principle was too thin—because it said nothing about the "positive relations" between *Großräume*.[48] An international law (*Völkerrecht*) with only two "foundational elements"—*Großraum* and nonintervention—would not suffice. What could be learned from these two concepts about the relationship between Germany and the two other members of the Tripartite Pact concluded in 1940—Japan and Italy—Höhn asked, other than that they should not intervene in the other *Großräume*? Höhn argued that Schmitt's insistence on the need for a revolutionary concept of *Großraum* indicates a lack of understanding that the real break in time already occurred six years earlier in 1933 (264).

After Werner Best critiqued Schmitt's first edition of the book in 1940,[49] Schmitt responded civilly: "That is an appropriate clarification. It relates, though, only to the inner structure of *Großraum* and leaves the other relational possibilities open."[50] But in a sharp rejoinder, Best chided Schmitt: "Schmitt thinks I only wanted him to amend one concept—'*völkerrechtliche* [international-legal] *Großraumordnung*' with a slightly different one—'*völkische* [racial] *Großraumordnung*.'"[51] But his critique went deeper, Best reminded his readers: "With the justification that the order of *Großraum* is an international-legal construct, subjects of hitherto existing international law could demand that they had to negotiate 'international-legal' contracts with the *Führungsvolk* of the order of *Großraum* as equal 'sovereign' partners, and that they, when necessary, could renounce their 'international-legal' agreements vis-à-vis the *Führungsvolk*." In short, Schmitt was too conservative with respect to traditional international law, with the result that states may believe they have retained rights that they should not have. These were rights that the profession still considered valid in the years 1933–35, when the Nazi regime still found it politically useful to contest the terms of Versailles with rhetoric asserting the essential equality of states. Höhn proffered the related critique that Schmitt applied the term "Reich" too ecumenically to nations other than Germany: "One should avoid a confrontation over whether precisely we Germans should abstract that name 'Reich,' which historically and spiritually is ours alone, into a concept that is arbitrarily applicable to the 'links between *Großraum*, *Volk*, and political ideas'"

(1534). Hans Frank, then governor-general of German-occupied Poland, made the same point: "The Reich is the political task given by history to the German people. Other peoples have founded states and empires . . . brought a Commonwealth or an 'Empire' into being . . . But the Reich is reserved for the Germans."[52] Nazi intellectuals, we realize, were engaged implicitly in a comparative practice: comparing the new German order in Europe with other empires in history. Comparison could provide succor and confidence or, conversely, cause anxiety.

Of course, one of the foundational assumptions of Schmitt's book on *Großraum* was the essential comparability of German ambitions in Central Europe to the prerogatives claimed by the United States in the Western Hemisphere in the Monroe Doctrine. For Ernst Wolgast, professor at Würzburg, comparison was enabling: "The idea of *Großraum* will doubtless have to be researched further."[53] "Altogether the study signifies a real and fundamental increase of the insight into the essence of the past and present interconnectedness of the world (*Weltzusammenhang*) by means of both clarifications of the *Großraum* concept and of the difference of England from other states" (24). In "The Myth of the Monroe Doctrine" (1942/43), the influential law professor and foreign policy advisor Friedrich Berber articulated a different, more critical view of the Monroe Doctrine: "[The doctrine] should be robbed of its mythological robe, American exceptionalism, and seen for what it is: an act of violence."[54] Nonetheless, Berber claimed the same rights for Germany. After the war, however, wrote Berber, Germany would replace it with "a real *völkerrechtliche* agreement, binding for all concerned, which rests on the basic principle of a clear separation of *Lebensräume* and continents, and which does not stand in the way of a true community of peoples, but rather makes this possible in the first place" (27).

Whether the constitution of a *Großraum* represented something more than an act of violence or assertion of power was, surprisingly, a pre occupation for many of the participants in the *Großraum* debate. An important touchstone was Heinrich Triepel's massive treatise, *Hegemony: A Guide for Leading States* (1938), and its distinction between domination (*Herrschaft*) and leadership (*Führung*).[55] The distinction reappears in essays by Hans Spanner,[56] a professor of law in Graz, then an occupation authority in the Netherlands, and Ernst Rudolf Huber, law professor, then in Strasbourg.[57] For Spanner, the distinction between the imperial behavior of France or England, on the one hand, and Germany, on the other, might be captured in the distinction between "*Herrschaftsraum,*" or "*Herrschaftsbereich,*" and *Großraum*:

> One could speak, perhaps, in contrast to *Großraum* for such cases, of a space of domination or area of domination (*Herrschaftsraum oder Herrschaftsbereich*), in the sense that there too, a people, a power, is in control first and foremost, which however sees its goal only in the expansion of its domination according to the singularly decisive principle of its interest in disregard of the interests of others within the dominated space of given peoples, and that, as a basic principle, pursues and attempts to realize this goal with all its available means.[58]

On the other hand, Spanner reflected on whether the difference may also be a question of perspective: the leader or the led. "The difference between *Großraum* and *Herrschaftsraum*, however, inheres particularly in for which final goal, with what justification and in what way the great power makes use of its power" (49). Spanner concluded sanguinely: in contrast to Germany, the United States, and Britain were "merely great powers with a region of domination (*Großmächte mit einem Herrschaftsbereich*), but not *Reiche* with a *Großraum*" (50).

E.R. Huber, by contrast, was at once more idealistic and more troubled by the conclusions suggested by the practice of comparison. Huber credits Schmitt's book with a cogent grasp of "political reality," but he was clearly troubled by the slipperiness of the distinction between the proposed German "*Großraum*" and the "*Großmächte*" associated with the "old imperialism" (*alter Imperialismus*).[59]

> The decisive question is whether today's *Großraumgedanken* confers the law-justifying and law-grounding inner power, in other words, how here a new *Völkerrecht* can unfold itself out of an old political system of power. Only when this question can be answered positively, would the related question of the difference between the impe-

rialism of the 19th century and the *Großraum* thought of the present be clarified . . . Whether today's *Großraumordnung* is merely a mere power-system (*faktisches Machtsystem*) or a true legal system. (40)

Huber wanted Schmitt to explain how, "according to his understanding the moment of order transforms and elevates the power-system of impe-rialism into the legal system of *Großraum* thought," the "legal content of *Großraum* order inheres inwardly in the fact that in effect here is not merely an external coercive violence vis-a-vis the conquered, but rather, that a leading people grants to other peoples allotted to it the possibility of development, support, aid, and protection" (41). Here Huber added in a footnote: "This is the justified core of the in itself considerable antith-esis of '*Herrschaft*' and '*Führung*' on which Triepel's *Hegemony* book is based" (41n1).

Huber concluded on this remarkable note, hard to explain in 1941: "The just exercise of power will be the criterion for the distinction be-tween the old imperialism (*Imperialismus*) and a true *völkerrechtliche Großraumordnung*" (42). Huber was writing at nearly the same mo-ment as Werner Best—the summer of 1941. On the subject of his cri-tique of Schmitt, Best's biographer Ulrich Herbert explains that Best's essay reached a wide audience and found positive resonance among the SS and Wehrmacht: "Best was considered since then both a brilliant ad-ministration specialist who stood for a 'sensible and rational politics of occupation,' as well as a leading *Großraum*-theoretician of the SS."[60] But if he was the theorist of "rational" or enlightened occupation policy, attempting to cleave closer to the pole of *Führung* than *Herrschaft*, the reality was that no firm line could—then or now—be drawn between the abstractions of *Großraumtheorie* and the practices of *Lebensraumpoli-tik*. That is, by the time Schmitt penned his fourth edition of the *VRGO* in July 1941, the Rubicon had been crossed: With the invasion of the USSR in June, there could no longer be any sense in these hair-splitting distinctions; a deliberate war of extermination had begun. If we recall that the first initiative of the group around Werner Best was the plan-ning of a *Festschrift* for the leader of the SS, Heinrich Himmler, we can also note that within those pages Best wrote what clearly amounted to a justification of genocide. As Herbert paraphrases Best: "If, then, there lived in the *Großraum* peoples . . . who were 'undesired' by the leading people and should not be integrated into the *Großraum*-order, then it was an imperative necessity—in accord with biological laws—that these peoples be either 'totally annihilated (or totally expelled from its area)'" (283). In an essay published the following year, "*Großraum* Order and *Großraum* Administration" (1942), condensing the longer essay in the *Festgabe für Himmler,* Best wrote, "Annihilation and expulsion of foreign races does not, according to historical experience, contradict the laws of life, when it happens completely."[61]

In addition to the conceptual and practical proximity of "*Großraum*," "*Vernichtung*," and "*Verdrängung*," we also find throughout the "scientific" literature of the period the concepts of *Großraum* promiscuously intertwined with "*Lebensraum*" and its cognates, like "*Lebensrechte*" or "*Lebensgesetze*." In an essay framed as an *Auseinandersetzung* with Schmitt on *Völkerrecht*, Herman Jahrreiss, a professor of public law and international law, wrote, "The German people desired for itself in its struggle against Versailles what every great people of the world naturally wants to have guaranteed: the freedom to organize its life in complete independence in its own state [that exists] for all like-minded settling *Volk*-comrades (*Volksgenossen*)."[62] In Jahrreiss, the discourses of *Lebensraum* and *Großraum* ran together. In Friedrich Berber's *The Myth of the Monroe Doctrine,* we find Schmitt's *Großräume* redescribed in terms of *Lebensraum*: "[The Monroe Doctrine] supposedly rests on the clear division of *Lebensräume*: the Americans are supposed to be in charge of their own house; that's why they didn't want to get mixed up anywhere else."[63] In another example, Berber spoke of "American *Lebensraum*" in contrast to "foreign" ones: "The entire East Asian policy of the United States since this time is a politics of intervention (*Einmischungspolitik*) in a foreign *Lebensraum* to the disadvantage of Japan, the leading power there . . . even though Japanese politics limited itself strictly to the East Asian space and by no means thought of intruding upon the American *Lebensraum*." Finally, Berber describes the Tripartite Pact of 1940, frequently referred to as an agreement between *Großräume* as "the clear division of *Lebensräume*" (27).

Many other examples from the discourse of the period show the porousness of the boundaries between the "geopolitical" and the "biopolitical" discourses, *Großraum* and *Lebensraum*. A 1941 text from Höhn illustrates the point particularly well, and warrants a full quotation:

> One champions with the *Großraum* concept the claim to an increased *Lebensraum*, which takes into account the *Dasein*-necessities of European peoples. *Großraum* thought opens a perspective on a new political order of Europe and the world which builds on the rights to life (*Lebensrechte*) of peoples, the necessities of space-shaping and the possibility of an impact according to the measure of its life- and achievement-power (*Lebens- und Leistungskraft*).[64] In Europe and in the *Lebensraum* connected with it, it is the German idea of Reich and the fascist idea of empire, which allow for the history and the contemporary meaning of these peoples. As long as we are speaking of the Reich, it does not present itself to us as an abstract magnitude, but rather as the life-kernel of *Großraum* as *Lebensraum* in its entire dynamics and in its orientation by the laws of life (*lebensgesetzliche Stellung des Reiches und seiner zwingenden inneren Kraft*). (262)

The porousness of the categories thus destroys the foundation of Schmitt's defense at Nuremberg.

On April 18, 1947, Carl Schmitt submitted his written reply to the question posed by Robert W. Kempner: "To what extent did you provide the theoretical underpinnings of Hitlerian Großraum politics (*Hitlersche Großraumpolitik*)?"[65] The answers form a rich archival source. Repeatedly, Schmitt argued that his work was purely theoretical and scholarly, and as such, had no meaningful connection to practical politics: by various means, Schmitt argued, he had attempted "to put beyond doubt the purely scholarly (*wissenschaftlich*) significance of my work and to distance myself from the catchphrases of propaganda" (459).

But Schmitt's book was written for a variety of practical purposes, including the effort to forestall the entrance of the United States in WWII. We do not know whether Schmitt's lecture on April 1 (on which the April 30 publication of the first edition was based) influenced Hitler, who mentioned the idea of a Monroe Doctrine for Europe, in his speech to the

Reichstag on April 28, 1939. "We Germans support a similar doctrine for Europe—and above all for the territory and interests of the German Reich." But we can infer that Schmitt considered taking credit for the idea from the fact that Hans Frank, an ally within the Nazi state, "advised him to stay quiet about the origin of the idea as 'the Führer prided himself on his originality.'"[66] Moreover, the notion that the theorist of the concrete concepts for combat would invoke the "purely scholarly meaning" of his work is hypocritical to the point of incoherence. While he is right that he did not actually coin the term "Großraum," the construction of the "Völkerrechtliche Großraumordnung" was original to Schmitt:

> I note first of all that the word 'Großraum' was not made up by me. It has belonged since 1923 to German usage and I in no way have a monopoly on it. It has remained a key term with an extremely wide range of meanings. I have attempted to promote and to formulate the clarification of a modern concept of space with the means and methods of my area of scholarly specialization. My activity was scholarly research, which did not rest with any finding, but rather used each newly won finding as a spur to further discovery. I have expressed this position, of unflinching scientific thinking, further, as pointedly as possible and in a conspicuous place, namely in a foreword to my Writings, and I have said, of myself and of this, my work: We are seafarers on the high seas and each book can be nothing more than a log-book.[67]

Schmitt, like his later defenders Kaiser, Maschke, and others, have claimed that the oftentimes strong critiques from the SS are compelling evidence of Schmitt's distance from the regime and its goals. Certainly this is what Schmitt sought to argue at Nuremberg:

> Höhn's essay was written with much effort, but it failed because of the deep incommensurability of biological-racial 'Lebensraum' and rationally constructed 'Großraum' . . . I understood this theoretically right away when I saw that Höhn did not notice the point of departure, namely a modern concept of space, but spoke right away of Großraum, without having even the slightest inkling of the most

difficult of all problems, precisely the concept of space. Being aware of the problem with respect to the concept of space has for me always been the criterion for a scientific consideration of the problem of *Großraum*. Otherwise the mist that encircles a clamorous catchphrase like '*Großraum*' remains entirely impenetrable . . . I perceived this sudden interest that an influential SS group took in my theories as grounds for immense caution. Whoever knows me and my life's work will not hit upon the thought that I could get involved with SS ideas or SS tendencies.[68]

But regardless of Schmitt's subjective intentions, his texts took on a life of their own. We have seen how the debate over *Großraum* became intertwined from a very early stage with the expansion of German empire on the ground and with the policies of resettlement and extermination. On these grounds, it is impossible for Schmitt to maintain the simplistic dichotomy of racist-*völkisch*-SS-*Lebensraum* and rational-scientific-*Großraum* thought. For Schmitt, "*Großraumpolitik*" in itself is a contradiction in terms, since Hitler's decisions and policies of expansion were devoid of any "specific meaning." As Schmitt continued,

If one compares the above-mentioned attempts at a theoretical underpinning for Hitlerian politics with the intellectual habitus (*geistiger Habitus*) of my works, then the question answers itself. My doctrine of *völkerrechtlicher Großraum* is a theory that has its place within broader scholarly contexts, and is also, because of its rigor, taken seriously. Hitler did not practice *Großraum* politics in the sense of this theory; rather, he practiced a mere politics of conquest inimical to the intellect and to principles, which one can only call it a *Großraum* politics if one denudes the word '*Großraum*' of its specific meaning and makes of it an empty catchphrase for any kind of expansion . . . Hitler's politics of expansion was so primitive that any scholarly analysis would necessarily have threatened it. In a global confrontation in which all the means of occidental rationalism were deployed, contact with a true scholarly concept meant for Hitler's politics not finding a foundation but rather being exposed. It would therefore be merely an unjustified, ideal gain for Hitler, undeservedly benefitting an anti-intellectual system, if my scientifically conceived construction were conflated with the Hitlerian politics of conquest. An inferior, fundamentally desperate kind of politics of power and expansion would thereby experience a posthumous valorization to which it can lay no claim. (463)

It is supremely ironic that the specter of emptiness and abstraction which bedeviled Schmitt in the wartime *Großraum* debate should return to haunt Schmitt at Nuremberg. This time it was Schmitt who charged Hitler with a concept lacking in real content, not the SS charging Schmitt. *Großraum* was full with meaning, Schmitt argued—not empty and abstract like Hitler's version. But the plenitude Schmitt claimed to find in *Großraum* was not that biopolitics of *Lebensraum* with which it was open to, steeped in, or promiscuously intertwined. Rather, Schmitt claimed that it was the tradition of "Occidental rationalism" which marks the impassable divide between the concepts. It was "science," once more, that forms Schmitt's alibi for his political choices and alliances. Scholars who wish to breathe new life into Schmitt's *Großraum* theory today should consider whether the concept enables critical and emancipatory views of international relations, or whether it contains any resources for resisting empire.

CHAPTER 4

The Making of a Realist

Wilhelm Grewe in the Third Reich

"GREWE'S ACHIEVEMENTS as a scholar of international law are truly exceptional. He is now the foremost figure in the German science of international law. That is not only an achievement and a task but a situation. May all good geniuses assist him."[1] So reads a 1948 diary entry by Carl Schmitt, one of the most influential, and notorious, German political and legal thinkers in the twentieth century. Wilhelm Grewe (1911–2000), a career diplomat, professor, and scholar of international law, today commands wide respect in Europe and the United States. He is remembered both for his scholarly accomplishments and his diplomatic service, especially under West German chancellor Konrad Adenauer (1949–63), whose reputation as the architect of West Germany's *Westbindung* rests in part on the labors of his devoted appointee.[2] For a lifetime of service, Grewe was honored with the *Großes Verdienstkreuz mit Stern* by both the German and Austrian governments. Unusually for a high-profile diplomat, Grewe is also remembered for his history of modern international law from 1490 to the present, *Epochen der Völkerrechtsgeschichte (Epochs of International Law)*, which is generally esteemed a "classic"—"a book of exceptional importance and influence" in the German-language historiography and beyond. [3] As a celebrated Atlanticist and self-described "realist," Grewe is a crucial figure for understanding the German-American dimensions of twentieth-century realism in international relations and international law. Moreover, prevailing interpretations of Grewe centered on the postwar career and the 1984 publication of *Epochs* have sundered both from his activities during the Third Reich. In Grewe's postwar autobiographical accounts, he describes himself as a figure in an "underground resistance" during the war. In more than fifty articles written between 1933 and 1945, Grewe energetically promoted the foreign policy goals of the

Third Reich. Through his teaching at the Friedrich Wilhelms-Universität Berlin (now the Humboldt) and his work at the Faculty of Foreign Studies, Grewe was personally enmeshed with both the Foreign Ministry and the SS. Grewe's significance for West German politics is well known, but the politics that conditioned *Epochs* itself is little understood. The effort to connect Grewe's opus in the intellectual and political contexts of the Third Reich has barely been attempted.[4] Reconstructing Grewe's wartime academic and institutional milieu in detail demonstrates that he was an active participant in academic and para-academic institutions fully politicized and instrumentalized to the war effort, and that Grewe's postwar claims to have resisted the Third Reich are false.

Grewe's *Epochs* divided the history of modern international law into Spanish, French, British, and Anglo-American "epochs," a framing adopted by leading textbooks in the field.[5] Koskenniemi has critiqued both Grewe's *Epochs* and Morgenthau's *Politics* on the grounds of their deep debts to Schmitt and their distortions in the ways they assess the relationship of international legal norms to the political power of nation-states and empires.[6] I share this skepticism. Koskenniemi is one of the only scholars who has dissented from the chorus of praise for Grewe's *Epochs* as "classic."[7] Rather, he calls it a "period piece from the discipline's least fortunate moment: infused with a cold realism that was *en vogue* as its author conceived it, insensitive to the worst crisis faced by Western civilization" (750). Koskenniemi is referring to the fact that while Grewe may not have known the full extent of Nazi atrocities in 1944 (though he must have known quite a bit), the same could not be said in 1984: "The fact that there is no mention of Germany's destruction of European Jewry during the Second World War . . . may be charitably credited to Grewe's ultra-realistic method. When such cold realism is applied to the catastrophes of the 20th century, with all sides portrayed as essentially 'similar', the result is a perverse exculpation of the German atrocities . . . a crime of forgetting" (750).

Reading Grewe's 1984 magnum opus in the light of the shorter essays, I demonstrate the pervasive influence of Carl Schmitt's writings. Building on the discussion in chapter 3, I draw out the connections between Schmitt's imperial comparison and invocations of the Monroe

Doctrine, and Grewe's reflections on the relation of international law and imperial politics. Grewe's *Epochs* is an exemplary Atlantic realist text because of the features it shares with other major works on the politics of international relations and international law written in the early Cold War such as Schmitt's *Der Nomos der Erde* (1950) and Hans Morgenthau's *Politics among Nations* (first edition, 1948). All three authors evince skepticism about international law as a restrainer of state action and emphasize the ways in which states instrumentalize law to their own political ends. Declarations of universal human rights, or the equality of states, are unmasked: for each norm there is an equally hidden exception. Postcolonial and Marxist theories of international law sometimes practice a similar hermeneutics of suspicion. But the Atlantic realism of the 1940s has particular features that militate against progressive appropriation.

Biography and Reception of the Work

Born in Hamburg, Grewe studied law in Hamburg, Berlin, Freiburg, and Frankfurt from 1931 to 1936, completing his dissertation and *Habilitation* in 1936 and 1941, respectively, under Ernst Forsthoff, a preeminent state and legal theorist and pupil of Carl Schmitt.[8] From April 1938 to March 1940, Grewe was lecturer (*Dozent*) at the Deutsche Hochschule für Politik (School of Political Science), an institution once famed for its commitment to liberal and republican values, but in 1933 purged of the majority of its faculty by Goebbels' Ministry of Propaganda. In 1940 the *judenrein* ("free of Jews") school was integrated into the newly formed Faculty of Foreign Studies (Auslandswissenschaftliche Fakultät; Berlin FFS hereafter) at the University of Berlin; as *Lehrbeauftragter* he began his teaching contract in March 1940. In October 1941, Grewe was given a dual appointment as *Dozent* in the Law and Political Science Faculty (Rechts und Staatswissenschaften) of the University of Berlin and its Faculty of Foreign Studies (Auslandswissenschaften). From 1942–45, he was first extraordinary professor and then full professor in the Berlin FFS, teaching courses including, notably, "Legal Foundations of Foreign Policy" and "Policy of International Law."[9] He also taught in the German Institute for Foreign Studies (Deutsches Auslandswissenschaftliches

Institut; DAWI hereafter), beginning in 1940, an institute directed by Franz Six, an SS-*Obergruppenführer* who was later sentenced to twenty years at Nuremberg.

Submitted in part as a *Habilitation* thesis in the spring of 1941,[10] the text was, according to Grewe, "finished in Berlin during the heavy air raids of August and September 1943 . . . On 4 December 1943, the partially set type was destroyed in an air raid of Leipzig" (xii). Grewe explained that "delays in printing" led him to publish his "most important findings in summary form" in 1943.[11] According to the prefaces to the first and second editions, the manuscript was complete by November 20, 1944, and the corrected page proofs were finished in early 1945. Grewe explained why it was not published that year: "When after the war the Leipzig publishing house Köhler and Amelang was licensed by the Soviet administration and could resume its activities, it was stipulated that a publication was now only possible under conditions which I was not prepared to accept. It had already been a remarkable accomplishment to avoid any alteration of the text by the censor during the Third Reich. I did not dare to make such an effort again, especially from the distance of the Western zones."[12]

In the denazification proceedings in the French zone, Grewe was designated "exonerated" (*entlastet*) and thus, like most other lawyers and diplomats active in the Third Reich, permitted to return to work.[13] His first employment was as full professor of law in Göttingen (1945–47), followed by Freiburg (1947–51). After Adenauer brought him into the Foreign Office in 1951, Grewe headed the German delegation that negotiated the end of Allied occupation of West Germany in 1955. A twenty-five-year career in the Foreign Office followed. From 1953–54 he served as director of the legal division of the German Foreign Office, and director of its political division from 1955–58. Three major overseas posts followed too: ambassador to the United States (1958–62), leader of the standing delegations to NATO in Paris (1962–67) and Brussels (1967–71), and finally ambassador to Tokyo (1971–76).

His signature political accomplishments as a diplomat are twofold. First, he drafted the 1954 Convention on Relations between the Three Powers (Britain, France, and the United States) and the Federal Republic of Germany, which accorded West Germany "the full authority of a sovereign state over its internal and external affairs," on condition of its integration into the Western defense alliance. The Allies committed themselves to no less than the future reunification of Germany—albeit one, as Article 7 specifies, "with a liberal-democratic constitution, like that of the Federal Republic, and integrated within the European Community." The second was his behind-the-scenes role as author of the "Hallstein Doctrine," named for Walter Hallstein, Konrad Adenauer's state secretary for foreign affairs from 1951 to 1957. The Hallstein Doctrine insisted that only West Germany was the legitimate representative of the German people; any state that recognized the East German government as de facto legitimate would forfeit diplomatic relations with West Germany. An example of a hardline Cold War policy, the Hallstein Doctrine guided West German foreign policy until the shift to détente in 1969.

From 1963–70, Grewe worked on *The Play of Power in World Politics*, a book he considered his "leisure-time hobby."[14] Despite his Adenauerian formation, Grewe remained an important diplomatic asset in the years of SPD-led coalition government (1969–82). In retirement, Grewe enjoyed the esteem of his colleagues as emeritus professor at Freiburg, published his memoirs[15] and a collection of essays on diplomacy, German foreign policy, and reunification,[16] and served as a member of the Permanent Court of Arbitration in the Hague until 1991.[17]

His magnum opus, *The Epochs of International Law*, was completed in 1944 but was not published in full until 1984. Written during the war and extensively revised between 1978 and 1984, the book spans the histories of Germany before and after 1945. Grewe returned to the book in the late 1970s, adding a new section on 1945–89, including references to decades of intervening scholarship. "After such a space of time, it was only possible to publish after fundamentally reworking and extending a presentation that had stretched only to 1939," Grewe noted in 1983 (xi). What finally appeared in print in 1984 was an unusual pastiche or hybrid—its basic thesis and architecture were designed in 1939–43 and revisited by one of the Cold War's preeminent diplomats. A new section assimilated the "Pax Americana-Sovietica," the phrase he used to describe the global order from 1945–89, in an effort to bridge historical gaps.[18] In

1998, Grewe added an epilogue on the post-1989 period for the English translation in 2000. This text has enjoyed a wide and mostly celebratory English-language reception ever since.

My contextualization makes it impossible to take at face value the anodyne prefatory note to the first English translation of *Epochs of International Law*, written in 2000 by the distinguished German professor of law Jochen Frowein:

> After his retirement Wilhelm Grewe finalized the book which he had written as a young researcher *during the Second World War* in Berlin . . . It is an indication of Grewe's attitude that it was *not necessary for him to change* the structure and content of a book on the history of public international law in any important manner. Indeed, Wilhelm Grewe had *abstained from mixing in politics* in any way during the Nazi period.[19] (emphasis added)

Grewe hardly "abstained" from politics. Not even Grewe characterizes his career this way. His defense of his actions was that he acted under duress. Grewe never spoke publicly about his complicity in the ideological state apparatuses of Nazism. In a 1992 lecture, during a discussion of Carl Schmitt, the most that Grewe could say was: "All I wanted to do here was to show you what kind of temptations and risks a German scholar of international law was subject to in those years."[20] As the legal scholar Detlev Vagts explained in an important article, "internal emigration" was possible: "A professor of international law could generally survive . . . [by] writing little or nothing, or writing only about safe subjects such as the history of international law and diplomatic immunity."[21] A prolific and polemical historian of international law *and* contemporary developments, Grewe chose the role of an active supporter of the regime.

Grewe's 1944 preface belies his claims to have escaped the "censors" of the Third Reich.

> The decision to complete and publish the book in wartime was motivated, above all, by the strongly felt need—experienced while teaching—for a book that would take students through the character and structure of international law from a historical perspective. At a

time when the traditional system of international law is shaken to its foundations, access to the remaining structural principles of the international legal order can only be provided on historical grounds.[22]

How strange, then, that Grewe and most of his readers treat the work as a classic that offers guidance to current generations, when it was originally intended as a work of clarification in a moment of crisis. He completed his history of the changing relationship between international law and political hegemony when Germany's bid for world hegemony was failing and America's looked imminent. This was no merely scholarly tome.

Schmitt dominated the intellectual field in which Grewe "won his spurs," in Erich Kaufmann's phrase.[23] As Fassbender writes, "Carl Schmitt is one of the most frequently (and usually approvingly) quoted authors in the *Epochen*"; and in an autobiographical speech in 1992, Grewe praised Schmitt "as the most brilliant and most publicly discussed" teacher of constitutional law and international law in the late Weimar Republic. That mutual esteem characterized the relationship between the two is evident from the diary entry of Schmitt's that forms this chapter's epigraph. Correspondence between Schmitt and Grewe reflects close personal ties spanning decades. As Fassbender reports, it was a relationship of mutual esteem.[24] In a letter to legal scholar Ernst Forsthoff in 1949, Schmitt mentioned that Grewe had made his own acceptance of Schmitt's old chair in law contingent on financial provision for Schmitt.[25] Fassbender adds, however, that "the extent to which Schmitt's ideas have influenced not only Grewe's analysis of specific development and events in the history of international law, but also the general conception of the book, is a question that is yet to be answered."[26] Martti Koskenniemi has offered a convincing answer: "Above all, however, Grewe's account of international law's 'epochs' . . . was the unmistakeable *analogon* of Carl Schmitt's *Großraumlehre*, first declared in a famous lecture in . . . 1939. In fact, the book reads almost like a commentary, or expansion, of Schmitt's *Der Nomos der Erde* (1950)."[27] This is true, but the basic thesis and architecture of Grewe's work was completed a half decade before Schmitt published his work.

Reading Grewe's *Epochs* in Context

> The stronger the leading position of the particular predominant power, the more that State marked the spiritual vision of the age, the more its ideas and concepts prevailed, the more it conferred general and absolute validity on expressions of its national-expansionist ideology.[28]

At first glance, Grewe's "ultra-realistic" method, to borrow Koskenniemi's words, appears to say little more than that law is conditioned by, and never wholly independent from, politics. The most fundamental goal of *Epochs*, Grewe explained, was to specify the "close connection between legal theory and State practice." His point was that both legal theory and state practice "are forms of expression of the same power." But Grewe does not interpret this power through the lens of political economy. The Westphalian system of sovereign nation-states, not the economy, is "necessarily the substrata which underlies the international legal order." The state system "is the pre-established, preordained order of the thing, in which the 'ambiance' of the law of nations . . . is realized."[29] Readers of Schmitt and Grewe who find them useful for a contemporary critique of global capitalism or Western imperialism should note how they treat the state, not the economy, as the source of social power in the last instance. Grewe carried *Epochs* with him, so to speak, through the war. Having begun work on it in the winter of 1939–40, he presented a summary of the book to a conference of the Nazi Federation of University Teachers (Arbeitstagung des NS-Dozentenbundes) in Weimar, on April 10, 1942. These lectures were published in 1943 as a two-part essay.[30] The essay offers a glimpse of the genesis of *Epochs* and provides additional insights into the text he ultimately published.

One passage (omitted from the 1944/84 text) illustrates the moral limits of Grewe's historicism:

> Since September 1939 there can be no doubt about the transitional character of this epoch [of Anglo-American world hegemony] . . . The battle is *only about* the question of whether we will enter an "American century"—in which control of the world goes

to the United States as a great power of Pan-American dimension and backed up by Great Britain, the Soviet Union and China—or whether the reorganization of the world personified by the powers of the Three Powers' Pact [Germany, Italy, and Japan] will succeed.[31] (emphasis added)

Describing World War II as a struggle between morally equivalent "great powers" is not the act of a resistance-fighter. When Grewe took the podium in April 1942, his listeners would have heard distinct echoes of Schmitt's 1920s critiques of liberal universalism and the postwar settlement but also of Schmitt's theory of *Großraum*. Grewe's 1942 lectures end with the arrival of the "transitional age of Anglo-American world hegemony, 1919–1939"—a wish for epochal change dressed up as a history of epochal shifts. Schmitt made a similar move in a July 1940 essay, "Empire and Space: Elements of a New International Law."[32]

Grewe faithfully reproduced the antinomy of *Großraum* and universalism ubiquitous in Schmitt's writings both before and after 1945. Grewe followed Schmitt's account of the Monroe Doctrine as the model *Großraum*:

> [What] the statesmen of the new world envisioned—that goes for Hamilton, Washington, Jefferson and Monroe as much as Bolivar—was an organized, coordinated state-system, that respects the natural, geographical and cultural context of the continent, closed unto itself . . . In a similar way, the Monroe delegation of 1823 proceeded from the idea of an intra-continental political and *völkerrechtlich* context, as a structurally necessary element of world order. (266)

Against these visions of an American *Großraum*, anchored by the real substance of continents and oceans, Grewe counterposed the wrecking ball of the British empire, whose colonies were "strewn in all parts of the world, accompanied by the inevitably universalistic thought-style, which must be correlated with any such geographically context-less world-empire."[33] Grewe, no less than Schmitt or Haushofer, internalized and reproduced a grand narrative of world history, in which "land" and "sea" constituted diametrically opposed models of power and law.

But here we encounter a paradox. Grewe elsewhere used the term "law of nations," rejecting Schmitt's division of international law into two different orders: that of land and sea. Schmitt had argued, "The usual non-distinguishing term 'law of nations' is false and misleading, because in reality two incoherent laws of nations are valid side by side" (274). Schmitt continued: "The continental land areas become State territory, the oceans remained 'free', i.e., free of State sovereignty. The astounding dualism of the European law of nations of the last centuries was born." Grewe openly rejected Schmitt's dichotomy of land and sea power. "Schmitt's thesis," responded Grewe, "in its strict application excluded the concept of one coherent international legal order, as this book assumes existed in the various epochs of the history of international law." International legal order emerged from a struggle between rival powers in which one leading power prevails. Against Schmitt, Grewe wrote, "[T]his author assumes that the continental and maritime conceptions of the law of nations did not oppose each other incoherently, but that they permeated each other in their mutual spheres of operation and that a more or less stable system of order developed in the different ages as a result of the greater weight of one or other conception."[34]

A key question in the internal Nazi debate on *Großraum* was how to specify the legal relationship of conquered or occupied nations to the German Reich in a way that differentiated Nazi imperialism from the "old imperialism." With apparent enthusiasm, Grewe euphemistically described the legal incorporation of hitherto sovereign states into the Nazi imperium: it yielded a productive "loosening and differentiation" of the once strictly separated fields of "*Staatsrecht*" and "*Völkerrecht*" (98). He wrote appreciatively of the Protectorate of Bohemia and Moravia and the *General Gouvernement* created in western Poland as examples of this "loosening" or "elasticity."[35] Nazi expansion by conquest and occupation resembled the British Commonwealth more than the imperialisms of the turn of the century, he agreed, pointing to the Commonwealth as an "instructive" example of imperial sovereignty, serving the same purpose as *Großraum*.

Grewe also followed Schmitt's emplotment of the interwar period as an epochal shift from the "substantive," or concrete, Christian public law of Europe to the abstract and deracinated (Jewish) "international law." As

Grewe wrote, "In the place of the *'Droit public de l'Europe'* emerged an international law whose undifferentiated general validity is captured in the expression Bentham coined [and accepted in] Anglo-Saxon *Völkerrechts-lehre*: 'International Law.'" For Grewe, the English term "international law" itself illustrated the incommensurability of German and Anglo-Saxon models of world order. International law was at its core an expression of Anglo-Saxon and French values.[36] This transition away from the old public law of Europe began in the nineteenth century, with the expansion of the British and French empires and their attendant civilizing missions and "humanitarian interventions." Grewe lamented an international community that had replaced the substance of its "Christian-European" identity with the anemic concept of "civilized states." Grewe's problem with the concept of civilization in this context was that it denoted "a very specific culture-consciousness . . . a specifically Western European, especially a British-French consciousness" (262). The devolution accelerated in 1919 when the community of states that recognized one another as states bound by law "was no longer a community of civilized nations, but rather was understood as a universal legal community of human beings, a fact of nature, as a 'society of nations', 'an international community', *'une societé internationale globale'*" (283).

Indeed, it is quite jarring to read in what is now considered a "standard textbook" history of international law, citations of the writings of Carl Schmitt in the 1940s without critical comment. And readers familiar with Schmitt's writings on *The Concept of the Political* (1928, 1932) will recognize the critique of false universalism in his narration of the negative impact of the French Revolution on international legal thought:

> The Revolution shook the foundations of the traditional legal community, anchored as they were in the European-Christian consciousness . . . It sought to replace the particular community of Christian Europe with the abstract idea of mankind—*le genre humain*—an ideological construct which was, in practice, unsuitable for containing national egoisms. However, this idea served as a point of departure for far-reaching, in large part utopian conceptions of a world state and of permanent world peace.[37]

In two sections of *Epochs*—"War against War: The Adversary as Criminal," and "Law Enforcement: The Outlawry of War, and Sanctions"—Grewe took up the classic question of just-war theory: the *jus ad bellum* and the *jus in bello*. Grewe claimed that the "discriminatory concept of war" originated in the French Revolution: "The ideas of the French revolutionaries had particularly strong consequences in respect of war. After more than a century of having been ignored they were seized upon by the founders of the Geneva League of Nations." The French war against Austria of 1792 was not war "in the traditional sense. It was the ultimate war against war without the traditional limits or hedgings of war. The enemy was no longer to be respected as '*iustus hostis*' but was criminalized, defamed as an 'enemy of the human race' who deserved no mercy in battle, no status as a prisoner of war."[38] Readers of Schmitt will immediately recognize Grewe's debts to Schmitt's critique of the Kellogg-Briand Pact (1927), which purported to outlaw war but only enabled war to proceed with a good conscience.[39] Grewe wrote that the pact "condemned 'recourse to war for the solution of international controversies.' However, it did not set out a general and principled renunciation of war . . . Wars for the purpose of imposing sanctions and enforcing international law against aggressors and others who threatened the existing world order indirectly acquired legitimacy."[40] But his argument that the nondiscriminatory concept of war (all wars are equal in the eyes of the law) dehumanizes combatants is belied by Grewe's astonishing argument in a September 1941 *Monatshefte* article, that the rules of war were "inapplicable"[41] on the battlefield in the Soviet Union since the USSR had already made clear their disregard for them: "After all that has become known until now about the way the Soviet troops fight, one can only perceive it as bloody mockery, when the . . . Soviet government communicated that it will, in the war against Germany, observe the Hague Convention concerning the laws on land-warfare, the Geneva Protocol about the ban on the use of choking, poisonous, and similar gases, as well as the Geneva Agreement about the treatment of prisoners of war" (750).

In 1942 Grewe wrote that Schmitt's idea of a *Völkerrechtliche Großraumordnung* was now "official policy," confirmed by both Article II of the German–Soviet Border Pact of September 28, 1939, and the Berlin Tripartite Pact of September 27, 1940.[42] Grewe's defense of the *Großraum* concept in April 1942 sheds light on Schmitt's defense of himself at Nuremberg. Schmitt and his numerous defenders contended that to argue for *Großraum* after the invasion of the USSR took courage. Grewe's reiteration of the *Großraum* concept well after the invasion suggests that there was nothing heterodox about the concept in mainstream foreign policy discussions. Late that year, Grewe hailed the creation of the Reichskommissariat Ostland, an occupation zone that encompassed Lithuania, Latvia, Estonia, parts of Belarus and of Ukraine, as a "revolutionary process of the reshaping of Europe that has obtained dimensions which transcend all existing ones . . . Wide expanses of Russian territory have thereby come under German administration. The conditions and requirements one will encounter require no further elaboration. An enormous effort will be necessary to conquer this space. Its conquest will decide the world-political contest in our favor." The phrase "requires no further elaboration" is chilling. Historian Detlev Vagts has noted the sharp difference in the behavior of German armed forces in eastern and western theaters: "In the east the rules were jettisoned completely. Nazi racial and imperial concepts, which had been reflected in the literature of the new international lawyers about the Grand Space and Living Space, made it possible to think of the war in the east as a phenomenon so different that the rules did not apply there."[43] In the 1980s, Grewe expressed regret for the essay, but still tried to excuse it. As one scholar who corresponded with him recounted, Grewe defended his former theses on the grounds that he lacked information regarding the practices of the German war in the East (e.g., the *Kommissarbefehl*[44]); and that his marital status cautioned him against commenting on what Grewe referred to as "its sensitive aspects." Grewe also described his hope that the war would lead to "collapse of the communist tyranny."[45] Grewe's retrospective excuses are unconvincing. His conclusions in the article follow a clear logic, namely, that the USSR is not a "normal" state: "[A] state (*Staatswesen*) that, according to its entire political, social, spiritual-cultural substance, fundamentally sets itself apart from the rest of the states in the community of *Völkerrecht*, which thanks to its particular essence (*Wesensart*) is capable of absolutely no true legal community with them, and that thanks to its political and ideological dynamics is oriented toward the destruction of the traditional order of states."[46] The subtext of this argument is that because the Russians are racially other, no legal "community" can be had between them. These subtexts render problematic Fassbender's argument that Grewe was a "moderate" in the context of the Third Reich.[47]

We do not know precisely what motivated Grewe to be so prolifically useful to the regime, although one can imagine a compound of ambition, enthusiasm, pressure from superiors, and fear. However, Grewe seems to have devoted himself with unnecessary zeal to legal questions that involved a detailed appreciation of military tactics and logistics. In his writings, he took up the laws of war as they pertained to various theaters: land, sea, and air.[48] In a June 1940 column on paratroopers, he noted, "Closed paratrooper formations did not yet exist [in WWI] in the way that the German *Wehrmacht* recently used them on a grand scale in Norway and in the West."[49] Grewe set to work envisioning new legal guidelines to keep pace with changes in "weapons and fighting techniques."

The future West German ambassador to the United States was, just a decade and a half prior to his appointment, composing searing critiques of US foreign policy. As examples, Vagts cites Grewe's *Destroyers for Naval Bases* (1942) and "The Fate of Neutrality in European Wars and in the Second World War" (1943).[50] There are also numerous essays on related topics that Grewe wrote during the war; it is clear that Grewe the future ambassador was very comfortable with American legal texts and had an excellent grasp of the intricacies of American political institutions and diplomacy.[51] His writings on "the fate of neutrality," or specifically, the rights of neutrals in wartime, was his signature variation on a Schmittian theme. Where Schmitt famously argued against the ways in which modern polities were depoliticized—we live in an "age of neutralizations," Schmitt wrote in the 1920s—Grewe applied the same logic to the unveiling of interests behind US claims to neutrality in World War II. Here Schmitt and Grewe had a valid point. As Vagts writes, "The Third Reich was not always wrong in its criticisms of the behavior of other countries vis-a-vis the laws of war. The actions of neutrals, above all the U.S., seemed to depart from the prohibitions under the old rules."[52] The Lend-Lease Act of January 10, 1941, was a shameful ploy "to develop a third possible legal status between 'belligerency' and 'neutrality.' This new status of 'non-belligerency' would permit one belligerent party to be favored over another."[53] In "The Destiny of Neutrality in European War and the Second World War" (1943), Grewe cited important American jurists like Philip Jessup and Quincy Wright as well as other authors published in the *American Journal of International Law*. He described the "destroyers for bases" deal as a "striking violation" of Article 6 of the 13th Hague Convention, and scorned Robert Jackson (then US attorney general, later the lead prosecutor at Nuremberg) for "justify[ing] the transaction on the grounds of existing neutrality law, an attempt deemed unsuccessful even in the eyes of American international lawyers." The US had "made a farce" of its neutrality.[54]

But Grewe's critique of the United States extended far beyond Lend-Lease aid and the other measures that President Roosevelt had used. Neutrality heralded the broader "age of neutralizations and depoliticizations" that Schmitt had written about in the late 1920s. Specifically, it was an omen of the American Century to come if the Third Reich were defeated: "The keyword of the 'American Century' is only the expression of a universalist missionary idea which has found its most active embodiment in Roosevelt . . . It is the picture of a regionally organized super-federation . . . with real executive power . . . the picture of a world federation, which may serve as the necessary instrument for the regulation of world peace and world order by the ruling north American supremacy. Such a universalistic conception is necessarily hostile to neutrality."[55] Grewe's arguments resembled Schmitt's arguments from the same period. If Schmitt was the "choirmaster" of the international lawyers of the Third Reich, Grewe was able to carry the tune.

A Legal Career in the Third Reich: 1933–1945

Grewe began his law studies three years before the Nazi takeover. His dissertation and *Habilitation* supervisor, Ernst Forsthoff, was a Nazi ideologue who took the chair of his purged Jewish predecessor at Heidelberg. In 1933, Forsthoff wrote an influential defense of the totalitarian state. Grewe dedicated his 1936 dissertation at Hamburg to Forsthoff,[56] following him to Königsberg in 1936–37 and completed his *Habilitation* with him in 1941.[57] Grewe's first published work, written when he was 21 (in 1932), provides a clue to his emerging worldview. In an essay in the journal *Die Junge Mannschaft*, Grewe proclaimed his beliefs in a revolution from the Right. The piece is noteworthy, both for the rare glimpse it affords of personal conviction, and because the rhetoric seems to prefigure some of his later commitments to the "realism" he evinced during the Cold War:

> A national opposition must necessarily stand, which protects German claims with unconditional, revolutionary decisiveness and may not step onto the ground of Versailles. We believed that the German youth was called to take up this task . . . The reconstitution of the state and the accomplishment of certain tasks, recognized to be necessary, requires an opposition that protects all actual concessions, all necessities of *Realpolitik* (*realpolitische Notwendigkeiten*) . . . with respect to the indispensable whole of the modern idea of the state and the eternal task of the Reich . . . Among the ranks of the oppositional youth of today, a political class must develop that is ready to carry out these tasks.[58]

Grewe first encountered Schmitt's thought as a twenty-year-old in 1931, when he reviewed Schmitt's *The Concept of the Political* for *Die Junge Mannschaft*.[59] A subsequent contribution to the volume, *What We Expect from National Socialism*, opened doors to write for *Deutsches Volkstum*, and brought him into personal contact with Schmitt for the first time in January 1932.[60] Six months later, Grewe was initiated into the small circle of Schmitt disciples in Hamburg with an invitation to a conference sponsored by the Deutschnationaler Handlungsgehilfen-Verband (DHV), at which elder Schmitt students such as Ernst-Rudolf Huber and Ernst Forsthoff were present. This appears to be the origin of the Grewe-Forsthoff relationship.[61] Breuer has turned up an astonishing number of "lost articles" that Grewe wrote in far-right youth journals, beginning in 1929. Taken together, they reveal him to be an energetic and precocious political thinker, and an active partisan of Hamburg's Nazi youth movement.[62] According to Breuer, while Grewe's ideas were shared by others in the "Hamburg School" of the German youth movement, Grewe can be identified as one of its "leading ideologues."[63]

In one essay, we find the "democratic political principle" and the related "bourgeois-Rechtsstaatlich and parliamentary elements of the state" contrasted with a superior principle—"an imperial principle, appropriate to a Reich."[64] Ideas such as these place Grewe at the heart of conservative-revolutionary thought. To what extent he outgrew these ideas is unclear. After 1933, moreover, it is even harder to recover Grewe's most personally cherished beliefs.

In 1937–38 Grewe worked as *Referent* for the German Institute for Foreign Policy Research (Deutsches Institut für Aussenpolitische Forschung; DIAF hereafter), an institution that was created at the behest of Joachim von Ribbentrop, who then controlled what was called the *Dienststelle Ribbentrop* in the Foreign Office (Auswärtiges Amt).[65] Historian Herman Weber has argued that the *Deutsche Dienststelle* and the DIAF were "practically identical"—their task was to "underpin the NS foreign relations with their publications."[66] According to Otto Abetz, a contemporary of Grewe's, the *Dienststelle* was a "cross between a diplomatic workshop (*Lehrwerkstätte*) and a type of foreign policy 'brain trust.'" The *Dienststelle* was composed of older men whom Ribbentrop could trust and younger men in the roles of assistants and adjutants. Among the latter were Abetz, Grewe, and Friedrich (Fritz) Berber.[67] These accounts make it hard to believe what Grewe claimed in a stormy letter after the war—that he had "never seen Ribbentrop outside of the newspapers and illustrated magazines."[68] From 1933 to 1941, there was a power struggle over the control of Nazi foreign policy research and propaganda between Ribbentrop and Goebbels' Propaganda Ministry that Goebbels ultimately lost.[69] Grewe's close working relationship with Berber enables us to locate Grewe on the Ribbentrop side of this conflict.

In November 1935, Berber became acting director of the prestigious Hamburg Institute for Foreign Policy (Hamburger Institut für Auswärtige Politik) and editor of its journal, the *Monatshefte für Auswärtige Politik*. In January 1937 Berber accepted a contract from Ribbentrop to turn the German Center for the Study of International Relations (Deutsche Zentralstelle für das Studium der Internationalen Beziehungen) into a German Institute for Foreign Policy Research (Deutsches Institut für aussenpolitische Forschung) (261). By April 1, 1937, Berber had cooperated with the *Gleichschaltung* of the once-important liberal foreign policy institute in the Hamburg institute (HIAP) with Ribbentrop's institute (DIAF).[70]

The institute's move to Berlin strengthened Ribbentrop's position vis-à-vis Goebbels. In late 1937, Berber joined the Nazi Party, and was named extraordinary professor of public law in Berlin.[71] In August 1939, Ribbentrop, now foreign minister, created the Deutsche Informationstelle (DI hereafter) as a division of the DIAF and appointed Berber acting director of both institutions.[72] Although Berber struggled at the end of the war to shake off "the impression of being a Ribbentrop protégé" (383–84), some of Berber's students referred to him as "little Ribbentrop" (387). In September 1939, Grewe went to work for Berber.[73]

After the war, both Berber and Grewe would insist that the work they performed at the DIAF was "scientific." But according to internal documents from 1942/43, there was virtually no difference between the DIAF and the DI: "Because they share the same work-tasks, the same researcher-colleagues (*Mitarbeiter*) and the same leadership, the two have in reality more and more coalesced into one scholarly *Dienststelle*."[74] Grewe was one of fifteen *Mitarbeiter* reporting to Berber at the DIAF.[75] On August 1, 1939, Grewe and Jürgen von Kempski were placed in charge of the international law section of the institute, which produced a monthly report on international legal developments.[76] Between 1939 and 1943, Grewe authored forty-two of these short but substantive examinations of international affairs and German foreign policy from a legal perspective.[77]

These monthly reports give us evidence of Grewe's assiduous contributions to the regime's foreign policy goals. In letters and memoirs written after the war, Grewe asserted that he had worked for Berber only under duress; that he had tried "to escape Berber"; and that he and other *Mitarbeiter* did not respect Berber.[78] But Grewe published in three journals or series edited by Berber and there is no archival evidence that their relationship was strained.[79] In 1937–38, when Grewe was *Referent* at the DIAF, he wrote four essays for the *Monatshefte*, and another twelve in 1939. Prior to 1933, the *Monatshefte* was the respected and nonpartisan journal of political science, *Europäische Gespräche*, edited by the liberal Albrecht von Mendelssohn Bartholdy.[80] These propaganda writings were oriented to the war with Western Europe and the United States.

After Germany's defeat at Stalingrad in February 1943, Berber ordered a stronger focus on Eastern themes. Until the end of his life, Berber denied he had produced "propaganda." But in letters from 1941 and 1942, Berber admitted that his work at the D1 was "directly under the command of the Foreign Minister of the Reich and during the war entrusted with special tasks."[81] Historians have suggested that Berber was not a committed ideologue.[82] Hermann Weber writes: "Certainly Reinhard Höhn and Franz Alfred Six were nearer to the core of NS race-ideology and dreams of *Lebensraum* than was Berber, but the breadth of opinion that was permitted as 'recognized National Socialist' afforded enough room for Berber."[83] Still, given that Berber was the designated expert for international law for the SS journal, *Reich, Volksordnung, Lebensraum* (1941–1944), Weber's assessment may be too lenient.[84] By late 1943, Berber fled to Switzerland, where he sought to rehabilitate his reputation through work with the International Red Cross. Even if there were some truth to the claim that Berber or Ribbentrop afforded protection to "outsiders" or nonconformists, the regime-supporting function of the spaces where Grewe worked is still clear.

Grewe also published in other journals that were fully *gleichgeschaltet,* that is to say, complicit with regime goals, and valuable to their realization. Grewe published four articles in the *Zeitschrift der Akademie für deutsches Recht,* the organ of the Academy of German Law.[85] The academy's main goal was to present a "respectable image among the international legal establishment," and "publiciz[e] the alleged inequalities and injustices perpetrated upon Germany as a result of the post-WWI settlement."[86] At Nuremberg, Schmitt distanced himself from the journal that he conceded was known for pieces of an "advocatory or apologetic character."[87] By writing several pieces for the *Jahrbuch der Weltpolitik*[88] and the *Zeitschrift für Politik,*[89] Grewe was working for Franz Six, a notorious SS officer and ideologue made Professor for Foreign Policy and Foreign Studies (Ordentlicher Professor für Aussenpolitik und Auslandskunde) at the University of Berlin.[90]

An SS *Untersturmführer*[91] in the SS intelligence service (*Sicherheitsdienst,* or SD) since 1935, Six was promoted by Heinrich Himmler to lead a division of the Reichssicherheitshauptamt (RSHA).[92] In 1940, Six enlisted in the *Waffen-SS* in April 1940, commanding a unit of *Einsatzsgruppe* B of the Security Police (*Sicherheitspolizei*) and the SD during the invasion of the USSR. He was promoted in November 1941 to *SS-Oberführer.* While the judges at Nuremberg in 1946 could not "scientifically prove" the charge of murder, Six was sentenced to twenty years' imprisonment for having been "an active participant in an organization that had committed acts of violence and crimes as well as inhumane treatment of the civil population."[93] He "irritated his American judges by . . . trying to pass off his work in the *Vorkommando* as a piece of scientific research. For instance, he presented the programs of teaching and research of the Deutsches Auslandswissenschaftliches Institut as an attempted 'east-west rapprochement'" (229). Serving only five years before resuming civilian life, he went on to have a successful career as an advertising executive with the Porsche company.[94]

Franz Six's deep involvement with the Holocaust and dissemination of Nazi ideology may only give us limited purchase on Grewe's political beliefs or activities. But reconstructing Grewe's milieu in the *gleichgeschaltet* institutions of the Third Reich casts light on the broader themes of his lifework, of great power behavior and the rise and fall of imperial hegemons. Six presented the DAWI as an effort to "catch up" with the Western powers by emulating them and, paradoxically, to revolutionize the study of international affairs by grasping its deepest German essence. Its mission was to support "German tasks in Europe and the European task in the world."[95] After departing in 1943, Six was replaced by Karl Heinz Pfeffer, a specialist on the British empire who wrote several books for the institute's book series.[96] Like Schmitt and Haushofer, Pfeffer and Six diagnosed the organization of German political science through a comparative Atlantic lens. Pfeffer compared the DAWI to the Institut d'études politiques (the forerunner of today's "Sciences Po") in France, the Istituto per gli Studi di Politica Internazionale in Milan, and the Council on Foreign Relations in New York. Much as Bowman had claimed the mantle of science for political geography, Pfeffer contrasted the DAWI's "autonomous research community which has scientific responsibility for itself," with the British Royal Institute of International Affairs, which he characterized as a mere propaganda arm of the Foreign

Ministry. The core, or foundational courses, included elements of history, political science, economics, law, and geography. Political geography and geopolitics (*politische Geographie und Geopolitik*) were central parts of the DAWI curriculum. In 1941, students were obligated to take a lecture course by the famous geopolitician Karl Haushofer. By 1943, the DAWI had awarded twenty students the equivalent of the bachelor's degree (*Diplom*) in Foreign Studies (*Auslandswissenschaften*) and twenty the doctoral degree.[97]

When Grewe received his first teaching contract in the Foreign Studies Faculty of the University of Berlin on March 6, 1941, he and Haushofer became colleagues. In the spring of 1941, Grewe offered two courses: "Seminar on Important Cases in International Law" and "History of State-Theories with Special Attention to State-Theoretical Foundations of Foreign Policy." In the (winter) semester of 1941/42, he taught "Current Questions in International Law."[98] A 1943 DAWI internal report (author unknown) included the proud claim that "finally the Institute has increasingly become the epicenter for a cultural-political discussion in which the questions of the new European order were clarified."[99] Grewe was also tasked with assembling a "Handbook" of basic concepts in Germany's policies vis-à-vis Europe (*Europapolitik*). In January 1942, Grewe discussed his plans with Six.[100] Grewe planned a second volume with contributions from Höhn, E.R. Huber, Karl Larenz, Theodor Maunz, Paul Rittersbuch, and Ulrich Scheuner.[101] Scheuner and Grewe would later find themselves in the same circles at the German Association for Foreign Policy, founded in 1954.

As Grewe completed the first draft of his *Habilitation*, the work that would become *Epochen der Völkerrechtsgeschichte*, he was entrusted with a number of priority projects for the institute. In addition, at the height of the war with the USSR, Grewe lectured on "Nation and State" and "Introduction to Basic Concepts in Legal Science," and taught seminars on "Contemporary International-Legal Questions" and "The Science of State" (*Staatswissenschaft*).[102] Grewe was also integral to a second massive handbook project, on concepts relating to foreign policy and international law. The goal of this "Dictionary of Foreign Policy" was to serve the generally educated but nonacademic reader, in addition to "those concerned with foreign policy in the Foreign Office, interested circles in the party and state, as much as students of relevant disciplines."[103] Fellow contributors were to include Six, Pfeffer, the future Social Democratic deputy Wilhelm Gülich, and high-ranking SS men Rudolf Levin and Horst Mahnke.[104] Grewe was seen as ideologically reliable enough to be tasked with formulating the "call for lexicon entries," and to be entrusted with all entries concerning international law.[105] Invited to give lectures at Leipzig in the winter semester of 1943, he lost the entire manuscript to the aerial bombing of Leipzig on December 4.

The fortunes of Karl Haushofer's son, Albrecht Haushofer, changed abruptly in May 1941. On the tenth of May, Deputy Führer Rudolf Hess flew to Scotland. Hitler suspected Albrecht might be to blame and sent him to prison for interrogation by the Gestapo. He was released after eight weeks, and permitted to return to the university, but now suspected of disloyalty. Karl Haushofer's home was searched and Hess's correspondence seized.[106] His son, Albrecht, was forced out for political reasons. A veteran of the *Dienststelle Ribbentrop* and the information office, Albrecht was later arrested for his ties to both the Kreisau Circle and the Red Orchestra, resistance groups that plotted Hitler's overthrow after the failure of the July 20, 1944 attempt on Hitler's life. Albrecht was executed at the end of April 1945. Given Grewe's postwar claims to have been a member of resistance groups, what to make of the fact that Grewe was called to take Haushofer's position? On November 11, 1943, the acting dean of the DAWI wrote to the Reich Ministry for Education, requesting that Grewe be promoted and take Haushofer's place:

> The DAWI has requested that the extraordinary prof. Albrecht Haushofer be removed and replaced, naming Grewe to Full Professor for Foreign Public Law and International Law at the *Auslandswissenschaftliche Fakultät*, with a salary drawn from the Full Professorship (*Ordinariat*) for Political Geography and Geopolitics . . . The reason is that Grewe has very quickly achieved a leading position among young international law scholars. Leipzig and other universities have offered him positions. We can't get a line for a Full Professor (*Ordinarius*) in *Rechtswissenschaft*.[107]

The half-Jewish background of Grewe's wife, Marianne Partsch, appears to have forced a vetting of his promotion. A memo dated September 27, 1944, states that while "his wife doesn't have the necessary documentation," Grewe, by contrast, "has pure German blood."[108] A subsequent letter confirming his promotion to *Ordinarius* on September 20, 1944, reads: "The director the Party-chancellor has raised no objections to the nomination. Prof. Grewe is exempt. There is no drawback in the milieu of the professor or among those to be granted the same rights as him."[109] Grewe plunged headlong into highly political and contemporary topics such as Allied plans for a United Nations.[110]

Coming to Terms with His Past

Erich Kaufmann was a distinguished jurist forced into exile by Nazi purges of German law faculties. In a heated correspondence between the two in 1952, Kaufmann charged that Grewe was deeply complicit with the Third Reich. Kaufmann's credibility stems from the fact that "more than anyone else, [he was] the person who helped Grewe get a new start" after the war.[111] Why did Kaufmann turn on his former protégé? Professional jealousy may have been a factor. Hallstein passed over Kaufmann when he selected Grewe, the younger man.[112] Remarkably, Carl Schmitt knew about the intimate exchange of recriminations between the two men. In a letter to Armin Möhler (June 29, 1952), Schmitt wrote that "Kaufman, who created Prof. Grewe, now sends around letters (*Rundbriefe*) in which he insults him as a Nazi and collaborator of Ribbentrop."

While Kaufmann charged that Grewe had "won his spurs" in the Ribbentrop office, Grewe responded that he had never seen Ribbentrop in his life. He insisted that his work with Berber was nothing to be ashamed of. The Hamburg Institute for Foreign Policy, he parried, had not yet set a "new course" with the outbreak of war. In fact, the institute was fully *gleichgeschaltet* by 1937, two years before Grewe began his work there. Grewe described his next career move, to the faculties of law and foreign studies faculty at the University of Berlin, as his "only chance to elude work with Berber," and described the ideological diversity at the university: "Next to the pronounced National Socialists," wrote Grewe to Kaufmann, "there was also a large circle of politically very reserved linguists from . . . the old Orientalist Seminar, and men like the [later] executed Albrecht Haushofer, or the present Social Democratic deputy Professor Gülich."[113]

Grewe went as far as to claim he had actively resisted in the last years of the war. In the same letter to Kaufmann, Grewe linked himself to a leading figure in the Red Orchestra in Berlin, noting that a Luftwaffe officer named Harry Schutze-Boysen, one of its leaders, had attended his lectures on the history of state theory at the University of Berlin, and asked Grewe to supervise his dissertation. Eventually, in the course of denazification proceedings in Freiburg (under French occupation), Grewe was "exonerated" ("*entlastet*") on the grounds of his "active resistance, especially on account of his participation in a resistance group connected to the July 20, 1944 [plot]." Nowhere else in the literature on Grewe has this extraordinary claim been corroborated. If it were true, one would expect it to be prominent in obituaries and other retrospective accounts of his life.

In his 1979 memoirs, he repeated the boldest of the claims made in his letter to Kaufmann from 1952. The "political coloration" of the faculty at the Faculty of Foreign Studies (AWF) was "as heterogeneous as in all other faculties."[114] He further asserted that by offering to supervise the thesis of a future leader of a resistance group, he knowingly lent support to an opponent of the regime: "I felt myself in sympathy and gave my agreement" to supervise a work that the student intended to function as a "concealed analysis of despotic regimes" (183).

Grewe claimed that his own resistance activities dated back to 1937. "It was not long [after my return to Berlin] that I became a member of one such underground circle. The official theme, with which we were supposed to be occupied with presentations (*Referate*) and discussions, sounded academically innocuous . . . The sole bond [between the group members] was resistance against the regime—two of the twelve-person group paid with their life . . . We met in the home of Otto Veit . . . After July 20, 1944, these meetings were naturally over" (180). In a questionnaire by the US government that Grewe filled out in 1957 or 1958 (presumably as part of his clearance as ambassador), Grewe listed Veit as one of three character references. After 1945, Veit became a prominent expert on monetary policy, president of the state bank of Hesse, professor of economics and banking at the University of Frankfurt, and a member of the international Mont Pelérin Society.

Grewe claimed too that he regularly met weekly for an evening drink with Berthold Graf von Stauffenberg (brother of Claus, the architect of the attempted assassination of Hitler on July 20, 1944), and Ernst Schmitz, director of the Kaiser-Wilhelms Institut für Öffentliches Recht und Völkerrecht: "We used these meetings chiefly to exchange information" (180–81). He also claimed a close relationship with Albrecht Haushofer:

> I soon found myself in close relationship with Albrecht Haushofer . . . When I met him at the beginning of the war, he was a determined opponent of the regime, prepared to run great personal risks—a professor of political geography, who was at the same time a highly sensitive poet. This breadth in his personality fascinated me. The same man who with as much shrewdness and erudition as cold-bloodedness and realism (*Realismus*) saw the catastrophe coming, and analyzed its causes and conditions, could, not much later—I experienced it in a small private circle of friends—recite his endlessly tender, foggy "Chinese Legends." (182)

The notion that Grewe and Albrecht Haushofer were co-conspirators seems unlikely. And given Grewe's extensive work on behalf of the regime, his romantic depiction of Haushofer as both poet and political realist seems self-serving.

When he drafted his reply to Kaufmann, Grewe had just joined Adenauer's circle of legal advisors, and the Foreign Office began to touch up its history. In the entrance hall of the new Foreign Office in Bonn sat a memorial dedicated to "those colleagues who gave their life in the struggle against the Hitler regime."[115] As historian Richard Evans wrote, "Gaining Adenauer's confidence . . . substantial numbers of old [Foreign Office] hands found their way back into the diplomatic and consular service and its administration in Bonn. One after another they were presented as having been distant from Nazism or even involved in the 1944 bomb plot" (179). Following on a public scandal in 2003, Foreign Minister Joschka Fischer appointed a historical commission that wrote a book on the Foreign Office during the Third Reich. Of it, Evans wrote, "The myth of the Foreign Office's resistance has been publicly exploded by this book" (182).

Grewe's legal career between 1937 and 1945 provides a window on another dimension of the destruction of the profession: the willingness of those who remained to subordinate themselves to the geopolitical and bio-political goals of the Nazi state. The fate of Jews in the international law profession in the Third Reich was even worse than in other professions. As historian Detlev Vagts explains, "The decimation of the profession represented a higher proportion than that of German professors in general, and law professors in particular."[116] While 16 percent of university faculty were forced out, and 22 percent of professors at law faculties lost their positions, the proportion of international lawyers was nearly twice that. Seven full professors were forced out between 1933 and 1935; six more followed between 1937 and 1939. "Of the tenured professors, several committed suicide (Fleischmann of Halle, Perels of Hamburg, and Neumeyer of Munich), several went into exile (Kelsen of Cologne, Mendelssohn Bartholdy of Hamburg, and Strupp of Frankfurt), and several were dismissed or went into premature retirement (Kaufmann of Berlin, and Schücking of Kiel)." Vagts explains that those international lawyers who remained had choices. Grewe did not choose "internal emigration," which Vagts describes as "disconnecting oneself from public life as much as was permitted" (679). Nor did Grewe take the path adopted by others like Viktor Bruns, founder of the Kaiser Wilhelm Institute for International Law, who "tried to pursue a normal career without identifying with Nazism internally." Lawyers like Bruns, writes Vagts, "would write obligatory pieces, putting in some obeisance to the new order and the theories that underlay it without indulging in racist rhetoric. He was attached to the system, of course, and in a way served it" (680). Can Grewe be described as an "opportunist" or "enthusiast," the category to which Vagts assigned both Schmitt and Berber?

> One could be an opportunist or a convinced Nazi, embracing all of the doctrines of race, *Volk, Lebensraum* and the *Führer* principle. This phenomenon occurred mostly among the assistant professors of

1933, partly because they had more to gain by currying favor with the powers, but also they belonged to the age cohort most vulnerable to Nazism.[117]

Vagts's characterization of Bruns is a partial fit for Grewe, although Bruns has the "testimony of reliable persons that his sympathies did not lie with the Government" while Grewe does not (683). Despite Bruns's lack of "inward commitment to the regime," reasons Vagts, "objectively," he was a highly useful ally. Those who remained and survived in the universities may not have all been "true believers," but most made accommodations to the regime that went beyond that which was necessary to survive. These were relationships of objective complicity, and Grewe's guilt can be measured in these terms.

In 1933, Arthur Nussbaum, the future author of a canonical history of international law, was forced from his position at the University of Berlin. While Nussbaum taught at Columbia Law School until his death in 1964, Grewe advanced as a result of the same *Gleichschaltung* that expelled Nussbaum. Grewe's *Epochs of International Law* is a product of the ethnic cleansing of the German universities in the Third Reich. Its celebrated "realism" is an artifact of the same historical processes that caused the scientific emigration and transformation of the German profession of international law. Grewe's realism, today perceived as an anchor of the transatlantic alliance, was less a worldview attuned to the exigencies of the Cold War than a residuum of the Third Reich's violent destruction of democratic institutions and the rule of law. Realism, one might say, is *was bleibt* (what remains).

CHAPTER 5

Geopolitics

Death and Rebirth of an Atlantic
Tradition during World War II

FROM 1939 TO THE END OF THE WAR, scholars and journalists in the United States devoted a surprising amount of attention to an academic super-weapon allegedly powering Nazi plans for world conquest: geopolitics. The year 1942 marked the height of this fascination. Across the spectrum of popular press, middlebrow literature, and academic tomes, all spotlighted the dangerous, foreign, and deeply German doctrine. Breathless, sensationalized reports appeared in publications as diverse as *Business Week* and *Fortune, Harper's* and *Life, Collier's* and *Time*.[1] Journalists grappling with the foreign concept of "geopolitics" tried to peer behind the curtain to find its wizard, alighting on Karl Haushofer (1869–1946), a WWI general and Munich professor of geography, who was depicted as the key strategic thinker behind Hitler's conquests. Even the mass circulation *Reader's Digest* published an article on the alleged "1000 Scientists behind Hitler," advancing the myth that Haushofer headed a "Munich Geopolitical Institute," where he kept "a file on almost everything and everybody in every country and in every part of the country on the face of the globe."[2] In fact no such institute ever existed. Haushofer and his son were teaching at the tightly controlled Faculty of Foreign Studies in Berlin alongside the international lawyers Wilhelm Grewe and Friedrich Berber, the sociologist Karl Pfeffer, and SS-*Oberführer* Franz Six. The Office of War Information film directed by Frank Capra, *Why We Fight: The Nazis Strike* (1943), depicted a hive of activity in Munich.

A score of hefty tomes were penned by prominent geographers and other academics, many German émigrés, and bearing titles like *The World of General Haushofer: Geopolitics in Action, Geopolitics: The Struggle for Space and Power,* and *German Strategy of World Conquest.*[3] The works differed on the exact extent to which Nazi imperialism had precedents in German history, and how much the theory of geopolitics guided actual strategy and foreign policy decisions. All agreed on one thing: understanding Karl Haushofer was the key to defeating Adolf Hitler.[4] As an article in *Time* magazine put it in 1942, West Point's "Colonel Beukema declares that history will rate Karl Haushofer, prophet of German geopolitics, more important than Adolf Hitler, because Haushofer's studies made possible Hitler's victories both in power politics and war."[5] Much as the Third Reich was often represented in contemporary accounts as a nation under the spell of one evil genius, the advent of geopolitics was said to be the work of just one man, Haushofer.

The demonization of Haushofer gave a name to inchoate anxieties about geopolitics. Imbuing geopolitics with a foreign national identity permitted Americans to forestall introspection into the geopolitical logic of their own empire. In chapter 2, I argued that an interwar Atlantic geopolitical tradition encompassing both Anglo-American and continental European thinkers has been neglected. Historicization breaks up later reifications of "Anglo-American" versus "German" geopolitics. As with other constructions of a peculiarly pathological German developmental pathway in history (the "*Sonderweg*" in historians' parlance), treating Germany as the exceptional bearer of an exceptional science risks missing the extent to which geopolitics was more norm than exception in the North Atlantic world. The American reception of German *Geopolitik* in the early 1940s had the effect of nationalizing and homogenizing a set of ideas that were in fact transatlantic.

After resuming the discussion of Haushofer and Bowman begun in chapter 2, I show how, at the height of the Third Reich's successes, US fears of being left behind triggered a search for an American equivalent. I trace how geopolitics became "German," distorting its roots in a common Atlantic discourse with global dimensions. The initial reaction of the American commentators on German *Geopolitik* was to denounce it as a dangerous and "politicized" form of science. But by 1942, Bowman and other commentators changed their tune. The debate shifted rapidly: the search was on for an "American Haushofer"—the intellectual who could help the Americans emulate the Germans' achievements. They identified candidates for this role and built institutions to help salvage the kernels of geopolitical truth from their German husks. While the salvage operation never prompted Americans to confront their own history of imperialism, the comparison did at least open up new possibilities of self-knowledge: Perhaps America and Germany were more comparable than they seemed?[6]

Americans Debate the Value of a "German Science," 1941–1945

A public controversy involving Bowman over the pedigree of German geopolitics broke out in 1941, illustrating the anxieties that fastened on the question of national origins. In 1941, Columbia University geographer George Renner published a series of maps in *Collier's* that lent legitimacy to Nazi and Japanese territorial ambitions. Renner defended the maps as "scientific," state of the art "geopolitics." After coming under attack, Renner invoked the authority of Bowman, whom he called "the dean of America's geopoliticians," in support.[7] In time, many came to refer to Bowman as "our" geopolitician, a label that irritated him greatly.[8] Bowman sued Renner for defamation.

To defend his reputation, Bowman wrote a series of articles arguing that (the good, American) political geography was fundamentally dissimilar from (the bad, Nazi) geopolitics. While the one was militaristic and mystical, the other was peace-loving and rational. His 1920 work, *The New World*, was objective, inductive, and realistic: "The method of my book was to deal *realistically* with the political problems of the postwar world. Its philosophy was one of gradualness of change by rational means. It interposed no ideological preconceived 'system' between a problem and its solution . . . It sought to analyze real situations rather than justify any one of several conflicting nationalistic policies" (emphasis added).[9] But Bowman's distinction between political geography and its evil twin, geopolitics, rested on essentialist and xenophobic arguments. Nonetheless, Bowman tried to claim the moral high ground of objective science: "Nothing has so clearly revealed the essential primitiveness of the German theories of government as the history of political thought in Germany for the past hundred years. Its 'laws' of national growth, its recent 'science' of geopolitics which assumes that 'political events depend upon the soil.' . . . These are among the doctrines that are separated from democracy by an abyss so wide that today only war can bridge it" (648).

The wartime context made it deeply uncomfortable for a figure like Bowman to acknowledge commonalities between American and German traditions of political geography. Bowman's protestations denied the complexity of the transatlantic intellectual exchanges that constituted the geopolitical realism of the interwar period. Instead, he insisted on an "either/or"—German or American geopolitics—in order to determine who had first sinned. "Geopolitics has migrated from Germany to America, not from America to Germany," wrote Bowman, denying that the historical traffic in ideas had gone in both directions (646). "It has recently been declared that American geopolitics was developed before it was taken up in Germany. The bad effect of this assertion touches more than personal or professional repute. It has given the question a national context." The debate touched a nerve because, as Smith explains, "Geopolitics was an acute disciplinary embarrassment for many geographers, but nowhere more so than in the US, where the national school was inspired by and built on German ideas."[10]

Bowman's strained distinctions between "scientific" political geography and "political" *Geopolitik* do not withstand critical scrutiny. While he sent hundreds of copies of the article to academics as well as business and political leaders, in private letters Bowman admitted these were "exercises in self-protection" (156).[11] But the line between "American" political geography and "German" geopolitics was made even harder to sustain by the fact that the Haushofer school had expressly taken Bowman as an important spur to their own work in the 1920s.[12] Bowman reasonably insisted that he was not responsible for the Haushofer school's formulations, however much they sought to emulate or rival his own, and that there were important differences between them. "Neither Mackinder nor Haushofer had theories that could stand up to the facts of air power . . . I might add that the mind of man is still a more important source of power than a heartland or a dated theory about it. It is always man that makes his history, however important the environment or the physical resources in setting bounds to the extension of power from any given center at a given time."[13] This theme of respect for human agency and freedom was also at the center of Weigert's characterization of the differences in the traditions: his "decisive objection to German geopolitics" was its neglect of the human being, his dignity (597).

Yet figures like Weigert and Bowman kept going back to the well, no matter how much they protested that the sources were tainted. Just two years earlier, for example, Bowman had boldly appropriated the concept "*Lebensraum*" from the continental tradition of Ratzel, Kjellén, and Haushofer—to describe the global economic supremacy envisioned by others under the labels "Pax Americana" or the recently coined "American Century." Bowman told the inaugural meeting of the Territorial Committee of the Council on Foreign Relations that if Hitler wanted *Lebensraum*, then "Lebensraum for all is the answer to Lebensraum for one," adding "it is an economic question."[14] Bowman's biographer, the critical geographer Neil Smith, interprets this as a direct appropriation from Ratzel but sidesteps the fact that this was, if anything, a creative misreading of Ratzel, since Ratzel aimed at the formal empire of territorial control. "An 'American economic Lebensraum' was exactly what Bowman, the State Department, and Roosevelt struggled to realize. Power would no longer be measured in territory. The Bretton Woods Conference established the IMF and World Bank to oversee the global economy. These represented the first planks of the economic infrastructure of the postwar American Lebensraum."[15] Bowman's balancing act was to appropriate something of the spirit of Ratzel, while simultaneously denying it by "brick[ing] a high wall between geopolitics and political geography" (289). Bowman's refusal of geopolitics as unscientific and ur-Deutsch did not last.

In the very same year that he sued Renner for defamation, he strongly endorsed two manifestos for an "American" geopolitics. The first was that of Yale political scientist Nicholas J. Spykman's *American Strategy in World Politics* (1942); the second, Robert Strausz-Hupé's *Geopolitics: The Struggle for Space* (1942).[16] Bowman gave a ringing endorsement to Spykman's reflections on the balance of power and power politics: "On grounds of merit and public value, [it] should be read in not less than a million homes. Every government official responsible for policy should read it once a year for the next twenty years—even if he may not agree with some of the remedies proposed"; isolationism was no longer an option: "our way of life is now planetary." But in the same essay, Bowman faulted Spykman for not recognizing his descent from the Americans— Mahan, Archibald Coolidge, and Morton Fullerton. "Professor Spykman picks up Fullerton's torch, and carries it magnificently."[17] "If I were to try to prepare the people of the US for the realities of power politics of chief concern to us here and now . . . I would prescribe four books to be read in the following order": "Mahan's *Interest of America in Sea Power, Past and Present* (1897), Mackinder's *Britain and the British Seas* (1902, last chapter only), A.C. Coolidge's *The US as a World Power*, and Morton Fullerton's *Problems of Power* (definitive edition, 1919)" (349). Bowman's recommended reading list gives the lie to the folk wisdom that the émigrés alone transplanted realism in America.[18]

If Bowman faulted Spykman for neglecting his American forbears, he appreciated Strausz-Hupé's efforts to construct an indigenous American tradition of geopolitics. In an essay in *Fortune*, Strausz-Hupé described the Monroe Doctrine as the original source for the theory of *Lebensraum*. "Memories of spacious early America flavored [Friedrich] List's book in 1841 . . . Thus List, the friend of Henry Clay and student of Alexander Hamilton, originated the theory of Lebensraum."[19] Of Strausz-Hupé, Bowman wrote, "He has an unfailing instinct for the weakness of the Haushofer school, and its 'science' of geopolitics," and his is a book "that every citizen should read" (656).

The popular press too found Spykman an attractive candidate to fill the role of the American Haushofer. Spykman, a Dutchman who had obtained his PhD at the University of California at Berkeley with a dissertation on Georg Simmel, became the founding director of the Yale Institute for International Studies in 1935.[20] He remained director until his sudden death in 1944. In a review of Spykman's book by *Time*, Malcolm Cowley applied the label "realism" to Spykman's geopolitical study. Bowman had reached for a similar construction—"the realities of power politics." At the University of Chicago, Hans Morgenthau had not yet embraced the label, and the paradigm remained inchoate until around 1950.

For Spykman accepts the fact "that there will always be conflict, and that war will remain a necessary instrument in the preservation of a balance of power." To some, *realism* so simple may well seem as devastating as frost in a hothouse for orchids. But such people may take comfort in the thought that Prof. Spykman is not infallible, that the cult of realism has its own limitations and cold-bloodedness leads to its own kind of distortion. To others, tired of statesmanship by euphemism and eye-catching phonies, Spykman's plain-talking seems a bracing corrective.[21] (emphasis added)

The metaphors for realism—as cult, and as cold-bloodedness—that appear in this popular review are fascinating to consider. Five years later, it would have been unthinkable that a mainstream media organ like *Time* would voice such doubts about "realism," let alone refer to it as a "cult." The prestige of realism developed in the late 1940s and 1950s in part through the routinization of such metaphors. "Cold-blooded" and "Cold War" are phrases that evoke the elemental and lend concepts the force of myth.[22] The partisans of geopolitics, and their critics, debated what counted as the real and the sensible. Was geopolitics part of common sense or its antithesis?

The press nominated a third figure after Bowman and Spykman to be "America's Haushofer." In January 1942, *Time* magazine profiled Col. Herbert Beukema as the architect of a breakthrough for geopolitics and military strategy in university education.[23] *Time* noted that a raft of new courses had been introduced at Ivy League schools. A new syllabus circulated by Columbia professor of government Grayson Kirk, *War and National Policy*, was under consideration at a wide range of national universities.[24] Kirk was an advisor to the State Department and would later attend the crucial conference on the future of the United Nations at Dumbarton Oaks. *Time* celebrated Beukema as an ordinary American enriched by the sophistication of German military thought. A "bronzed, lean artilleryman at West Point," Beukema was a "Michigan-born son of a small-town newspaperman" who "met three brilliant young German officers whose sensational theories about total war launched on him on a career in geopolitics."[25] While Kirk won over the intellectuals, *Time* depicted a geopolitics at home in the American heartland.

The intellectuals who favored developing an "American" geopolitics to match Germany's also argued that it was a necessary tool for constructing any future peace. Strausz-Hupé argued in *Geopolitics: The Struggle for Space* in 1942 that *Geopolitik* was a degenerate form of an objectively valid set of observations about international relations. What *Geopolitik* got right is that space is power, and international relations a perennial struggle for space.[26] Hans Weigert, another émigré, then teaching at Trinity College in Connecticut, opined in *Harper's* that the Americans must "learn their own geopolitics": "The lack of centers where American students and soldiers can, like the German youth in Munich, be trained to understand the facts and to think in terms of political geography and geopolitics seems to me to be a regrettable flaw [in our war effort] . . . It will be inexcusable if the Army General Staff cannot be supplied with as many enthusiastic experts on geopolitics as Haushofer was able to offer to the German General Staff."[27] Weigert thus repeated the fantasy of a geopolitical institute in Munich described in the army's propaganda films. The real geopoliticians, Karl Haushofer and his son Albrecht, were teaching students from all over the Nazi-allied world, at a different institute: the German Faculty for Foreign Studies (Deutsche Auslandswissenschaftliches Institut) in Berlin.

In the same year, the German émigré jurist Andreas Dorpalen published a selection of primary texts in translation from Haushofer and the *Zeitschrift*. Colonel Beukema provided the introduction. As Dorpalen wrote, "The great danger of geopolitics therefore lies, not in the system as such, but in the uses to which it can be put. If applied to the realization of legitimate objectives it is fully acceptable."[28] Beukema claimed that Haushofer had swerved from the "objective" Anglo-American tradition, and that was the fateful turning point: "It is precisely here that the Munich Institute breaks from the line of reasoning developed by Mahan and Mackinder."[29] Beukema and Dorpalen resolved to set the crooked path straight.

The same year, Derwent Whittlesey, professor of geography at Harvard University and president of the Association of American Geographers, published *German Strategy of World Conquest,* with two co-authors— Charles Colby, a professor at the University of Chicago, and Richard Hartshorne of the University of Wisconsin. Hartshorne, a student of Ratzel's work and of leading American geographer Ellen Semple, would later head the geography division of the Office of Strategic Services (OSS), the forerunner of the CIA. Like Dorpalen, Weigert, and Strausz-Hupé,

Whittlesey described geopolitics as a German pseudoscience, rooted in a thousand-year quest for *Lebensraum* to its East. But this scathing characterization of geopolitics notwithstanding, Whittlesey still sought to salvage a benign version of it.[30] Whittlesey next contributed an entire chapter on Haushofer to a major volume, *Military Thought from Machiavelli to Hitler*, assembled by Princeton's Edward Earle, written with the assistance of German émigrés Alfred Vagts and Felix Gilbert.[31]

Like Bowman, Whittlesey attempted to affirm political geography while distancing it from geopolitics. But he acknowledged that with a figure like Ratzel the boundaries between the two fields were too blurry to separate cleanly. At the end of Ratzel's life, Whittlesey wrote, he got carried away by enthusiasm for German naval power—but this was but an aberration. "His departure from scientific discipline is far from the method of the geopoliticians, who glory in manipulating their findings to serve the presumed interests of the German state."[32] Whittlesey tried to thread a needle: Ratzel was not a bona fide geopolitician, but "nevertheless [contributed] significantly to geopolitics" as its "progenitor." Ratzel understood that the resemblance of states to organisms was merely "a useful analogy. Although in practice he overworked it, he was aware of its limitations." By contrast, the geopoliticians absolutized the analogy, failing to grasp the fundamental distinction of the biological from the political worlds. The obscure lineages of fin de siècle German thought had somehow become relevant to understanding the latest news from the battlefronts of Europe.

Bowman and Spykman, Whittlesey, Hartshorne, Colby, and Beukema were interconnected through networks that crisscrossed an elite host of US universities and wartime institutions. Whittlesey's book originated from a report commissioned by the National Planning Association in April 1941 entitled, "A Proposed Study of the Principles of German Geopolitik: In the Interests of the National Defense of the US and of World Reconstruction in the Postwar Period."[33] Bowman, Beukema, and Hartshorne prepared a five-point program for an army-specialized training in geography.[34] In August 1944, Whittlesey wished Beukema "the best of luck in introducing geography formally to West Point."[35] Beukema found an ally in Edward M. Earle, who initiated a strategy seminar at the Institute for Advanced Study at Princeton in 1940.[36]

Earle knew Spykman well too. Since 1939, Earle had been director of the American Committee on International Studies. Earle developed courses on war strategy that ran at Spykman's home institution, Yale University, among other places. Earle, Spykman, and Whittlesey were also part of a short-lived group of academics mobilized by Lt. William S. Culbertson under the auspices of the War Department in June 1942.[37] Culbertson organized various conferences on geopolitics and, in October 1942, convinced Henry Luce to convene a meeting of top publishers and newspaper editors and reporters (133). Beukema selected a textbook authored in 1935 by two scholars affiliated with the Yale Institute of International Studies, Brooks Emeny and Frank Simonds.[38] Its title recalls the discourse on *Weltpolitik* at the turn of the century represented by Paul Reinsch and Archibald Coolidge: *The Great Powers in World Politics.*

Revealing doubts about geopolitics were aired in private correspondence between leading geographers. Whittlesey's ties to the Yale Institute were strong. On November 24, 1943, Whittlesey wrote to Frederick Dunn, one of the three directors of the Yale Institute, regarding his hopes for geography at Yale: "During the years I have been at Harvard I have been earnestly hoping that Yale would embark upon a program of geography . . . Whatever its associations, it is bound to develop rapidly as a result of the war."[39] Whittlesey approached Bowman in 1945 about forming a new journal of political geography.[40] Bowman replied, "I very much doubt the wisdom of establishing a periodical in political geography, for I believe it will promote the publication of dreamy stuff in the field of geopolitics. There are few men in the US who are qualified to handle diplomatic history, power politics and the like to provide more than an occasional article in existing journals."[41] Robert Gale Woolbert, from the University of Colorado, was more enthusiastic, but still worried that it could easily be misunderstood: "Naturally you have to be extremely careful that the magazine will not appear to be an American version of Haushofer's propaganda organ. At the same time you can easily run it into the ground by making it too esoteric."[42] Bowman and Woolbert were expressing anxieties of influence—the influence of German paradigms on American academe.

"Geopoliticians without Portfolio":
The Equivocations of Edmund Walsh

Less than a year after Germany's capitulation in the war, Karl Haushofer and his wife, Martha, committed suicide by poisoning. On September 25, 1945, the 76-year-old Haushofer was interviewed in Munich
while under house arrest. The interviewer was an American professor
named Edmund Walsh. Called in by the US military government, Walsh
was a Jesuit priest, founder and regent of the School of Foreign Service
at Georgetown University. In a colorfully written article describing an
encounter with Karl Haushofer in *Life* magazine, Walsh described the
scene when he arrived at Haushofer's home. Haushofer had pleaded with
him: "Why could not your government send some experienced American
such as Isaiah Bowman or Owen Lattimore [an expert on the Far East]?
Then too there is a priest in a university in Washington who has written
much against me and whose writings I have collected. Any one of these
men would understand what I meant and what I endeavored to achieve
by my geopolitics."[43] Haushofer did not realize that the priest he named
was standing before him.

Robert Jackson, the lead prosecutor at Nuremberg, excused Haushofer
from testifying in exchange for writing a mea culpa.[44] In his "Defense"
of March 1946, the last text he wrote before committing suicide, Haushofer argued that his version of geopolitics was part of a larger Western, or specifically Anglo-American, tradition. Not only was German
Geopolitik comparable to Anglo-American geopolitics—it was derived
largely from it. The "basic inspirers of my teaching," he wrote, included
the Americans Mahan, Brooks Adams, and Ellen Semple, in addition to
the Britons Joseph Chamberlain, Thomas Holdich, and Alfred Kitch-
ener.[45] English and American political geographers had developed the
teachings of Ratzel "for the sake of power expansion."[46] "These theories, originally derived from [Ratzel] . . . and from those who continued
his theories in the United States (Semple) and in Sweden (Kjèllen), were
formed to a larger extent from sources among English-speaking peoples
than from continental peoples.'"[47] Given their defensive purpose, these
look at first glance like purely opportunistic and apologetic remarks;

Haushofer played the comparability card well: "Up to the disturbance in its natural growth from 1933 on," German geopolitics "had originally— from 1919–32—goals similar to American geopolitics" (348, 351). The goal had been identical to that of US geopolitics: "to achieve the possibility of excluding disorders in the future like those of 1914–18" (352). But there is more here than apologetics: Haushofer made similar arguments twenty years before, when he hadn't similar need to distort the truth.

In 1948, Walsh published a much longer assessment of Haushofer, and general reckoning with German geopolitics, in his study-cum-memoir, *Total Power: Footnote to History.* In florid prose, Walsh recounted his meetings with Haushofer in Germany after the end of the war:[48] "For more than twenty years the voluminous writings and manifold activities of this German general . . . had engaged my attention and furnished material for many university courses and seminars at Georgetown University . . . [and formed] the topic of teaching assignments at the Army's command and General Staff School, Ft. Leavenworth, Kansas " (2).

Walsh's account of Haushofer's geopolitics was self-contradictory, swinging wildly from demonization to qualified endorsement. "While agreeing with Karl Haushofer in a great percentage of his teachings . . . I admitted to him, as I did to my German audience in Frankfurt, that he often reached 50 percent or somewhat better of sound truth . . . 10 percent evil may sink the vessel. That is exactly what happened to German geopolitics" (40). The difficulty American intellectuals had with coming to terms with the simultaneous proximity and "otherness" of German geopolitics was captured in Walsh's illustrative— indeed, practically comic—assertion that German geopolitics was about 50 percent—maybe 70 percent—valid and true. Walsh's simultaneous "yes" and "no" to German geopolitics was symptom of a practice of comparison that Atlantic realists engaged in—in this case, the object of the cross-national comparison was traditions of scholarship. Walsh could not ultimately decide whether German geopolitics represented a slight deviation from an imagined Western norm or was simply beyond compare. Attendant on these practices of comparison are the usual difficulties we face in the effort to gain self-knowledge—of ambivalence, denial, and projection.

These difficulties are on full display in Walsh's writings and are symptomatic of the broader wartime moment. Walsh's intimate familiarity with Haushofer's texts had "convinced [him] of the dangerous international objectives underlying his teachings" (9). Even its style was degenerate: "One stared in awe at the ponderous expressions in Haushofer's journal . . . and marveled at his travail in clothing simple geography with political mysticism . . . But beneath the mass of verbiage [in his writings from 1919 forward] reposed a theory of territorial expansion, which, in essence, was simply an apology for international theft" (4). By indoctrinating the German people, Haushofer had made a "considerable" contribution to the Nazi order. At the same time, Walsh implied that the essence of Haushofer's thought was fundamentally unproblematic. As he wrote, there is a "very large degree of validity to be found in Haushofer's factual and doctrinal exposition of the geographical elements of an enlightened national polity" (40). Walsh thus dramatically downplayed the fact that as early as 1931 Haushofer had compromised with the Nazi Party's race ideologues, and abetted his discipline's *Gleichschaltung* after 1933: "I agreed with Haushofer's chronology of geopolitics in modern Germany and the legitimate function it can exercise in supplying a helpful and informative body of knowledge or the guidance of statesmen in the form of domestic policy and the conduct of international relations" (6). Haushofer was, in the final analysis, a colleague—a fellow Atlantic realist, as it were.

Despite his equivocations, Walsh agreed with Haushofer that geopolitics was a science with North Atlantic contours that encompassed Germany, England, and America. Walsh asserted that Haushofer "borrowed copiously" from the writings of two Englishmen, John Fairgrieve and Halford Mackinder. Walsh pivoted to claim geopolitics was as American as apple pie. Frederick Jackson Turner's *Frontier* "was a striking geopolitical monograph." Theodore Roosevelt and Homer Lea were also geopoliticians avant la lettre: "All these precursors of the Munich specialists lacked only classification; they were geopoliticians without portfolio."[49] But in contrast with Bowman, who sought to rehabilitate Ratzel while denouncing Haushofer, Walsh identified Ratzel as a branch of a rotten tradition that began with the earlier German geographer, Karl Ritter. "The corruption of pure geographic knowledge" began with Ritter:

"The organicist conception of the state . . . is the basic geographic heresy that led to the irrational and one-sided policy of German geopoliticians during the Nazi regime." Walsh, the devout Catholic, was pronouncing a Ratzel a geopolitical heretic (39). Other authors were writing intellectual histories in the same mode, looking for the moment in the past when Germany's fate was sealed, the turning point of Germany's deviant path through modernity.[50]

Geopolitics could be a force for good, Walsh concluded. "These evil consequences of false geopolitics and its concomitant provocations must not blind us to the power for good in a true geopolitics . . . Is there such a thing as legitimate geopolitics? Assuredly. I have conducted courses on that subject for many years at Georgetown and at Army schools for the training of staff and commanding officers." The key to a legitimate geopolitics was to delink it from a one-sided focus on national interest. Haushofer's sin was that he "[interpreted] geographical phenomena mainly in their relationship to the interests of Germany" (49). Legitimate, "scientific" geopolitics, by contrast, must adopt a global perspective, remaining agnostic on questions of national interest: "On the basis of sound facts and knowledge, the nations of the world must come to a reasonable and humane solution of boundary problems and to an equitable distribution of the fruits of the earth" (50).

But within the same volume, Walsh stressed the need for a specifically "American geopolitics" built on recognition that the US was "encircled" by Europe and Asia. His formulation represented a remarkable inversion of the prevailing notion that the US occupied a continent endowed with the protective barrier of two oceans. This was ideology parading as geopolitical reason. "Geographically we are encircled . . . and it will be a prime principle of American geopolitics to recognize and forestall any combination of overseas powers which . . . could overwhelm us" (303). "Wistful expectations must be controlled by the realism of facts"—the facts of "undiminished production of armament behind an iron curtain" (304). Like Bowman, who spoke of "facing realities" and "the realities of power politics," Walsh had alighted on the similar phrase "realism of facts." Both understood the liabilities of the geopolitical tradition and offered solutions to the reputational problems it faced in America.

The Critics Have Their Day

In a *New Republic* review of Spykman's *America's Strategy in World Politics*, the New York–based critic Malcolm Cowley turned the tables on Spykman rhetorically.[51] "Mr. Spykman's realism—the quality on which he insists—is blinding him to the realities of our own time . . . In spite of all he says about the balance of power, Mr. Spykman never presents a valid defense of it." The book is being presented to the public as, Cowley writes, "the first geopolitical analysis of the position of the US in the world. Since geopolitics is now a magical and incantatory world; since everybody is interested in geopolitics as being—perhaps—the secret of Hitler's victories, one reads the book for whatever light is may cast on this new science." But geopolitics excludes too many factors from consideration: "human institutions, human hopes and fears and judgments of right and wrong." Skeptics like Cowley were marginalized by the vogue for geopolitics. Cowley's description of geopolitics as a kind of magical thinking was echoed by Hans Speier.

Speier, a German émigré and then an itinerant professor in the US, and later a leading defense intellectual, echoed Cowley with his description of how German propagandists "turn geography into a kind of magic."[52] Speier used *The War in Maps*, the same volume that Renner had, as an example of how "lines [representing 'large-space economies'] which are strong, smooth and sweeping . . . cut the world into four 'natural zones'." These were North America–South America; Europe-Africa; Japan-Australia-India and Western China; Europe east of the Ural Mountains, and the remainder of China. Speier rejected the "implicit devaluation of political boundaries . . . For example, the Philippines, India, Australia . . . and large parts of China are included in the 'natural' sphere of Japanese interests."[53] Andrew Georgy, another émigré, and author of the most impressive study in the genre, *Geopolitics: The New German Science*, described Spykman's work as "incisive "and "a pioneering work of prime importance." He added, however, that it was "surprisingly similar to that of the Nazi German geopoliticians (*Wehrgeopolitiker*) . . . a defensive geopolitical survey of the Americans as against the offensive geopolitics (*Wehrgeopolitik*) of a militarized National Socialist Germany." Spykman's "determinist geopolitical interpretation leads him into several contradictions," Georgy added. Georgy broadened his critique beyond Spykman, highlighting

his comparability with Haushofer and Renner. All three offered a "biologi-
cally inspired dynamic conception of politics" which argues by analogy from
the individual life cycle—youth, maturity and old age—to that of nations.
The problem with it is that this "sharp division of young and old, mature
and immature, leads . . . moreover to an unlimited and sincere glorification
of power as the sole and final arbiter in international relations."[54]

Given the manufactured hysteria in the press about German geopolitics,
and the anxieties about the national identity of geography versus geopolitics
in academe, Alfred Vagts (1892–1986) stood apart as one of the most sober
and independent voices. In 1941 Vagts published a lengthy account of the US
and the balance of power, anticipating the revaluation of balance of power
politics that Morgenthau made one of his signatures beginning after 1945.[55]
In a 1943 review, Vagts reviewed Dorpalen's Haushofer book, as well as
the most recent work of the famous British strategist, Halford Mackinder,
whose ideas had become influential in the US through Spykman and Walter Lippman.[56] Lamenting the grandiose claims and false laws it tended to
make, Vagts became one of its most incisive detractors:

> Many things and much power were conceded to *Geopolitik* at once.
> For some it was like a new all-around explanation of a phenomenon
> for which they were not otherwise prepared, a pan-determinism
> compared with which historical materialism became almost a spiri-
> tual sensification of history and politics. "The facts of geography
> condition the destiny of our world," it was stated, whereas even
> the most school-bound German geopolitician would have insisted:
> that these facts co-condition it, and probably more so in war than
> in peace. Numerous articles were written on *Geopolitik* and books
> dealing with it were published, whose number was clearly not ra-
> tioned in accordance with the true importance of the subject and
> the sustained national interest in it. In fact, the saturation point for
> geopolitics would seem to have been reached by now, which may al-
> low the contemplation of its theories more at leisure.[57]

Vagts was an émigré from Nazi Germany too. A historian who had studied in Munich, he had also attended Yale University on an exchange in the
1920s. The star student of one of the leading liberal international lawyers in

Germany, the Hamburg-based professor Albrecht Mendelssohn Bartholdy, he emigrated to London in the fall of 1932. Married to Miriam Beard, the daughter of the historian Charles Beard, he was a prolific independent scholar of German militarism and international thought. Beard thanked him in the acknowledgments of his landmark work, *The Idea of National Interest* (1934), for his assistance with documents on German foreign policy. Through Vagts, Beard came to know the work of Eckart Kehr, the great critic of German naval imperialism and theorist of the "Primat der Innenpolitik" (primacy of domestic policy). Beard critiqued Roosevelt's naval buildup in the 1930s using concepts he acquired from Kehr. Vagts brought a Kehrite skepticism about militarism to his analysis of geopolitics. Geopolitics had not reached the "saturation point," as he had hoped.

Writing from the heart of the OSS in 1942, Franz Neumann, the German émigré political scientist, contributed a landmark work in the study of the Third Reich: *Behemoth*.[58] Neumann's account of geopolitics and Haushofer was as deflationary as the views of Speier, Georgy, and Vagts. Neumann considered ideas of a "Greater German Reich" (*Großdeutsches Reich*) prominent among the ideological roots of National Socialism. Nazi geopolitics was a subset of this broader tradition of German imperialism, or "thinking in large spaces." Neumann had known Schmitt, the most famous *Großraum* theorist, personally in Berlin during the Weimar Republic. Together with Morgenthau, he had worked as a legal clerk for the famed Social Democratic jurist and labor lawyer, Hugo Sinzheimer.[59] Of the Third Reich's ideologists he wrote, "They did not invent geopolitics any more than they invented the idea of a *Großdeutsches Reich*" (138). The "prehistory of Nazi geopolitics" could be traced to Ratzel, the Swede Kjèllen, the Englishman Mackinder, and the German theorist of "*Mitteleuropa*," Friedrich Naumann (137).[60] But "[all] these strains reach their ultimate formulation with Karl Haushofer" (142). Neumann's damning assessment of geopolitics recalls the critiques leveled by that other, earlier member of the Frankfurt School, Karl Wittfogel, some of which Haushofer allowed to appear in his *Zeitschrift für Geopolitik*.[61] But even though he was highly connected as a member of the brain trust of the Office of Strategic Services, Neumann's skeptical voice was no more effective than that of the other critics in arresting a conservative geopolitics' advance.

From Geopolitics to "Realism"

Realism became the dominant paradigm in the American study of international relations between the end of the war and the mid-1950s. The diverse usages of the term "realism" and its cognates by Bowman, Spykman, and Cowley illustrate that realism remained inchoate until the end of the war. As numerous émigré intellectuals taught Americans to fear the foreignness of German geopolitics, labeling it both undemocratic and unscientific, "realism" became an attractive alternative category with which a certain type of political thinker could identify. Realism became the semantic refuge for fugitives from the discredited discourse of Nazi geopolitics. The debate on geopolitics gave momentum to "realism" as a synonym for "power politics." Not just a discourse of counter-Enlightenment conservatism, as Guilhot characterizes it, realism in the US was also what remained after the debate on the German science of geopolitics had ended. While some of the early realists explicitly distanced themselves from "geopolitics," and some of the geopoliticians considered themselves explicitly anti-realist, there was considerable overlap in the intellectual networks that solidified realism as a paradigm within international relations.[62]

Morgenthau and the members of the Yale Institute for International Studies were all geopolitical thinkers in the Atlantic mode.[63] The historiography of realism has offered no explanation for why the 1890s discourses of "classical geopolitics" deposited no historical traces in the interwar period. That so many Americans initially feared and disavowed German geopolitics in the 1940s for its illiberalism may account for historians' difficulties in recognizing the connections between "realism" in the 1930s and 1940s and the realism of the generation of 1898, that of Mahan, Reinsch, and Semple.

The demand to find, or recover, a "lost" American geopolitics proved stronger than any objection Bowman had raised about its foreignness or alleged lack of scientific rigor. This was ironic since Bowman, more than any other single figure, embodied the mix of liberal and realist worldviews that had never truly been lost. But for those caught up in the debate about the foreignness of geopolitics, something had to be done. It would not do to throw geopolitics out with the Nazi bathwater. With the exception of

Strausz-Hupé, Bowman, and Mattern, the most common assumption in American accounts of German geopolitics was that Americans had not thought in those terms before WWII. Therefore, I agree with Gearóid Ó Tuathail's assessment: "What was important was to assert a globalist geopolitics to counter the isolationist geopolitics of US political culture" (140). As Ó Tuathail writes, "US narrations of German geopolitics during World War II saved geopolitics from itself and resecured its functioning." For critical geographers like Ó Tuathail, Bowman's tendentious claims to scientific objectivity established an unhelpful pattern of treating geopolitics as the constitutive "other" to properly scientific political geography. Bowman's articles about German geopolitics were "wartime propaganda," but left a lasting stain on the reputation of geopolitics in Anglo-American geography through the early 1980s (154). Bowman's narrations of US geopolitics therefore not only aligned it with the intensified globalism of post-1945 US foreign policy but impeded the development of a critical geopolitics that could have described this globalism as imperial.

Geopolitics in the interwar Atlantic invited leaders to a specific way of seeing. This mode of seeing required cultivation and training—in short, an educational habitus. Figures like Weigert, Beukema, Whittlesey, and Earle seized the career opportunities and built up the academic infrastructure. As Colonel Beukema, a professor at the US Military Academy, wrote in 1941, "Intelligent America can no longer afford to ignore geopolitics . . . Geopolitics can give us a first long step toward the realism needed if peace is to be something more than another Versailles."[64] The problem of *Geopolitik* would metamorphose into the questions faced by the young discipline of international relations in the United States. As we will see in the case of Hans Morgenthau above all, realists sought to assemble an educational habitus that turned political judgment into a transmissible art and science. Haushofer's aspiration to make geopolitics into a doctrine of art (*Kunstlehre*) is part of that genealogy.[65] The history of German *Geopolitik* in the US, both its foes and partisans, is an important and neglected part of that story.

CHAPTER 6

An American Power Politics

Hans Morgenthau and the Making of a
Realist Orthodoxy, 1940–1960

THE RELATIONSHIP OF REALISM to the history of the Cold War
is dialectical. The writings of academic realists like Morgenthau and
semi-academic ones like Kennan and Niebuhr shaped the broad lenses
through which Cold War policy was made. The doctrine of containment
and the broad discourses on national security owe much to Kennan,
Morgenthau, Lippmann, and Nitze, as David Milne and others have
shown.[1] At the same time, scholars such as John Gaddis and Melvyn
Leffler have treated geopolitical concerns as the main explanation for the
Cold War's origins.[2] By doing so, John Thompson argues, they implicitly
rely upon "realist assumptions that considerations of power and security
are both primary in shaping states' behavior and essentially objective in
character."[3] Furthermore, the history of the Cold War's unfolding was
often presented as evidence of the validity of the theory. "Widely seen
as the quintessential realist balancing of power in operation," international relations scholar Beate Jahn wrote in 2013, the history "in turn
support[ed] the primacy of the realist paradigm in international affairs."[4]
Constructivist critics of realism, generally speaking, by contrast, argue
that threat perception is socially constructed and geopolitical theories
unsupported by the real world.[5] As Thompson argues in regard to the
Cold War, "[in] the case of American anxiety about the danger of the nation being overwhelmed by a hostile power controlling all the resources
of the Old World, the extent of underdetermination by reality would
seem to be extreme, to put it mildly." The "universalist interpretation
of US security requirements," he argues, far exceeded what would have
been required by "hard-headed geopolitical calculations" alone.[6] The
career of the German refugee jurist Hans Morgenthau (1904–1980) in
America offers an invaluable vantage point from which to assess the

American understanding of the threats and challenges it faced in the Cold War in the 1940s and 1950s.

As the author of *Politics among Nations* (1948), Morgenthau came to shape the minds of generations of students at the University of Chicago and across the country. It was immediately "adopted as a textbook for foreign policy and international relations [courses] at Harvard, Yale, Princeton, Columbia, and Notre Dame. The following year, ninety colleges adopted it—more than all other previous textbooks combined."[7] Although he was never a central policy-maker, he was an influential voice on the margins of policy-making, and a regular at the Council on Foreign Relations. Hardly a stranger to the corridors of power in Washington, DC, he carried on a correspondence with Secretary of State Dean Acheson; with George Kennan, the director of the Policy Planning Staff at the State Department; and had a collegial and long-term relationship with Henry Kissinger, although they exchanged deep recriminations over Vietnam by 1968.[8] Historians of the American discipline of international relations agree that Morgenthau is the single most consequential figure in the making of the discipline before 1960, and along with Kenneth Waltz, the most influential representative of the broad realist current in IR theory.

Hans Morgenthau is one of the most celebrated figures in twentieth-century international thought, and not surprisingly therefore, one of its most contested.[9] His relationship to realist tradition, and the nature of his identity as a "realist," is complicated. Though he at times identified with the label, he also chafed against it. While in the 1980s, Stanley Hoffmann referred to Morgenthau as the "founding father" of international relations in the US and the "Pope of Realism," William Scheuerman, the leading revisionist scholar of Morgenthau, names him an "uneasy Realist," emphasizing his increasing discomfort with what the Cold War intellectual establishment understood as "realism" during the Cold War.[10] In his important study *The Weimar Century*, Greenberg argues that the leitmotif of Morgenthau's career was a desire to balance the pursuit of the national interest and power-political calculation with "moral and ethical considerations."[11] As he argues correctly, "As the 1950s progressed, Morgenthau became increasingly frustrated with diplomats who espoused his realist theory to justify policies he opposed. While such tension remained largely latent during this period, it presaged his subsequent opposition to Cold War policies" (225–26). For Koskenniemi, IR realism drew on Hobbesian and Schmittian themes and argument.[12] For Nicolas Guilhot too, Morgenthau is a deeply Schmittian thinker whose realism was fundamentally influenced by political theology. As he writes, "Schmittian ideas could remain influential because they found in the US a cultural receptacle in the neoorthodoxy represented by Niebuhr and the Christian realists. Once translated into the indigenous language of conservative Christian realism, this import became undetectable."[13] Guilhot concludes that Schmitt and Morgenthau developed "essentially an identical understanding of the political" and a shared aristocratic nostalgia for an elite-managed politics. In Guilhot's telling, the realists in general and Morgenthau in particular represented a broader midcentury project of "counter-enlightenment," aiming to stem the commitment of modernist social science to a deepening of American democracy.[14] On the narrower question of Morgenthau's debts to Schmitt I follow both Koskenniemi and Guilhot, but on the broader issue of the character of his realism I reframe the debate.

Like Wilhelm Grewe, Morgenthau was a close and important reader and transmitter of Carl Schmitt's ideas about international political theory and geopolitics for the postwar world. Grewe's Schmittian realism is an enduring face of Atlantic realism that remained after the Nazis purged and destroyed both the traditions and representatives of liberalism and cosmopolitanism in German law and political science, including many of its Jewish practitioners. As Grewe rebuilt his career after the Third Reich, a generation of German-Jewish scholars, often trained in law, and who had been forced into exile, became the vanguard of a similar Schmitt-colored "realism" in American political science and its splinter, international relations.[15] Carl Schmitt's legacy for Morgenthau's power politics is very important. But overemphasizing it misses the extent to which Morgenthau's thought evolved across the Atlantic. Both those who argue for a Schmittian Morgenthau and those who suggest an anti- or non-Schmittian Morgenthau, treat Morgenthau as essentially fully formed by the age of 35 in 1940. This has the effect of unduly discounting the importance of his encounter with American culture, politics, and academe. An adequate genealogy of Morgenthau's power politics requires greater attention to the resistance he encountered from the American intellectual field. Morgenthau rejected certain German forms of power politics. But he invented a modified version in America.

Morgenthau's career is of the greatest significance for interpreting the German-American connection in international thought. His complex relationship with the label "realism" reveals symptomatic ambiguities of the tradition. Was realism a theory of international relations, a foreign policy posture, or an academic identity? One of the ironies of Morgenthau's life is that though no one was more responsible for turning the label into an identity, he did not himself always identify with the label. The revisionist defenders of Morgenthau as a philosophical moderate, uneasy with the oversimplified narrative of realism as power politics, have to contend with the inconvenient fact that Morgenthau was his own worst popularizer. Morgenthau complained bitterly about misunderstandings of the proper place of power politics in his work. His defenders argue that Morgenthau can therefore hardly be characterized as an unproblematic realist (let alone its archetypal figure). But he cannot avoid responsibility for these readings. His rhetoric is often highly reductive. Morgenthau's texts made power politics appear metaphysical and substantive, the very signature of the real. He energetically promoted recognition of power politics as the sine qua non of the statesman.

Any progressive inclined to dismiss Morgenthau as a representative of conservative thought or a hard-line Cold War posture must contend with his unsparing and early criticisms of the Vietnam War as neither moral nor in the national interest, however. He was the first government official to do so, and an inspiration to influential critics of the war like Senator William Fulbright. The Institute of Policy Studies in Washington, DC, a group founded by members of the antiwar Left disillusioned with the Kennedy administration like Richard Barnet, invited Morgenthau onto their advisory board, where he was active from 1963 to 1971.[16] Barnet and Marcus Raskin wrote moving tributes to him late in his life.[17] Clearly he was no simple conservative.

Although the realists were not the primary shapers of Cold War foreign policy, and lost many battles on specific policy questions, their worldview shaped the contours, and came to dominate the academic field of international relations in the US. The IR scholars Groom and Olson have identified 1945 to 1960 as the "realist period" in the discipline, wherein "power politics" was the analytic core.[18] Through academic writings and in his various public roles, as intellectual and counselor, Morgenthau built realism into a Cold War orthodoxy. Morgenthau's thought is an important chapter in the making of an Atlantic tradition of realism. Hans Morgenthau was more than an ordinary academic theorist or public intellectual. Through passionate rhetorical performances of his key themes—the centrality of the national interest in contrast to international or global interests, and power politics as the signature of the real—Morgenthau showed as much as told us what it meant to be a "realist." The charisma of his ideas is entwined with his personal charisma and his personae.

A German Jurist in America

Born in Coburg, a small town in northeastern Bavaria, Morgenthau grew up in an educated German-Jewish secular and bourgeois household. In his youth in the 1920s he was a devoted reader of Weber and Nietzsche.[19] He began in philosophy at Munich but switched to law in Frankfurt and Berlin. In 1929, he wrote his dissertation on the justiciability of international disputes.[20] In the late 1970s, Morgenthau wrote a short self-portrait in which he describes an encounter with Schmitt that he had arranged after receiving a flattering letter from him about his dissertation. "The disappointment was total. When I walked down the stairs from Schmitt's apartment, I stopped . . . and said to myself, 'Now I have met the most evil man alive.'" Morgenthau claimed next that Schmitt had stolen ideas from his dissertation without attribution.[21] Differences between the original 1927 and 1932 versions of *The Concept of the Political* reveal a shift, with Schmitt adopting the idea of "intensity" as an integral characteristic of the sphere of "the political" in the 1932 text. Not all Morgenthau scholars are convinced.[22] There is more evidence that Morgenthau borrowed a great number of Schmittian themes in turn when he came to America. His 1946 work, *Scientific Man versus Power Politics*, rehearses many distinctive Schmittian themes.

Nonetheless, as Scheuerman has emphasized, Morgenthau belonged to a progressive left-liberal milieu in Frankfurt.[23] In May 1928, he joined the law office of Hugo Sinzheimer, one of Weimar's most famous left-wing lawyers. He also worked as assistant to Sinzheimer at the law faculty at the university. Future intellectual luminaries Franz Neumann, Ernst Fraenkel, and Otto Kahn-Freund were employed at the same time by Sinzheimer. Like another figure regarded as a classical realist, E.H. Carr, he was influenced by the left-wing Hungarian sociologist Karl Mannheim, who overlapped with him in Frankfurt.[24] From early days he was drawn to questions of raison d'état. As Jütersonke points out, one of his diary entries from August 1929 reads, "Have given up the plan for the Machiavelli, as Meinecke's book on Raison d'Etat already contains much the same thing."[25] Like the earlier Atlantic realists Ratzel, Mahan, and Reinsch, Morgenthau experimented with ideas about how best to develop a realistic approach to international politics. Against a backdrop of artistic currents known as the *Neue Sachlichkeit* ("New Objectivity"), it is not surprising that intellectuals like Morgenthau also strove for an austere style of representation. In a 1929 essay, he applauded the Social Democratic foreign minister Gustav Stresemann for his foreign policy prowess. Morgenthau admired the way Stresemann leveraged a "static," status quo–oriented tool—international law, and the League of Nations, to which Stresemann had initially been opposed—for the "dynamic" ends of increasing Germany's power position in Europe by peaceful means. What the Germans needed, Morgenthau argued, was "a politically fruitful relationship to international law." Before World War I, he continued, the Germans had rejected it tout court; now, the Germans appeared to be leaning too far to the other extreme. He worried that this would "lead to a forgetting of the actual problems and a misjudgment of reality and produce an unpolitical *Haltung*."[26] *Haltung*, or "posture," is a word that reappears often in Morgenthau's oeuvre and is an important motif of this chapter.

What Morgenthau admired in Stresemann was the way he built a cultural bridge across the Atlantic: The ideas and institutions of international law originated with one *Haltung*—the "spiritual-intellectual posture" of the "European-American world," and "alien to the German essence (*Wesen*)." Stresemann's dramatic accomplishment was to Europeanize the German "spirit." By filling Euro-American international legal forms with German "spiritual and political content," Morgenthau wrote, Stresemann was the first German politician to bridge the gap "that first opened in the Wilhelminian period" between Germany and Europe. Having now "declared German thoughts in forms which are understood and trusted by the world—insofar as he spoke as a European, without giving up being a German—he has provided an example for the *geistige Haltung* (spiritual posture) of Germany overall, and beyond the legal-political realm" (176). The Europeanization of the German spirit did not last.

In March 1932, Morgenthau received a letter from his mentor, Hugo Sinzheimer, in which he described Nazi electoral successes: "On Sunday is the vote. I am prepared for a hullabaloo to ensue. All lies in darkness. Germany is once more ruined. The political metaphysics and the belief in miracles, that is, the absolute escape of the Germans from reality."[27] The same month, the Rockefeller Foundation rejected his research proposal.[28] On July 11, 1933, Morgenthau was fired from his job as acting president of the labor law court in Frankfurt in accord with the law purging Jews from the civil service.[29] Morgenthau and Irma Thormann, whom he married in 1935, left Germany in 1933 for Geneva. As Morgenthau considered his personal and professional options, he wrote to Karl Loewenstein, another jurist, who had been stripped of his legal faculty position in Munich but had secured employment at Yale. Loewenstein cautioned Morgenthau that opportunities in the US for a German legal scholar were slim: "It gives me great sadness to report that I can't do anything for you here, Yale overall is hopeless, because besides me there are already two younger well regarded jurists, among them a Völkerrechtler (Dr. Von Elbe) in the same situation as you."[30]

On July 17, 1937, Morgenthau and his wife boarded a ship in Antwerp, bound for New York. The previous five years had not been easy. He had encountered fierce antisemitism in Geneva and his *Habilitation* had been rejected. A twelve-month position in Madrid was renewed, but then interrupted by war, and his property confiscated by the Popular Front government in March 1937. His first contacts in New York included an individual who introduced him to Philip Jessup, then a professor of international law at Columbia University. Like hundreds of German refugee scholars, Morgenthau's major preoccupation was finding employment. In a letter dated September 27, 1937, he wrote: "Yale is one of the universities on which I have set my sights. I have been told that Wolfers has a great deal of influence there." Sixteenth months of poverty in New York followed before he accepted a position at the University of Kansas City in January 1939.[31]

An unsuccessful fellowship application to the Guggenheim Foundation, submitted in 1937, provides a glimpse of his realistic approach to law and politics before he had embraced the label "realist." His guiding questions concerned the "theoretical structure of international politics" and the relationship between international politics and international law. "This work will continue attempts for (sic) a realistic understanding of international politics, which I undertook in preceding publications."[32] In a substantial article published in 1940, Morgenthau outlined a version of legal realism that he called legal functionalism.[33] But as Jütersonke has convincingly argued, it was easily confused with prevailing forms of legal realism in the US academy and Morgenthau rapidly distanced himself from the label.[34] His legal functionalism built on his 1929 thesis and argued that law could evolve to respond to changing power relations. He called this "improving international relations by means of the law." "Not infrequently the disillusioned idealist becomes a cynic and pessimist," he wrote to the American international lawyer Philip Jessup in 1941. "In both cases he takes the same unscientific attitude towards reality with only a different emphasis . . . For those who have not shared the illusions of the twenties and thirties, I see therefore no reason for despondency and pessimism about the future of international law."[35] Letters to Quincy Wright and Percy Elwood Corbett from the early 1940s corroborate this picture of a Morgenthau still very much identified with his training in law and believing that international law could be realistic about power and politics. Corbett was professor in the Department of Government and International Relations at Yale, and a distinguished international lawyer who had emigrated from Canada.[36] In December 1943, Morgenthau had written to Corbett, "I feel greatly disappointed that I am unable to cooperate with you at the present time in the work you are undertaking . . . If I can be of any assistance to you in Chicago . . ."[37] In 1943, Morgenthau arrived at the University of Chicago political science department as a replacement faculty member for Quincy Wright.[38] Wright was one of the *grand seigneurs* of international law in the US.[39] While Morgenthau would soon put great rhetorical distance between himself and international lawyers, in 1945 he remained part of discussions that included more traditional internationalists such as Jessup, Wright, and Corbett.[40] This appears to have changed rapidly after he attained tenure in 1946. From July 9–13, 1945, for example, Morgenthau worked alongside Wright at the 21st Institute of the Norman Wait Harris Memorial Foundation.[41] In October, they published the proceedings as "The United Nations and the Organization of Peace and Security." In his contribution to the discussions, and in essays he published the same year, we find a shift away from the law and toward the power politics pole, but not as complete as one would expect from the author of *Scientific Man versus Power Politics*, with its rhetorical assaults on legalism. A state-of-the-field essay on international relations, published the same year, affords a glimpse of the paradigm shifts ahead in the US study of world politics. As Grayson Kirk, then a professor of government at Columbia University, explained, hitherto IR had been the preserve of "historians, lawyers and idealists—this must change."[42] With his customary brilliance and economy of prose, Morgenthau cut incisively to the essence of the UN Charter's decision not to upend the prerogatives of the most powerful countries: "The Charter does not replace, according to its explicit and implicit purposes and principles, the traditional balance of power and power politics; it presupposes their continuous operation, and therefore it is unrealistic to ask whether the Charter can succeed all by itself or whether it is a good thing to have it or whether it would be better not to have it. For by itself, the Charter can do nothing."[43] The charter was what Schmitt might have called a "decisionist" document. Morgenthau described it in Schmittian terms: peace cannot be preserved without the application of sanctions; sanctions depend upon the "decision of concrete cases"; and this in turn depended on the unity of the "Big Powers." What the charter did not offer, he pointed out, was any "instrumentalities by which this unity can be established." Therefore, "what is decisive is that the whole structure of the Charter, its whole operation, depends upon the premise of successive diplomatic action which establishes and maintains the unity of the Big Powers" (4). The new charter merely rebottled the "the old traditional methods of diplomacy," proving the "intimate connection" between the two.

Several scholars of Morgenthau's work have argued that "Machiavellian" is a misleading way to describe his subtle efforts to balance moral and political considerations. In this respect, he is closer to Machiavelli himself, whose effort to balance *fortuna* with *virtù* is not captured by the caricature of "Machiavellianism." But Morgenthau's writings from the time lend themselves to misconstrual so easily that their author has to take some responsibility for any misreadings. Given the sober mood of his remarks on the charter's "decision" for the power pole of the morality-power dyad, as it were, it is frustrating to find Morgenthau damning the architects of the Security Council at Dumbarton Oaks as failures. The politicians there "refused to face" this "basic truth of social experience," namely, the moral basis of legal order.

> Wilson tried to obliterate the gap [between the quality of our political intelligence and the quality of our political practice] by superimposing a defective brand of political intelligence upon a *reluctant political reality*. The men of Dumbarton Oaks, preoccupied with the mechanics of government and haunted by the memory of Wilson's failure, *refused to transcend the political reality at all*. (emphasis added)

As I show in the next section, Morgenthau will turn the same rhetorical maneuvers against the other side the following year. He continued:

> By doing so, they overlooked what even the men of the Holy Alliance were fully conscious of—that common moral standards are part of the political reality itself which goes into the making of government—nay, its very foundation. Wilson's failure was at least the failure of greatness, of too great a vision. Nobody will say as much for the epigones of Machiavelli.[44]

Was Wilson—his avatar of liberal idealism—also a visionary of greatness? There are not one, but two, utopianisms Morgenthau wished to avoid: "Whether they swear by Wilson or by Machiavelli, they are always Utopians pursuing either nothing but power or nothing but justice." The twentieth-century heirs of nineteenth-century liberals "see in power politics nothing but an irrational atavism." They need to recognize "that the end of power politics is yet to come. They welcome the new legalistic diplomacy of the UN as a step toward the ultimate victory of law over politics."[45] He reiterated the point in another essay that year, contrasting "Wilsonian utopianism" with its equally unrealistic "Machiavellian" counterpart.[46] But in constantly seeking ways to balance considerations of power and morality, he tangled himself in knots. He claimed that he had never wavered from the view "that whereas international politics cannot be understood without taking into consideration the struggle for power, it cannot be understood by consideration of power alone." But the same year, he described E.H. Carr, who made a virtually identical statement in his 1939 work, *The Twenty Years' Crisis*, as a "utopian of power," concluding archly: "It is a dangerous thing to be a Machiavelli. It is a disastrous thing to be a Machiavelli without virtù."[47]

Scientific Man vs. Power Politics: Morgenthau's American Debut

If there was any doubt where Morgenthau stood on the "great debate" that he believed cleaved public opinion of the UN in 1945, the publication of his work *Scientific Man versus Power Politics* in 1946 erased most of this ambivalence. *Politics among Nations* is often treated as the most important text for evaluating Morgenthau's international political theory and its influence. But the less-read *Scientific Man versus Power Politics* is more revealing of the man and his beliefs. Published in 1946, the book remained Morgenthau's personal "favorite" until the end of his life.[48] The 1946 text does not mark a clear break in the substance of his thought, in part because we know the roots of the project reaches back to at least 1940.[49] But in terms of its rhetoric, the book is a watershed. It is extreme—shrill and unconvincing—a *cri de coeur*. Generations of students who have imbibed Morgenthau from the much more famous *Politics among Nations*, and its simplifying formulae, the "Six Principles of Political Realism"—only added through the encouragement of the publisher in the 1954 second edition—have neglected one of the most important texts of Morgenthau's mature thought.

Admittedly, the extremism of the tone can be chalked up, one imagines, to the feelings of alienation he experienced in Chicago, where a behaviorism foreign to his training reigned in political science. It was this alienation that "led to his polemical reaction against all forms of scientism and his eventual withdrawal from cutting edge academic debates in both international and political science, in favor of a more 'common sense' approach to US foreign policy and international politics,"[50] argues a leading scholar of Morgenthau's work, Oliver Jütersonke. Charles Merriam, chair of the department from 1923–40, steered the discipline to the search for causal laws of political behavior that could be useful to New Deal policymakers. Merriam's 1922 essay, "The Present State of the Study of Politics," set in motion developments that led to the creation of the Social Science Research Council (132). One of Merriam's leading "disciples" at the University of Chicago was Harold Lasswell, a figure whose writings Morgenthau forthrightly disdained.[51] Morgenthau might well have remained more friendly to the international law community, Jütersonke argues, had he not been afraid that his functionalism would be conflated with legal realism—then associated in the public mind with a problematic moral relativism.[52]

Over the course of two decades in the United States, between 1940 and 1960, Hans Morgenthau developed this "common sense" approach so effectively that it became part of the common sense of public discourse on international affairs. As vehemently as E.H. Carr had seven years before, Morgenthau derided liberal internationalist and pacifist meliorisms as forms of rationalist utopianism. Not until the transatlantic peace movement and the Frankfurt School began to rehabilitate the concept of the "utopian" in the 1970s did the damage Morgenthau and Carr inflicted by their work on this score subside. In *Scientific Man*, Morgenthau constructed "liberalism" as the hegemonic tradition within modern international thought, with "power politics" as its most important corrective. *Scientific Man* contains his reflections on power politics in their most dramatic form. The intensity of the rejection of international law in his 1946 work contrasts sharply with the collegial tone of his conversations with Jessup, Corbett, and Wright in the preceding half-decade. Its ferocity derives some of its pathos and force from the fact that *Scientific Man* is partially an exercise in self-critique, namely, of the internationalist legalism Morgenthau had imbibed in Weimar.[53]

Although Morgenthau retreated to a more balanced position by the end of the 1950s, *Scientific Man* captures Morgenthau at a liminal moment in his career, as the beleaguered partisan of unpopular ideas: "No political thinker can expect to be heard [today] who would not, at least in his terminology, pay tribute to the spirit of science and, by claiming his propositions to be 'realistic,' 'technical,' or 'experimental,' assume their compliance with scientific standards." The abstractions of scientific rationalism can only fail to disclose the logic of concrete political situations. Scientific experts cannot replace politicians and their role as decision-makers (31). Morgenthau's primary goal in the book was to discredit the Wilsonian liberalism that he believed—incorrectly—dominated interwar American thought. It could pass as a description of the atmosphere at Chicago, but Morgenthau turned this local history into a universal critique of US tradition.[54] Like the American commentators of the 1940s who denied that the United States had its own indigenous tradition of geopolitics, Morgenthau ignored the imperial tradition of geopolitics and strategy that stretched from Mahan, Reinsch, and Coolidge to Root, Bowman, and Lippmann. Indeed, in two odd passages, he dismissed Reinsch and Charles Beard both as lacking in the realism he prescribed.[55]

Though his proximate target was the regnant Wilsonianism, he painted on a much broader canvas. By constructing "scientific man"— the allegedly perennial figure in Western culture who failed to respect "power politics"—as his target, Morgenthau built an escape route from recent Atlantic history. Gone were the imperial realism of Reinsch and Mahan, Bowman and Wilson. In their stead, he placed Wilson on one side, Thucydides, Machiavelli, Richelieu, Hamilton, Disraeli, and now himself, on the other. In contrast to the church fathers and eighteenth-century "anti-Machiavellian writers," Bacon, Bentham, Spencer, Wilson, and Cobden, Morgenthau adumbrated a canon of thinkers who conceived "the nature of international politics as an unending struggle for survival and power." He quietly omitted the qualification that Machiavellianism could easily degenerate into "utopianism" he had made so passionately the year before.

Morgenthau went further, making "modernity" itself a core part of the problems afflicting scientific man. There was something quintessentially "modern" about the Western retreat from power politics allegedly embodied by Wilson. The "liberal internationalism" of Spencer and Wilson was symptom of a deeper "sterility of the modern mind" (39). The moderns were guilty of an "original sin"—conceiving of politics and economics as mutually exclusive alternatives (90). Influenced by the neo-Augustinianism of contemporary thinkers like his friend, Reinhold Niebuhr, and in parallel to the writings of the historian Herbert Butterfield, Morgenthau's "realism" is ostensibly secular—the descendant of Nietzsche and Weber's "disenchanted" worlds. But there is a strong element in his thought of what Nicolas Guilhot calls "counter-enlightenment" thinking, endebted to political theology, and ultimately conservative in politics and traditional in morality.[56] Although he insisted that power politics could not be eliminated, Morgenthau acknowledged that something had to be done to tame the "destructiveness of power politics." But the remedies Morgenthau recommended are traditional ones. Modern social and political problems must be read "in the light of the pre-rationalist Western tradition" (10).[57] Morgenthau made a valid point in recommending resources "different from and superior to the reason of the scientific age" to tame destructive dynamics in modern societies, but he makes it too easy for himself by claiming the authority of science when it suits him, and of tradition when it does not.

The central failing of liberalism, Morgenthau believed, was its excessive faith that "rational argument will reveal as misunderstanding what uninformed opinion has taken for unbridgeable conflict" (106). Rationalism usurps the place of practical rationality. It is striking that one of the examples Morgenthau uses to illustrate his point about the strength of "concrete" concepts as opposed to abstract ones is the *Großraum*, or great space, theorized by Schmitt: "While nonliberal political concepts such as Roman Empire, new order, living space, encirclement, national security, haves vs. have-nots, and the like, show an immediately recognizable relationship to *concrete political aims*; liberal concepts, such as 'collective security,' 'democracy,' 'national self-determination,' 'justice,' [and] 'peace,' are abstract generalities which may be applied to any political situation but which are not peculiar to any particular one" (72; emphasis added). Morgenthau argued that because they are instrumental to a specific political purpose, nonliberal political concepts are superior to liberal ones. Their very instrumentality is a guarantee of their superior "concreteness": destined to "disappear and be replaced by others as soon as they have fulfilled their temporary political function . . . they will be relatively immune from the danger of being at variance with reality and therefore of falling into disrepute."[58] Liberal ideologies, on the other hand, "are kept alive after they have outlived their political usefulness and [are] . . . disavowed by the realities of international politics, which by their very nature, are concrete, specific and dependent on time and place" (73). These statements are remarkably outrageous and inimical to a twenty-first-century liberal sensibility. It is hard to square this preference for immanence with his transcendental commitments to truth, morality, and justice articulated in the same work. Can Morgenthau truly be recovered for a progressive liberalism?

Furthermore, his logic is syllogistic: "Reality" is perennially and inevitably constituted in part by power politics. Liberalism cannot grasp power politics. Therefore, liberalism cannot grasp reality.

> Liberalism, therefore, is able to accept only international aims which can be justified in the light of reason. Since however the rationalist conception of international affairs does not fit political reality where power is pitted against power for survival and supremacy, the liberal approach to international problems has necessarily an ideological quality. Liberalism expresses its aims in the international sphere not *in terms of power politics, that is, on the basis of the international reality,* but in accordance with the rationalist premises of its own misconception. (71; emphasis added)

Morgenthau charged that liberalism moves within a closed circle of its own device, but his own brief for power politics relied on logic that is circular. For its "reality effect," realism depended on certain rhetorical moves. For the age always in search of the scientific formula, "an *obstinate reality* again and again makes the solution of today the fallacy of tomorrow" (101; emphasis added). One cannot avoid the impression that it is Morgenthau's rhetoric itself that engenders these reality effects, conjuring the object it represents.

From Insurgent to Authority: Morgenthau and
the Making of a Cold War Orthodoxy

"Throughout the 1940s, Morgenthau distanced himself from the Realist label. Beginning in 1950, however, he fervently embraced it," William Scheuerman has written.[59] Why did this happen? Between 1945 and 1954, the US field of international relations developed a new identity as something other than a hodgepodge of diplomatic history, international law, and policy advocacy. The Social Science Research Council (SSRC hereafter) and Rockefeller Foundation sponsored discussions and lent support to competing camps of academic protagonists. Historian Nicolas Guilhot has reconstructed these debates in illuminating detail. In April 1948, the SSRC established a Committee on International Relations that aimed to clarify priorities and paradigms in the study of international affairs. The initial discussions were convened by Frederick Dunn, director of the Yale Institute for International Studies, and attended by Chicago's Quincy Wright, by this time viewed as a major rival of Morgenthau; the Columbia University political scientists William T.R. Fox and Grayson Kirk; Malcolm Davis of the Carnegie Endowment for International Peace; and Rupert Emerson, a political scientist from Harvard.[60] They saw their task as putting the field on a firm footing in the social sciences. Not surprisingly, Morgenthau was not invited (17). The committee disbanded, unsuccessful, in July 1950. Guilhot argues that the SSRC committee foundered in no small part due to the divisiveness of Morgenthau's *Scientific Man*. As Guilhot explained, in a passage worth quoting in full:

> In the end, the focus on value-orientations and on the domestic determinants of foreign policy . . . could not coexist with the realist vision of the state not as a pluralist arena but as a sovereign and quasi-ontological reality . . . Nor could the connivance between the social sciences and the progressive idea of modernization coexist with the pessimistic outlook characteristic of realism. The incompatibility between liberalism and historical pessimism sealed the fate of the SSRC initiative. (19)

Although today Morgenthau is considered a founder of an integral branch of political science—the subfield of IR—he had scarcely veiled contempt

for the American political science of his day. In *Scientific Man* he ridiculed
the effort to make politics into a science: "Liberalism, by conquering the
state, freed an ever increasing domain from direct political domination
and, finally, seemed even to expel politics from the state and to make statecraft itself a science . . . Finally, there is no field of governmental activity
which would not be regarded as a proper branch of 'political science.'"[61]
The book, Morgenthau later recalled, caused a "big fight" in political
science that "dragged on until 1954."[62]

By the end of the 1940s, Kenneth Thompson, Grayson Kirk, William Fox, and others had begun to craft a distorted image of interwar
scholarship in line with Morgenthau's own account to legitimate the new
realist approach.[63] Thompson completed a doctorate with Morgenthau
in 1950 and became the head of Rockefeller's Program for International
Studies.[64] On May 7–8, 1954, Thompson hosted a conference on international politics for the foundation, the task of which was to discuss
"the nature, boundaries, and future of their field" (148). The attendees
included a group from varied disciplinary and professional backgrounds:
Fox, Arnold Wolfers, Morgenthau, and Niebuhr were academics, the latter
two famous public intellectuals; Walter Lippmann and James B. Reston
were distinguished journalists from the *New York Herald Tribune* and
New York Times, respectively; Dorothy Fosdick, Robert Bowie, and Paul
Nitze came from policy-making backgrounds. Thompson's list "excluded
scholars associated with international law and organizations" (148). When
Thompson drew up a list of centers and scholars doing research in IR in
February 1954, he included Morgenthau's Center for the Study of American Foreign Policy at Chicago, but not Wright, or any scholar from the
political science department (146–47). By excluding both the ascendant
behaviorist political scientists and the old legalist international lawyers
alike, Thompson put institutional flesh on the antiscientific and antile-
galist brief for power-political realism Morgenthau had made in 1946.[65]
This was what Guilhot has convincingly described as "the realist gambit":
by establishing a defensive "demarcation line vis a vis the behavioral sciences" (151), the realists carved out a distinctive space for a realism anchored in less scientist approaches to international relations. This was
a tricky business, for the conference attendees both wished to articulate

a theory of international politics and simultaneously insist on "the 'limits' of theory: a clear reminder, against the cognitive pretension of the social sciences, that power politics [resisted] . . . complete rationalization. In fact, IR theory not only had limits; it was essentially defined by those limits" (151). This was Morgenthau's gambit too.

Just as Morgenthau tried to have his cake and eat it too when it came to the dyad of power politics and morality, he also fundamentally equivocated on the question of whether IR could be scientific. At the 1954 conference, among his elite peers, he could admit that "a theory of IR must . . . guard against the temptation to take itself too seriously and to neglect the ambiguities which call it into question at every turn. A theory that yielded to that temptation would become a metaphysic, superimposing a logically coherent intellectual scheme upon a reality which falls short of such coherence." But later in the same proceedings Morgenthau argued that what makes theory possible is the assumption of rationality: "Foreign policy is pursued by rational men who pursue certain rational interests with rational means."[66] Three years later, he would describe the international realm as governed by natural laws: "The balance of power, you may say, is for foreign policy what the law of gravity is for nature; that is, it is the very essence of foreign policy."[67] Morgenthau never resolved these tensions.[68]

In the same years that the SSRC and Rockefeller Foundation were promoting international relations as an adjunct of the new globally interventionist United States, the future of Germany, the fate of Eastern Europe, the Chinese revolution, and the atomic arms race with the USSR were all focusing the minds of intellectuals and policymakers. Reading Morgenthau's works in late 1946, George Kennan recognized a deeply kindred thinker. In 1949, Kennan, since 1947 director of the Policy Planning Staff at the State Department, brought Morgenthau to the department as a consultant. In June 1949, Morgenthau took part in discussions of European affairs alongside John J. McCloy, the US high commissioner to Germany, Niebuhr, and the incoming CIA director.[69] Between 1948 and 1952, Morgenthau published a series of articles of enduring value, in which he began to embrace the label "realist" forthrightly for the first time.[70] It was at this juncture that Morgenthau alighted on the "national interest" as his signature concept.[71] In the interests of being heard and exerting influence, Morgenthau simplified his message, ironing out its ambivalent oscillations between power and morality, art and science. First as a consultant to, and then as a member of, the Council on Foreign Relations, he found himself in the elite circles where political and military policy and strategy was being shaped.[72] But in the early 1950s, Morgenthau still felt he had an uphill climb to earn an audience for his brand of realism.

He felt locked in a struggle to have his realism correctly understood. His critics seemed to cherry-pick "words out of context to prove that realism in international affairs is unprincipled and contemptuous of morality."[73] "Political realists," he wrote in 1958 "are not amoral, they just make different choices between moral values . . . for if he does not take care of the national interest nobody else will, and if he puts American security and liberty in jeopardy the cause of liberty everywhere will be impaired" (85). In a 1952 letter to George Kennan, he complained bitterly that the elite Council on Foreign Relations was dominated by Wilsonians. Of his correspondence with longtime editor of the journal *Foreign Affairs*, Hamilton Fish, he wrote, "I did of course not need that correspondence to become aware of the difficulty people of my persuasion have in making their views known to the general educated public by way of articles." While the journal contains a number of articles, he told Kennan, "which implicitly deviate from the legalistic-moralistic position, [you] will not find a single article that takes [explicit] issue with that position. I might add that quite a number of people with whom I have discussed the matter, including Lippmann and Hans Simons, have told me of Fish's personal bias in favor of Wilsonianism." The reviews of his book, *In Defense of the National Interest* (1951), were decidedly mixed, as the reviews of *Scientific Man* had also been. Myres MacDougall, of the Yale Law School, wrote, "In our contemporary disillusionment it is again becoming the fashion to minimize both the role that law presently plays in the world power process and the role that, with more effective organization, it could be made to play in maintaining the values of a free, peaceful, and abundant world society."[74] *The Economist* disparaged the book as a "theology of realpolitik."[75] Carl Friedrich, another German-Jewish émigré, described it as "an American version of the German Realpolitik, stressing as it does military potential and natural resources." His book offered "a valuable check on excess enthusiasm" and utopianism, but Morgenthau's exasperation with "moralizing" was so intense that it became "oppressive."[76] Morgenthau was outraged by the historian A.J.P. Taylor's negative review in *The Nation*, prompting an angry letter to its editor, Freda Kirchwey. Taylor faulted Morgenthau for urging America "to go back to the realities of power politics. The object of foreign policy should be the defense of the national interest, neither more nor less."[77] To Kirchwey he wrote, "The lot of a writer on American foreign policy who does not consistently follow the 'popular' line is difficult and risky enough as it is, and he must see to it that the record be kept straight."[78]

Five years later, the tone of his writing had shifted dramatically, and the satisfaction of an outsider who has overcome resistance is palpable: "I remember very well that when I used the term 'balance of power' at the beginning of my academic career in the early '30s I met with an unfavorable reaction . . . [it] was then a kind of dirty word—something which respectable scholars would not use, at least not in an affirmative sense . . . it was something to be abolished."[79] An exchange of letters between Morgenthau and Philip Jessup in January 1954 captures how much the relationship between international law and international relations had changed since Morgenthau abandoned the field in 1940, and Grayson Kirk had described the relation of the disciplines. "Thank you for [sending me] your article, 'International Law in 1953 AD,'" Jessup protested to Morgenthau. "However I cannot help regretting the content and really think you have done an injustice to me and to those who think like me." Jessup explained, "There's a so-called 'Great Debate' going on . . . academic warfare between the international lawyer and the realist . . . I cannot claim to be a member of any school . . . This gives me the unfair advantage of escaping the dilemma of having to choose between being a 'realist' and a 'Utopian'. I sympathize with those who might be cross-examined under oath: 'Are you or have you ever been a Utopian?'"[80] Between 1952 and 1957, Morgenthau's position in the American intellectual field shifted dramatically. The insurgent became an authority. From demanding satisfaction in intellectual duels, Morgenthau became a satisfied and powerful man (a "satisfied power," as it were). In his writing from these years, discussed below, Morgenthau learned to move more easily across the Atlantic than he had before.

A Natural Comparativist

At times Morgenthau, with his thick German accent, played the role of Old World tutor to the new, scolding the Americans for their naivete about the age-old truths of international affairs. At other times, Morgenthau found it more prudent to flatter the Americans by congratulating them on their own indigenous tradition of realism: "the extraordinary qualities of political insight, historic perspective and common sense which the first generation of Americans applied to affairs of state." In this way, Morgenthau, the German Jewish outsider, could present himself as merely an aide in the recovery of the "classic age of American statecraft."[81] At the same time, however, Morgenthau presented himself as the educator of Americans on the "peculiarities" of their experience: "This aversion to seeing problems of international politics as they are and the inclination to viewing them instead in non-political, moralistic terms can be attributed both to certain misunderstood peculiarities of the American experience in foreign affairs" (836). Having crossed the Atlantic and been forced to adjust to the peculiar difficulties of intellectual exile, Morgenthau was a natural comparativist. "Two potent historic accidents" led the US to believe in the "uniqueness of American foreign policy in its freedom from those power-political blemishes which degrade the foreign policies of other nations" (837). Echoing the geopolitical thinking of Schmitt, Nicholas Spykman, and Wolfers, Morgenthau endorsed thinking in terms of spheres of influence: "The Monroe Doctrine and the policies implementing it express that permanent national interest of the US in the Western Hemisphere" (834).[82] But Morgenthau's characterization of the Monroe Doctrine as an expression of American exceptionalism elided the transatlantic history of the doctrine itself. Recall that Alfred Mahan fashioned the Monroe Doctrine into the *ur*-symbol of America's foreign policy realism. But Mahan understood the doctrine as the expression of a norm—one dictated by the nature of international relations and the vital "energies" of the nation as natural organism. Not surprisingly, Morgenthau did not wish to suggest too great a familiarity with the doctrines of *Großraum* that had provided a realist gloss on Nazi imperialism and biopolitics. It was not long before that the American public had been riled up by propaganda films about Haushofer and his devilish Institute for Geopolitics. But to describe the Monroe Doctrine as a testament to American peculiarities repressed the comparable questions raised by the pursuit of continental or hemispheric hegemony, be it by the Germans in Europe or the US in North America, South America, and the Caribbean.[83]

Morgenthau's comparativism illustrates that the rhetorical force of Atlantic realism depended in part on its practice of making comparisons. Comparisons both establish norms by which to measure deviation and promote discourses of exceptionalism. America was no more exempt from power politics than any other nation—only its protection by two oceans had led it to entertain these illusions—but it was also exceptionally able to ensure that its realism about power served the liberal goals of a global American hegemon. After saluting George Washington's refusal of entangling alliances, Morgenthau wrote that this "retreat from European politics, as proclaimed by Washington, could, therefore, be taken to mean retreat from power politics as such" (837). From this very abbreviated history of American foreign policy, Morgenthau constructed a schematic typology that included the category "realist": "Out of the struggle between these two opposing conceptions three types of American statesman emerge: the realist . . . the ideological . . . and the moralist . . . To these three types, three periods of American foreign policy roughly correspond" (840). Over the course of the 1950s, realism would evolve into something considerably more robust than an ideal-type.

Morgenthau, for one, would soon construct his realism in terms that suggested a gendered, embodied subject. The opposite of "the realist" was the "escapist." Totalitarianism and liberalism shared a common denominator: they both offered a different route of "escape from power."[84] Or, as he put it in his essay on Bernard de Jouvenel, power is "the central problem of our age," but "the modern tendency [is] to face the problem of power, but to face it as it were with a squinting eye."[85] The trope of the necessity of "facing" power depends on a masculine rhetoric that has echoes of Nietzsche or Weber, with their fear of the feminine and emphasis on courage and bravery as masculine qualities. His use of the verb "facing" implies a human face. The image recurs often in his writings of the period. As he put in 1950, "Isolationism, then, is in its way as oblivious to political reality as is Wilsonianism—the internationalist challenge, to which it had thought to have found the American answer . . . Both refused to face political reality either in realistic or ideological terms. They refused to face it at all."[86] Realism was a tool for building a consensus on the new global-facing posture of a hegemonic, interventionist United States.[87]

Morgenthau also experimented with the rhetoric of psychoanalysis, a language that enjoyed widespread cultural recognition at least among his American readers in in the 1950s.[88] His encounter with Freud began in late 1920s Frankfurt, and there is a Freudian strand in his mature thought too.[89] In his 1950s writings, Morgenthau sometimes adopted the posture of a psychoanalyst with the authority to distinguish rationality from mere emotion: "It is only by ingenuously taking public statements at their word that US policy can be described plausibly in terms of the theory of the coordinate state." By coordinate state, Morgenthau meant the principle of federation between states as opposed to the balance of power. "In truth, it is not the disinterested contemplation of facts which has given birth to the theory of the 'coordinate state.' That theory is rather the response to an emotional urge, and since this emotion is not peculiar to a particular author but typical of a popular reaction to the new role which the US must play in world affairs, it deserves brief analysis."[90] Morgenthau continued: "We expected from that war (World War II) a reaffirmation of the secure, detached, and independent position in world affairs which we had inherited from the founding fathers." A "happy chapter in the history of the nation and in one's own way of life has come to an end," he wrote as if addressing a forlorn child. Beseeching his readers to face this "disappointing and threatening reality," he warned against the temptation to escape into a fantasy realm: "Three such escapist fantasies have arisen in our midst in response to the challenge of American world leadership and power: the fantasy of needless participation in war, the fantasy of American treason, and the fantasy of American innocence" (62). The word "fantasy" does not appear in *Scientific Man versus Power Politics*. Morgenthau adopted the fashionable Freudianism of Cold War America, becoming a decoder of the dream-work of nations. Nations pursue objectives that are not only unnecessary for its survival but tend to jeopardize it. Second-rate nations which dream of playing the role of great powers, such as Italy and Poland in the interwar period, illustrate this point. So do great powers which dream of remaking the world in their own image and embark upon worldwide crusades, thus straining their resources to exhaustion. Here scientific analysis has the urgent task of pruning down national objectives to the measure of available resources in order to make their pursuit compatible with national survival. (74)

Morgenthau thus shunned the kind of scientific analysis and recommendations for political behavior associated with Charles Merriam and Harold Lasswell's political science in the 1940s, but embraced the scientificity of psychoanalysis. The antiscientific wing of the realists opposed the alliance of social science with democratic reform in part to insulate elite decision-making from the demos.[91] Paradoxes abound. Morgenthau adopts the elite role of cultural psychoanalyst but claims it is only to serve the common man: "The man in the street, unsophisticated as he is and uninformed as he may be, has a surer grasp of the essentials of foreign policy and a more mature judgment of its basic issues than many of the intellectuals and politicians who pretend to speak for him and cater to what they imagine his prejudices to be" (64). Clearing the national mind of the cobwebs spun by misguided intellectual elites, Morgenthau depicts himself as mere auxiliary to the already wise people. Far from antidemocratic, it is a populist Morgenthau who re-enfranchises the people and their common sense. But in the closed seminar room of the 1954 conference on international politics, Morgenthau confessed his true worries about democracy: "A theory of international relations must be conscious of the fact that foreign policy is deflected from its rational course by errors of judgment and emotional preferences, the latter especially where foreign policy is conducted under the conditions of democratic control."[92] That he toiled so long in public to make the case against the war in Vietnam illustrates that Morgenthau was not just a mandarin.[93]

But in the 1950s, his mandarinism still dominated. Implicit in Morgenthau's exhortations for Americans (and others) to distinguish between dreams and illusions and fantasies and reality are ideal yardsticks of maturity and rationality of which Morgenthau was qualified to judge. Recognizing that this could appear patronizing, Morgenthau wrote: "It is often said that the US is in need of maturing . . . [but] it would be truer to say that this generation of Americans must shed the illusions of their fathers and grandfathers and relearn the great principles of statecraft which guided the path of the republic in its first decade and—in moralistic disguise—in the first century of its existence."[94] Indeed, the Americans did not need to "grow up"; rather, they needed to clear their heads of the moralistic clutter that prevented them from accessing their "instinctive" common sense:

> The intoxication with moral abstractions which as a mass phenomenon started with the Spanish American war, and which in our time has become the prevailing substitute for political thought . . . Underneath . . . there has remained alive an almost instinctive awareness of the perennial interests of the United States. This has been especially true with regard to Europe and the Western Hemisphere; for in these regions the national interest of the US from the beginning has been obvious and clearly defined. (834)

Describing knowledge of the national interest as "instinctive" naturalizes political decisions. Like earlier generations of Atlantic realists, Morgenthau sought to cultivate the art of imperial statesmanship as "second nature."

Bildung, or The "Art" of Statesmanship

At the same time that Morgenthau flattered the American public with these descriptions of its common sense, he had an even stronger inclination to idealize the wisdom of the elite statesman. The practical wisdom of the properly realist statesman cannot be captured by science, but is rather an "art." As he wrote already in Scientific Man, "The social world, deaf to the appeal of reason pure and simple, yields only to that intricate combination of moral and material pressure which the art of the statesman creates and maintains."[95] In an essay on the "greatness" of Winston Churchill, from 1952, Morgenthau described the realist Haltung as something greater than the sum of its parts, ineffable and eliding precise formulation: "The secret of Sir Winston's greatness . . . cannot be explained in this space, if it can be explained at all; it can only be adumbrated." He also depicted realism as a mode of seeing: "What is required of the statesman is, first of all, to see clearly: himself, the enemy, and then himself again as the enemy sees him." The typically sober Morgenthau allows his rhetoric to reach romantic heights of exuberance: "The outstanding quality of that intellectual force is the ability to see a problem in its true proportions, by not allowing the involvement of will and emotion to interfere with understanding."[96] Through these metaphors drawn from the senses and references to emotion, Morgenthau groped toward the description of a realist posture that was embodied. Morgenthau's description of Churchill's art of statesmanship reminds us of similar evocations of ineffable and intuitive ways of knowing in Haushofer, Ratzel, and Mahan. The German admiral Maltzahn had recommended his officers read Ratzel's writings on the "ocean as a source of national greatness," and let it seep into their blood (*ins Blut übergehen*). For Morgenthau, too, the definition of a realistic politics was connected to questions of aesthetic truth and representation. As Michael Williams explains, when Morgenthau said in a lecture of 1946 that statesmen have a "kind of artistic feeling for the political possibilities which a particular problem offers," and that "an element of art enters into the solution of political problems," these were not just figures of speech.[97]

Part of Morgenthau's genius was to formulate a realist stance, posture, or *Haltung* that capitalized on the authority of science while strategically emphasizing the ineffable qualities of statesmanship and decision. After 1950, Morgenthau often described the realist's essential tool as political prudence. Many erudite commentators have emphasized the roots of this prudence in the ethics of responsibility articulated by Max Weber in his famous essay of 1919, "Politics as a Vocation."[98] The Weberian roots of Morgenthau's posture is obvious and indisputable. But Morgenthau's realist *Haltung* grew out of his experiences in America too. In academic combat against a hostile establishment, he had found new rhetorical strategies for describing the responsibilities of political actors. Speaking to the Naval War College on October 2, 1957, Morgenthau addressed the male youth who were the audience best placed to practice his teachings. There are two and only two "fundamental attitudes that a man can take towards a political and a social problem," he explained. One was that reform can solve problems once and for all; the other that problems can only be mitigated, never eliminated. The root of these ineliminable problems lay in "the very essence of human nature."[99] Morgenthau describes his philosophical anthropology as conservative. Conservatism, he wrote, "is part and parcel of the American political tradition . . . [It] holds—as we saw the realist philosophy of international relations to hold—that the world, imperfect as it is from a rational point of view, is the result of forces inherent in human nature. To improve the world one must work with these forces, not against them."[100] The *Haltung* of the statesman is conservative in two senses therefore. It describes an art of engaging with recalcitrant forces in the world. But only the rarest (and implicitly male) figure can attain the skill necessary to practice it.

As Robbie Shilliam has written, "Morgenthau quarantined Bildung to a policy elite institutionally buffered from direct political responsibility to follow the will of the masses. And here we arrive at Morgenthau's 'conservative liberalism.'"[101] At the same time that Morgenthau adumbrated the prerequisites of "greatness" in statesmanship, he was growing increasingly comfortable in American academe. Even in Chicago, that bastion of behaviorism in political science, Morgenthau's relationships with Robert Hutchins, Mortimer Adler, and Leo Strauss were congenial to the practices of self-cultivation and reflection, of *Bildung*, the tradition of the educated German bourgeoisie. Leo Strauss, his contemporary and friend at the University of Chicago, argued that the dominant political science "had come into being 'through an attempted break with common sense.'" He and Morgenthau were among "the 'old fashioned political scientists' [who] . . . continued their 'old fashioned practice' of adhering to 'Aristotelian political science,' albeit with 'a somewhat uneasy conscience.'"[102] While he had expressed extreme skepticism about the very possibility of a political science in *Scientific Man*, Morgenthau found recognition in the postwar US conversation of political theory. Perhaps the academy could recover from the "tragedy" of behaviorism and stay focused on "the great political issues."[103]

Debating Morgenthau's Legacy, or, Taking Responsibility

While some scholars insist that Morgenthau's reflections on the "world state" in *Politics among Nations* are evidence of at least an incipient cosmopolitan outlook, others interpret these elements, added later, as opportunistic and insincere.[104] Scheuerman concedes that Morgenthau's endorsement of the world state "was qualified by deep reservations about even modest efforts to begin building it. Like Schmitt, Morgenthau occasionally seemed to presuppose that intrastate conflicts represented the most authentic expression of the political" (39). Emphasizing the human aspiration for power was not tantamount, as many of Morgenthau's commentators supposed, to claiming that an amoral struggle for power was the only form of political action. Indeed, Morgenthau complained in prefaces to the second and third editions of the textbook that it was "not pleasant for an author to be blamed for ideas he has not only never expressed, but which he has explicitly and repeatedly refuted, and which are repugnant to him."[105] "Power, Morgenthau kept insisting, was not to be equated with material strength," writes Oliver Jütersonke. "On the contrary what he termed power had much to do with . . . the *virtù* of the individual involved, either in theory or in practice, with political action."[106] But the same author recognizes that Morgenthau's writings played an important part in the genesis of a "veritable aversion to international law in academic and policy circles" (185). Morgenthau's "frustrations did not prevent him from reinforcing these misinterpretations of his ideas with talk of a 'realist theory of international politics' in the second edition [of *Politics among Nations*]. When the options were academic obscurity or considerable public prominence . . . the choice for Morgenthau was nonetheless an easy one. If the book sells better by reiterating and emphasizing what your readers declare you to have said, then so be it" (182). In the preface to the 1967 edition, he "conceded that his commitment to realism may have led him into exaggeration." Morgenthau must share the burden for these misunderstandings.

While revisionists have emphasized the normative elements in Morgenthau, they have not made the power-political pole of the dyad disappear but only put it into tension with the normative one.[107] Other readers of

Morgenthau have described him as successfully overcoming the either-or of morality and power politics, resolving it through synthesis. Clearly that is how Morgenthau saw himself. But that is not the Morgenthau that became most legible in the American public sphere.[108] Nothing but power, or nothing but justice; Morgenthau claimed to offer a *via media* between the two, but the constant oscillation suggests confusion or difficulties at a deeper level.

Morgenthau's account of power remained blurry throughout the 1950s. Morgenthau became a balancer of power considerations. In a representative statement from 1955, he wrote:

> When the times tend to depreciate the element of power, [political science] must stress its importance. When the times incline towards a monistic conception of power, it must show its limitations . . . When the reality of power is being lost sight of over its moral and legal limitations, it must point to that reality. When law and morality are judged as nothing, it must assign them their rightful place.[109]

His position has its merits. At times, he insisted on proper respect for "the political" as the sine qua non of realistic perception and choice. At others, he played the role of "balancer" and "restrainer," demanding that we avoid the "excesses" of power politics.

Neither the utopian rationalist nor the totalitarian achieves the right balance between power politics and other dimensions of life: "So the gap between the political ideal and political reality, which perfectionism tried to resolve in favor of the ideal, totalitarianism also tries to eliminate but by the opposite procedure, that is by tearing the ideal down to the level of the brute facts of political life."[110] But while Morgenthau took pains to emphasize that power is less than the totality of human relations, his self-fashioning as a balancer of power considerations is equivocal. As John Herz wrote in 1960, "contrary to uninformed criticism, political realists have indeed always insisted on distinguishing morality from 'moralism', but where, in particular, do they propose to draw the line?" Peter Stirk suggests that it will not suffice to "replace a story about amoral theorists of power politics with a story about moral theorists of power politics."[111] The underlying problematic remains unresolved.

Another reason it does not suffice is that it allows the midcentury an-titotalitarian consensus to overshadow the postcolonial problematics of North-South relations that emerged with renewed force after 1945. Al-though Morgenthau was an early and vocal dissenter from the Vietnam War—already in 1965—it is important to note the limits of his critique. Arguing that the war was not in the national interest, and that the end could not justify the means, nowhere did he question the prerogative of the United States to order the entire world's affairs in its interests; in short, its imperial prerogative. The same can be said of his close friend Rein-hold Niebuhr. While trenchant in their critique of the messianism and hubris that distorted its imperial conduct, Niebuhr's searing books and articles on the conduct of the Cold War did not rebut the basic premises of American empire themselves.

The story of Morgenthau's American years offers an important cor-rective to the ahistorical realist canon. While canonizers are quick to place him in a lineage that links him to *Realpolitik*, he shunned the term. Scheuerman is right that "critics misread his insistence on the en-during and central importance of power in all political relationships as an endorsement of European style *Realpolitik* and its axiom that might makes right."[112] But the definition of *Realpolitik* is highly contested too.[113] Morgenthau had more in common with Ludwig Rochau than Treitschke. In *Scientific Man*, he rejected Hobbes and Machiavelli as an "accident without consequences, a sudden flash of lightning, illuminating the dark landscape of man's hidden motives but kindling no Promethean fire for a grateful posterity."[114] It was a dangerous thing to be a Machiavelli—with or without *virtù*.[115]

It was only in the 1940s and 1950s—and therefore, only in America—that Morgenthau came to identify as a political "realist" and developed his mature understanding of what that meant. Throughout his American years, according to one biographer, Morgenthau downplayed again and again his debts to German thinkers, preferring to quote from English and American authors. Historical genealogies of Morgenthau's thought have revealed his deep debts to Schmitt, Weber, and Meinecke, Nietzsche, Kelsen and Freud. The legal realism that he abandoned in 1940 was shaped not only by the dialogue with Schmitt in the late 1920s but also by the leading legal minds of the Social Democratic left in Weimar as well. His insistence on ethics demarcates him from the German *Realpolitiker*. Neither, obviously, was Morgenthau a Schmittian statist *tout court*. He was an antitotalitarian liberal with a conservative temperament and an elitist sensibility. His project of making Americans into realists involved more than just the deployment of concepts from the old world. Constructing power politics as the signature of the real, and realism's key concepts—the national interest and power politics—as common sense, involved more than just academic infighting and disciplinary politics. Realism was not just a tradition of texts, but an emotional style and a posture that Morgenthau cultivated and practiced. Morgenthau enthusiastically disseminated this realist *Haltung* (posture) as pedagogy. Morgenthau's realism sutured together a bricolage of Schmittian, Weberian, and Freudian elements, adding a dash of Hamilton, Jefferson, and Judeo-Christian tradition. Realism's keywords—national interest and power politics—have long conceptual histories that are important for the story of realism's development as a tradition. But Morgenthau taught what it was to be a realist not just through the dissemination of his ideas but through the performance of a role. The role illustrated that realism was a way of seeing and a way of being in the world. Hans Morgenthau's cultivation, articulation, and performance of realism as a worldview and sensibility naturalized historical choices with the force of myth and generated the common sense of the Cold War. Born of the Atlantic passage of a refugee scholar from one legal and political culture to another, Morgenthau's work illustrates not just the transplantation and growth of ideas and ideal-types but the reinvention of the realist habitus for his generation of Americans.

CHAPTER 7

Realism's Crisis and Restoration

West Germany, 1954–1985

THE CAREER OF HANS MORGENTHAU is emblematic of the success of the realist paradigm in the American theory of international relations from 1940 to 1960. The dominant figure in West German politics in the overlapping years of 1949–63 was the Christian Democratic Union's Konrad Adenauer. Many scholars have examined the development of West German political culture and academia through the lens of "Americanization," the gravitational pull of the American colossus. But realism was not immediately adopted in West German academia. Hans Morgenthau's *Politics among Nations* was not even translated into German until 1963. Nor was Georg Schwarzenberger's *Power Politics* (1941) until 1955. This chapter traces the history of realism's development in West German international relations theory and diplomatic practice. It claims that realism's fortunes rose and fell with the dialectic of *Westbindung*, or "orientation to the West," and *Ostpolitik*, the effort to relax tensions with East Germany, the Eastern bloc, and the Soviet Union. The cycles of *Westbindung, Ostpolitik,* and the return of *Westbindung* were the broad political context in which the intellectuals debated realism in the academic realm and in foreign policy. Realism thrived during a first period characterized by *Westbindung* from 1954 to 1967. It entered a crisis and was reformulated during the highwater mark of détente between 1967 and 1974, and made a dramatic return after 1975, accompanying the breakdown of detente and the reheating of the Cold War.

Realism was burdened by its associations in the public mind with the undiluted *Machtstaatspolitik* of the Third Reich. Would-be West German realists therefore faced a problem akin to that faced by American geopoliticians in the 1940s who had had to fight free of the associations of their thought to that of Karl Haushofer and German *Geopolitik*. For the West German thinkers who championed it in the 1960s and 1970s, realism seemed overdue. But the realists' effort to popularize the writings of Hans Morgenthau, for example, had to contend with the demand of New Left radicals in the 1960s that any realism worthy of the name must be boldly future-oriented. The survival of humanity was at stake. Elder statesmen of the Frankfurt School like Herbert Marcuse and Erich Fromm argued powerfully that realism needed to develop its imaginative capacities and set the pace for humanity, not just meekly catalogue its failures. These West Germans drew on developments in the antiwar movement in the United States. Many of the intellectuals discussed here attempted to align American and German understandings of realism, but these efforts to synchronize the Atlantic time of realism did not always succeed. Realism developed differently in these two major theaters of the postwar Atlantic.

The Deutsche Gesellschaft für Auswärtige Politik, Gottfried-Karl Kindermann, and Realism's Halting Return to Germany, 1954–1967

From 1954 to 1967, West Germany regained its sovereignty from the Allied occupiers. It reacquired what the political scientists of the era called the "freedom to act" (*Handlungsspielraum*). But there were real limits to this sovereignty.[1] As sovereignty was passed back to West Germany, a group of leading industrialists, diplomats, and academics created the German Society for Foreign Policy (Deutsche Gesellschaft für Auswärtige Politik; DGAP hereafter), with the goal of equipping its elite to navigate the Cold War. It had the blessing of the ruling Christian Democratic Union and the support of the conservative wing of the Social Democratic Party. The DGAP believed it was necessary to catch up to the latest strategic thought coming from the United States. The perception that West Germany had fallen behind spurred an effort to synchronize the "time" of German and American foreign policy thought. By building the infrastructure and concepts of an "Atlantic security community," the DGAP created an intellectual space that seemed optimally designed to receive the realist currents that dominated international relations theory in the US, and contributed to the broad contours of Cold War foreign policy. Morgenthau had founded the

Center for American Foreign Policy at the University of Chicago in 1950, and won powerful allies at the Rockefeller Foundation, the State Department, and the Council on Foreign Relations. But his thought did not have a similar impact in West Germany. Why? Through transatlantic links with the US and Great Britain, the DGAP succeeded in creating a series of institutions dedicated to the transatlantic partnership. But the reception of realism in Germany was halting, incomplete, and ultimately overtaken by events. Still, between 1955 and 1967, the DGAP did bring together notable realists such as Henry Kissinger, Robert Osgood, Hans Morgenthau, and Wilhelm Grewe. In a historical twist common in the Adenauer period, Grewe, the partisan of *Großraum* in the Third Reich, became the theorist of American *Großraum* in the 1950s. The accomplishments for which Grewe would be most well-known, the formulation of the Hallstein Doctrine and the "Deutschlandvertrag," which restored German sovereignty, stem from this period. The Hallstein Doctrine was a quintessential realist doctrine—it denied diplomatic recognition to any country that maintained diplomatic relations with East Germany.[2] By forcing a decision, it recapitulated the Schmittian concept of the friend-enemy distinction as the essence of politics. By the early 1960s, however, American IR theory had taken a behaviorist turn and was becoming more oriented to cybernetic theories and computing. The "classical realism" barely canonized by the mid-1950s was already being perceived as passé.[3]

The DGAP combined idealism about European integration with a pragmatic approach to the German question. Explicitly conceived as a German version of Great Britain's "Chatham House" (the Institute for Security Studies), or the US's Council for Foreign Relations, the DGAP was envisioned in a memorandum by the first president of the country, Theodor Heuss, as "a school of sobriety (*Nüchternheit*)." It would provide a bit of "solid ground" in a "time of intellectual (*geistig*) oscillations."[4] Herbert Blankenhorn, a legal advisor to Adenauer who, like Grewe, had served in the Nazi Foreign Office, helped convince Adenauer that an institution that could produce "basic and long-term studies" would be useful (71). Founded on March 29, 1955, the DGAP had the express support of Chancellor Adenauer. Both Foreign Minister Hallstein and his advisor Grewe were involved in discussions of its finances and structure in early

1955, and Grewe was designated the main point of contact between the Foreign Office and the DGAP. The three leading candidates for director were Tübingen historian Hans Rothfels (1891–1976), Bonn international lawyer Ulrich Scheuner (1903–1981), and Freiburg political scientist and sociologist Arnold Bergstraesser (1896–1964). Hallstein and Grewe supported Bergstraesser, a Jewish former student of Alfred Weber who spent the war years in exile in California, before becoming the first political science professor at the postwar University of Freiburg.[5]

The choice of Bergstraesser and his "cultural-sociological" or "synoptic" approach to world politics meant choosing an émigré familiar with postwar American political science, and underscored the transatlantic security relationship; he was also the least politically conservative of the three.[6] At the same time, it expressed a nostalgic preference for someone who wrote in a mandarin style of Weimar-era *Kulturkritik* (71).[7] His students, who later became famous as scholars and public intellectuals––Karl Sontheimer, Hans Maier, Dieter Oberndörfer, and Karl-Gottfried Kindermann––were known collectively as the "Freiburg School" of political science. Under Bergstraesser's leadership, the DGAP rebuilt German foreign policy as an elite practice based on social science, and generally insulated from the public.[8]

From the mid-1950s, the DGAP became a resource for American experts looking for information about German sources. In 1955, with the backing of the Council of Foreign Relations, Harvard professor of government Henry Kissinger convened a study group on the impact of nuclear weapons on the strategic thinking of the Federal Republic that resulted in the 1957 publication of *Nuclear Weapons and Foreign Policy*.[9] Even before it was translated at the behest of the DGAP into German in 1959, the book was widely discussed. From 1955 to 1961, the DGAP's journal, the *Europa Archiv*, reprinted important essays from the US nuclear strategy discussion authored by Kissinger, Arnold Wolfers, Klaus Knorr, Albert Wohlstetter, and John Foster Dulles, the US secretary of state from 1953 to 1959 (119).[10] By 1960, the notion of Western nuclear primacy was giving way to calls for "managed bipolarity" and "stability." Intellectuals associated with the RAND Corporation, founded in Santa Monica, California, in 1948, developed a new social scientific paradigm for the discussion of nuclear strategy called "systems-analysis." In 1961, a major book on the subject of nuclear strategy, *Arms Control, Disarmament and National Security*, was published, drawing on conference papers printed in the journal *Daedalus* the year before.[11] The following year, the DGAP's Uwe Nerlich edited a German translation of the volume, one that became a major vehicle for the reception of American strategic thought in West Germany (140). The reactions of two DGAP members, Carl Friedrich von Weizsäcker and Helmut Schmidt, reveal how these German figures viewed the technical expertise then in vogue in the Kennedy administration. While von Weizsäcker spoke of a "Daedalus language" (referring to the journal) that was "not only an American but above all a modern one that we Germans must learn" (141), Schmidt expressed greater skepticism, referring to the discussion as a kind of "glass bead game with computers"(140n67). But he added that "there is something important here . . . We Germans, we Europeans, must finally move away from the 'Bertha von Suttner–Noel Baker' thought, as well as from geopolitical and historical conceptions."[12] Schmidt saw himself steering a kind of middle path, much as Kindermann would present Morgenthau as a mediator of the extremes. Yet by the time the German edition of the arms control book appeared, some leading figures in the DGAP were growing skeptical of the arms control school's talisman, "stability." In his afterword, Cornides wrote that a "strategy of war-prevention that is focused exclusively on arms control (*Rüstungspolitik*) cannot produce a stable order deserving of the name peace" (143). Still, the dominant view was that Robert McNamara's deployment of computers to rethink military strategy was the direction of the future. In 1964, Ulrich Scheuner, the head of the DGAP's research arm, went so far as to see in the Cuban Missile Crisis a "successful" example of the application of scientific methods to strategic decision-making that would help the US gauge the reactions of the USSR and China to its escalation in Vietnam (172). In January 1965, the Bundestag made plans to create a research institute in Germany on the model of the RAND Corporation. The cabinet confirmed these plans for a *Stiftung Wissenschaft und Politik* in Ebenhausen near Munich in May 1966.[13]

The DGAP helped synchronize the discussions of arms control and security policy in the US and Germany in the first half of the 1960s. Despite major political turmoil in the "Atlantic partnership" between 1963 and 1965, these initiatives survived and grew.[14] In the early 1960s, NATO allies began to seek more control over nuclear weapons to reduce their reliance on the American deterrent. But the Americans wanted to limit proliferation. A scheme, called the Multilateral Force (MLF), represented a possible solution to this dilemma. The MLF plan was to create a fleet of ships armed with Polaris ballistic missiles, manned by crews from various nations, but under joint NATO command. In January 1963, French president Charles de Gaulle vetoed British participation in the European Defense Community. The French decision effectively to exit joint NATO command and to control its own nuclear deterrent threw the Kennedy administration's "Grand Design" into chaos. The Americans pressured the West Germans to join the MLF. Debates between so-called "Gaullists" and "Atlanticists" roiled the DGAP.

While the new chancellor, Ludwig Erhard, favored the MLF—and sent Grewe to Washington to expedite its passage—Franz Joseph Strauss of the Christian Social Union represented the "Gaullist position," stating that "Europeans should not place blind confidence in the reliability and trustworthiness of the Americans . . . So long as Europe has no nuclear weapons, Europe has no sovereignty."[15] In the midst of this controversy, major figures from the DGAP such as Theo Sommer, Helmut Schmidt, and Uwe Nerlich were invited to a conference held at Harvard at the end of May 1963.[16] There they encountered Hans Morgenthau who, against the Atlanticist majority in the study group, defended France's striving for nuclear independence. De Gaulle "was right in principle," Morgenthau insisted. ". . . In the atomic age no one can expect a state to commit suicide for another. The whole system of alliances has lost its meaning, and each state must fall back on its own strength and protect its own interests."[17] Two months earlier, Morgenthau had defended de Gaulle in an article in *Commentary*.[18] In a letter to Dean Acheson, a few weeks later, he articulated the deeper philosophical stakes:

> What I find so disturbing in the Washington scene today is the dearth of men who are capable of thinking in political terms. It is not so much a question of evaluating Cuba, Berlin or de Gaulle one

way or other as it is the congenital inability to bring political categories to bear upon these issues. It is as though people were to judge
paintings not in view of their intrinsic aesthetic value but in terms
of say, the cost of their production, the chemical composition of the
paint, or their physical relations to each other. I suspect that this de-
ficiency is not limited to the American scene and not even to democracies but rather is of a general nature. Reading 19th century history,
as I do from time to time for intellectual stimulation, I am struck by
the political isolation of Bismarck and Cavour whose most brilliant
and successful moves were understood by hardly anyone at the time
and were actively opposed by those who were to benefit most from
their success. Still I feel the same ambivalent longing and trying my
hand at doing better what is being done so badly.[19]

Acheson, the former secretary of state, was then serving as an advisor to
Kennedy. The two men had carried on a friendly correspondence since
1957. What is so extraordinary about Morgenthau's reflections here are
the clear debts to Schmitt's writings on the concept of the political in the
1920s and 1930s—and relatedly, the extent to which he believed that political thinking was a "capacity" that eludes most contemporary politicians.

In response to the crises of the year, the Ford Foundation approved a
research program in "Atlantic Policy Studies" at the end of 1963 to support the development of NATO (187). By the end of 1963, Uwe Nerlich
reflected with pride that the DGAP had placed itself "in manifold ways
at the center of the strategic debate in Germany." Grewe published an
article in support of the MLF in 1964.[20] Plans begun in 1961 came to
fruition in 1964 at the first annual Colloquium on Questions of International Security, which assembled over fifty participants to hear presentations by Grewe, then ambassador to NATO. Subsequent colloquia with
transatlantic participation followed in 1966 and 1967. The contributions
of realist figures like Morgenthau and Grewe to the transatlantic security
conversation made a strong impression in the public mind: they could rest
assured that the "political-security debate in the Bundesrepublik between
1963 and 1966 was characterized by a sober regard for the facts (*sachlich-
nüchterner Stil*)" (169). The DGAP recognized both Morgenthau and

Grewe as experts on security questions bearing on the Western Alliance. Remarkably, given the extent to which each of their careers resembled the other's, there is no correspondence between the two men in either man's personal archive. The bridges between the US and German realist communities were still under construction. The DGAP's history helps compensate for the missing dialogue between the two men.

Championing Morgenthau: Kindermann and the Return of Realism to German International Relations Theory

One of Bergstraesser's protégés was Gottfried-Karl Kindermann (b. 1926), an Austrian political scientist who had earlier been a pupil of Morgenthau's. Bergstraesser brought Kindermann to the DGAP shortly after it opened its doors.[21] Kindermann met Morgenthau as an exchange student at the University of Chicago in 1949, returning twice as his research assistant in 1951–53 and 1954–56 at the Center for the Study of American Foreign and Military Policy.[22] In 1956, the Rockefeller Foundation's Kenneth Thompson, another Morgenthau student, supplied a grant to create a series of "yearbooks" of international affairs, for which the model was Chatham House's annual surveys. Kindermann was put in charge of the section dedicated to East Asia.

A correspondence between Kindermann and Morgenthau from 1957 to 1966 records Kindermann's evolution from deferential student to peer. In 1961 he concluded that Morgenthau belonged to a realist tradition that was transatlantic, not merely German. Crucially, realism was to be distinguished from a German tradition of *Realpolitik*.[23] In 1957, Kindermann wrote to his former mentor Morgenthau with a list of earnest questions about his philosophical relationship to the thinkers Friedrich Meinecke, Max Weber, and Reinhold Niebuhr, with whom he seemed comparable. To one query, Morgenthau replied, "To call me a disciple of Meinecke is untrue from a strictly historic point of view and somewhat far-fetched from any point of view."[24] This is an interesting disavowal given Morgenthau's documented appreciation for Meinecke's work on raison d'état in the 1920s. Is there much distance between your positions and Niebuhr's? Kindermann asked. Morgenthau replied that there was not: whereas "Niebuhr addresses the moral and philosophic aspects of international politics," Morgenthau was concerned with "its technical aspects, the rules of the political art."[25] How does your position differ from that of Treitschke? Kindermann asked next. "This is a complete misunderstanding of my position. Treitschke was the ideologist of the nation-state of Bismark (*sic*) and of power. I am an analyst of the nation-state and of power and have time and again emphasized their negative moral connotations. More particularly, I have emphasized their obsolescence as a principle of political organisation."[26] But Morgenthau's conception of power was hardly always a "negative" one, nor was his insistence on the obsolescence of the nation-state consistent with his consecration of the "national interest."

For six years, Kindermann played the role of Morgenthau's champion, seeking a German publisher for Morgenthau's magnum opus, *Politics among Nations* (1948). Owing to his connections at the DGAP, it was finally published in a series on "War and Peace," edited by Uwe Nerlich at Oldenbourg.[27] Kindermann provided the introduction while Morgenthau added a foreword.[28] In his foreword, Nerlich wrote that the problems of war and peace in the present world situation posed "existential questions" for humanity more than they had for previous generations. "Political science is called to address these pressing questions with a realistic clarity" (7). In his introduction, Kindermann constructed a "realist school" composed of Niebuhr and Morgenthau, one that allegedly kept its distance from traditional German *Realpolitik*. Kindermann's interpretation of *Realpolitik* is an important moment in Morgenthau's West German reception. All too often, Kindermann wrote of *Realpolitik*, "in this tradition (*Richtung*) power (*Macht*) was equated with, even exchanged for violence, especially military violence (*Gewalt*)." Both Niebuhr and Morgenthau warned against the "pseudo-realistic military interpretation" of the problem of power. Kindermann's essay attempted to insulate Morgenthau's realism from any "idealizing or naturalistically grounded glorification of state power (*Staatsmacht*)." *Realpolitik* was a mode by which the state sought to become an "organ of national vitality" and a "vehicle of its self-actualization."[29] Kindermann was correct that Morgenthau's realism was not a direct descendant of *Realpolitik*. Both Morgenthau's and Grewe's realism evolved from a transatlantic *Weltpolitik*, for which, however, a conception of the state as an organism, and empire as a form of vitality, were central. Skipping over the fin de siècle contexts, Kindermann removed the taint of empire in the Atlantic world from Morgenthau, framing the "rules of the political art" as a species of political ethics. In Kindermann's hands, Morgenthau was presented as a descendant of the Weber of "Politics as a Vocation" with its dueling ethics—immature conviction and mature responsibility—not the Weber of Wilhelmine imperialism.

In his 1963 foreword, Morgenthau addressed his German readers: "Written in 1947," he lamented, the book was "the fruit of twenty years' experience. It resulted from lonesome and apparently ineffective reflections on the essence of international politics and also how a falsely conceived foreign policy, that of the Western democracies, undoubtedly conjured the horror of totalitarianism and war" (8). Readers had said that the book's lessons were valuable for the United States only in a particular phase of its history, since the lessons had allegedly been learned by Europeans long before. But that was not the case. West Germans needed reminding of the errors committed by German foreign policy makers after the departure of Bismarck.[30] Morgenthau generalized wildly about the entire German national experience:

> The specific German misunderstanding was to a certain extent the opposite of the American. While the US tended to underestimate the significance of power, finding a replacement in vague legalistic and moralistic aspirations, Germany on the other hand shows the propensity to understand power in narrow "material" terms and in practice rely on coercion, above all in its military form. They neglected the more subtle manifestations of power in theory and praxis. The German mistakes were different than the American ones, but they were mistakes nonetheless. So may this book serve as a corrective for German mistakes, as much as it has done for the American ones. (10)[31]

The book was not an immediate success. In May 1965, Kindermann sought to reassure Morgenthau that sales were slow in part because there was only one *Ordinariat* for International Politics in all of West Germany. "I have heard that within the next 2–3 years such *Ordinariate* will be created at Hamburg, Tübingen, Munich and a number of the newly established universities."[32] In June, he noted, the German Association for Political Science had founded a section for international politics, but the section was tiny and marginalized. Kindermann explained that the conditions for the reception of his work were not ideal: "In general, our political scientists are not that intellectually impressive. Figures like Weber, Heller, and Mannheim are long gone. Bergstraesser was the last of the greats." Morgenthau responded well: "What you say about the state of political science in Germany of course explains the lack of immediately audible resonance" of the German translation of *Politics among Nations*. Kindermann echoed Morgenthau's claim in the Foreword: realism was the ideal mediator of extremes. After four decades, when a "power-glorifying *Realpolitik*" dominated German social and political science and historical thinking, the "pendulum" had swung in the opposite direction—"a power-denying moralism. Today it seems to me, that both extremes are beginning to narrow and the basis for a realistic middle-position is becoming visible."[33] The image of realism as a "middle position" echoed Morgenthau's observation made two years before. It also reflects Morgenthau's labored efforts to become a balancer of power considerations against moral ones in his debates with American colleagues. From its beginning—the German Political Science Association was reestablished in West Germany in 1950—political science faced stiff opposition from the more traditional disciplines of philosophy and law. With the exception of the Free University of Berlin, which had two chairs in international politics, there was no chair in the territory of the Federal Republic until 1966/67, and by 1977 some universities in West Germany still had none (204). Kindermann faced an uphill battle to bring Morgenthau home.

When Kindermann assumed the first West German chair in international politics in Munich in 1967, he named his approach "neorealist."[34] He explained that the label meant that neorealists were "clearly but not exclusively shaped by realist thinkers (Niebuhr, Morgenthau, Kennan, Spykman, Schwarzenberger, Lippmann, Herz, Kissinger, Osgood, [and] Tang Tsou)."[35] "[The] other important influences [who] have shaped the posture (*Haltung*) of the neorealist tendency" were Bergstraesser and the foreign policy decision-theorists Richard Snyder, H. Bruck, B. Sapin,

Glenn Paige, and Karl Deutsch. Characteristically for realists writing in the neo-Augustinian tradition like Morgenthau and Niebuhr, he made humility a leading virtue: "For us, 'realism' (*Realismus*) does not constitute a claim to superior knowledge. It is the posture of the will (*Willenshaltung*) that we share." But despite the "will" to share this paradigm, this sensibility—this *Willenshaltung*—with his fellow West Germans, it did not find many supporters in West Germany. Writing in 1980, two experts on IR theory claimed that "as far as we can see, Kindermann, along with his assistants in Munich, seems to be the only one who has explicitly continued using it."[36] They surmised, "At any rate his concept of power politics was not easily applicable to the powerless situation of the Federal Republic of Germany, which perhaps also explains the poor response."[37] Still, by 1969, the political scientist (and future research director of the DGAP) Karl Kaiser wrote in an encyclopedia of international relations, "The approach of the national interest, as Morgenthau developed it, remains the most influential approach in the discipline of international politics . . . This approach . . . is the broadest attempt to date to create a general theory of international politics."[38] But practice was outstripping theory; and thus the demand for new theories. Kaiser's essays from 1970 reveal how Morgenthau's reception in Germany was essentially stillborn. By the time German IR theory was in a position to synchronize, the moment of opportunity had passed. Kindermann's project was out of sync in part because of a crisis of classical realism that was transatlantic. The Munich school of "neorealism" remained relatively marginal for the rest of the discipline's history in the Federal Republic.

Détente, Peace Research, and the Crisis of Classical Realism, 1966–1970

Realist theory entered crisis in Germany just as the missionary liberal anticommunism of the containment policy entered its reductio ad absurdum in Vietnam. Ironically, *Ostpolitik* made realism seem passé even as it emphasized the priority of the two Germanies' national interests and deemphasized ideology. Environmental concerns and the communications revolution of the early 1970s also pointed beyond the nation-state to a world of interdependence in which naked raison d'état was obsolete.

Between 1966 and 1970, as classical realism sank into crisis, in the United States the technocratic optimism characteristic of the early 1960s was losing its luster because of Vietnam.[39] The peace movement was growing, and figures like Morgenthau from the center and Erich Fromm from the left (both German émigrés in the US) challenged the technocratic optimism of the wizards of Armageddon. In 1966, the SPD joined the ruling coalition for the first time in postwar history. While the Social Democrats had been well represented in the bipartisan consensus on *Westbindung* favored by the DGAP, other voices pushed for a broader relaxation of tensions, an *"Entspannung,"* or détente, with the Eastern bloc countries and the USSR. This meant questioning the Hallstein Doctrine and eventually renouncing it. Realism seemed to dictate recognition of the facts on the ground: the GDR wasn't going anywhere. The Schmittian logic of friend-enemy lost favor in the CDU to its "reluctant realists." The meaning of realism was shifting from nonrecognition of the enemy to recognition.[40]

Willy Brandt's 1969 victory encouraged scholars to develop peace research (*Friedensforschung*) into a new intellectual field with strong institutional support. Its leading figure was Ernst-Otto Czempiel (1927–2017), who trained a generation of important researchers in Frankfurt.[41] The peace movement brought a "utopian" perspective into the conversation about realism, and figures of the establishment DGAP like Karl Kaiser moved left. Interdependence became a buzzword for both American and German security thinkers. Thus, by the time Kindermann founded his school of neorealism, he was forced to mediate between two camps—utopian and realist—rather than assuming the more orthodox realist view he had championed five years earlier.[42] Émigrés such as Karl Deutsch and John Herz contributed to the broad shifts in the discussion from East-West conflict to North-South and ecology.[43]

In 1966, a "Great Coalition" formed between the two major postwar West German parties. The CDU's Kurt Kiesinger invited Social Democrat Brandt to join his ruling coalition as foreign minister. The DGAP had been questioning one of the linchpins of *Westbindung*, the Hallstein Doctrine, since September. Karl Carstens noted that the "dam" that denied recognition to the DDR was weakening; its breaking "appears only a matter of time."[44] On December 12, 1966, Kiesinger attended a meeting of the DGAP's study group where the Hallstein Doctrine was discussed, and the next day he declared Bonn's readiness to "improve the relationship to our eastern neighbors, and where conditions allow, to also rebuild diplomatic relations" (206). Over the next three years of the coalition, but more intensively after the SPD won the 1969 elections, the West German government pursued a policy of "*Entspannung*," or détente, with East Germany. This was made possible and underpinned by the decision of the Nixon administration to pursue détente between the US and the USSR.[45] At the same time, France's 1966 exit from NATO united command raised questions about the transatlantic relationship. As observers at the Council on Foreign Relations in New York worried about the slowing pace of European integration, Stanley Hoffmann at Harvard summed up the mood: "There is no Atlantic partnership, and no drive for European integration."[46] The advent of the SPD-FDP coalition marked the beginning of a hopeful chapter for West German progressives. The success of negotiations with the Soviet Union over German-German relations seemed to confirm the practicality of Brandt's *Ostpolitik* and the aspiration to reduce the threat of war in Europe. In October 1969, the Brandt-Scheel government came to power. On October 28, the West German government acknowledged for the first time that there were "two states" in Germany, both of which were legally valid. The early success of détente in Germany rendered obsolete the principles of the Hallstein Doctrine. Vietnam symbolized the murderous consequences of the goal of "containing" Communism on a global scale. Technocratic elites lost credibility and moral reputation. Realism appeared unhinged from the higher moral concerns it had always claimed to serve. As a new generation demanded answers to fundamental questions, classical realism entered a sustained crisis of legitimacy that endured until the waning of détente in the mid-1970s.

A first sign of questioning of realist orthodoxy appeared in the arena of arms control. The decade had begun with optimism about achieving nuclear balance and "stability" among German and American strategists, but skepticism about the ability to fight "limited nuclear war" grew. Could the nuclear arms race be managed, or did it represent the specter of death, a form of organized insanity? Morgenthau challenged the views of Herman Kahn's *On Thermonuclear War* (1960), which considered limited nuclear wars to be winnable. In 1961, Morgenthau gave a lecture in which he insisted that the shadow of the bomb had set international relations a critical task: a merger of the "realistic and utopian approaches to politics in general and to international relations in particular."[47] The "unprecedented revolutionary force" of nuclear weapons compelled international theorists to join the ranks of "great political utopians" whom he credited with both starting from a "realistic analysis of the status quo" and suggesting ways to move beyond it (76–77). This represented a major shift from both the substance and rhetoric of his work of the 1950s.[48] In the 1940s and 1950s, Morgenthau argued that nuclear weapons had revolutionized warfare, not international relations per se. Influenced by Karl Jaspers's dire warnings in *The Future of Mankind* (1958), Morgenthau developed a substantial critique of nuclear weaponry and the arms race, especially the theorists Edward Teller ("limited nuclear war") and Herman Kahn (*Thinking about the Unthinkable,* 1962) (146–49).[49] In 1967, Kindermann was granted the first West German chair in international politics. Just as Kindermann finally acquired the resources to develop a German version of IR realism, the meaning of realism was becoming less clear and more contested. Morgenthau was questioning the premises that had guided him in the 1950s. Kindermann recognized that the ground was shifting beneath his feet and followed Morgenthau in revaluing perspectives the two men had once derided as utopian.

They were not alone. Morgenthau's fellow German émigré, Erich Fromm, contributed an essay to the 1960 *Daedalus* volume in which he advocated unilateral disarmament.[50] Fromm had authored a book called *The Sane Society* (1955), which became the source of the name of an influential citizens' group: SANE (later SANE-FREEZE). Fromm was not the only member of the neo-Marxist Frankfurt School to have an influence on the transatlantic discussion of nuclear strategy and the Cold War. In the context of his participation in the antiwar movement against the Vietnam War, Marcuse developed a concept of "positive peace" that envisioned something more than the mere absence of war.[51] Frankfurt School perspectives commingled with ideas from the American peace movement to seed the budding German field of "peace research" (*Friedensforschung*). Its leading figure, Ernst-Otto Czempiel (1927–2017), helped reanimate utopian perspectives by lending his authority to the young people's questions and demands. He had spent the 1965/66 year at Columbia University. The peace movement became transatlantic, allowing American and German thought to cross-fertilize. If the DGAP was the first incubator of a "transatlantic" identity for strategic thought, the peace movement was its successor. As critique circulated across the Atlantic, the crisis of classical realism grew in both countries.

On July 26, 1970, the Peace Research Institute in Frankfurt was created, the first such institute in West Germany. Relentlessly opposed by the CDU in Hesse from the beginning (17), the Peace Research Institute Frankfurt (PRIF) nurtured a generation of important scholars of international relations. In 1968, Czempiel and his assistant, Egbert Jahn, initiated a national organization, the Working Group on Peace and Conflict Research.[52] After studies at the Humboldt University in Berlin in 1947–48, and in Mainz, 1948–53, he became assistant to Eugon Kogon at the Technischen Hochschule Darmstadt (1957–64), and wrote his *Habilitation* thesis on American foreign policy in the postwar period. For the first generation of German peace researchers—Dieter Senghaas, Klaus Jürgen Gantzel, Egbert Jahn, and Volker Rittberger—he was an important mentor. In 1969, Czempiel also published an anthology of essays on the scope and methods of international relations. Nearly all of the texts reproduced there were authored by Americans.[53] Czempiel thus furthered the work of intellectual synchronization of American and German strategic thought, just as Uwe Nerlich had done with his *War and Peace* series. After four years as professor of international politics at Marburg (1966–70), Czempiel moved to Frankfurt (1970–92).

In a July 1968 letter to the state government of Hesse, Czempiel argued that Germany lagged behind its peer countries in the industrial democracies of the North Atlantic. Aided by a speech of Gustav Heinemann on the thirtieth anniversary of the outbreak of WWII, on September 1, 1969, Hesse's new minister president, Albert Osswald, called on the state's universities to develop a "work and research program for peace research."[54] In June 1970, the Hessian minister of culture convened a preparatory scientific commission to outline the scope of research and work methods. It included figures with national reputations such as Jürgen Habermas,

Wolfgang Abendroth, Iring Fetscher, and Eugon Kogon, as well as a younger generation of the German Left: Klaus Jürgen Gantzel, Gerhard Brandt, Theo Hermann, Claus Koch, Hans Nicklas, and Dieter Senghaas. Fetscher and Senghaas were already active in Frankfurt, working to bring "together the more recent American approaches to peace research and the traditions of the Frankfurt School for research purposes" (16). Czempiel was the commission's driving force. Czempiel began on the German Left but after his long march through the institutions—the PRIF and the University of Frankfurt—arrived at a progressive liberalism shorn of its radical edge. As we will see shortly, his career forms a kind of mirror image of the DGAP's Karl Kaiser, since it was Kaiser who helped legitimate peace research in the eyes of more conservative thinkers with a major survey of the state of the field supported by the Volkswagen Foundation.[55]

In September 1968, Austrian radio convened an extraordinary conference in Salzburg, the transcripts of which were published two years later as *Peace in the Nuclear Age: A Controversy between Realists and Utopians*.[56] The participants included a range of European scholars, but the event's major protagonists were American and German. On the more conservative "realist" side were Stefan Possony, then of the Hoover Institution at Stanford University; Hans Speier of the New School for Social Research and RAND; Morgenthau; and Kindermann. Representing the "utopian" or antirealist perspectives were Herbert Marcuse, Erich Fromm, and French sociologist Lucien Goldmann; Austrian newspaper editors Gunther Nennig and Ernst Fischer; theologian Hans-Eckehard Bahr; and writer and "futurologist" Robert Jungk.[57] Edited by Austrian radio journalist Oskar Schatz, the volume records nuanced explorations of the categories of utopian and realist and possibilities for synthesis akin to those Morgenthau had gestured at in 1961. As Schatz explained, the utopians in the group believed "*Realpolitik*" could at best deliver "negative peace," a peace that does not address the origins of conflicts.

> Has the condition of nuclear age, which puts total power over man's future in his own hands, erased the boundary between reality and utopia, such that only utopia can guarantee man's survival? . . . While the so-called realists expect to secure and maintain peace

primarily through the techniques and instruments of classical politics of power and interests, the so-called utopians (*Utopisten*) mistrust this type of *Realpolitik*.[58]

As Schatz writes, we succumb to a false "sense of reality" (*Realitätsinn*) that neglects the historical-social dimensions of peace. Peace research "cannot be the exclusive domain of a theory of international politics," but must address the domestic causes of war using multiple disciplinary tools. Peace research otherwise risked "degenerating" into technocratic scenario-planning (9).

In their essays, Fromm and Marcuse depicted realism as an ideology of the status quo. As Marcuse put it, "The realist confuses the given reality with reality: That is, I believe, the essence of realism" (11). As Kurt Grüssing, a student and editor of the Austrian journal *Neues Forum*, explained, the "so-called 'realists' . . . lack the capacity to think in terms of the possible." The "atomic sandbox-games (*Sandkastenspiele*) they rehearse, only permit us to hear the past" (209). "The maintenance of peace is a cynical misnomer. Because no peace exists, not only because we're in war in Vietnam and Czechoslovakia, but that for the majority of mankind, conditions dominate that in reality are war-like ones" (210). Vladmir Horsky, a sociologist from Prague, echoed the sentiment: "[In contrast to the realists] we have ambitions that go beyond 'preventing nuclear war between the US and USSR'" (221). The designated "utopians" concurred that peace meant more than managing the balance of terror.

Morgenthau responded archly: "If one wishes to speak of 'realism' (*Realismus*) one must above all speak of respect for facts (*Respekt vor den Tatsachen*)" (255). Still, Morgenthau concurred with the other critics of limited nuclear war who referred to it as a "Clausewitzian illusion": "Nuclear weapons, if used as instruments of national politics, would destroy the real goal of politics as much as the warring parties themselves. Therefore, as a means of national politics they are unnecessary" (35).

Kindermann also struck a rather imperious tone. Marcuse had not taken into account the permanence of conflict: "I can scarcely imagine even in utopian fantasy a human existence without conflicts" (202). He continued: "It is the thankless task of the so-called 'Realists' to depict the human condition, an unhappy one because it demonstrates the impotence of the will to progress and peace faced with the force of established power. It is naturally very easy to say that the realists, the atomic theorists, the war theorists, engage in sandbox games." But if that were true, should Khrushchev and Kennedy have been able to sleep through the Cuba crisis undisturbed (211)?

Neither the utopians nor the realists formed united fronts, however. Indeed, the labels themselves had long been an obstacle to the clear exchange of ideas. Disagreements between Fromm and Marcuse showed that there was no one "utopian" line. Fromm labeled the ideas of Marcuse about the "new men" "vague and for the most part rhetorical" (227). Fromm also crossed the increasingly blurred battle lines when he agreed with Morgenthau that the inherent goodness of man had been overstated (244). Akin to Marcuse's contemporary celebration of the "new sensibility" of American and German youth aroused by global struggles, Fromm similarly found inspiration in American voters rallying around Senator Eugene McCarthy's antiwar presidential campaign. Fromm argued that the "only realistic path" and "hope for peace is in the mobilization of all citizens who share a fundamental "humanistic" stance, to protest "in the name of life against bureaucratization, against war, against the automatisation of life" (243). Peace depended on more than respect for the facts, the management of interstate competition, or the strategy of nuclear war. "What we need is a new stance (*Haltung*) . . . a combination of cynical realism (*zynischer Realismus*) and faith, an avoidance of all sentimentality, of all irrationality, bound up with faith in the real possibilities" (245). Fromm countered Kindermann's realist *Haltung* with an alternative of his own.

The Vietnam War scrambled Morgenthau's priorities for "realism." Policies that he detested were being carried out in the name of a realist orthodoxy that had escaped his control.[59] Morgenthau visited Vietnam for first time in late 1955, the year after the fall of the French garrison at Dien Bien Phu and the signing of the Geneva Accords. As early as 1956, he was raising concerns about the wisdom of the US commitment to South Vietnamese leader Ngo Dinh Diem. In 1964, Morgenthau became the most visible former government official to take a public stand against the war. His value to the antiwar movement was widely recognized. From activists to the politicians who were quietly recalibrating their policy options, "they believed that opposition on the part of a Cold War realist to anti-Communist diplomacy would carry a special weight in shaping the United States' diplomatic priorities."[60] Now it was President Johnson, not the Wilsonians who had bedeviled him in the early 1950s, whom he damned as a "crusading moralist."[61] By 1965, he was publicly rebuking the Johnson administration for living in a fantasy world and succumbing to psychopathology. But for all his farsightedness and moral passion, Morgenthau still worried about the problems of "saving face." In a revealing correspondence with Martin Herz, a US embassy official in Saigon, Morgenthau sought to explain the logic of his antiwar position. He wrote, "My attitude towards our involvement in Vietnam is a logical application of one of the principles of diplomacy formulated in the first edition of *Politics Among Nations* in 1948, to wit: 'Never put yourself in a position from which you cannot retreat without losing face and from which you cannot advance without grave risks.' This is exactly what we have been doing."[62] Morgenthau saw consistency in his realist opposition to the war, but his denunciations of the war planners as fantasists and crusading moralists attest to a discourse in flux.

Perhaps sensitive to the price Morgenthau had paid for his criticisms of the war in Vietnam, Kindermann referred to the "so-called realists" and "so-called utopians" in his concluding remarks. The quotation marks indicate the waning of the "high realist" orthodoxy Morgenthau had championed in the 1950s. Kindermann's diplomatic suggestion to synthesize and transcend the positions of utopianism and realism passed without objection from his former teacher: "The realists are charged with missing the constructively new, possible, and necessary." But "the utopians are accused of a posture (*Haltung*) that is so tied to the future and to hope that it refuses to deal with the here and now" problems of the atomic age other than to negate the given. Both "progress-oriented future planning" and "'realistic' analysis of power-political structures of the present" are critical; a political science must be "as based in reality as it is future-oriented." The aspiration to transcend inherited power structures represents a "Promethean [effort] to make man the master of his own history," Kindermann wrote, but "even as Prometheus sought to grab fire, he did not attempt it floating ghost-like in the clouds, but as a man with both feet on the earth."[63] Kindermann thus played the role of mediator and reconciler.

Kindermann's diplomatic approach to the clash of realist and utopian perspectives on the Cold War illustrates that the old consensus—the one the DGAP had forged on the basis of *Westbindung*, the Hallstein Doctrine, and technocratic arms control—was critically weakened. Classical realism would have to yield to some new dialectical synthesis of the "realistic" and the "utopian." E.H. Carr's famous refusal of the utopian was obsolete.

"Interdependence" as Critique of Realism

Mounting doubts about the "realism" of arms control and the sanity of "mutually assured destruction," the term Robert McNamara coined in 1967, were one source of the transatlantic crisis of classical realism at the end of the 1960s. The second, more academic source arose from within the fields of political science and international relations.[64] By decade's end, a younger generation "with the political and social reformist ambitions of the leftist social democrats and the liberals" represented a majority of the profession.[65] This generational shift coincided with the end of twenty years of CDU rule, together creating an opening for new perspectives to gain traction.

Two articles published in 1963 addressing the relationship between foreign and domestic policy prefigured realism's destabilization by perspectives then considered "utopian."[66] These articles represented a return to the historian Eckart Kehr's challenge to the "primacy of foreign policy" in the late 1920s, with his groundbreaking critique of the domestic forces propelling German naval construction and imperial *Weltpolitik* in the 1890s.[67] Around the same time, in the United States, William Appleman Williams was generating his own version of the *Primat der Innenpolitik* (primacy of domestic policy), in his seminal 1959 work, *The Tragedy of American Diplomacy*.[68] The fifth, sixth, and seventh congresses of the International Politics section focused exclusively on this subject. Czempiel, still at Marburg, presided over each congress. Gathering critiques of classical realist notions of sovereignty that were presented at the German Political Science Association conferences from 1966–69, he published *The Anachronistic Idea of Sovereignty*. Contributions from scholars residing in the US—James Rosenau, Karl Deutsch, and Wolfram Hanrieder—illustrate the transatlantic character of the conversation. Klaus Jürgen Gantzel expressly resumed the discussion inaugurated by Kehr forty years earlier, in his essay on how domestic and external forces combine to escalate the contemporary arms race.[69]

If Czempiel can be seen as bringing the peace researchers of the left wing of German political science to the mainstream of policy debate, the political scientist Karl Kaiser moved the center to the left during this period. Kaiser, a member of the DGAP since 1962, was based at Harvard University from 1963–68, and became an affiliate of London's International Institute for Strategic Studies in 1966. From 1963–65, he worked as a research associate for Henry Kissinger's Project on Germany.[70] He served as an advisor to Chancellors Willy Brandt and Helmut Schmidt, and was director of the DGAP's research institute from 1973–2003. In April 1969, the DGAP and Chatham House co-hosted a conference in London that Kaiser and Czempiel both attended. Kaiser's presentation, published subsequently as "Interdependence and Autonomy: The Federal Republic of Germany and Great Britain in the Multinational Environment,"[71] offered what one historian of the period names a powerful "critique of the traditional 'realistic' (*realistisch*) idea of a foreign policy centred on power-driven nation-states."[72] Kaiser argued that "new forms of political interaction are gaining in significance . . . direct horizontal transactions between the social actors of different nation-states which do not control ruling institutions but strongly influence them" (51). The traditional view of "'international politics' postulated sharp boundaries between the environment and the purportedly 'sovereign,' state actor," but its many linkages (*Verflechtungen*) with the outside world challenged the idea of the state as "walled off." "*Verflechtung*," meaning interdependence and interconnection, and implying interlocking and entwinement, is a central concept in Kaiser and Czempiel's 1969 writings. Kaiser's reflections recall the contemporaneous discussion between "realists" and "utopians" at Salzburg, and their dueling conceptions of what "respect for the facts" entailed. Endorsing the view of John Herz that nuclear weapons have "broken through the hard shell of the territorial state," (55) Kaiser wrote that the permeability of sovereignty in the nuclear age generated a shared will to survive that is a force of international solidarity.

The historian Hans-Peter Schwarz, like Kindermann a student of Bergstraesser's, also contributed to the 1969 conference sponsored by the DGAP and Chatham House. His essay "The Role of the Federal Republic in International Society" echoed the points Czempiel and Kaiser had made, and contributed to the rising tide that produced a crisis for classical realism in Germany.[73] What distinguished Schwarz's essay was the way it questioned the category of the "great power," a concept that predates but becomes especially important to discussions of realism in the Atlantic world beginning at the turn of the twentieth century. Indeed, his reflections corroborate the argument made in chapter 1 that German elites in the two decades before the First World War were preoccupied with maintaining their "rank" among the other European powers (225). Today, "Germany is no longer a world power (*Weltmacht*)—but what is it then?" Schwarz asked. In lieu of concerns about rank, Schwarz proposed a different understanding of West Germany's "role." West Germans should no longer measure themselves in terms of "status groups like '*Großmächte*' or '*Mittelmächte*' but rather through a functional understanding of their role, in English what one calls a consciousness of 'interdependence'" (227). While many experts at the time, such as Stanley Hoffmann, depicted international society as comprising three "classes"—"superpowers," "middle powers," and "small powers" (228)—Schwarz observed that the categories themselves were inadequate for describing countries that were economically strong but "geopolitically handicapped" like West Germany and Japan (230). Comparisons that purported to measure power objectively missed key differences in "strategic position, self-understanding, foreign policy style, and room to maneuver" (231). The "so-called freedom to act of a state is nothing other than the greater or lesser chance to freely choose its main roles" (235). "The most difficult question faced by a state that acts on the international stage consists in the numerous roles which are given to [it], and how [it] may play them without assuming the sad figure of a schizophrenic international-legal subject" (234). That West Germans chose one role above all for themselves—that of *homo economicus*—has been overlooked (237). Should the Germans choose to define its roles

"relative" to different "issue-areas," it would shed absolutist constructions of identity such as *"Weltmacht"* or *"Großmacht"* (238). Beginning
in the mid-1960s, many discussions at the DGAP turned on the question
of "whether the Federal Republic stands last in the circle of the [great
powers] *(an letzter Stelle im Kreise der Großen)* or first among the [small
powers]."[74] From this perspective, Schwarz's reflections represented a
significant break. With his claim that power was not objectively measurable, Schwarz challenged one of the foundations of Atlantic realism, the
practices of imperial comparison that were important from Ratzel and
Mahan to Haushofer, Schmitt, Grewe, and Morgenthau.

Westbindung in the 1970s and 1980s and the Renaissance of Realist Fundamentalism

The question of whether the new "interdependence" of nations had rendered classical realist notions of state sovereignty obsolete caught the
attention of Grewe in Brussels, where he was the ambassador to NATO
from 1963–70. In these same years, he composed a lengthy book, *The
Play of Forces in World Politics*, published in 1970, which he referred to,
modestly, as his "leisure-time hobby."[75] In it, Grewe described the 1960s
as an era of astonishingly rapid technical change and shrinking of global
space. Generational and intellectual changes would also produce changes
in the "style of world politics" (344–46). "Forms of thought and action
in the time of the Congress of Vienna are not satisfactory any more in
the technical and intellectual world of our time" (247). The division of
Europe would continue through the 1970s. The Soviet reaction to the
Prague Spring made clear that it would not permit its control of Eastern
Europe to erode. Grewe argued that as the preponderance of the superpowers continued to grow, the gap between the traditional great powers
(Großmächte) and the middle states would narrow. Yet he noted that the
meaning of the rank order of powers had shifted: the superpowers would
not find it easy to translate their nuclear superiority into political influence
(354–55). By discussing world politics through the lens of the "rank order
of powers," Grewe emphasized the continuing salience of the framework
of imperial comparison. Neither détente nor economic interdependence
had changed the fundamentals.

Grewe soberly reminded readers that "a pacifist age cannot be expected." We would continue to "live with the bomb," as with a sword of Damocles, and "fear of the bomb will remain a dominant factor in world politics." Grewe was concerned that the media's use of the term "détente" missed its realistic core: "Détente is no goal in itself, but rather, a means to an end. It offers no solutions, rather it creates the conditions for the solution of contentious questions (*Streitfragen*) and conflicts of interest. It is no end goal but rather a stage on the path towards [peace]." He concluded, contra the *Ostpolitiker*, "Disarmament cannot precede détente: only the reverse is worth discussing" (339).

In the US, Morgenthau made nearly the identical argument.[76] *Ostpolitik* was hardly an unqualified success, said Morgenthau. He wrote that its effect was "to minimize if not expel the influence of the United States from Western Europe—to emasculate NATO; to isolate West Germany and then to unify Germany under Russian auspices." Earlier that year, Morgenthau had argued that technology transfer from West Germany to the USSR could be construed as a "new Rapallo," a reference to the German-Soviet rapprochement of the 1920s. He fretted that these agreements would weaken the US–West German strategic partnership and play into Soviet ambitions for a "radically new alignment of forces in Europe." John Herz, for one, found him unduly alarmist: "Hans Morgenthau perceives such a risk in Soviet détente efforts now. I cannot agree."[77] In his writings of 1974, Morgenthau worried that if "Western Europe may be absorbed, nation by nation into the Soviet orbit," a process of "Finlandization" would result.[78] By contrast, when the October 1973 war broke out in the Middle East, the US appealed to the USSR to approach the conflict "in the spirit of détente."[79] "The idea that the Soviet Union would all of a sudden forget about power politics . . . that it would allow itself to be pushed out of the Middle East in the spirit of détente, was of course an absolute illusion" (75). He added, "Americans have a tendency to take the desired end result of a policy to be inherent in the policy itself," Morgenthau opined. "'Détente' is as abstract and meaningless as the concepts the USSR has [used to pose] as the defender of peace or security or peaceful coexistence . . . all the other similarly abstract concepts which the Soviet Union has floated in order to muddle our thinking" (78). He concluded:

"How vaporous, to the point of lack of meaning, the concept has become."[80] Morgenthau's skepticism of détente represents another turning point in the realist revival. It also problematizes the general interpretation of Morgenthau as "uneasy Realist" and progressive reformer.[81]

Grewe also worried that each of the four most popular prognoses for the 1970s—convergence, de-ideologization, introversion, and change in the axes of power—offered too rosy a prognosis of superpower détente. The idea that the Communist and capitalist blocs would converge was "illusionary wishful thinking"; de-ideologization was a "fantasy" because the Soviet elite could not do away with Communist ideology without giving up its own basis of legitimacy and domination. Further, the notion of the USSR "turning inwards" in the 1970s was improbable for any superpower ("A superpower, which indulges itself with too long a breathing spell, cannot remain a superpower"), Grewe asserted axiomatically. And finally, Grewe rejected the idea which had been important for Brandt that North-South inequalities should be a priority for the North Atlantic powers: "the north-south opposition/polarity would not supercede and replace the east-west axis but will only enlarge it" (358). According to an influential report by Carl Friedrich von Weizsäcker, in the next two decades a major hunger crisis would occur in the developing world and cause "major destabilizing effects" on countries not directly affected. The decisive question of world order in the 1970s was therefore to what extent the superpowers could cooperate in "coming to terms with poverty, hunger and underdevelopment but also the maintenance of peace" (359). Grewe predicted that the superpowers would continue to compete but would likely have to share responsibility for international security.[82] The nuclear arms race could be managed, but "no illusion should exist that the gaping chasm between East and West will not persist." The USSR, he insisted, was not a conservative power but remained a revolutionary "expansionist world power (*expansive Weltmacht*) which will seek to exploit every situation of instability and every power vacuum (*Machtvakuum*) to augment its own power position (*Machtstellung*) and to frustrate the West" (361). In the late 1970s, therefore, Grewe and Morgenthau spoke the same language and arrived at very similar conclusions about Soviet power.

For decades, Hans-Peter Schwarz (1934–2017) was a highly visible writer in West Germany, and an influential professor of political science and contemporary history.[83] In 1973, Schwarz lauded the appearance, three years before, of Grewe's *Spiel der Kräfte in der Weltpolitik*. Schwarz's article exemplifies the "change in tendency" (*Tendenzwende*), the term used to describe the conservative backlash to the reform currents that had come to power with Brandt in 1969. The ideological shift was reflected in the election of Helmut Schmidt in 1974, and Helmut Kohl's rise to national prominence in 1973. It also illustrated Schwarz's turn away from the more critical and reflective stance he had adopted in his critical analysis of Germany as a "great power" four years before. Most important, it revealed the different tempos of realism in the US and Germany. Intellectuals who sought to synchronize realism across the Atlantic had to contend with the unevenness of intellectual development.

But Schwarz's argument that the book was a "late German echo" of the realism of Hans Morgenthau and other classical realists raised important questions that shaped this study. Grewe's respect for historical approaches distinguished him from the newer scientisms that had grown fashionable in the field of international politics in the 1960s.[84] In Grewe's "decisive plaidoyer for the 'realistic' (*realistische*) approach in the realm of international relations," Schwarz found an unsolved problem of the Federal Republic's history: "Clearly endebted to the thought-style and terminology of the 'realistic school,' (he names Hans J. Morgenthau. George Kennan, Kenneth W. Thompson, and Raymond Aron) . . . it is worth pondering why this line of thought, despite favorable conditions in West Germany, could not gain a foothold" (123). Noting the belated translations of Morgenthau's major work, and George Schwarzenberger's *Power Politics*, Schwarz lamented that they had "scarcely influenced the political and theoretical discussion in the Federal Republic."[85] E.H. Carr's *The Twenty Years' Crisis* was still untranslated at the time of his writing. Kindermann had struggled to find an audience for Morgenthau in the mid-1960s, running out of time as peace studies approaches became ascendant in political science. Schwarz's plaudits for Grewe as an outlier corroborate our picture of the loneliness of the realist in early 1970s West Germany.

Schwarz also offered a convincing explanation for the failure of German thought to sync with the American discussion: "An essential role was played by the fact that the concepts *Realpolitik* and *Machtpolitik* aroused, on the basis of the experiences with National Socialism, associations as unfavorable as the concepts nation or *Volk* in other contexts." Despite reassurances by Morgenthau and others of this school that *"Realismus"* had nothing to do with the *"Machtstaatspolitik"* that found many spokesmen in Wilhelmine Germany and the Third Reich, the demands of close integration with the Western world made this type of foreign policy theory "unsuitable."[86] Schwarz's narrative helps explain why Kindermann felt he needed to banish *Realpolitik* from the realist canon and Americanize realism's image. Schwarz argued that West Germany lacked the essential preconditions for a realist school to take hold. In Britain and the United States, the "realistic" school understood itself as "the necessary corrective to the exuberance of utopianism." But in West Germany, "progressive-liberal foreign policy ideologies and concepts" never dominated. While these currents were "not without influence" in Germany before 1933,[87] it is "only since the beginning of the 1960s that we find in the parties, the universities and in the public sphere something like a response to pent-up demand for progressive-liberal ideology and activity, which displays all the recognizable characteristics of the idea-syndrome (*Ideensyndrom*) familiar to us from England and the USA" (124). Among these characteristics, Schwarz included, "anthropological optimism, sympathy for all attempts to secure peace through international organization, treaties and agreements, anti-imperialism, anticolonialism, pacifism, mistrust of the military, alliances, the munitions industry, and all types of *Machtpolitik*, trust in the power of the good example, and unilateral concessions" (124). It was "symptomatic," therefore, that just when "elements" of this foreign policy worldview "have for the first time begun to prevail," a book such as Grewe's appeared that "reject[ed] some of the basic premises of this tendency and marked out a counterposition" (124). Schwarz's psychologizing and pathologizing of these ideas as a "syndrome" was tendentious and unconvincing. He also overstated the hegemony of the peace camp in West German debates. Schwarz's description of Grewe as a "belated German echo" of American realism overlooked the realism of the DGAP and the importance of Grewe and Hallstein in the Adenauer chancellorship. It also sundered Grewe neatly from his complicitous career in the Third Reich. But his review contained an important truth: realism's return to Germany was halting and delayed by the ascendance of competing ideas on the liberal and left side of the political spectrum.

Schwarz's championing of Grewe made sense. The year 1973 was the nadir of *Westbindung*. SALT I was signed in May 1972, and the German-German Basic Treaty in December. Since 1970, Schwarz worried, as Morgenthau and Grewe had, that European Security Conference negotiations that began in 1973 could lead to Western Europe's "Finlandization."[88] "Successful as it was, detente's high-wire act did not salve divisions within the Atlantic Alliance; instead it raised the specter of a hyperpower 'condominium' from which the Europeans would be excluded."[89] Denmark, Ireland, and Great Britain joined the European Economic Community. US diplomats, for their part, worried that the West had entered a "transitional stage" in which pressures from détente, European integration, and the end of Bretton Woods might break the alliance apart. Kissinger's strategic response, an initiative of 1973 called the "Year of Europe"—which aimed at a new comprehensive "Atlantic Charter" spanning military, monetary, trade, and energy policy—was, in the words of one historian, "a dud" (156).[90]

In 1974, a scandal involving an East German spy in the chancellor's office brought down the Brandt government. Brandt's replacement with Helmut Schmidt stanched the bleeding that détente maximalists and critical peace research had inflicted on establishment notions of *Westbindung*.[91] As he put it, *Westbindung* had never "seriously been placed into question by Eastern pressure"; it was the "guilt feelings" (*Schuldgefühle*) of Western elites that had posed the real difficulty (333). Reiterating the argument he made in his 1973 review of Grewe, Schwarz expressed irritation about the "syndrome" of liberal ideas of foreign policy that dominated the left wing of the SPD (334). These ideas derived from an emotional posture, in many ways the opposite of the "sober" *Haltung* that Kindermann and Morgenthau had made de rigueur. Schwarz named this *Haltung* the "deep-rooted longing (*Sehnsucht*) for international harmony," recycling ideas that exercised Schmitt in the 1920s, Carr in the

1930s, and Morgenthau in the 1940s. But if Schwarz complained of the hegemony of these ideas in 1973, just two years later, he was more sanguine toward them. Schwarz concluded his 1975 discussion of the Federal Republic's Western orientation by emphasizing the "tenacity" of the idea (337). "Despite some of the escapades at the beginning of the 'new Ostpolitik'," when the irrational "enthusiasm for an 'all-European peace order' was at its greatest," even then, the SPD "understood itself as part of the Western convoy" (336). Pacifist strategies of unilateral disarmament, Schwarz continued, were successfully sidelined and contained by the SPD's acceptance of the American arms control school and its commitment to the necessity of a "balance of power idea" (335). Despite the drift that Kissinger and Nixon feared, Germany's orientation to the Atlantic Alliance remained intact.

But Schwarz's 1975 declaration of victory over the pacifists was premature. A decade later he still found it necessary to write a book on the Germans' "forgetfulness of power," updating his plaidoyer for realism. He could not have foreseen how Schmidt's commitments to *Westbindung* would undo him in the Euromissile crisis of 1979–81, and lead to the fall of the SPD-FDP coalition in 1982.[92] The Brandt government, as we have seen, directed considerable resources to the work of institutes of "peace research" in West Germany in the 1970s.[93] When Karl Kaiser was elected chair of the board of trustees of the DGFK in 1971, he envisioned a continuation of the agenda of "classical peace research," a tradition characterized by Jeffrey Herf as a "liberal, social democratic, and 'dovish' perspective on inter-state conflicts . . . focused on arms control and limitation, mediation and negotiation, international organizations, and foreign aid" (186). Over the course of the decade, the DGFK supported the publication of nearly a hundred books and over three hundred articles but hardly any focused on Soviet foreign and security policy.[94] By 1980, however, Kaiser resigned from his position because, according to Herf, it had become a "vehicle of 'critical peace research' and had failed to follow the transitional, more reformist strategy he advocated in 1970" (186).[95] By then, the state's network of peace research institutes was militantly opposed to Schmidt's interpretation of *Westbindung*. When 250,000 people demonstrated against the NATO missile deployments in Bonn on October

10, 1981, it was the largest demonstration in West Germany's history. The rejection of NATO's vision of *Westbindung* by a large percentage of the SPD (against Schmidt's will) convinced the FDP's leader Hans-Dietrich Genscher to resign as foreign minister, and the FDP to align with Kohl's CDU. After Kohl was elected, the Bundestag voted in favor of the missiles. The guerillas won the battle but lost the war.

In March 1980, the CDU held a conference to discuss "the new realism" necessary to steer the nation beyond the anti-NATO sentiment that had prevailed in the Euromissile affair. The proceedings were subsequently published as *The New Realism: Foreign Policy after Iran and Afghanistan*.[96] In his introduction, Kohl explained the volume's rationale: "The Soviet invasion of Afghanistan raises new and radical questions which in the past ten years have been tabooed, especially the question of the political and geographical boundaries of détente, the goals and perspectives of the Soviet Union" (8). He noted the rise of anti-American sentiment and asked, "Do the Germans no longer seek their future, unconditionally, in the Western community? One cannot take these questions seriously enough" (9). Kohl called for a paradigm shift. The new situation "demands a new realism in international politics, one which is characterized by a sober (*nüchterne*) recognition of the changed situation," as well as fidelity to certain ideals and values: "peace, freedom, human rights and more social justice in the world" (11). In his essay, Kohl wrote that "we are entering a decade in which the element of power will again play a leading role" (227). It is no surprise to find Grewe among the included authors. Grewe's rhetoric belongs to the same subculture of Atlantic realist discourse as that of Kohl, Kindermann, and Schwarz.

In his essay and others from the same period (1980–82) discussed below, Grewe assumed the role of an elder statesman vindicated by the collapse of détente and persistence of the Cold War. The world-political situation at the beginning of the 1980s "entered a new stage," Grewe asserted. The invasion of Afghanistan threatened control of the Gulf region, and therefore constituted an "existential question" of survival: the avoidance of economic "strangulation" (72). Like previous crises in Berlin, Hungary, Cuba, and Prague, this threatened the "lifeblood (*Lebensnerv*) of the Western world" (72). Hopes embodied in *Entspannungspolitik* since the late 1960s that the East-West conflict would diminish, were disappointed.[97] "No one can any longer avert one's eyes from the fact that the West has allowed severe deficits to develop during the years of *Entspannungspolitik,* ones that are difficult to correct" (81). Using the metaphor of continental collision that he borrowed from Kissinger, Grewe wrote: "For the first time in history, economic, political and military power no longer coincide, as Kissinger has stated, we live in an epoch of tectonic shifts" (79). Long-term tendencies pointed in a different direction from the present conjuncture: though the economic and technological factors that favored the West continued, we have arrived "at the uncomfortable conclusion that there is no substitute for military power" (80). In an essay published in 1982, Grewe expressed optimism nonetheless: "We stand at a critical turning point in the development of world politics: America has been healed of its Vietnam-Watergate syndrome; it has become more sober (*nüchterner*), freer of illusions and readier to act" (19).[98] But a good outcome is not guaranteed: "Either the West allows things to drift, i.e., it allows the intra-Atlantic differences to proliferate and the military balance to worsen. Then in short order there will be more Afghanistans and the West will experience a rapid decline in power." We can't just preach détente, Grewe concluded, when our "adversary takes every opportunity to alter the global balance of power" (20).

Surveying a range of historical precedents that "might serve the present," Grewe selected the 1907 Anglo-Russian agreement on Persia and Afghanistan as the most suitable model for managing superpower cooperation and competition. Spheres of influence and interest played an important role in the decade before World War I in Central Asia. It could be a model again today. "I'm the last person to take pleasure in this idea," Grewe wrote, "but whether we like the forms of world politics or not, we have to reckon with the realities of power politics, not just in Europe but in Asia and Africa too." Grewe suggested that while the actual wording of the agreement was obsolete, the "fundamental idea is salvageable."[99] "We find ourselves in a historical-political situation in which moral prejudices and ideal principles are not helpful sources of orientation. When it comes to survival and the avoidance of an atomic war, only the coldest realism is appropriate" (90–91). Grewe was not the only Atlantic realist to use the metaphor of coldness to describe the emotional cast of the realist *Haltung*. In a radio address on the subject of "Machiavelli and the Style of World Politics," delivered July 19, 1981, Grewe asked rhetorically, "The cold-blooded calculations and unscrupulous practices of *Machtpolitik*, of which Machiavelli was the great master, are they not still present in today's world politics?"[100] When Hans-Peter Schwarz sought a descriptor for the power and precision of Grewe's formulations in *Spiel der Kräfte*, he came up with the colorful and evocative "Hanseatic cold-bloodedness" (*hanseatische Unterkühltheit*).

Schwarz's appreciation for Grewe spanned a decade. After reading his 1984 magnum opus, Schwarz complimented him in a personal letter: "I believe that this work will achieve the rank of a classic. It is a lovely thought to imagine that in the 23rd or 24th century, a clever Japanese, Chinese or American colleague will study it as respectfully as we today study Suarez, Vattel or Pufendorf."[101] A year later, Schwarz published *The Tamed Germans: From Power-Obsession to Power's Oblivion*, where he continued to praise Grewe: "He can be understood as the crucial but also sole German exponent of a school of thought of responsible power-politics (*Machtpolitik*)" (136). He called Kindermann's neorealism an "eclectic systematic of international relations . . . a legitimate undertaking, to be sure but not one that really be grasped as a continuation of the fundamental realistic approach (*realistischer Grundansatz*)" (137). Schwarz claimed that a "theoretical vacuum resulted from the discrediting of one-sided power-political theories (like geopolitics)." The paradigm of peace research exacerbated that existing problem. In 1969, Schwarz had joined Kaiser, Czempiel, and others who were scrutinizing the utility of the category of the "great power" and the notion of foreign policy as "foreign." In the mid-1980s, however, a significant section of the intellectuals returned to the fundamentals of realism. As Schwarz wrote in 1985, "In the 1970s promises of global and regional interdependence stood at the center of attention. This was equally true for politics, public opinion, and the theory of IR. In the 1980s, a factor forgotten for a time was remembered: power and the power-politics of great powers and small states."[102] Schwarz's portrayal of a paradigm shift is overly stylized and too neatly periodized, but it does capture a real change in political culture.

In the late 1960s, realism entered a crisis that widened its horizons and held the potential to renew it. By the early 1980s, the new experiments in moving beyond the realism-utopianism binary were eclipsed by a return to realist fundamentalism. What Schwarz interpreted as the tragic forgetting and triumphant remembering of the ancient laws of power in international politics is better emplotted as comedy: the recurrence of the same Atlantic realism that claimed to transcend its epoch in the 1890s was now recycled as an up-to-date truth. The DGAP's effort in the 1950s to construct a transatlantic "community" based on NATO was outflanked by an insurgent transatlantic protest movement of students and radical intellectuals. Schwarz lamented the paucity of realism in Germany and Grewe's work as a "late German echo" of more robust American, British, and French traditions. His thesis that Grewe was a belated realist can only be sustained if Grewe the Adenauerian is viewed in isolation from the Grewe of the Nazi Foreign Office. But by doing so, Schwarz gave realism a post-1945 pedigree, the posture that best embodied the spirit of *Westbindung*. Schwarz was right that *Machtpolitik* had become enduringly damaged by its association in the postwar West German mind with the Third Reich. Kindermann's difficulties promoting Morgenthau's ideas attest to that too. Kindermann, Grewe, Schwarz, and Kohl each tried to make realism into a symbol of a revitalized North Atlantic "West." Critics like Czempiel, Kaiser, Marcuse, and Fromm, even Morgenthau, insisted that any realism worth the name would have to adapt to the world being created by globalization in the 1970s, the declining importance of East-West competition, and the growing significance of the North-South division. The return to realist fundamentalism in the 1980s, not the alleged forgetting of power politics in the 1960s and 1970s, was the real tragedy.

Conclusion

THIS BOOK BEGAN ORIGINALLY as a study of a triangle of figures: Carl Schmitt, Hans Morgenthau, and Wilhelm Grewe. How, I wanted to know, had major concepts of Schmitt's political theory seeded postwar American and German foreign policy discourses and practices? A robust literature on the intellectual emigration of German-Jews, most trained in law, and their reception in American political science, encouraged my first steps into the Morgenthau papers in the Library of Congress. Given the obvious echoes of Schmitt's Weimar writings in Morgenthau's of the 1940s, I expected to find substantial archival traces of the Schmittian inheritance. But I did not. There are a mere handful of terse letters between the two. Grewe's relationship to Schmitt was easier to document. But to my surprise, the two great self-described realists of the postwar North Atlantic, Morgenthau and Grewe, appear to have never corresponded with one another. They moved in the same Atlantic security circles in the 1960s, but never cited each other, never wrote each other. This was a disorienting discovery at the outset of my project.

It was at this point that I came upon the writings of Dirk Bönker and Jens-Uwe Guettel on the parallels between American and German navalism at the fin de siècle, and concepts of imperial liberalism, respectively. Both scholars described the robust Social Darwinism that flowed back and forth across the Atlantic, including in the writings of the German geographer Friedrich Ratzel and American naval captain Alfred T. Mahan. As I dove into the German *Weltreichslehre*, and the historiography of *Weltpolitik*, I encountered the ways in which Paul Reinsch, Archibald Coolidge, and others were describing America's attainment of the status of a "world power" at exactly the same time that Germany was rethinking its international vocation. It became clear to me that the careers of

Ratzel, the theorist of *Lebensraum*, and Mahan, the prophet of sea power, formed a mirror of each other. Both combined racial and spatial dimensions of thought into a potent geopolitics, though the word "geopolitics" was not coined until 1899. As I argued in this book, foundational notions of classical realism—such as the primacy of the national interest, and the notion of state as an organism possessed of an *élan vital*—are an artifact of a transatlantic, and yet peculiarly provincial, history of European and American thought during the closing decades of the nineteenth century.

The similarities between the geopolitical discourses of the 1890s and the ideas labeled "classical realism" associated with thinkers of the mid-twentieth century were too compelling to ignore. Although the word "realism" as a term for a formal theory of international politics only dates back to the 1930s—the *locus classicus* being E.H. Carr's *The Twenty Years' Crisis* (1939)—it became clear to me that there was a critical connection between the 1890s and the 1930s. I began to excavate the writings of Karl Haushofer and returned to Schmitt in a new light, in the hopes of identifying some of the key relays from the fin de siècle to the interwar years. It was relatively easy to establish the biographical links between Ratzel and Haushofer, Haushofer and Mackinder, and between those three thinkers and Schmitt.[1] When confronted at Nuremberg by interrogators who asked Schmitt whether his theory of *Großraum* had underwritten the Third Reich's imperialism and extermination of the Jews, he claimed that his 1939 reflections on *Großraum* met the highest international standards of scholarship and had nothing to do with politics. This denial motivated my explorations of Nazi discourses on *Lebensraum*. What I found was that *Großraum* and *Lebensraum* were often used as synonyms in the writings of the most committed Nazi ideologues. Although he was faulted by the SS for not being racist enough, Schmitt's geopolitical reflections could nevertheless not be divorced from their biopolitical effects on the ground. Like Schmitt, Haushofer after 1945 tried to use these minor differences between their conceptions of geopolitics and the Nazi practice of it to exonerate himself. Conveniently left aside, however, was the extent to which Haushofer had bent over backwards to accommodate the Nazification and *Gleichschaltung* of his discipline.

As unsavory as Haushofer and Schmitt were as characters, therefore, their writings posed challenges to my initial assumptions. Schmitt did offer a critique of American imperialism, no matter how inconsistent his support for Nazi empire in Europe was with his normative standpoint. When Haushofer insisted to his interrogator, the Jesuit priest and Georgetown professor Edmund Walsh, that his geopolitics was a derivative of Anglo-Saxon forerunners among the languages of empire, this was not just the cynical pretext of a condemned man. Haushofer was partially right. The two figures whose careers placed them at the heart of the Third Reich, Schmitt and Haushofer, pointed me to a broader Atlantic context for their geopolitics. Isaiah Bowman, advisor to Presidents Wilson and Roosevelt, became important for disentangling American from German geopolitics. I traced the relationship of Bowman and Haushofer from the 1920s to the 1940s, examining the claims each had made about the other and his colleagues. Haushofer's intellectual debts to earlier Anglophone traditions of geopolitics corroborated my suspicion that realism in the United States long predated the 1930s.

The notion that realism was developed by German émigrés—liberals traumatized by Nazism in the 1920s and 1930s—whose realism reflected the traumatic learning processes of the century, is a fixture of what Charles Maier has called our "moral narratives." We want to believe that the hard edges of power politics are consistent with, or at least ultimately sanctioned by, our liberal values. We want to believe that *Realpolitik* can be our shield and sword. But this story is too good to be true. Realism has a different pedigree. Realism is not just the child of the midcentury emigration, the Shoah's bitter fruit. The myth of realism's birth from the spirit of totalitarianism improperly sunders realism from 1890s *Weltpolitik* and imperial geopolitics. It also reinforces a second myth, that the Wilsonians were idealistic anti-imperialists—truly liberal and internationalist. They were nothing of the sort.

Nor did realism descend from Bismarckian *Realpolitik*. It is not the romantic expression of Old World truths, the métier of Metternich or Bismarck. Instead, realism descended from the concept of *Weltpolitik* that was, paradoxically, invented precisely as a counter to *Realpolitik*.[2] Where *Realpolitik* spoke of balance, equilibrium, and the consolidation of contiguous continentally bound power, *Weltpolitik* had been based on a British model of noncontiguous or spatially deterritorialized imperialism, a combination of colonies and preferential access to trade. Realism was born from the spirit of fin de siècle American and German imperialism.

Toward a Cultural History of the Realist Habitus

Realism as a theoretical position on world politics is beset by paradoxes. This is why the tropes used to figure out the "real" are so important for authorizing it.[3] Throughout I have sought to highlight the rhetoric employed by realists and their critics. For example, realists sometimes claimed the authority of science for their views. At other times, they claimed that realism's prudential qualities made it more of an "art," a form of political judgment that could not be formally taught. Whether via art or science, the realists enjoined their readers to see and represent the world in accord with "the nature of things." Again and again, we find metaphors drawn from the register of the visual. In his study of European literary realism, critic Peter Brooks has described "how centrally realist literature is attached to the visual, to looking at things, registering their presence through sight. Certainly realism more than any other mode of literature makes sight paramount—makes it the dominant sense in our understanding of and relation to the world."[4] Gearóid Ó Tuathail has described the "cartographic gaze" of the modernist geographer and geopolitician in suggestive and fruitful ways.[5] Admiral Alfred T. Mahan, a crucial turn-of-the-century figure for my story, pioneered the application of this trope to international politics: "To look with clear, dispassionate, but resolute eyes" at the fact that "the face of the world has changed, economically and politically." Or, as Morgenthau put it in one of his essays from the 1950s, power is "the central problem of our age," but "the modern tendency [is] to face the problem of power, but to face it as it were with a squinting eye."[6]

Realism was a way of seeing. Throughout, I have emphasized the recurrent description of realism by its adherents in the German-language texts as a *Haltung*, or posture toward the world. These exhortations were structured by language that included metaphors referring to the body, to emotions, and to gender. The discourse of realism contrasted the sobriety and rationality of the realist statesman or counselor to the intoxication and emotionality of the idealist reformer. To give one example, the German political scientist Hans-Peter Schwarz memorably commented on Grewe's "Hanseatic cold-bloodedness." But while my treatment has remained at the level of the discursive, *Haltung* points the way beyond discourse to a cultural history focused on practices of statesmanship as an art. Like much "high culture" in modern Western history, realism was not available to all equally. There were barriers to entry, codes to be taught. From Maltzahn's celebration of Ratzel as a great artist, to Haushofer's *Kunstlehre*, to Morgenthau's art of the statesman, realism was imagined as an art for a worldly elite. The enduring allure of realism in the Atlantic lies in its transformation of an elite practice into the democratic idiom of common sense. How was this accomplished? We need to know more about how precisely realists rooted the prestige of realism in the Atlantic world in the twentieth century. How did people come to believe that a specific set of axioms and habits of mind offered a privileged glimpse of international "reality"? How did the romantic image of statesmanship— the solitary decisionmaker guided by his conscience, heroically disciplining his emotions and reason—offered by the realists become naturalized as common sense?

Despite generations of challenges to realism as a theory of international relations, something about its picture of the world has a remarkable staying power. While many see this endurance as proof of its transcendent analytic value, in writing about the origins of realism in geopolitics I have come to see it more as a set of embodied attitudes and mental habits that can be historicized. My intellectual history offers part of the story, for the ideas discussed here were charismatic enough to be routinized by the elites. They became the common sense and sensibility of the foreign policymakers, commentators, and academics most responsible for the conduct of US and German foreign policy in the last century. In his work on the profession of international law between 1870 and 1960, a different but not unrelated "sensibility," Martti Koskenniemi writes of the "rather surprising hold that a small number of intellectual assumptions and emotional dispositions have had on international law during its professional period."[7] My intellectual history of realism as a "sensibility" in the United States and Germany unearths the similar hold of a distinct set of assumptions and dispositions.[8] I hope the present work may inspire other scholars to use mine as the foundation for a more robustly cultural-historical approach to the realist sensibility. Realism is often described as a tradition, an ensemble of texts and commentaries. But traditions are not just invented, they are also—as Pierre Bourdieu has amply shown—instruments of socialization and habituation. Scholars might draw successfully on Pierre Bourdieu's theory of practice, the methods of the history of emotions, and feminist challenges to the male-dominated canon of "classic" international relations texts.

Bourdieu's theory of the habitus may enable us to theorize the enduring power and prestige of realism despite generations of challenges to it at the level of theory. Bourdieu has defined the habitus as a "system of lasting transposable dispositions which, integrating past experiences, functions at every moment as a matrix of perceptions, appreciations, and actions and makes possible the achievement of infinitely diversified tasks, thanks to analogical transfers of schemes permitting the solution of similarly shaped problems."[9] Following the pathbreaking scholarship of historian Frank Costigliola, an expert on the realist George Kennan, a leading textbook in the history of US foreign policy now includes entries entitled "Gendering American Foreign Relations," "The Senses," and "Reading for Emotion."[10] T.J. Jackson Lears has given us a model for relating masculinity to militarism and empire in the history of US foreign relations. He explains that "many educated men embraced [a] militarized definition of manliness . . . In the rhetoric of empire, there were few (usually no) alternatives between heroism and cowardice."[11] As I have shown in my discussion of Hans Morgenthau, even while he dissented from the Vietnam War he argued that it was important that the United States be able to "save face."[12]

The IR scholar Patricia Owens and the historian Katharina Rietzler have brought our attention to the unjustly neglected women theorists and public intellectuals in international thought, including F. Melian Stalwell, whose 1926 work, *The Growth of International Thought*, gave our field its name. Their *Women in International Thought: A New History* demonstrates how what counts as international thought itself is historically produced by exclusions based on race and gender.[13] The theorist Christine Sylvester has written about how gender was constitutive of modern international relations theory, and Cynthia Enloe has written about the intersections of gender and geopolitical thought. With the exception of Ellen Semple, all of the protagonists in this book are men. This is a reflection of the marginalization and exclusion performed by realists in developing their tradition. This marginalization of important women thinkers like Merze Tate, Dorothy Fosdick, and Vera Michaeles Dean resulted in an incomplete picture of the development of Atlantic realism and the contestations over its meaning. As Owens and Rietzler write, "Tate, for example, can be described as a small 'r' realist, [but] she clearly lacked the blinkers of many 1950s realists when it came to race and empire. We may speculate what a more sophisticated realism might have looked like had African American thinkers like Tate not been systematically marginalized from the academic discipline of IR."[14] While women have become increasingly visible in positions of leadership in foreign policy making, academic international relations, and commentary, the difficulty women have had in convincing publics of their fitness on questions of "national security" attests to the legacy of a gendered realist sensibility of "statesmanship." Without more scholarship on realism from a feminist historical perspective, we will not have a satisfactory account of the persistence of the realist habitus in the Atlantic world.

Finally, inspired by the research program of historians at the University of Bielefeld led by Angelika Epple, I have outlined how realism can be viewed as an intellectual practice of comparison. I have situated the discourses on *Weltpolitik*, "great powers," and "world power" in their political and intellectual contexts, but more could be done to flesh out the infrastructure of these meditations on the "world stage." As I have shown throughout, the Atlantic realist imagination was a comparative one, and the practices of comparing were integral to the habitus. In his recent book, *International Pecking Orders: The Politics and Practice of Multilateral Diplomacy*, Vincent Pouliot uses Bourdieu to develop an account of the social negotiation of hierarchy and roles.[15] In this respect, IR theory has returned to the productive questioning of the construction of power relations in international society, not simply their reification.

Beyond Tragedy and Restraint: Realism after Atlantic Realism

Today may seem an inopportune time to be criticizing elements of the realist worldview from a cosmopolitan perspective. As Michael Zürn points out, for many on the populist Right in Europe, "international institutions are not only superfluous but they epitomize the political enemy . . . [N]ew despots in Russia and Turkey manage to centralize power in the name of national pride . . . The common major enemy is the EU and global governance. Any form of governance that cannot be associated with strong national governments is duly rejected."[16] National interests seem as real and recalcitrant as ever. World federalism or a deepening of global governance seem to be off the table. In his tour de force, *The Realist Case for Global Reform*, political scientist William Scheuerman proved that the classical realists were not hostile to every vision of global political integration and international law. Even Morgenthau believed that eventually a world-state would be necessary. Scheuerman notes too that while the classical realists Herz, Morgenthau, Wolfers, Schwarzberger, and Schumann brought with them from Germany an intellectual legacy, he emphasizes these authors' ties to left-wing and liberal milieux.

Despite the cogency of Scheuerman's effort to recover and recuperate the cosmopolitanism and progressivism of the midcentury émigré realists, I do not think they point the best way forward. The mid-twentieth-century classical realists do have some attractive features: their ethical seriousness and their Burkean caution, for example. They form the trunk of the family tree of realism. But the roots and branches of the Atlantic realist tradition point away from cosmopolitan political outcomes.

By locating Atlantic realism's origins in the German-American intellectual discussion of what it means to be a world power, I have tried to right an imbalance—not to forestall any attempt to rethink realism from the margins but to emphasize the challenges of doing so. Much attention has been profitably paid to realism at the mid-twentieth-century moment in its evolution, when the emigration of German-speaking refugee scholars, many of them Jews, stimulated changes in American political sensibility and foreign policy outlook, what has been described as a dramatic "sea change" in American social thought and culture. Their remarkable impact on academia and public discourse is incontestable and rightly celebrated. But the success of figures like Morgenthau had its price too. By emplotting the clash between power and morality under the figure of the tragic, the midcentury realists turned a particular moment of American hegemony into an exemplar of truths true for all time. By making a strawman of Wilson and interwar "idealism," they both misrepresented Wilson's own brand of power politics and overstated their own novelty. Their ideas did encounter some resistance, but their success was also a function of the émigrés' ability to pick up threads of American thought about international affairs that had "realist" features already. Two master-categories dominate contemporary accounts of realism: "tragedy" and "restraint." Both exert a conservative pull on our politics that I find unhelpful and that makes a reconception of realism both make necessary and more difficult.

Twentieth-century Atlantic realists used the genre of tragedy to emplot the "hard choices" and dirty hands involved in statesmanship. But the invocation of tragedy barely conceals a fascination with the gap between the aspirations of the ethicists and the necessities of power politics. "The tragic" is also a romantic ideal. Max Weber famously stylized the man with the "calling" for politics as the man who can resist the seductions of pure idealism. Politics, the slow boring of hard boards, by necessity entails discreet liaisons with violence, and the *Gesinnungsethiker*, or pure ethicist of conviction, will never have the "maturity" required to be a responsible politician capable of making hard choices. Weber presented politics as the activity of the solitary, male statesman, alone with his conscience and difficult decisions: "Here I stand I can do no other," he wrote, appropriating Luther. Courage and masculinity were cited as key aspects of what it took to face reality without the crutch of religious faith. The disenchanted, secular world had left man tragically orphaned in a prison of his own making.

Weber's notion of tragedy derived in part from Nietzsche, whose reflections on "great politics," power, and tragedy deeply influenced him.[17] Weber's *Haltung*, like Morgenthau's, owes more than a little to Nietzsche's aristocratic individualism, his "pathos of distance" (*Vornehmheit*) from the ordinary man. The Nietzsche-Weber line set in motion a cultural dialectic of decadence, diagnosis, and revitalization, and this was the seedbed of a discourse that fully flowered and was globalized in the middle of the twentieth century when an American discipline of international relations, its theorists, and canon made itself hegemonic.[18] There is a realist revival in political theory today that looks to Weber too.[19] From Weber, Morgenthau, and Kissinger, to Mearsheimer and Walt today, realists have used an array of metaphors and figures to create a "reality effect": illusions vs. truth, tragedy vs. innocence, ethics vs. power politics. As democratic publics demand more accountability of their elites, perhaps the time of romanticizing the solitary decisionmaker and his conscience alone as the tribune of reason can yield to a more robust democratic form of decision-making in foreign affairs.[20] Describing foreign affairs through the lens of the tragic exacerbates realism's democratic deficit.

Realism's democratic deficits are linked to its imperial blind spots through the figure of the elite decisionmaker insulated from the demos. Empire is a central dimension of the story of Atlantic realism I have told here. Still, this narrative must contend with the fact that some realists appear to resist empire. Morgenthau was applauded by some important thinkers on the American Left. Today, a number of leading thinkers in the field of US foreign policy have laid out a vision of imperial restraint anchored in principles of classical realism. But the image of realism as "restraint" has only limited value. As Richard Ned Lebow argued in 2003, the problematics of tragedy and restraint are linked by the notion of hubris.[21] Informed by the neoconservative debacle in Iraq, classical realism gained an understandable appeal. Andrew J. Bacevich has eloquently articulated the costs of American imperial overstretch in the Middle East, costs which include the loss of his own son in the Iraq War. His is a dissenting and progressive face of realism, an aspect of the tradition I have neither focused on nor emphasized. Because of its imperial pedigree, I find the Atlantic realist tradition fatally flawed. But most traditions can be reconstructed to be more inclusive and progressive. A truly progressive realism will have to address my critique of the provincial Atlanticism of realism, the postcolonial critique of the Eurocentrism of Western international relations theory, the turn to race, gender, and empire in the historiography of US foreign policy, and the feminist critique of the constitutive exclusions of the realist canon, and of IR theory itself.

A major counterargument is that realism is already an anti-imperial tradition, as progressive a way of viewing international relations as is possible given that some measure of power politics is hard-wired into the architecture and logics of international relations today. Compelling voices have been raised in defense of a realist tradition characterized by prudence, pragmatism, and restraint.[22] In a brilliant essay, historian T. Jackson Lears argued for an American pragmatic, anti-imperial tradition that links William James and Randolph Bourne to Charles Beard and Senator Robert Taft, and to George Kennan and Senator William J. Fulbright. The Quincy Institute for Responsible Statecraft, a newly created think tank in Washington, DC, seeks to revive this tradition of imperial restraint. In 2019, Andrew Bacevich became its first president.[23] Harvard University political scientist Stephen Walt, the faculty chair of the International Security Program at Harvard University, wrote an op-ed in *Foreign Policy* on July 22, 2019, under the title, "Restraint Isn't Isolationism and It Won't Endanger America." Of the Quincy Institute, Walt wrote, "The founding of a new, restraint-oriented think tank—the Quincy Institute for Responsible Statecraft—whose supporters include the odd couple of George Soros and Charles Koch, suggests that realism and restraint are ideas whose time has come."[24]

In an impressive recent book, the Quincy Institute–affiliated international security scholar Patrick Porter writes that "classical realism" is still the best guide to the contemporary crisis of liberal order. Marxist, critical, or postcolonial perspectives in IR scholarship that seek a "new humanist order" beyond imperialism and raison d'état fail to recognize the constraints of "the tragic nature of international life."[25] I agree with the logic behind the Quincy Institute's initiatives, namely, to remind defenders of the so-called "rules-based liberal international order" that a post-Trump restoration of globalism will not suffice. Militarism and the national security state exact too high a cost on the American people to continue unreformed. But while the new realist-restrainers claim to want a foreign policy shorn of American exceptionalism and the expectation of primacy, I believe that the lesson of my German-American story is that the imperial blind spots and democratic deficits of Atlantic realism run too deep for it to be an effective resource for contesting the prerogatives of empire or renewing democracy.

There is much to be learned from the dissenting, pragmatic tradition of realism. But this is not the realism that dominated academia or public life during the Cold War. The history of realism in the Cold War shows that realism was not always at odds with the American empire. It may have restrained it, or wished to restrain it, at certain moments. But realism has also done a great deal of damage. Even though William Fulbright had learned much from Morgenthau, he concluded in 1972 that "hard-headed realism" concealed an "intoxicatingly romantic notion of power," one that needed to be stripped of its "façade."[26] Realism and restraint are not an adequate recipe for a recalibration of American power in the world. Americans can no longer afford to be provincial in their conceptions of what constitutes realistic national behavior. If the realists have taught us anything, it is that we are not beyond compare.

Acknowledgments

It is a pleasure to rehearse the debts, intellectual and institutional, that I have incurred over the course of a decade, not least those from 2020, the year of the global pandemic. My wife, Marjan Mashhadi, read every word of the final draft and edited it brilliantly; she has been always been there to reassure and motivate me. Stefan Eich gave advice in conversation and made outstanding editorial suggestions on multiple drafts of key chapters; Michael Behrent advised me on Bourdieu and gave encouragement and close readings when I needed them most. Daniela Blei, a Stanford-trained historian and freelance editor, read and improved every chapter. Two anonymous readers for Stanford University Press raised important questions and made valuable suggestions for the book at an early stage. Their detailed and valuable comments on the final version of the manuscript, both stylistic and theoretical, helped me identify areas that could be revised and improved. I thank them both heartily for their willingness to read my manuscript at the height of the pandemic and US electoral chaos, and returning it so promptly.

For suggestions, comments, and encouragement I received on individual chapters, I am grateful to the following scholars: Martin Jay, Carl Landauer, Tony La Vopa, Thomas Müller, Daniel Bessner, Katharina Rietzler, Milorad Lazic, Emily Levine, Johannes Nagel, Mark Bassin, Adi Gordon, Eliah Bures, Claudia Koonz, Nicolas Guilhot, and Seth Rogoff. Karl Kaiser kindly accepted my invitation to interview him over Zoom. Speaking with him was one of the high points of the entire project. Milorad Lazic and Daniel Bessner generously answered my questions about the historiography of the Cold War, and offered detailed feedback on specific passages. Steve Poland, Andrea Volpe, Vince Brown, and Margo Irwin all gave valuable advice on writing in general.

No one can write about foreign policy realism and *Realpolitik* without incurring debts to the scholars who have made the field of international political thought and its history so vibrant. The writings of two scholars in particular have been especially important inspirations: Bill Scheuerman and Nicolas Guilhot. I'm grateful for their intellectual example and personal generosity. Conversations with them in Durham, NC, and New York have been among the highlights of my research process. I also want to acknowledge the following authors—in a list which is in no way exhaustive—for work that was especially important in lighting my path: Brian Schmidt, Stefano Guzzini, Duncan Bell, David Milne, John Bew, Ulrike Jureit, Mark Bassin, Dirk Bönker, Geoff Eley, Gearóid O'Tuathail, Gerry Kearns, Samuel Zeitlin, Michael Stolleis, Peter Stirk, Michael Byers, Bardo Fassbender, Martti Koskenniemi, Neil Smith, Oliver Jütersonke, Udi Greenberg, Daniel Eisermann, John Thompson, and Richard Barnet.

There were other specific moments in my education that helped me formulate the methods and perspectives adopted here. Johannes Grave gave a memorable lecture on comparative viewing practices in art history at Wesleyan University's Center for Humanities in 2016 that first inspired me to think about practices of comparison. Bill Reddy at Duke introduced me to the history of emotions. Alfons Söllner's writings on Morgenthau were an important early inspiration. And thanks to Joseph Nye for a seminar on ethics and foreign policy I still remember thirty-five years later. John McCole and Mary Gluck inspired me to pursue intellectual history as a vocation; the Duke History Department and the Triangle Intellectual History Program made me into a professional historian.

I am also grateful to the following institutions for their financial and logistical support: the American Council on Germany for a Richard H. Hunt research fellowship; the Department of History and Dean of Arts and Sciences at Central Connecticut State University; the Institut für die Wissenschaften vom Menschen in Vienna for a visiting fellowship in Fall 2013; the Center for Humanities, Wesleyan University, for a visiting fellowship in 2015–16; the Department of Political Science, and the Institute for European Studies, at UC Berkeley, for a visiting scholar appointment and Senior Fellow appointment, respectively, in 2017–18; the

Duke University Center for Global and International Studies, for a visiting research scholar appointment in 2019–20.

The following institutions hosted lectures, seminars, or workshops where I presented work-in-progress. In chronological order these were: the Danish Institute of International Studies; the Institut für die Wissenschaften vom Menschen; the History and Culture Colloquium, Drew University; the Ralph Bunche Institute, City University of New York; the German Studies Association; the "History of Political Ideas in the 1970s" workshop at Yale University; the College of Social Studies, Wesleyan University; the Institute for European Studies, UC Berkeley; the DAAD Center for German and European Studies, University of Wisconsin; the Triangle Intellectual History Seminar, North Carolina; the Collaborative Research Centre on Practices of Comparing, and the Department of History, both of the University of Bielefeld; the Center for Global Security and Governance, University of Aberdeen; and the Center for Advanced Security, Strategic and Integration Studies, University of Bonn. I'm grateful to all of these institutions for their invitations, and the individuals who organized the events, whether in person or over Zoom: Edward Baring, John Torpey, Isaac Nakhimovsky, Duncan Kelly, Donald Moon, Akasemi Newsome, Pam Potter, James Chappel and the other directors of the Triangle Intellectual History Seminar, Angelika Epple, Thomas Weber, and Ulrich Schlie.

Giovanni Zanalda, the director of the Duke University Center for Global and International Studies, deserves special mention for his devotion of substantial resources and personal attention to a workshop that I designed with Daniel Bessner on realism and liberal internationalism. The workshop that met in February 2019 was a milestone in the development of my thinking in this book. Thank you to Malachi Hacohen for introducing me to Giovanni, and to Danny for being the ideal collaborator. Thanks also to Amanda Frederick who organized a flawless event, the Duke faculty who participated in our forum for students, and all the participants.

At UC Berkeley, I have been fortunate to find intellectual community and collegial spaces in which to work. Jeroen DeWulf, Akasemi Newsome, Julia Nelsen, and Gia White made my year as a Senior Fellow at the Institute for European Studies a successful one. Claire Talwalker and Alan Karras first helped me get situated in the Program in Global Studies; Max Aufhammer, You-tien Hsing, Steve Vogel, Crystal Chang, and Darren Zook extended a warm welcome to the Global Studies and Political Economy teaching programs. Hector Murillo managed an enormous workflow of library requests. Varsha Venkatasubramanian, a PhD candidate in History, helped me manage my research and bibliography over a two-year period, researched the early 1960s debates on the MLF, and gave editorial feedback on chapters. She has my gratitude for all of her hard work.

For memorable and helpful conversations about my project, some dating back more than a decade, I wish to thank Hauke Brunkhorst, Andreas Kalyvas, Nicolas Rengger, Richard Beardsworth, Larry McGrath, Jeannette Samyn, Gavriel Rosenfeld, Robert Nelson, Tim Snyder, Pam Potter, Geoff Eley, Giuliana Chamedes, Patrick Iber, Adi Armon, Nils Gilman, Samuel Moyn, Daniel Steinmetz-Jenkins, Stephen Poland, Philip Nielsen, Jeremy Kessler, Grey Anderson, Stephen Sawyer, Malachi Hacohen, Lloyd Kramer, Steven Vincent, Seth Rogoff, Jana Puglierin, Alexandra Kemmerer, Mark Bassin, Cemil Aydin, Katharina Rietzler, Adam Tooze, Stuart Schrader, Robert Kaufmann, Udi Greenberg, John Connelly, Daniel Sargent, Sam Zeitlin, Joseph Ledford, Varsha Venkatasubramanian, and Martin Jay.

I am deeply grateful to Emily-Jane Cohen, the editor who first brought the manuscript to Stanford University Press; to Kate Wahl for her professional advice; to the entire Editorial Board of the Press for their deliberations and endorsement; and to Margo Irwin for superb guidance and encouragement at every turn. I also thank Cindy Lim for her professionalism and outstanding guidance through the production process. It has been a great pleasure working with this team. Thanks are also due to Wiley-Blackwell and to *History & Theory*, for permission to reuse material from a 2016 article of mine originally published in *History & Theory*.

I would also like to extend my singular thanks to my friend, and colleague from *History & Theory*, Ethan Kleinberg, for the invitation to the Wesleyan Center for the Humanities, for hosting a productive semester of discussions and lectures under the theme of "Comparison," and for introducing me to Emily-Jane Cohen at Stanford.

Childcare during the pandemic posed a major challenge that threatened to derail the book. Thanks to the devotion of my children's teachers at the Black Pine Circle School in Berkeley, my wife and I were able to maintain a semblance of regular working hours. We are immensely grateful to the Black Pine Circle administration, faculty, and staff for saving our daughter's third-grade year. I could also not have completed this book without the creativity, love, and attention of Aimee Cuellar to our preschool son. Aimee ran a one-room schoolhouse, or "pod," in our basement for four children. My mother-in-law, Sedi Afshari, assumed a major share of the childcare responsibilities too. I am deeply grateful to her for her devotion to our family. I also wish to thank my mother, for enduring the pandemic alone in New York City, and keeping us well stocked with books, clothes, toys, and newspaper clippings. With the help of three siblings from the block, Cyrus, Darius, and Ariane Bolandgray, our kids managed to have a summer camp experience in 2020—"Camp Camino"—and their parents got the time they needed to work. Thanks also to all my neighbors on the block and denizens of "La Playa" for helping us keep our good humor.

Liz Phillips, Shirin Khanmohamadi, Susan Head, Munis Faruqui, Vince Brown, Ajantha Subramanian, Rob Steinman, Dillon Cohen, Max Stevens, Jay Zimmerman, Chris Thomas, and many other dear friends provided moral support and distanced companionship in the difficult circumstances of 2020.

I would also like to thank my father, David Kenneth Specter, who died in 2013, nine months after my daughter Leila was born. I learned everything I needed to know about being a father from his marvelous example. I am certain he would be happy to see me flourishing in my work and life alike. My final words of thanks are for my wife, Marjan, and children, Leila and Kiran, for their patience, endurance, and tolerance of the years of work I invested in this project. I could not be more grateful to them for their love and support.

Notes

Introduction

1. Hedley Bull, *The Anarchical Society. A Study of Order in World Politics*, 4th ed., with forewords by Andrew Hurrell and Stanley Hoffmann (London: Palgrave, 2012), 23.

2. For a powerful critique and defense of classical realism, see Richard Ashley, "The Poverty of Neorealism," *International Organization* 38, no. 2 (Spring 1984): 225–86; Daniel Bessner and Nicolas Guilhot, "How Realism Waltzed Off: Liberalism and Decisionmaking in Kenneth Waltz's Neorealism," *International Security* 40, no. 2 (2015): 87–118.

3. For the context and debates around Carr's classic, see Brian Schmidt, ed., *International Relations and the First Great Debate* (London: Routledge, 2012).

4. Stanley Hoffmann, "International Relations: An American Social Science" (1977), repr. in Hoffman, *Janus and Minerva: Essays in the Theory of International Politics* (New York: Westview Press, 1987), 14.

5. Kenneth N. Waltz, *The Theory of International Politics* (New York: McGraw Hill, 1979). Where the classical realists treated the sinfulness of man, or the lust for power (*animus dominandi*), as the deepest cause of the conflict and violence characteristic of international politics, neorealists shifted attention to the structural tendencies in the international "system," abandoning the more controversial claims about human nature.

6. See the exchange in Colin Elman and Michael A. Jensen, eds., *The Realism Reader* (New York: Routledge, 2014), 481–523.

7. Nicolas Guilhot, ed., *The Invention of International Relations Theory: Realism, the Rockefeller Foundation, and the 1954 Conference on Theory* (New York: Columbia University Press, 2011), 23.

8. Nicolas Guilhot, *After the Enlightenment: Political Realism and International Relations in the Mid-Twentieth Century* (Cambridge: Cambridge University Press, 2018), 5.

9. For the connection between neoconservatism and the realist revival, see also Guilhot, *Invention*, 5–7. In early 2019, Steven Wertheim observed that they were reinventing themselves as "neo-neoconservatives" or "post-neoconservatives," which suggests that this may have already begun to change. See Wertheim, "Return of the Neocons," *New York Review of Books*, January 2, 2019.

10. Thirty-three leading American IR scholars signed a statement displayed as an op-ed in the *New York Times,* "War in Iraq Is Not in America's National Interest," September 26, 2002.

11. See, for example, Karl E. Meyer, "Weighing Iraq on Morgenthau's Scale," *World Policy Journal* 20, no. 3 (2003): 89–92; Michael Williams, "Morgenthau Now: Neoconservatism, National Greatness, and Realism," in *Realism Reconsidered: The Legacy of Hans Morgenthau in International Relations,* ed. Michael C. Williams (Oxford: Oxford University Press, 2008).

12. Robert D. Kaplan, *The Revenge of Geography: What the Map Tells Us About Coming Conflicts and the Battle against Fate* (New York: Random House, 2012).

13. See, for example, David Lane and Vsevolod Samokhvalov, eds., *The Eurasian Project and Europe: Regional Discontinuities and Geopolitics* (London: Palgrave Macmillan, 2015)

14. See, for example, Aaron L. Friedberg, "An Answer to Aggression: How to Push Back against Beijing," *Foreign Affairs* 99, no. 5 (September–October 2020): 150–64.

15. See, for example, Yan Xuetong, *Leadership and the Rise of Great Powers* (Princeton, NJ: Princeton University Press, 2019).

16. "As a mytho-history that provides an account of origin and a guide to action, the false memory of order obscures what power politics involves. And it turns attention away from where it can lead, especially when the powerful inhale their own mythology. The task should not be to adapt, reform, refresh, repackage or rebrand this vision. That vision put the USA where it is now. The prudent response is instead to correct or at least restrain its flaws." Patrick Porter, *The False Promise of Liberal Order: Nostalgia, Delusion, and the Rise of Trump* (Cambridge: Polity, 2016), 16.

17. However oblivious to the finer points of diplomacy," Bacevich continues, "candidate Trump correctly intuited that establishment views about the United States' proper role in the world had not worked"; Andrew J. Bacevich, "Saving America First: What Responsible Nationalism Looks Like," *Foreign Affairs* 96, no. 5 (September–October 2017): 61.

18. John Lewis Gaddis, *Strategies of Containment: A Critical Appraisal of American National Security Policy during the Cold War* (Oxford: Oxford University Press, 1982). In his biography of Kennan, Gaddis wrote: "Others determined, to be sure, what 'containment' required: hence Kennan's disillusionment with that strategy from the moment he ceased to make those determinations." In John Lewis Gaddis, *George F. Kennan: An American Life* (New York: Penguin Press), 695. I thank Dr. Milorad Lazic for help with this point and references.

19. For a discussion of this irony in Morgenthau's career, see Udi Greenberg, *The Weimar Century: German Emigres and the Ideological Foundations of the Cold War* (Princeton, NJ: Princeton University Press, 2014).

20. Summarizing the work of many recent scholars, Beate Jahn writes, "The

Cold War is, indeed, widely seen as the quintessential realist balancing of power in operation, thus, in turn, supporting the primacy of the realist paradigm in international affairs." Jahn, *Liberal Internationalism: Theory, History, Practice* (New York: Palgrave Macmillan, 2013), 19.

21. The "realist liberalism" proposed by John H. Herz was an effort to bridge the perceived gap but was not very influential at the time. See John H. Herz, *Political Realism and Political Idealism: A Study in Theories and Realities* (Chicago: University of Chicago Press, 1951).

22. See, for example, the account of Brian Schmidt, "The National Interest Great Debate," in *International Relations and the First Great Debate*, ed. Brian Schmidt (London: Routledge, 2012), 94–117.

23. These historians have shown how rooted modern British international relations thinkers, such as Alfred Zimmern, Norman Angell, and others, caricatured as unworldly "idealists," were actually perceptive students of late nineteenth-century dynamics of globalizing capitalism, imperial nation-state competition, and the possibility—not inevitability—of interdependence. See Jens Steffek and Leonie Holthaus, et. al., eds., *Jenseits der Anarchie: Weltordnungsentwürfe im frühen 20. Jahrhundert* (Frankfurt: Campus Verlag, 2019); David Long and Peter Wilson, eds., *Thinkers of the Twenty Years' Crisis: Inter-War Idealism Reassessed* (Oxford: Clarendon, 1996); Brian Schmidt, ed., *International Relations and the First Great Debate* (London: Routledge, 2012).

24. See Tony Smith, *Why Wilson Matters: The Origin of American Liberal Internationalism and Its Crisis Today* (Princeton, NJ: Princeton University Press, 2017); Adam Tooze, *The Deluge: The Great War, America, and the Remaking of the Global Order, 1916–1931* (New York: Viking, 2014).

25. As Jahn writes, brilliantly, "Unlike liberalism . . . realism offers at best a very few ground rules for the conduct of international politics. This paucity suggests that realism is not, in fact, a competitive political project but rather a product of the exclusion and subsequent systematization of the essential role of power politics within liberalism . . . The separate theorization of the power-political dimension of liberal world politics helps to present and promote liberalism as a genuine alternative to 'realist power politics.'" In Jahn, *Liberal Internationalism*, 174.

26. Jahn, *Liberal Internationalism*, 15.

27. Guilhot, *After the Enlightenment*, 24, 83.

28. "The three most fundamental Realist assumptions . . . evident in [their] books [are] that the most important actors in world politics are territorially organized entities (city states or modern states); that state behavior can be explained rationally; and that states seek power and calculate their interests in terms of power, relative to the nature of the international system that they face." Cited in Brian Schmidt, *The Political Discourse of Anarchy: A Disciplinary History of International Relations* (Albany: SUNY Press, 1997), 28.

29. John Mearsheimer, *The Tragedy of Great Power Politics* (New York: W.W. Norton, [2001] 2014), 2. For insight into this tradition, the work of Duncan Bell

is indispensable. See his "Anarchy, Power and Death: Contemporary Political Realism as Ideology," *Journal of Political Ideologies* 7, on. 2 (2002): 221–39; Bell, *Political Thought and International Relations: Variations on a Realist Theme* (Oxford: Oxford University Press, 2009).

30. David Armitage, "The International Turn in Intellectual History," in Armitage, *Foundations of Modern International Thought* (Cambridge: Cambridge University Press, 2012), 17–32.

31. David Armitage, "The Fifty Year's Rift," *Modern Intellectual History* 1, no. 1 (2004): 97–109; Duncan Bell, "International Relations: The Dawn of a Historiographic Turn?" *British Journal of Politics and International Relations* 3, no. 1 (April 2001): 115–22.

32. Key revisionist works are well summarized in Schmidt, *International Relations*.

33. For the different preoccupations of Hobbes and Locke from their modern "realist" and "liberal" epigones, see, for example, Armitage, *Foundations of Modern International Thought*, 59–90; and for Thucydides and Hobbes, see Beate Jahn, ed., *Classical Theory in International Relations* (Cambridge: Cambridge University Press, 2006).

34. John Hobson, *The Eurocentric Conception of World Politics: Western International Theory, 1760–2010* (Cambridge: Cambridge University Press, 2012). On the hegemonic status of American IR globally, see Ole Waever, "On the Sociology of a Not-So International Discipline," *International Organization* 52, no. 4 (1998): 687–727; Knud Erik Jørgensen, "After Hegemony in International Relations, or, the Persistent Myth of American Disciplinary Hegemony," *European Review in International Studies* 1, no. 1 (2014): 57–64.

35. This book aims in part at a Chinese audience that is growing interested in this tradition.

36. See Martti Koskenniemi, "Out of Europe: Carl Schmitt, Hans Morgenthau and the Turn to 'International Relations,'" 413–509, in *The Gentle Civilizer: Rise and Fall of International Law, 1870–1960* (Cambridge: Cambridge University Press, 2001). Skepticism toward international law became a signature of the realist critique.

37. See Nicolas Guilhot, "The Realist Gambit: Postwar American Political Science and the Birth of IR Theory," in Guilhot, ed., *The Invention of International Relations*, 148.

38. Inderjeet Parmar, *Foundations of the American Century: The Ford, Carnegie, and Rockefeller Foundations in the Rise of American Power* (New York: Columbia University Press, 2015). For a critique of Parmar's interpretation of the Yale Institute for International Studies' "realism," see Robert Vitalis, *White World Order, Black Power Politics: The Birth of American International Relations* (Ithaca, NY: Cornell University Press, 2015), 90–92. For the shifting geography of IR in the elite American universities, see Guilhot, *Invention*.

39. Hoffmann, "American Social Science," 6.

40. Alfons Söllner, *Deutsche Politikwissenschaftler in der Emigration: Studien zu ihrer Akkulturation und Wirkungsgeschichte* (Wiesbaden: VS, 1996); Koskenniemi, *Gentle Civilizer*; Guilhot, *Invention*; Guilhot, *After the Enlightenment*; Greenberg, *Weimar Century*; Jana Puglierin, *John H. Herz: Leben und Denken zwischen Idealismus und Realismus, Deutschland und Amerika* (Berlin: Duncker & Humblot, 2015); Daniel Bessner, *Democracy in Exile: Hans Speier and the Rise of the Defense Intellectual* (Ithaca, NY: Cornell University Press, 2018); Felix Rösch, ed., *Émigré Scholars and the Genesis of International Relations: A European Discipline in America?* (London: Palgrave Macmillan, 2015); Jeremy Suri, *Henry Kissinger and the American Century* (Cambridge, MA: Harvard University Press, 2009).

41. Nicolas Guilhot and Robert Vitalis converge on the 1930s. Guilhot asserts that the term "realism" was first used in the US in the 1930s: "The call for a 'realist' approach to contemporary issues first resonated in theological circles of the 1930s, long before it became a stable category in political theory." See his *After the Enlightenment*, 79. Vitalis writes, "A new and subsequently crucial concept (and identity) for writers and students of international relations— 'realism' and 'realist'–was introduced in the United States in the 1930s," at 83. For "the protean nature of mid-1930s American realist discourse," see Vitalis, *White World Order*, 88–92.

42. Vitalis, *White World Order*, ix, 59–66.

43. Charles Maier, *Leviathan 2.0: Inventing Modern Statehood* (Cambridge, MA: Harvard University Press, 2012),16.

44. See Eric Grimmer-Solem, *Learning Empire: Globalization and the German Quest for World Status, 1875–1919* (Cambridge: Cambridge University Press, 2019).

45. Friedrich Meinecke, *Machiavellism: The Doctrine of Raison d'État and Its Place in Modern History*, trans. Douglas Scott (New York: Praeger, 1965).

46. Hans Morgenthau, "The Mainsprings of American Foreign Policy: The National Interest vs. Moral Abstractions," *American Political Science Review* 44, no. 4 (December 1950): 836.

47. Rochau was a member of the German National Liberal party, and of the generation that sought to make of the Prussian monarchy a constitutional one in the failed revolution of 1848. See Bew's impressive work, *Realpolitik: A History* (Oxford: Oxford University Press, 2015).

48. Bew, *Realpolitik*, 47–64.

49. Bew has examined how "Realpolitik" became an epithet or term of endorsement thrown at a wide range of American policymakers but in every case missing the originally intended meeting represented by its coiner, Ludwig Rochau. Bew argues that in the period from 1900–1914, "America might be said to have awoken to the Realpolitik that was causing such a stir in Europe." He mentions Theodore Roosevelt, Mahan, and Lippmann as examples of "what might be described as a new 'realism' in American foreign policy debates . . . From

its inception this was clearly distinct from that associated with Germany"; Bew, *Realpolitik*, 108. Bew's narrative depends on an Americanization of *Realpolitik* but does not identify the American or German sources or channels by which the translation was made, and ultimately downplays the German connection in favor of a British one: "The Lippmann version of Realpolitik in fact owed more to traditional British than German ideas of strategy. It held that America had a broader interest in the stability of the international system . . . It was, in essence, a form of robust internationalism" (108). He concedes, however, that "in the US, Realpolitik never had the same pejorative connotations as in England" (146), but offers no explanation why. My approach stresses a much more robust transnational connection between Germany and the US, anchoring the Mahan-Roosevelt moment in that context.

50. See Michael Heffernan, "The Origins of European Geopolitics, 1890–1920," 51–70, in *Geopolitical Traditions: A Century of Geopolitical Thought*, ed. Klaus Dodds and David Atkinson (New York: Routledge, 2000); Irene Diekmann, Peter Krueger, et al., *Geopolitik: Grenzgänge im Zeitgeist*, 2 vols. (Berlin: Verlag für Berlin-Brandenburg, 2007); Gerry Kearns, *Geopolitics and Empire: The Legacy of Halford Mackinder* (Oxford: Oxford University Press, 2009).

51. John Bew ascribes to Alfred Mahan and Theodore Roosevelt a proto-realism ("what might be described as a 'new realism'") that flowered in the intellectual circle around Lippmann at the *New Republic*. The first American text that he names "realist" is an essay of Walter Lippmann's from 1915, "A Little Realpolitik." At that time, Lippmann and his circle at the *New Republic* were arguing for the US entrance into World War I.

52. Coined by the Swedish political scientist Rudolf Kjellén in 1915, the term did not catch on internationally until it was translated into the German as *Geopolitik*. For the next twenty-five years, the word used in England and America had, as *Realpolitik* had, an unavoidable aura of "Germanness" about it.

53. See Carroll P. Kakel III, *The American West and the Nazi East: A Comparative and Interpretive Perspective* (London: Palgrave Macmillan, 2011).

54. The view that Germany's development from 1848–1945 was pathologically deviant from a Western norm represented by Britain and France, and secured to them by "successful" bourgeois revolutions, is called the "Sonderweg" or "special path" thesis. It was commonly held by postwar historians until convincingly overturned by Geoff Eley and David Blackbourn, *The Peculiarities of German History* (Oxford: Oxford University Press, 1984).

55. Daniel Immerwahr, *How to Hide an Empire: A History of the Greater United States* (New York: Farrar, Straus, and Giroux, 2019); Daniel Bessner and Nicolas Guilhot, *The Decisionist Imagination: Sovereignty, Social Science, and Democracy in the Twentieth Century* (New York: Berghahn Books, 2019).

56. Dirk Bönker, *Militarism in a Global Age: Naval Ambitions in Germany*

and the United States in Germany and the United States before World War I (Ithaca, NY: Cornell University Press, 2012).

57. See Emily Levine, *Allies and Rivals: German-American Exchange and the Making of the Modern Research University* (Chicago: University of Chicago Press, 2020)

58. Bradley Naranch and Geoff Eley, eds., *German Colonialism in a Global Age* (Durham, NC: Duke University Press, 2014), 38.

59. Jens-Uwe Guettel, *German Expansionism, Imperial Liberalism and the United States, 1776–1945* (Cambridge: Cambridge University Press, 2012); Andrew Zimmerman, *Alabama in Africa: Booker T. Washington, the German Empire and the Globalization of the New South* (Princeton, NJ: Princeton University Press, 2012); James Q. Whitman, *Hitler's American Model: The US and the Making of Nazi Racial Law* (Princeton, NJ: Princeton University Press, 2018).

60. Geoff Eley, "Empire by Land or by Sea? Germany's Imperial Imaginary, 1840–1945," in Naranch and Eley, *German Colonialism,* 39.

61. The phrase "German Atlantic" was coined by Andrew Zimmerman in *Alabama in Africa.*

62. Willibald Steinmetz, ed., *The Force of Comparison: A New Perspective on Modern European History and the Contemporary World* (New York: Berghahn Books, 2019); Angelika Epple, Walter Erhardt, and Johannes Grave, eds., *Practices of Comparing: Towards a New Understanding of a Fundamental Human Practice* (Bielefeld: Bielefeld University Press, 2020).

63. The record of their correspondence in the Morgenthau Papers at the Library of Congress contains nothing of real substance.

64. While the Anglo-American connection is important, it is one that also obscures a lot and (falsely) creates the impression of a monolithic, Anglophone "West." See Duncan Bell, *Reordering the World: Essays on Liberalism and Empire* (Princeton, NJ: Princeton University Press, 2016); Jeanne Morefield, *Covenants without Swords: Idealist Liberalism and the Spirit of Empire* (Princeton, NJ: Princeton University Press, 2005).

65. Sometimes called "the history of international thought," this is a dynamic field in European and American academies right now—an intersection of history, sociology of knowledge, political theory, and IR. David Armitage calls it "international intellectual history." See Armitage, *Foundations of International Thought.* Important syntheses include Lucian Ashworth, *A History of International Thought: From the Origins of the Modern State to Academic International Relations* (London: Routledge, 2014), and Brian Schmidt and Nicolas Guilhot, eds., *Historiographical Investigations in International Relations* (London: Palgrave, 2018).

Chapter 1

1. Sönke Neitzel, *Weltmacht oder Niedergang. Die Weltreichslehre im Zeitalter des Imperialismus*. Mit einem Geleitwort von Winfried Baumgart (Paderborn: Schöningh, 2000); Dirk Bönker, *Militarism in a Global Age: Naval Ambitions in Germany and the United States before World War I* (Ithaca, NY: Cornell University Press, 2012).

2. Geoff Eley, "Empire by Land or Sea? Germany's Imperial Imaginary, 1840–1945," in *German Colonialism in a Global Age*, ed. Bradley Naranch and Geoff Eley (Durham, NC: Duke University Press, 2014), 26–27; see also Bönker, *Militarism in a Global Age*, 27–30, 33. For an important influence on my own thinking, see also Eley, 'Empire, Ideology and the East: Thoughts on Nazism's Spatial Imaginary," in *Nazism as Fascism: Violence, Ideology and the Ground of Consent in Germany, 1930–1945* (New York: Routledge, 2013), 131–55.

3. Eley, "Empire," 34. *Weltpolitik* had a range of meanings and encompassed diverse policies—from economic expansion to outright conquest and settler colonialism.

4. Sweeney points out that the Pan-German League, long thought to advocate only continentalist and migrationist colonialist positions (described ideal-typically by Woodruff Smith as *"Lebensraum"*), actually had a much more complex stance that included a sophisticated appreciation for the advantages of *Weltpolitik*. In a text like *World Policy, Imperialism and Colonial Policy* (1908), written by the league's leader Ernst Hasse, Sweeney "argue[s] that pan-German conceptions of a Greater Germany figured not a spatially fixed and racially enclosed nation-state but rather a complex 'imperial formation': an uneven and 'mobile macropolity' centred on a nation-state core but radiating outward in a complex 'architecture' of multiple, ambiguous and gradated zones of territorial and nonterritorial sovereignty"; Dennis Sweeney, "Pan-German Conceptions of Colonial Empire," in *German Colonialism in a Global Age* (Durham, NC: Duke University Press, 2014), 267.

5. For the complexities and overlap between the discourses of *Lebensraum*, *Mitteleuropa*, and *Weltpolitik*, see Woodruff D. Smith, *The Ideological Origins of Nazi Imperialism* (Oxford: Oxford University Press, 1986), 52–82, 196–212.

6. Ratzel, "Flottenfrage und Weltlage" (1897), in *Kleine Schriften* II (München: R. Oldenbourg, 1906), 377–78. I am indebted to Mark Bassin for the reference. Mark Bassin, "Imperialism and the Nation State in Friedrich Ratzel's *Political Geography*," *Progress in Human Geography* 11, no. 4 (September 1, 1987): 482.

7. For more on Rochau, see Natascha Doll, *Recht, Politik und 'Realpolitik' bei August Ludwig von Rochau (1810–1873): Ein wissenschaftlicher Beitrag zum Verhältnis von Politik und Recht im 19. Jahrhundert* (Frankfurt am Main: Klostermann, 2005); Duncan Kelly, "August Ludwig von Rochau and *Realpolitik* as Historical Political Theory," *Global Intellectual History* 3, no. 3 (2018): 301–30.

8. August Ludwig von Rochau, *Grundsätze der Realpolitik: Angewendet auf die staatlichen Zustände Deutschlands* (1853), 2nd ed. 1859. The second volume was published in 1868.

9. John Bew, *Realpolitik: A History* (Oxford: Oxford University Press, 2018), 47.

10. Wolfgang J. Mommsen, *Max Weber and German Politics, 1890–1920* (Chicago: University of Chicago Press, 1984), 42.

11. Looking back in 1913, Weber praised "that kind of 'Realpolitik' that has brought our policy so many noteworthy successes in the past 27 years." But in letters dating from 1887, 1906, 1909, and 1913, he denigrated the "Realpolitik" he found manifested in his contemporaries. See Mommsen, *Max Weber*, 43n32.

12. Max Weber, letter of April 25, 1887, cited in Mommsen, *Max Weber*, 9.

13. See Mommsen, *Max Weber*, 69.

14. Max Weber, *Weber: Political Writings* (Cambridge: Cambridge University Press, 1994), 26.

15. For an enlightening discussion of the Rochau-Treitschke relationship, see Bew, *Realpolitik*, 68–76.

16. Treitschke, "Bundesstaat und Einheitsstaat" (1864), in *Aufsätze, Reden und Briefe*, ed. Karl Martin Schiller, vol. 3 (Meersburg: F.W. Hendel, 1929), 20. Cited in Peter Winzen, "Treitschke's Influence," in *Nationalist and Racialist Movements in Britain and Germany before 1914*, ed. Paul Kennedy and Anthony Nicholls (New York: Palgrave Macmillan, 1981), 159.

17. Treitschke, "Die Freiheit," *Preussische Jahrbücher* 7 (1861): 388. In another essay of 1864, he wrote, "This Germany cannot become a great power in the best sense of the word within that time span the present generation may survey." Both cited in Winzen, "Treitschke's Influence," 159.

18. The source of the quotation is Harry Denicke, "Ein kolonialpolitisches Nachwort," *Deutsche Kolonialzeitung* 1, no. 9 (January 1892).

19. Holstein and von Bülow "and a large part of the generation of officers to which they belonged never really adjusted their thinking about policy from the Bismarckian mode [which emphasized] security, balance of power and alliance politics." See Smith, *Ideological Origins*, 56–57.

20. Smith characterizes Tirpitz as an opportunist who "used Weltpolitik arguments but subordinated them to his prime concern . . . building a battle fleet second to none"; Smith, *Ideological Origins*, 58.

21. Bönker, *Militarism in a Global Age*, 46.

22. Jens-Uwe Guettel, *German Expansionism, Imperial Liberalism and the United States, 1776–1945* (Cambridge: Cambridge University Press, 2012), 80.

23. The main elaboration was published in 1901 in a *Festschrift* for the German sociologist Albert Schäffle. Friedrich Ratzel, *Der Lebensraum: Eine biogeographische Studie* (Tübingen: Laupp, 1901).

24. The best overviews of this Darwinian background can be found in Ulrike Jureit, "Mastering Space: Laws of Movement and Grip on the Soil," *Journal of Historical Geography* 61 (2018): 81–85; Mark Bassin, "Friedrich Ratzel's

Travels in the United States," *History of Geography Newsletter* 4 (1984): 11–22. See also Smith, *Ideological Origins*, 145–50; Jureit, *Das Ordnen von Räumen: Territorium und Lebensraum im 19. und 20. Jahrhundert* (Hamburg: Hamburger Edition, 2016).

25. See Guettel, *German Expansionism*, 99–101.

26. Ratzel, *Wider der Reichsnörgler: ein Wort zur Kolonialfrage aus Wählerkreisen* (München: R. Oldenbourg, 1884).

27. Friedrich Ratzel, *die Erde und das Leben: Eine vergleichende Erdkunde*, 2 vols. (Leipzig: Bibliographisches Institut, 1902) 1:590–606.

28. See Jureit, "Mastering Space," 84.

29. Ratzel, "Lebensraum: A Biogeographical Study," trans. Tul'si Bhambray, *Journal of Historical Geography* 61 (2018): 14.

30. Ian Klimke and Mark Bassin, *"Lebensraum* and Its Discontents," *Journal of Historical Geography* 61 (2018): 54.

31. Ratzel's travels in the United States as a journalist in 1874–75 were what inspired him, as a biologist trained in zoology, to become a geographer. The US features prominently in his subsequent publications, including a two-volume study he completed in 1893. See Mark Bassin, "Friedrich Ratzel's Travels in the United States," *History of Geography Newsletter* 4 (1984): 11–22; C.O. Sauer, "The Formative Years of Ratzel in the US," *Annals of the Association of American Geographers* 61, no. 2 (June 1971): 245–54, at 253.

32. Friedrich Ratzel, *Die Vereinigten Staaten von Nord-Amerika*, 2nd ed., vol. II (München: R. Oldenbourg, 1893 [1880]), 85.

33. Ratzel, *Die Vereinigten Staaten*, vol. II (1893), 4, cited in Bassin, "Ratzel's Travels," 14.

34. Friedrich Ratzel, *Politische Geographie* (1897) 3 Aufl. (München/Berlin: R. Oldenbourg, 1923), 257, cited in Bassin, "Travels," 17.

35. From Ratzel, *Glücksinseln und Träume: Gesammelte Aufsätze aus den Grenzboten* (Leipzig: F. Grunow, 1905), 476, cited in Bassin, "Ratzel's Travels," 18. The phrase appears to be taken verbatim from the writings of his teacher Oscar Peschel.

36. "I believe I learned the following in America and that I am justified in applying the lesson to Europe: the art of politics consists to a great extent of directing political conflicts out of restricted spaces where they corrode on each other like ulcers." Quoted in Bassin, "Imperialism," 480. See Bassin for an insightful discussion of what distinguishes his views on race from the more overt racism of Ernst Haeckel, Arthur de Gobineau, and Houston Stewart Chamberlain.

37. Jureit, "Mastering Space," 85n35. For "neoracism," I follow Thomas McCarthy, *Race, Empire and the Idea of Human Development* (Cambridge: Cambridge University Press, 2009).

38. Ratzel, "Nationalitäten und Rassen," *Kleine Schriften* II (München, 1906), 483, cited in Jureit, "Mastering Space," n. 32.

39. Ratzel sometimes used the term *Großraum* to describe a way that states

could achieve *Lebensraum*. Ratzel did not coin the term *Großraum*—it already been used by Theodor Inama von Sternegg, a political economist, in 1869. The United States, Australia, Russia, and China were all *Großräume*, wrote Ratzel in his 1897 *Political Geography*: "The European system of small but intensively used spaces is retrograde in the face of [contemporary states based on *Großraum*] because it cannot be [the pattern] of the future: a pattern which today, as it has for millennia, strives unremittingly after ever-larger spaces. The large states, such as represented by the US, are the modern expression of a political state in which new developments take place." Ratzel, *Politische Geographie*, 270, cited in Bassin, "Imperialism," 479.

40. Friedrich Ratzel, "Die Nordatlantischen Mächte," *Marine Rundschau* 14 (1903): 911–39, 1047–62.

41. Ratzel, "Die Nordatlantischen Mächte," 1054.

42. Ratzel, "Vorbemerkung," (January 24, 1900) in *Das Meer* (see following note).

43. Ratzel, *Das Meer als Quelle der Völkergrösse: Eine politisch-geographische Studie* (München: R. Oldenbourg, 1900), 84–85.

44. Hassert, "Friedrich Ratzel: Sein Leben und Wirken," *Geographische Zeitschrift* 11, no. 7 (1905), cited in Bassin, "Imperialism," 482.

45. Bonker, *Militarism in a Global Age*, 263.

46. Curt von Maltzahn, "'Friedrich Ratzel: Ein Gedenkwort,'" *Marine Rundschau* 16 (1905): 218.

47. I borrow the notion of the "charisma" of ideas from Anna Tsing, "The Global Situation," in *Schools of Thought: Twenty-Five Years of Interpretive Social Science*, ed. Joan W. Scott and Debra Keates, 104–38 (Princeton, NJ: Princeton University Press, 2001).

48. Archibald Cary Coolidge, *The United States as a World Power* (New York: Macmillan, 1909).

49. John A. Thompson, *A Sense of Power: The Roots of America's Global Role*, 1st ed. (Ithaca, NY: Cornell University Press, 2015), 31.

50. See Brian C. Schmidt, *The Political Discourse of Anarchy: A Disciplinary History of International Relations* (Boulder, CO: SUNY Press, 1997). "This marked the beginning of an illustrious career in political science, a discipline that Reinsch would do much to help establish in the US." Schmidt adds that in 1900, "Apart from Reinsch's work, a discrete discourse devoted to international relations did not really exist"; *Discourse*, 70–75.

51. William Olson and A.J.R. Groom, *International Relations Then and Now: Origins and Trends in Interpretation* (London: HarperCollins, 1991), 47.

52. Paul S. Reinsch, *World Politics at the End of the Nineteenth Century* (London: Macmillan, 1900), 310–11. Compare: "The change, however, has occurred, and no force of logic can reverse the current of history," at 310. Reinsch may have discovered Ratzel in his studies with Turner. Turner and Ratzel were mutual admirers, and Turner cited Ratzel's 1893 work on the US appreciatively in an 1896 essay. See Guettel, *German Expansionism*, 94–95, 100–101.

53. Schmidt, *Discourse*, 70.

54. The school was directed by Richard Ely, a professor of political economy active in the American Progressive movement and who had been influenced by the Historical School of Economics in Germany.

55. Schmidt, *Discourse*, 81; Noel H. Pugach, *Paul S. Reinsch, Open Door Diplomat in Action* (Millwood, NY: KTO Press, 1979), 14.

56. Max Weber, "National State and Economic Policy," in *Weber: Political Writings* (Cambridge: Cambridge University Press, 1994), 26.

57. Reinsch, *World Politics*, 294, 313, 361.

58. Reinsch, *World Politics*, 312. For additional examples, see 361–62.

59. Charles Beard, *The Idea of the National Interest* (1934), republished with Alfred Vagts and William Beard, eds. (Chicago: Quadrangle Books, 1966), 2, 316, 439.

60. Bew argues that figures like Walter Lippmann and Herbert Croly at the *New Republic* were the first realists, but built on a Mahan-Roosevelt moment: "In arguing that the US needed to engage with the rest of the world—in a more front-footed and assertive manner—there emerged what might be described as a new 'realism' in American foreign policy debates, embodied by Theodore Roosevelt and Alfred Mahan." See Bew, *Realpolitik*, 108. In his nuanced portrait, Milne refers to Mahan's "instinctive realism." See David Milne, *Worldmaking: The Art and Science of American Diplomacy* (New York: Farrar, Straus and Giroux, 2015), 45.

61. A.T. Mahan, "A Twentieth Century Outlook" (September 1897), in *The Interest of America in Sea Power, Present and Future* (Boston: Little, Brown, 1917), 224–25.

62. For the same trope, see Mahan, "The Future in Relation to American Naval Power" (October 1895), in *Interest of America*, 146.

63. Mahan, "The Future," 148.

64. Mahan, "The United States Looking Outward" (December 1890), in *Interest of America*, 18.

65. Mahan, "Outlook," 165–66.

66. Mahan, "Possibilities of an Anglo-American Reunion" (November 1894), in *Interest of America*, 118.

67. Mahan, "Looking Outward," 7–8.

68. Mahan, "The Persian Gulf and International Relations" (1902), in *Retrospect and Prospect: Studies in International Relations, Naval and Political* (New York: Kennikat Press, 1968), 249.

69. Mahan, "Possibilities," 130; "Persian Gulf," 241–51.

70. Mahan, "Outlook," 258–59.

71. Mahan, "The Naval War College" (July 1912), in *Armaments and Arbitration, Or, The Place of Force in the International Relations of States* (New York: Harper and Bros., 1912), 204. He applied the label "doctrinaire" to the British Labor Party's foreign policy, "Armaments in Arbitration" (25), as

well as to President Wilson.

72. Mahan, "Monroe Doctrine" (1903), in *Naval Administration and Warfare: Some General Principles, with Other Essays* (New York: Little, Brown, 1908), 376. Mahan used similar metaphors in his 1894 essay "The Future in Relation to American Naval Power," 156.

73. Jay Sexton, *The Monroe Doctrine: Empire and Nation in Nineteenth-Century America* (New York: Hill and Wang, 2011), 203.

74. See Nancy Mitchell, *The Danger of Dreams: German and American Imperialism in Latin America* (Chapel Hill: University of North Carolina Press, 1999).

75. See Coolidge, *World Power*, 106.

76. See Juan Pablo Scarfi, *The Hidden History of International Law in the Americas: Empire and Legal Networks* (Oxford: Oxford University Press, 2017), 59–86, which contains an enlightening discussion of the contestation of the meaning of the Monroe Doctrine by Pan-Americanist lawyers such as the Argentine Luis María Drago and the Chilean Alejandro Alvarez.

77. Sexton, *Monroe Doctrine*, 229.

78. Mahan, "Monroe Doctrine," 408.

79. For example, in 1898, regarding the Caroline Islands, see Alfred Thayer Mahan, "The Deficiencies of Law as an Instrument of International Adjustments" (November 1911), in *Armaments and Arbitration,* 80. In "The Great Illusion" (March 1912), he writes: "Can we wonder if the Germans ask themselves whether there would be fundamental iniquity if they took in hand the development of the Amazon valley?" In idem, *Armaments and Arbitration*, 137.

80. Mahan, "Diplomacy and Arbitration," (July 1911) in idem, *Armaments and Arbitration*, 42–43.

81. Mahan, "Deficiencies of Law" (1911), 91.

82. Mahan, "Looking Outwards" (1890), 17

83. Mahan, "The Future," 155.

84. Mahan, "The Great Illusion" (1910), 121–26.

85. Mahan, "Deficiencies of Law," 83.

86. Mahan, "Persian Gulf and International Relations," 216.

Chapter 2

1. See John Bew, *Realpolitik: A History* (Oxford: Oxford University Press, 2018), 108; David Milne, *Worldmaking: The Art and Science of American Diplomacy* (New York: Farrar, Straus & Giroux, 2015).

2. See Nicolas Guilhot, ed., *The Invention of International Relations Theory: Realism, the Rockefeller Foundation, and the 1954 Conference on Theory* (New York: Columbia University Press, 2011).

3. Oliver Jütersonke explains that the systematic use of the term "realism" in the context of legal realism dates to a brief exchange of views between a young Karl Llewelyn and Roscoe Pound in 1930. See Jütersonke, *Morgenthau, Law,*

Realism (Cambridge: Cambridge University Press, 2012). Nicolas Guilhot argues that "[the] call for a 'realist' approach to contemporary issues first resonated in theological circles of the 1930s, long before it became a stable category in political theory." See Guilhot, *After the Enlightenment: Political Realism and International Relations in the Mid-Twentieth Century* (Cambridge: Cambridge University Press, 2018), 79. And Robert Vitalis argues, "[a] new and subsequently crucial concept (and identity) for writers and students of international relations— 'realism' and 'realist'–was introduced in the United States in the 1930s." Vitalis, *White World Order, Black Power Politics: The Birth of American International Relations* (Ithaca, NY: Cornell University Press, 2015), 83.

4. William T.R. Fox, "Interwar International Relations Research: The American Experience," *World Politics* 2, no. 1 (October 1949): 67–79.

5. Vitalis, *White World Order,* 88–92.

6. Karl Haushofer, *Dai Nihon: Betrachtung über Groß-Japans Wehrkraft, Weltstellung und Zukunft* (Berlin: E.S. Mittler und Sohn 1913). The authoritative study of Haushofer and Japan is C.W. Spang, *Karl Haushofer und Japan: Die Rezeption Seiner Geopolitischen Theorien in der Deutschen und Japanischen Politik* (München: Iudicium, 2013).

7. Wolfgang Natter, "Geopolitics in Germany, 1919–45: Karl Haushofer and the *Zeitschrift für Geopolitik,*" in *A Companion to Political Geography,* ed. John Agnew, Katharyne Mitchell, and Gerard Toal (Oxford: Blackwell, 2003), 186–203, at 193. The other editors were Erich Obst, Kurt Lautensach, Otto Maull, and, slightly later, Fritz Termer.

8. The novel's author was Hans Grimm. David T. Murphy, *The Heroic Earth: Geopolitical Thought in Weimar Germany, 1918–1933* (Kent, OH: Kent State University Press, 1997).

9. Mark Bassin, "Race contra Space: The Conflict between German Geopolitik and National Socialism," *Political Geography Quarterly* 6, no. 2 (April 1987): 125.

10. Karl Wittfogel (1896–1988), an active member of the Communist Party in 1929, had been invited to join the Frankfurt Institute of Social Research in 1925. Despite his scathing critique of geopolitics as the ideology of "monopoly capitalism" in the 1929 essay "Geopolitics, Geographical Materialism and Marxism," Haushofer deemed the essay important enough to republish it in the *Zeitschrift* in 1932. They also published other articles by him. On Wittfogel, see Gearóid Ó Tuathail, *Critical Geopolitics: The Politics of Writing Global Space—The Barrows Lectures* (Minneapolis: University of Minnesota Press, 1996), 143–47.

11. William E. Borah, "Wie es zum Krieg kam: Keime eines zukünftigen Weltkrieges," *Zeitschrift* 6, no. 8 (1928): 619–20. Quoted in Andrew Georgy, *Geopolitics: The New German Science* (Berkeley: University of California Press, 1944), 239n14.

12. In total, the *Zeitschrift* published 1,200 articles by over 600 authors. For details on the *Zeitschrift,* see Natter, "Geopolitics," 192–99; Holder H.

Herwig, *The Demon of Geopolitics: How Karl Haushofer 'Educated' Hitler and Hess* (London: Rowman and Littlefield, 2016), 121; Murphy, *Heroic Earth*, ix; Trevor J. Barnes and Christian Abrahamsson, "Tangled Complicities and Moral Struggles: The Haushofers, Father and Son, and the Space of Nazi Geopolitics," *Journal of Historical Geography* 47 (2015): 47–63.

13. Edmund A. Walsh, *Total Power: A Footnote to History* (New York: Doubleday, 1948), 347.

14. Bassin, "Race contra Space," 125.

15. Bassin argues in defense of Haushofer that absent this pressure, race "appeared always as a lesser element and one directly dependent on the all-important factor of *Raum*, or environment." Bassin, "Race contra Space," 121.

16. Barnes and Abrahamson, "Tangled Complicities," 68.

17. The Munich State Archives record eight visits with Haushofer and Hess, according to Holder Herwig who provides this source: "Herr Hess. Besuche," Justizvollzugsanstalt Nr. 15161/5, Nr. 27, from the Staatsarchiv München. Cited in Herwig, *Demon of Geopolitics*, 93 and 93n2; Barnes and Abrahamson assert that a considerably greater number of visits took place: "Wednesdays from 24 June to 12 November"; "Tangled Complicities," 67.

18. Othmar Plöckinger, *Geschichte eines Buches: Adolf Hitler's 'Mein Kampf'*, *1922–1945* (München: Oldenbourg, 2006), 145; Herwig, *Demon of Geopolitics*, 99.

19. Herwig, *Demon of Geopolitics*, 96. Citing Friedrich Ratzel, *Erdenmacht und Völkerschicksal: eine Auswahl aus seinen Werken*, Hrsg. Karl Haushofer (Stuttgart: A. Kröner, 1940), xxvi.

20. Jacobsen, *Karl Haushofer: Leben und Werk*, Bd. I (Boppard am Rhein: Boldt, 1979), I:241. For the view that the Hess-Haushofer-Hitler genealogy is unproven, see Dan Diner, "Grundbuch der Planeten: Zur Geopolitik Karl Haushofer," *Vierteljahrshefte für Zeitgeschichte* 32, no. 1 (1984): 1–28, at 26.

21. "Hitler did not really engage himself with Haushofer's work and the conceptual framework behind the professor's term. Rather, he was attracted by *Lebensraum* because it gave a name to something he had been thinking about [already]." See Thomas Weber, *Becoming Hitler: The Making of a Nazi* (New York: Basic Books, 2017), 321.

22. Natter, "Geopolitics," 201.

23. Bassin, "Space contra Race."

24. Neil Smith, *American Empire: Roosevelt's Geographer and the Prelude to Globalization* (Berkeley: University of California Press, 2004), 301. The scholarly investigation did nothing to alleviate the plight of refugees and was terminated by President Truman in 1945.

25. Smith, *Roosevelt's Geographer*, 309. Smith's source is an interview with Owen Lattimore, dated January 12, 1983, at 515n58.

26. Smith, *Roosevelt's Geographer*, 325. The War and Peace Studies project produced "some 670 reports, held 361 meetings, involved over 100 individuals and spent almost $300,00 of Rockefeller Foundation funds in the process. The

CFR's dream of power and influence now came to fruition." Smith, *Roosevelt's Geographer*, 330.

27. Bowman, "Geography and Geopolitics," 648.

28. See, for example, Steven J. Bucklin, *Realism and American Foreign Policy: Wilsonians and the Kennan-Morgenthau Thesis* (Westport, CT: Praeger, 2000), 9: "The record of these men reveals a much different interpretation of Wilsonianism than that which has been forwarded in the works of the realist school." For discussion of the neglected Schumann, see Robert Vitalis, *White World Order*, 11, 87–88, 90, 141, 161, 164, 168.

29. Edward Hallett Carr, *The Twenty Years' Crisis, 1919–1939: An Introduction to the Study of International Relations* (New York: Harper and Row, [1939] 1964).

30. For a good summary of the debates, see Peter Wilson, "The Myth of the 'First Great Debate'," in *International Relations and The First Great Debate*, ed. Brian Schmidt, 16–32 (London: Routledge, 2012). See also Jens Steffek and Leonie Holthaus, et. al., eds., *Jenseits der Anarchie: Weltordnungsentwürfe im frühen 20. Jahrhundert* (Frankfurt: Campus Verlag, 2019); David Long and Peter Wilson, eds., *Thinkers of the Twenty Years' Crisis: Interwar Idealism Reassessed* (Oxford: Clarendon, 1996); Brian Schmidt, ed., *International Relations and the First Great Debate* (London: Routledge 2012); Tim Dunne, Michael Cox, and Kenneth Booth, *The Eighty Years' Crisis: 1919–1999* (Cambridge: Cambridge University Press, 1999).

31. In 2006, Anne-Marie Slaughter described Root as a "Wilsonian," and precursor of her 1990s "liberal internationalism." See "Rereading Root," in *American Society of International Law Proceedings* 100 (March 29–April 1, 2006): 203–16.

32. Samuel Moyn, "Beyond Liberal Internationalism," *Dissent* 64, no. 1 (Winter 2017): 116–22.

33. Juan Pablo Scarfi, *The Hidden History of International Law in the Americas: Empire and Legal Networks* (Oxford: Oxford University Press, 2017), xxv.

34. Smith, *Roosevelt's Geographer*, 92.

35. Isaiah Bowman, *The New World: Problems in Political Geography* (New York: World Book, 1923); Ó Tuathail, *Critical Geopolitics, 153*.

36. Ó Tuathail, *Geopolitics*, 15.

37. "The trustees of financially strapped Clark University sold the *Journal of Race Development / International Relations* to the mix of millionaire lawyers, bankers and professors who in 1921 had founded the New York's Council of Foreign Relations," 60. The journal was founded in 1910, and subsequently renamed. See Vitalis, *White World Order*, 57, 60.

38. Smith, *Roosevelt's Geographer*, 152n16.

39. Smith, *Roosevelt's Geographer*, 181–207, at 193.

40. Vitalis has pointed out that Coolidge, who earned his PhD in Freiburg in 1892, was also influenced by Grant.

41. Vitalis, *White World Order*, 72. Isaiah Bowman, "The Pioneer Fringe," *Foreign Affairs* 6 (October 1927): 49–66. According to Smith, Bowman strongly

rejected Turner's 1890 frontier thesis: "From time to time it is announced that the pioneer has vanished, that the world has filled up with humanity. This is like saying that the age of exploration is over because man has reached the two poles." In Smith, *Roosevelt's Geographer*, 216.

42. Scarfi, *International Law in the Americas*, xxiii, xxv.

43. I borrow the phrase from Benjamin Coates, *Legalist Empire: International Law and American Foreign Relations in the Early Twentieth Century* (Oxford: Oxford University Press, 2016).

44. Carl Landauer has portrayed the "genteel" tradition of the American Society of International Law with both panache and penetrating insights in "The Ambivalences of Power: Launching the *American Journal of International Law* in an Era of Empire and Globalization," *Leiden Journal of International Law* 20, no. 2 (2007): 325–58.

45. Bew describes the moment when Lippmann joined Bowman on the Inquiry as illustrative of a brief moment of "synergy between the geopolitical awakening of the US and the liberal internationalist movement of the era" (*Realpolitik*, 129). Bew asserts that it was in the hands of the editors of the *New Republic*—William Weyl, Herbert Croly, and Walter Lippmann—that the term "Realpolitik" first shed its negative connotations in the US. In "A Little Realpolitik," (1915), Walter Lippmann advocated a "liberal realism" that drew on Theodore Roosevelt and Mahan. The "temporary marriage" collapsed when Lippmann rejected Wilson's commitment of the US to the League of Nations on the grounds that it was not in the national interest. See Bew, *Realpolitik*, 131.

46. On Bowman's debts to Mackinder, see Smith, *Roosevelt's Geographer*, 27–28; James Trapier Lowe, *Geopolitics and War: Mackinder's Philosophy of Power* (Washington, DC: Rowman and Littlefield, 1981), 86–87; Gerald Kearns, "Closed Space and Political Practice: Frederick Jackson Turner and Halford Mackinder," *Society and Space* 2, no. 1 (March 1984): 23–34.

47. Gerry Kearns, "Geography, Geopolitics and Empire," *Transactions of the Institute of British Geographers* 35, no. 2 (2010): 191–92.

48. See Michael Heffernan, "Fin de Siècle, Fin du Monde? On the Origins of European Geopolitics, 1890–1920," in *Geopolitical Traditions: Critical Histories of a Century of Geopolitical Thought*, ed. David Atkinson and Klaus Dodds (London: Routledge, 2002).

49. Mark Bassin, "What Is Classical Geopolitics?", unpublished paper, Conference at Duke University, Center for International and Global Studies, February 8–9, 2019.

50. Cited in Bernhard Streeck, "Diffusionism and Geopolitics in the Work of Friedrich Ratzel," in *Europe between Political Geography and Geopolitics: On the Centenary of Ratzel's 'Politische Geographie'* (Roma: Societá Geografica Italiana, 2001), 62.

51. See S. Holdar, "The Ideal State and the Power of Geography: The Life and Work of Rudolf Kjellén," *Political Geography* 11 (1992): 307–23.

52. Haushofer, *Dai Nihon*; Rudolf Kjellén, *Die Großmächte der Gegenwart* (Leipzig: B.G. Teubner, 1914).

53. Herwig, *Demon*, 117.

54. Haushofer, "Zur Geopolitik," reprinted in Jacobsen, *Karl Haushofer: Leben und Werk*, Bd. I (Boppard am Rhein: Boldt, 1979), 544.

55. Natter, *Geopolitics*, 192.

56. Herwig, *Demon of Geopolitics*, 160–63. The letter from Hess is in Jacobsen, *Haushofer*, Bd. I: 370–75, cited in Herwig, *Demon of Geopolitics*, at 167.

57. In 1904, Ellen Semple was a founding member of the Association of American Geographers (AAG). In 1906, she joined the Department of Geography at the University of Chicago, the first department in the United States to offer graduate training in the subject. Semple had an influential career at Chicago until 1923 when she moved to Clark University. Many of her students went on to become leaders in the field: Derwent Whittlesey (1890–1956) of Harvard University, Carl O. Sauer (1889–1975) of the University of Michigan and the University of California–Berkeley, and Richard Hartshorne (1900–1992) of the University of Wisconsin. She was elected president of the AAG in 1921, and her students Whittlesey, Sauer, and Hartshorne each held the same prestigious position in turn.

58. Davis and Shaler created a formal course in physical geography that helped the US discipline define its scientific raison d'être and identity. Davis founded the American Association of Geographers in 1904 with the goal of excluding "the mere traveller, the lover of outdoor nature," and the dilettante. See Susan Schluten, *The Geographical Imagination in America, 1880–1950* (Chicago: University of Chicago Press, 2001), 74. According to Jens-Uwe Guettel, during the 1890s "Ratzel's ideas found a second home among Harvard geologists and geographers" like Shaler. In *Nature and Man in America* (1891), Shaler "introduced Ratzel's ideas to American readers." See Jens-Uwe Guettel, *German Expansionism, Imperial Liberalism, and the United States, 1776–1945* (Cambridge: Cambridge University Press, 2012), 99–100. Ratzel had met Louis Agassiz (1807–1873), on a trip in the 1870s; Agassiz later taught Shaler, and Shaler, Davis. See Mark Bassin, "Friedrich Ratzel's Travels in the United States," *History of Geography Newsletter* 4 (1984): 11–22; Smith, *Roosevelt's Geographer*, 223.

59. Ellen Elizabeth Adams, "Ellen Churchill Semple and American Geography in an Era of American Imperialism" (PhD diss., College of William and Mary, 2011), 16.

60. Ellen Semple, "Review of *Anthropogeographie*, by Friedrich Ratzel," *Annals of the American Academy of Social and Political Science* 16 (1900): 137–39; "Review of *Der Staat und Sein Boden*, by Friedrich Ratzel," *Annals of the American Academy of Social and Political Science* 9 (1897): 102–4; "Review of *Politische Geographie der Vereinigten Staaten von Amerika*, by Friedrich Ratzel," *Annals of the American Academy of Social and Political Science* 4 (1894): 139–40.

61. Adams, "Semple and American Geography," chap. 2.

62. Ellen Semple, *American History and Its Geographic Conditions* (New York: Houghton Mifflin, 1903), 433.

63. William A. Koelsch, "Miss Semple Meets the Historians," *Journal of Historical Geography* 45 (2014): 50–58.

64. Ellen Churchill Semple, *Influences of Geographic Environment: On the Basis of Ratzel's System of Anthropo-Geography* (New York: Henry Holt, 1911), 11. "It became a standard textbook on historical geography and human geography (anthropogeography) for secondary school teachers, at some universities, and was "adopted by every ship's library in the US Navy, and included in the list of required reading for students entering the government military at West Point." Innes M. Keighren, *Bringing Geography to Book: Ellen Semple and the Reception of Geographic Knowledge* (London: I.B. Tauris, 2010), 34.

65. Mark Bassin, "Politics from Nature: Environment, Ideology and the Determinist Tradition," in *A Companion to Political Geography*, ed. John Agnew, Katharyne Mitchell, and Gerard Toal (London: Wiley 2003), 13–29.

66. Ellen Churchill Semple, "Two Works on Political Geography: *Leitlinien der allgemeinen politischen Geographie: Naturlehre des Staates* by Alexander Supan and Erich Obst; *Politische Geographie* by Friedrich Ratzel," *Geographical Review* 17, no. 3 (1927). Bowman's name does not appear in the original version of the 1927 review. Semple, *Geographical Review* 14, no. 4 (October 1924): 665–67.

67. Bowman, "Some German Works on Political Geography," *Geographical Review* 17, no. 3 (July 1927): 511–13.

68. Smith, *Roosevelt's Geographer*, 279–84.

69. See, for example, Murphy, *Heroic Earth*, and Gerry Kearns, *Geopolitics and Empire: The Legacy of Halford Mackinder* (Oxford: Oxford University Press, 2009).

70. Jacobsen, *Haushofer*, Bd. I:153.

71. Karl Haushofer, Erich Obst, Hermann Lautensach, and Otto Maull, *Bausteine zur Geopolitik* (Berlin-Grunewald: Vowinckel, 1928).

72. Haushofer, "Politische Erdkunde und Geopolitik" (1925), in *Bausteine*, 60.

73. A German translation of Mahan, Alfred T. Mahan and Julius Sachs, *Die weisse Rasse und die Seeherrschaft* (Wien: Lumen, 1909), or *The White Race and Seapower*, is also mentioned in Lautensach, "Geopolitik in Schule," in *Bausteine*, 319; this is the rather remarkable translation of Mahan's important work, *The Interest of America in Sea Power, Present and Future* (1897).

74. Haushofer, "Geopolitik und Kaufmann," 271. Reprinted from *Handwörterbuch des Kaufmanns: Lexicon für Handel und Industrie*, ed. Paul Arndt, Karl Bott (Hamburg: Hanseatische Verlagsanstalt, 1927).

75. James Fairgrieve (1870–1953) was a British geographer, who studied part-time at the London School of Economics with Mackinder and spent most of his career as a reader at the University of London Institute of Education. He was president of the British Geographic Association in 1935.

76. James Fairgrieve, *Geographie und Weltmacht: eine Einführung in die Geopolitik*, trans. Martha Haushofer, with an introduction by Karl Haushofer (Berlin-Grunewald: Vowinckel, 1925).

77. Karl Haushofer, "Zur Geopolitik," Ausarbeitung für den Rundfunk (1931), repr. in Jacobsen, *Leben und Werk*, Bd. I:542–51, at 542. Compare "Geographische Grundzüge auswartiger Politik," *Süddeutsche Monatshefte* (January 1927), repr. in Jacobsen, *Leben und Werk*, Bd. I:537–42, at 541.

78. Karl Haushofer, "Politische Erdkunde und Geopolitik," in *Bausteine*, 57. Original in *Freie Wege vergleichender Erdkunde: Erich v. Drygalski zum 60. Geburtstage gewidmet von seinen Schülern* (München: R. Oldenbourg, 1925). For this translation, see Andreas Dorpalen, The *World of General Haushofer: Geopolitics in Action* (New York: Farrar & Rinehart, 1942), 28. Compare Haushofer, "Geopolitik und Geojurisprudenz," *Zeitschrift für Völkerrecht* 14 (1928). The geopoliticians were interested in synthesizing geography and international law, and some lawyers were interested in their work. As Murphy points out, Manfred Langhans-Ratzeburg's major treatise on "geo-jurisprudence," published in 1932, had similarities with Schmitt's theory of *Großraum*. But the two men's biographies intersected little. There is no mention of Haushofer in the index of Reinhard Mehring's massive biography of Schmitt, for example, and Schmitt rarely cited him. In the index to *Frieden oder Pazifizismus*, a collection of Schmitt's essays from five decades, Haushofer's name appears only once.

79. In English, see Christian W. Spang, "Karl Haushofer Re-examined: Geopolitics as a Factor of Japanese-German Rapprochement in the Interwar Years," 139–58, in *Japanese-German Relations: War, Diplomacy and Public Opinion*, ed. Christian W. Spang and Rolf-Harald Wippich (New York: Routledge, 2006).

80. Christian W. Spang, *Karl Haushofer und die OAG: deutsch-japanische Netzwerke in der ersten Halfte des 20. Jahrhunderts* (München: Iudicium, 2018), 92–107.

81. Kearns, "Geography, Geopolitics and Empire," 187,

82. See the essays in Haushofer, *Bausteine der Geopolitik*.

83. For example, Haushofer, "Zur Geopolitik" (1931), 545. At 546, "die Kunst der Politik."

84. Letter to Martha Haushofer, June 4, 1917, Privatarchiv H.H. Hartschimmelhof, cited in Jacobsen, *Haushofer*, Bd. I:483; Haushofer, "Zur Geopolitik," 544.

85. Haushofer et al., "Historische Entwicklung,"19.

86. "Zur Geopolitik" (1931), paraphrased by Jacobsen, *Haushofer*, Bd. I:488.

87. Kurt Vowinckel to Karl Haushofer (August 26, 1941), Jacobsen, *Haushofer*, Bd. II:520.

88. Haushofer, "Politische Erdkunde und Geopolitik" (1925), *Bausteine*, 57.

89. Haushofer recommends Bowman's *The New World* as a "useful introduction" to the problems faced by the Germans after WWI because the book "conceives of the whole world as geopolitical raw material."

90. See Michael Williams, "Morgenthau and Aesthetic Realism," in

Historiographic Investigations in International Relations, ed. Brian Schmidt and Nicolas Guilhot (London: Palgrave, 2019).

Chapter 3

1. See Chantal Mouffe, "Schmitt's Vision of a Multipolar World Order," *South Atlantic Quarterly* 104, no. 2 (2005): 245–51.

2. See Carl Schmitt, *The Concept of the Political* (1932), trans. George Schwab (Chicago: University of Chicago Press 1996), 30.

3. Gerry Kearns, *Geopolitics and Empire: The Legacy of Halford Mackinder* (Oxford: Oxford University Press, 2009), 16.

4. See Dirk von Laak, "Von Alfred T. Mahan zu Carl Schmitt: Das Verhältnis von Land und Seemacht," in *Geopolitik: Grenzgänge im Zeitgeist*, Bd. I:1890–1945, ed. Julius H. Schoeps et al. (Berlin: Verlag für Berlin-Brandenburg, 2000), 257–82.

5. Carl Schmitt, *Völkerrechtliche Großraumordnung mit Interventionsverbot für Raumfremde Mächte: Ein Beitrag zum Reichsbegriff im Völkerrecht*, Dritte, Unveränderte Auflage der Ausgabe von 1941, 2nd ed. (Berlin: Duncker & Humblot, 2009). Cited in Claudio Minca and Rory Rowan, "The Question of Space in Carl Schmitt," *Progress in Human Geography* 39, no. 3 (Fall 2015): 277.

6. Schmitt, *Völkerrechtliche Großraumordnung*, 29.

7. Schmitt, "Vorbemerkung," in *Der Nomos der Erde* (Berlin: Duncker & Humblot, 1950).

8. Werner Best, "Völkische Großraumordnung statt Völkerrechtsgroßraumordnung," *Deutsches Recht* 11 (1941): 1533–36.

9. David T. Murphy, *The Heroic Earth: Geopolitical Thought in Weimar Germany, 1918–1933* (Kent, OH: Kent State University Press, 1997); Mark Bassin, "Race contra Space: The Conflict between German *Geopolitik* and National Socialism," *Political Geography Quarterly* 6, no. 2 (April 1987): 115–34.

10. Dan Diner, "'Grundbuch des Planeten': Zur Geopolitik Karl Haushofers," *Vierteljahrshefte für Zeitgeschichte* 32, no. 1 (January 1984): 12–13.

11. According to his contemporary Nicholas Sombart: "Ever and again he [Schmitt] posed the question to himself (and me): What kind of war is this in which we are engaged? . . . Did it have any sense at all after the defeat of Poland and France? The revision of the Versailles Diktat, that was Hitler's historical mission. Those were conventional land wars. But now? What should one think of this? In the East we are conducting an ideological war of annihilation, in the West a worldwide sea war. We simply aren't up to this." Sombart, *Jugend in Berlin: Ein Bericht* (München: C. Hanser, 1984), 266. Cited in Samuel Zeitlin, "Propaganda and Critique: An Introduction to Land and Sea," in Carl Schmitt, *Land and Sea: A World-Historical Meditation*, ed. Samuel Zeitlin and Russell A. Berman (Candor, NY: Telos Press, 2015), xl. I have discussed the translation of the Sombart quote with Zeitlin personally and rendered it very slightly differently than he.

12. As Samuel Zeitlin has explained, with reference to the third and fourth editions of *Völkerrechtliche Großraumordnung*, and to *Land and Sea* (1942),

"'Land powers' in Schmitt's vocabulary in *Land and Sea*, are anthropologically identified with peoples who base their existence on the land. In connecting Germany and Russia through a shared humanity—one that in Schmitt's view, Germans do not share with the English, the Americans, and the Jewish people, Schmitt may seem to subtly imply that the annulment of the Hitler-Stalin Pact was a geopolitical error for Nazism." In Zeitlin, "Propaganda," xlvi. I thank Sam Zeitlin, both for sharing his deep historical insight on this point, and for clarifying his interpretive position. Although he has noted the text's oblique criticism of the regime in regard to the invasion, the book remains for Zeitlin, unambiguously, a work of "Nazi propaganda." See Zetlin, "Propaganda," lxix.

13. Friedrich Ratzel, *Die Vereinigten Staaten von Nord-Amerika*, vol. II, 2nd ed. (München: R. Oldenbourg, 1893), 85.

14. Joseph Kaiser, "Europäisches Großraumdenken: Die Steigerung geschichtlicher Grössen als Rechtsproblem," in *Epirrhosis: Festgabe für Carl Schmitt*, vol. II, ed. Hans Barion (Berlin: Duncker & Humblot, 1968), 538.

15. See Minca and Rowan, "The Question of Space in Carl Schmitt," 276. Stirk concurs: "Developments had left a mark on his texts. The early emphasis on central and Eastern Europe had given way to a more expansive conception." See Peter Stirk, "Carl Schmitt's *Völkerrechtliche Grossraumordnung*," *History of Political Thought* 20, no. 2 (1999): 361.

16. Ulrich Herbert, *Best: Biographische Studien über Radikalismus, Weltanschauung und Vernunft, 1903–1989* (Bonn: J.H.W. Dietz, 1996).

17. Schmitt, "Antwort an Robert Kempner" (April 18, 1947), in *Carl Schmitt: Antworten in Nürnberg*, ed. Helmut Quaritsch (Berlin: Duncker & Humblot, 2000), 77.

18. "Question: You however admit that the absolute is a *Völkerrechts*-theory of *Lebensraum*? "Answer: I say *Großraum*. Question: Hitler was also for *Großraum*. Answer: Indeed they all were, including members of other states." In *Carl Schmitt: Antworten in Nürnberg*, 54.

19. As he does in Section 10 of *Land and Sea* and in the prologue to *Gespräch uber den neuen Raum* (Santiago de Compostela: Univ. de Santiago de Compostela, 1958). Schmitt often used the terms *Großraum* and *Lebensraum* seemingly interchangeably and understands German expansion into German-speaking territories to be consistent with his notion of a *Völkerrechtliche Großraumordnung* even if "'international law' may be cited to the contrary." Samuel Zeitlin, "Propaganda and Critique: An Introduction to Land and Sea," Carl Schmitt, *Land and Sea: A World-Historical Meditation* (New York: Telos Press, 2015), 62.

20. Stirk, "*Grossraumordnung*," 358.

21. Diemut Majer, "Die Perversion des Völkerrechts unter dem Nationalsozialismus," *Jahrbuch des Instituts für Deutsche Geschichte* 14 (1985): 329.

22. Carl Schmitt, *Staat, Großraum, Nomos: Arbeiten aus den Jahren 1916–1969*, ed. Günter Maschke (Berlin: Duncker & Humblot, 1995), 371. Cited in Stirk, *Grossraumordnung*, 358n6.

23. Stirk, "*Grossraumordnung*," 359.

24. Michael Stolleis, *The History of Public Law in Germany, 1914–1945*, trans. Thomas Dunlap (Oxford: Oxford University Press, 2004), 412.

25. Stirk, "*Grossraumordnung*," 372.

26. Schmitt, *Völkerrechtliche Großraumordnung*, 22.

27. Tracing the concept of *Großraum* back to the Middle European Diet founded by economist Julius Wolf in 1904, Berghahn describes Wolf as an advocate for informal empire who looks "across the Atlantic . . . what was needed was the creation of a *Großraum* stretching from the English Channel to the Balkans." While the stabilization of the Weimar economy with American loans in the mid-1920s gave credence to the notion of transatlantic economic cooperation and open markets, the crash of 1929 caused that vision of *Großraum* to recede: "Conceptions of economic bloc-building now made a strong comeback . . . The new debate was merely about how closed and autarkic the *Großraum* should be in which German business expected to predominate." Völker Berghahn, "German Big Business and the Quest for a European Economic Empire in the 20th Century," in *Quest for Economic Empire: European Strategies of German Big Business in the Twentieth Century*, ed. Völker Berghahn (Oxford: Berghahn Books, 1996).

28. Stirk, "*Grossraumordnung*," 370; Schmitt, *Völkerrechtliche Großraumordnung*, 14. Schmitt credits Viktor Weizsäcker with the coinage of "Leistungsraum." See Weizsäcker, *Der Gestaltkreis: Theorie und Einheit von Wahrnehmen und Bewegen* (Leipzig: Georg Thieme, 1940).

29. Berghahn, *Economic Empire*, 17.

30. Berghahn mentions Arno Solter, Andreas Predohl, and Werner Daitz as advocates of giving formal equality to foreign-owned companies within the cartel. See Berghahn, *Economic Empire*, 22.

31. Schmitt, *Völkerrechtliche Großraumordnung*, 13. Daitz was also author of "True and False Versions of Lebensraum" in the leading SS journal. See "Echte und Unechte Großräume: Gesetze des Lebensraumes," *Reich, Volksordnung, Lebensraum: Zeitschrift für völkische Verfassung und Verwaltung* 2 (Darmstadt: L.C. Wittich Verlag, 1942), 75–96.

32. Berghahn, *Economic Empire*, 23.

33. Stolleis, *Public Law*, 411.

34. Stolleis asserts that Schmitt's thesis is derivative of Triepel's *Hegemonie* [1938]: "[*Hegemonie*] was not a National Socialist book . . . and [it was] by a national conservative emeritus who was removed from National Socialism. Yet this fundamental book . . . did initiate the debate about the formation of mutually differentiating empires with a ring of hegemonic relationships. An updated and pointed expression of this idea in geopolitics led to the notion of *Großraum* (large space)"; Stolleis, *Public Law*, 418.

35. Herbert, *Best*, 278.

36. "Whereas Höhn, like Best, referred to the 'Volk' as a living organism and as a legitimizing point of departure for 'völkischer' politics, Schmitt's thinking

lacked such a 'natural' category; the center of his political thought was, rather, power." Herbert, *Best*, 274.

37. The journal was edited by Wilhelm Stuckart, Werner Best, Gerhard Klopfer, Rudolf Lehmann, and Reinhard Höhn.

38. See Schmitt, "Antwort an Kempner" (April 18, 1947), in Carl Schmitt, *Staat, Großraum, Nomos*, 460–62.

39. Schmitt, *Völkerrechtliche Großraumordnung*, 11.

40. See Raphael Gross, *Carl Schmitt and the Jews: The "Jewish Question," the Holocaust, and German Legal Theory*, trans. Joel Golb (Madison: University of Wisconsin Press, 2007).

41. Schmitt, *Völkerrechtliche Großraumordnung*, 79n93; Schmitt credits Walter Hamel with overcoming this problem in his book, *Das Wesen des Staatsgebietes* (Berlin: O. Liebmann, 1933).

42. At n. 94, Schmitt cites Ratzel, *Der Lebensraum: Eine biogeographische Studie* (Tübingen: H. Laupp, 1901), 12.

43. Schmitt cites Viktor von Weizsäcker, *Der Gestaltskreis: Theorie der Einheit von Wahrnehmen und Bewegen* (Leipzig: Georg Thieme,1940), 102.

44. Schmitt, *Völkerrechtliche Großraumordnung*, 80: "Only now have the ideas of an empty dimension of depth and of a purely formal category of space been definitively overcome. Space becomes 'Leistungsraum.'"

45. Reinhard Höhn, "Großraumordnung und völkisches Rechtsdenken," in *Reich, Volksordnung, Lebensraum* 1 (1941), 269.

46. Compare Höhn, "Großraumordnung," 267: "The substance, which first makes the enemy an enemy, is confusingly negated as the concept of the enemy . . . The definition of the political . . . contains blood and life only if one knows why one chooses it, and on which political grounds the friend-foe grouping is sharpened."

47. Süthoff-Gross, "Deutsche Großraum-Lehre und Politik," *Deutsches Recht* 1943, H. 23/24, 567, cited in W. Mallmann, "Zur Weiterentwicklung der Großraumlehre," *Geistige Arbeit* 1943, Nr. 6.

48. Höhn, "Großraumordnung," 274–75.

49. Werner Best, "Völkische Großraumordnung," *Deutches Recht; Zentralorgen des Nationalsozialistische Rechtswahrerbundes* 10, no. 25 (1940): 1006–7.

50. Schmitt, *Völkerrechtliche Großraumordnung*, 3rd ed., 47, cited in Werner Best, "Nochmals: Völkische Großraumordnung statt 'Völkerrechtliche Großraumordnung,'" *Deutsches Recht* 11, no. 29 (1941): 1533. Schmitt also offers this concession to Höhn's critique in his "Raum und Großraum im Völkerrecht" (1940), reprinted in Schmitt, *Staat, Großraum, Nomos*, 235.

51. Best, "Nochmals," 1533.

52. Hans Frank, "Das Reich," *Zeitschrift der Akademie für Deutsches Recht* (April 1939), 218–19, cited in Ernst Wolgast, "Großraum und Reich: Bemerkungen zur Schrift Carl Schmitts 'Völkerrechtliche Großraumordnung'," *Zeitschrift für öffentliches Recht* 21, no. 1 (1941): 29n2.

53. Ernst Wolgast, "Großraum und Reich," 29.

54. Friedrich Berber, *Der Mythos der Monroe-Doktrin*, 2. Veränderte Auflage in Schriftenreihe des Deutschen Instituts für Aussenpolitische Forschung (Essen: Essener Verlagsanstalt, 1943), 26.

55. Heinrich Triepel, *Die Hegemonie: Ein Buch von Führenden Staaten* (Stuttgart: W. Kohlhammer, 1938).

56. Hans Spanner, "Großraum und Reich: Bemerkungen zu Bd. I der Zeitschrift, '*Reich, Volksordnung, Lebensraum*," *Zeitschrift für öffentliches Recht* 22 (1942): 28–58. Trained in Vienna, Spanner was from 1942 to 1944 leader of a legal division of the General Commissariat for Justice and Administration in the German-occupied Netherlands.

57. Ernst Rudolf Huber, "Positionen und Begriffe: Auseinandersetzung mit Schmitt," *Zeitschrift für die gesamte Staatswissenschaft* 101, no. 1 (1941): 1–44. Huber, a student of Schmitt's in Bonn, was professor of law in Kiel (1937–41) and Strasbourg (1941–44).

58. Hans Spanner, "Großraum und Reich," 48–49.

59. Huber, *Positionen*," 39n1: "We speak of an age of imperialism and the political concept of a *Großmacht* was always used . . . Schmitt discusses the difference between '*Großraum*' and '*Großmacht*' in *Reich und Raum* [1940: 201], without clarifying the difference."

60. Herbert, *Best*, 290.

61. Werner Best, "Großraumordnung und Großraumverwaltung," *Zeitschrift für Politik* 32, no. 6 (June 1942): 407.

62. Hermann Jahrreiss, "Wandel der Weltordnung: Zugleich eine Auseinandersetzung von mit der Völkerrechtslehre Carl Schmitt," *Zeitschrift für öffentliches Recht* 21 (1941): 527. Jahrreiss was professor for public law, international law, and philosophy of state and law at various universities between 1933 and 1945: Greifswald, Köln, Göttingen, and Innsbruck.

63. Berber, *Der Mythos*, 22.

64. Höhn, "Großraumordnung" (1941), 260.

65. Schmitt, "Antwort an Kempner" (April 18, 1947), in Schmitt, *Staat, Großraum, Nomos*, 453.

66. Cited in Claudio Minca and Rory Rowan, *On Schmitt and Space* (New York: Routledge, 2016), 170. They give as their source, Timothy Nunan, ed., *Carl Schmitt: Writings on War* (Cambridge: Polity, 2011), 13.

67. Schmitt, "Antwort an Kempner," in *Staat, Großraum, Nomos*, 453.

68. Schmitt, "Antwort an Kempner," in *Staat, Großraum, Nomos*, 461.

Chapter 4

1. Carl Schmitt, *Glossarium: Aufzeichnungen der Jahre 1947–1951*, ed. Eberhard Freiherr von Medem (Berlin: Duncker & Humblot, 1991), 203.

2. Grewe often reflected on his role in these historic events. See, for example,

"Westbindung und Deutsche Frage: Wie weit reicht die Interessengemeinschaft mit den westlichen Partnern," in *Deutsche Frage und Westbindung*, ed. Klaus Weigelt (Melle: Verlag Ernst Knoth, 1986), 89–118.

3. In one of the only historical treatments of Grewe's work, legal scholar Bardo Fassbender describes *Epochs* as "the only thorough description of [the modern history of international law] in the last 50 years in any language, with no successor being in sight." Fassbender calls it "the standard work of the German-language historiography of international law, particularly in light of the strong influence the book had." Bardo Fassbender, "Stories of War and Peace: On Writing the History of International Law in the 'Third Reich' and After," *European Journal of International Law* 13, no. 2 (2002): 481.

4. Hermann Weber and Gideon Botsch touch on Grewe's wartime career, but only Fassbender makes it his focus. Weber, Botsch, and Fassbender cited in note 8 below.

5. The work was soon acknowledged as a standard text on the history of modern international law. Bardo Fassbender and Anne Peters, "Introduction: Towards a Global History of International Law," in *The Oxford Handbook of the History of International Law*, ed. Fassbender and Peters (Oxford: Oxford University Press, 2012), 22. Some scholars, however, have critiqued his approach for overstating the discontinuities between so-called epochs; for example, Oliver Diggelman, "Periodization of the History of International Law," in Fassbender and Peters, 1004.

6. Martti Koskenniemi, "Out of Europe: Carl Schmitt, Hans Morgenthau, and the Turn to 'International Relations,'" in *The Gentle Civilizer of Nations: The Rise and Fall of International Law, 1870–1960* (Cambridge: Cambridge University Press, 2001), 413–509.

7. Martti Koskenniemi, "Review of *The Epochs of International Law*," *International and Comparative Law Quarterly* 51, no. 3 (July 2002): 747.

8. For the chronological reconstruction of his biography, I have used the Lebenslauf, which forms part of the Grewe Nachlass in the (former) Max-Planck-Institut für Europäische Rechtsgeschichte (NL 7), but corroborated these with documents from the files of the Reichsministerium für Wissenschaft, Erziehung und Volksbildung (REM hereafter) housed in the Bundesarchiv in Berlin. R4901/13264, Fiche 069 contained biographical information through October 1941. R4901/1250a contained information through December 1942, as well as a first-person Lebenslauf ("Wissenschaftlicher Werdegang," August 15, 1944). Information about his teaching was obtained from the annual reports of the Archiv des Deutschen Auslandswissenschaftlichen Instituts, available in R4902/6028, R4902/4999, and R4902/4720. Three other sources based on extensive research in the primary documents were invaluable: Hermann Weber, "Rechtswissenschaft im Dienst der NS-Propaganda: Das Hamburger Institut für Auswärtige Politik und die deutsche Völkerrechtsdoktrin in den Jahren 1933 bis 1945," in *Wissenschaftliche Verantwortung und politische Macht*, ed. Klaus Jürgen Gantzel (Berlin: Dietrich

Reimer Verlag, 1986), 185–425; Gideon Botsch, *"Politische Wissenschaft" im Zweiten Weltkrieg: Die "Deutschen Auslandswissenschaften" im Einsatz 1940– 1945* (Paderborn: Ferdinand Schöningh, 2006); and Fassbender, "Stories," which relies in part on Hermann Weber, above.

9. See also Fassbender, "Stories," 494n62.

10. Accepted by the law and political science faculty of Königsberg University in March 1941. According to Grewe, "Preface to the First Edition" (1944), in *The Epochs of International Law*, trans. and rev. Michael Byers (Berlin: Walter de Gruyter, 2000), xiii.

11. Ibid. The title is "Die Epochen der modernen Völkerrechtsgeschichte," *Zeitschrift für die Gesamte Staatswissenschaft* 103, Bd. I, H. 1 (1943): 38–66; Bd. II, H. 2 (1943): 260–94.

12. A second unchanged version of the second edition (1984) was published in 1988. The 2000 version includes a new section on the period since 1945, "Part Six: United Nations: International Law in the Age of American-Soviet Rivalry and the Rise of the Third World, 1945–1989," 639–700, in Byers (trans.), *The Epochs of International Law*.

13. A FOIA request of records relating to Grewe in the IRR Image Files of the National Archives and Records Administration turned up an American questionnaire relating to denazification that Grewe had completed, probably in 1955 or 1956. In this questionnaire, he answered question XVI—"Denazified on—by—decision" with the following: "1947, Denazification Panel, Freiburg Br., V-exonerated." Freiburg was in the French zone. Grewe made the same claim in a letter to Erich Kaufmann from 1952. In general, and according to both statistics and contemporary commentaries, denazification was implemented most strictly in the American zone and "most leniently" in the French zone, as illustrated by the fact that 52% of legal proceedings (the highest percentage of the four zones) were suspended. As one of only .5% of interrogees deemed "exonerated," Grewe fell between two much larger groups—the 44.7% who were deemed *"Mitläufer"* (follower) and 52.2% whose proceedings were suspended. In the same document, Grewe replied "No" to the question of whether he had been a member of "any organization whose aims were inimical to the Weimar Constitution," an answer demonstrably untrue given the records indicating his party membership began in 1933. The date of his membership of the Nazi Party is given in his own hand as May 1, 1933, with *Mitgliedsnummer* 3125858, in the "Parteistatistische Erhebung 1939," R 9361-I002, Bundesarchiv Berlin.

14. Wilhelm Grewe, *Spiel der Kräfte in der Weltpolitik: Theorie und Praxis der Internationalen Beziehungen* (Düsseldorf: Econ-Verlag, 1970).

15. Wilhelm G. Grewe, *Rückblenden, 1976/1951* (Frankfurt/Main: Propyläen, 1979). The memoirs are widely praised in letters to Grewe from conservative luminaries of the German legal and historical establishment such as Carl Schmitt (August 22, 1979), Hans-Peter Schwarz (March 14, 1978), Roman Schnur (May 14,

1979), Franz Wieacker (May 19, 1979), Ernst Nolte (October 12, 1979), and Hans Maier (May 21, 1979). See Grewe *Nachlass*, Max Planck Institut-Frankfurt am Main, NL 7:2:16:1.

16. Wilhelm G. Grewe, *Machtprojektionen und Rechtsschranken: Essays aus vier Jahrzehnten über Verfassungen, politische Systeme und internationale Strukturen* (Baden-Baden: Nomos, 1991).

17. Grewe was first nominated in 1954 and the nomination renewed in 1961, 1967, 1973, and 1979. Letter from the Permanent Court of Arbitration, June 7, 2001, on file with Bardo Fassbender, cited in Fassbender, "Stories," 484n13.

18. W.G. Grewe, *Epochen der Völkerrechtsgeschichte* (Baden-Baden: Nomos, 1984).

19. Grewe, "Foreword," *Epochs*.

20. Fassbender, "Stories," 511.

21. Detlev Vagts, "International Law in the Third Reich," *American Journal of International Law* 84: 661, 679. Cited in Carl Landauer, "Review of Grewe, *The Epochs of International Law*," *Leiden Journal of International Law* 16, no. 1 (2003): 192.

22. Grewe, "Preface" (1944), *Epochs*, xii.

23. Personal letter, Erich Kaufmann to Wilhelm Grewe, March 17, 1952, Grewe *Nachlass*, Politisches Archiv, Auswartiges Amt, Berlin. Erich Kaufmann (1880–1972) was one of the most important jurists in the Weimar Republic, and like Schmitt a critic of the Labandian legal positivism dominant before 1914, but unlike him a democrat, a republican, and an advocate of natural law. Baptized Protestant, he was nonetheless considered Jewish by the Nazi regime, and forced from teaching in 1934. He fled Germany in 1938, returning to a position as professor of international law in Munich from 1946–50, and consultant to the Foreign Office from 1950 to 1958.

24. According to the index of the Schmitt *Nachlass* in Düsseldorf assembled in 1993, there are 69 items of correspondence between Grewe and Schmitt, 325 notes and materials concerning Grewe, and several books and articles by Grewe in Schmitt's library (422 et seq. and 567 et seq.). Cited in Fassbender, "Stories," 504n123. Not all of this is reproduced in the Grewe *Nachlass*.

25. Schmitt to Forsthoff, September 18, 1949, *Briefwechsel Schmitt-Forsthoff,* ed. Angela Reinthal (Berlin: Akademie Verlag, 2003).

26. Fassbender, "Stories," 504.

27. Martti Koskeniemmi, "Review of *The Epochs of International Law*," *International and Comparative Law Quarterly* 51, no. 3 (July 2002): 747.

28. Grewe, *Epochen*, 23.

29. Grewe, *Epochs*, 6.

30. Grewe, "Die Epochen der Völkerrechtsgeschichte," *Zeitschrift für die gesamte Staatswissenschaft* Bd. 103, H. 1 (1943): 38–66; H. 2 (1943): 260–94. "The following remarks were the basis of a lecture which the author gave at the

Arbeitstagung des NS-Dozentenbundes in Weimar on the 10th of April 1942. It offers a summary overview of the results of his book 'Epochs of the Modern History of International Law' which will shortly appear from Verlag Köhler and Amelang, Leipzig." In "Die Epochen der Völkerrechtsgeschichte," *Zeitschrift für die gesamte Staatswissenschaft* Bd. 103, H. 1 (1943): 38.

31. Grewe, "Epochen," 1943, Pt. II, 283.

32. Schmitt, "Reich und Raum," *Zeitschrift der Akademie für Deutsches Recht* Jg. 7, H. 13 (July 1, 1940): 202.

33. Grewe, "Epochen," 1943, Pt. II, 266.

34. Grewe, *Epochs*, 275.

35. Grewe, "Protektorat und Schutzfreundschaft," *Monatshefte für Auswärtige Politik* Jg. 6, H. 4 (April 1939): 341ff.

36. Grewe, "Epochen," 1943, II, 267.

37. Grewe, *Epochs*, 414.

38. Grewe, *Epochs*, 422–23.

39. Carl Schmitt, *The Concept of the Political*, trans. George Schwab (Chicago: University of Chicago Press 1996).

40. Grewe, *Epochs*, 621, cf. Grewe, "Zwischen Neutralität und Kollektivsicherheit: Zur Aussenpolitik der Vereinigten Staaten," *Monatshefte für Auswärtige Politik* 4 (October 1937): 637. The Kellogg Pact was never legally valid because of its "indeterminate formulations and numerous reservations."

41. Grewe, "Die Neue Kriegsphase," *Monatshefte für Auswärtige Politik* 9, no. 9 (September 1941): 751: "To the extent that positive norms of the received Völkerrecht have become inapplicable through the growing dissolution of the hitherto existing order of states, one will in the future have to orient oneself to the ordering value of these mutual objectives."

42. Grewe, "Die Völkerrechtlichen Grundlagen der Stellung des Reiches in Europa" (1942), 99.

43. Grewe, "Stellung des Reiches" (1942), 111.

44. The Commissar Order of June 6, 1941, was a secret directive to the armed forces on the eve of the invasion of the USSR, counseling disregard for the laws of war: "When fighting Bolshevism one cannot count on the enemy acting in accordance with the principles of humanity or International Law."

45. Personal correspondence, Grewe to Hermann Weber (November 18, 1985), cited in Weber, "Rechtswissenschaft," 365–66n3.

46. Grewe, "Die Neue Kriegsphase," 748.

47. Legal scholar Bardo Fassbender argues that "spheres of influence" and "hegemony" were among "the buzzwords of the group of comparatively moderate internationalists of the 'Third Reich,'" which included Heinrich Triepel, Schmitt, and Grewe. "The notions of *Hegemonie, Reich, Europa,* and *Weltordnung* allowed this group to support Hitler's foreign policy through an adoption of geopolitical ideas grounded on, or at least related to, older Pan-Germanic and imperialistic

views which were still common among conservative Germans after the First World War." Bardo Fassbender, "On Stories of War and Peace: On Writing the History of International Law in the 'Third Reich' and After," *European Journal of International Law* 13, no. 2 (April 2002): 497.

48. Grewe, "Probleme des Luftkriegsrechtes," *Archiv für Luftrecht* Bd. XI, H. 3/4 (1942): 125 ff.

49. Grewe, "Fallschirmjäger," *Monatshefte für Auswärtige Politik* Jg. 7, H. 6 (June 1940): 422

50. Grewe, *Zerstörer gegen Stützpunkte* (Schriftenreihe Deutsches Institut für Aussenpolitische Forschung, 1942), cited in Detlev Vagts, "International Law," 699. Grewe, "Das Schicksal der Neutralität im europäischen Kriege und im zweiten Weltkrieg," *Jahrbuch der Weltpolitik* 2 (1943): 86–106.

51. See Grewe, "Zwischen Neutralität und Kollektivsicherheit"; Grewe, "Die Beschlüsse von Havana," *Monatshefte für Auswärtige Politik* 11, no. 8 (August 1940): 583–86; Grewe "Der Status der Nichtkriegsführung," *Zeitschrift der Akademie für Deutsches Recht* 7 (1940): 206ff.; Grewe, *Der Dritte Wirtschaftskrieg* (Berlin: Junker & Dünnhaupt, 1940); Grewe, "Die Bestimmung des Kriegszustandes," *Zeitschrift der Akademie für Deutsches Recht* 7, no. 22 (November 15, 1940); Grewe, "Stellungswechsel der amerikanischen Völkerrechtspolitik," *Zeitschrift für Politik* 31, no. 5 (May 1941): 21ff.; Grewe, "Das Englandhilfsgesetz," *Zeitschrift für gesamte Staatswissenschaft* 101 (1941): 606–26; Grewe, *Probleme des Luftkriegsrechts* (Königsberg/Berlin: Ost-Europa Verlag, 1942), 125ff.; Grewe, 'Der Zweite Weltkrieg," *Monatshefte für Auswärtige Politik* 9, no. 1/2 (January–February 1942): 7–13

52. Vagts, "International Law," 699.

53. Grewe, *Epochs*, 634.

54. Grewe, "Das Schicksal der Neutralität," 99.

55. Grewe, *Epochs*, 105.

56. Fassbender, "Stories," 491n40: "In the fall of 1922, Grewe left Freiburg for Frankfurt where Forsthoff had been appointed [Herman Heller's] successor . . . It seems that Grewe followed Forsthoff to Hamburg in 1935 . . . Forsthoff taught [there] from 1 April 1935 to 31 March 1936 . . . In 1933, Forsthoff was 31 years old, and Grewe 22."

57. Grewe's dissertation, *Gnade und Recht* (*Mercy and Law*), 1936, was dedicated to "my teacher, Prof. Ernst Forsthoff in sincere gratitude and the bonds of friendship." See Angela Reinthal et al., eds., *Briefwechsel Ernst Forsthoff—Carl Schmitt* (Berlin: Akademie Verlag, 2003), 12n65.

58. Grewe, "Die Umbildung der Republik," *Die Junge Mannschaft*, H. 1 (1932): 5–6.

59. Grewe, "Der Begriff des Politischen-Politik und Moral," *Die Junge Mannschaft* 1, 1931/1932, H. 6 (December 1931). Cited in Stefan Breuer, *Carl Schmitt im Kontext: Intellektuellenpolitik in der Weimarer Republik* (Berlin: Akademie Verlag, 2012), 212.

60. See Schmitt, *Tagebücher 1930 bis 1934* (2010), 147, 157; Grewe to Schmitt, January 7, 1932, in the Carl Schmitt *Nachlass* (Papers), RW 265–5150. Both cited in Breuer, *Carl Schmitt*, 212n75.

61. Cf. Breuer, *Carl Schmitt*, 212, 242. The DHV, the German National Association of Commercial Employees, was a *völkisch* and antisemitic lobbying group founded in 1893. Tending to align with the Deutschnationale Volkspartei (DNVP), it grew closer to the National Socialists (NSDAP) after 1930.

62. See the detailed notes in Breuer, *Carl Schmitt*, 242–47. The journals were *Die Kommenden, Deutsches Adelblatt, Der Junge Sturm, Die Junge Mannschaft,* and *Deutsches Volkstum.*

63. Breuer, *Carl Schmitt*, 243. For the "leading ideas" of the "Hamburg School," see ibid., 244.

64. Grewe, "Verfassungspolitischen Aufgaben eine nationalsozialistischen Staates," in *Was wir von Nationalsozialismus erwarten: Zwanzig Antworten,* ed. Albrecht Erich Günther (Heilbronn: E. Salzer, 1932), 92.

65. Fassbender, "Stories," 491n43.

66. Peter Longerich, *Propagandisten im Krieg: Die Presseabteilung des Auswärtigen Amtes unter Ribbentrop* (München R. Oldenbourg, 1987), 52.

67. Weber, "Rechtswissenschaft," 277.

68. Grewe to Erich Kaufmann, March 23, 1952, in Politische Archiv, Auswärtiges Amt, Berlin.

69. Goebbels had wanted since 1933 to subsume the Deutsche Hochschule für Politik under his Ministry of Research but with Ribbentrop's prompting, Hitler opted for the Foreign Office (AA), in Weber, "Rechtswissenschaft," 327 and 327n3.

70. Weber, "Rechtswissenschaft," 274.

71. Longerich, 53n39. He was promoted to *Ordinarius* in 1940.

72. Weber, "Rechtswissenschaft," 275.

73. The DI shared a *Referat* structure with the DIAF and was financed by the Foreign Office. The Foreign Office paid the DI 696,000 marks in 1941/42 and 360,000 marks in 1942/43 and 1943/44. Weber, "Rechtswissenschaft," 279. While Grewe and von Kempski were responsible for the international law section (*Völkerrechtsreferat*), the scholar responsible for the Near East and *Geopolitik* was Albrecht Haushofer, Karl Haushofer's son. Ibid., 282.

74. Quote from "AA, Rechtsabteilung, geh. Völkerrecht/Wissenschaft, RI und R II, Bd. 1., Jahresbericht f. 1942/43," cited in Longerich, *Propagandisten im Krieg,* 52n35.

75. In mid-1941, this number increased to twenty. Weber, "Rechtswissenschaft," 281.

76. Archives of the Reichsministerium für Wissenschaft, Erziehung und Volksbildung (REM), Bundesarchiv Berlin, R4901-1250a.

77. Grewe's curriculum vitae, REM, R-4901-1250a, 2–5.

78. According to a letter of Grewe from July 22, 1983, Berber did not enjoy a

reputation as an authority in the discipline (*"fachliche Autorität"*) and overestimated his own abilities to an embarrassing extent. Cited in Weber, "Rechtswissenschaft," 335n3. See his memoirs for the same: Grewe, *Rückblenden*, 183.

79. Berber was the editor of *Monatshefte* and the *Jahrbuch für Auswärtige Politik* in the years Grewe published there.

80. In 1934, Paul Marc (brother of the painter Franz Marc) renamed it the *Hamburger Monatshefte für Auswärtige Politik*. Later, when the HIAP was folded into the Berlin DIAF in 1939, the name was shortened to the *Monatshefte für Auswärtige Politik*. Weber, "Rechtswissenschaft," 310n3.

81. Ibid., 335n5. "In a message to the author, Berber denied being involved in any propagandistic activity, which, given the materials at hand, must be described as entirely misleading." Longerich, *Propagandisten,* 53.

82. Fassbender, "Stories," 491n46. He relies on Longerich, *Propagandisten,* 52–68.

83. Weber, "Rechtswissenschaft," 385 and 385n6.

84. Herbert, *Best,* 284.

85. Grewe, "Wehrbereitschaft und Verfassungsrecht," *Zeitschrift der Akademie für Deutsches Recht* 4 (February 15, 1937): 110ff.; Grewe, "Wirtschaftliche Neutralität" (May 1, 1940): 141–44; Grewe, "Der Status der Nichtkriegsführung," *Zeitschrift der Akademie für Deutsches Recht* 7 (1940): 206–7; Grewe, "Die Bestimmung des Kriegszustandes," *Zeitschrift der Akademie für Deutsches Recht* 7, no. 22 (November 15, 1940): 355–56.

86. Dennis LeRoy Anderson, *The Academy for German Law* (New York: Garland, 1987), 464–65.

87. Schmitt, "Antwort an Kempner" (April 17, 1948), in *Staat, Großraum, Nomos,* 459.

88. Grewe, "Die Völkerrechtlichen Grundlagen der Stellung des Reiches in Europa," Sonderausgabe aus dem *Jahrbuch der Weltpolitik*, Deutsches Auslandswissenschaftliches Institut (Berlin: Junker & Dünnhaupt, 1942), 90–111; Grewe, "Das Schicksal der Neutralität im Europäischen Krieg und im Zweiten Weltkrieg," *Jahrbuch der Weltpolitik* Jg. 2 (1943): 86–106.

89. Grewe, "Krieg und Frieden: Proudhons Theorie des Völkerrechts," *Zeitschrift für Politik* 30, no. 6/7 (June–July 1940): 233–45; Grewe, "Rechtsformen des ökonomischen Imperialismus im 19. Jahrhundert," *Zeitschrift für Politik* 31, no. 4 (April 1941): 230–42; Grewe, "Das Bündnissystem der Allierten," *Zeitschrift für Politik* 32, no. 7 (July 1942): 483–89; Grewe, "Von den 'Allierten und Assoziierten Mächten' zu den 'Vereinigten Nationen," *Zeitschrift für Politik* 33 (1943): 262–66; Grewe, "Die Völkerbundspläne der Alliierten," *Zeitschrift für Politik* 34, no. 7/8 (1944): 266–86.

90. Regina Urban and Ralf Herpolsheimer, "Franz Alfred Six," in *Zeitungswissenschaftler im Dritten Reich: Sieben biographische Studien,* ed. Arnold Kutsch, et. al. (Köln: Studienverlag Hayit, 1984), 180. See also REM 4902–4800. The DAWI was linked with but distinct from the University of

Berlin's Faculty of Foreign Studies (*Auslandswissenschaftliche Fakultät*). Both were created at the behest of the Reich's Education and Propaganda Ministries by an order of January 5, 1940.

91. The lowest-ranking officer's commission, equivalent to a second lieutenant in many modern militaries.

92. The RSHA, formed in September 1939, consolidated the SD with the Sicherheitspolizei (*SiPo*), which in turn was composed of the Gestapo (*Geheime Staatspolizei*) and the Kripp (*Kriminalpolizei*). Cf. Charles Ingrao, *Believe and Destroy: Intellectuals in the SS War Machine*, trans. Andrew Brown (New York: Polity, 2013), esp. 228–30; Peter Klein, ed., *Die Einsatzgruppen in der besetzten Sowjetunion, 1941/42* (Berlin: Edition Hentrich, 1997), 180–84; Lutz Hachmeister, *Der Gegnerforscher: die Karriere des SS-Führers Franz Six* (München, 1998), 237ff.

93. Ingrao, *Believe and Destroy*, 231.

94. See Lutz Hachmeister, *Der Gegnerforscher: Die Karriere des SS-Führers Franz Alfred Six* (München: Beck, 1988).

95. F.A. (Franz) Six, "Das Deutsche Auslandswissenschaftliche Institut im Jahre 1941," *Archiv des DAWI Berlin*, no. 4 (April 4, 1942). REM, R4902–6028, 1124/1, unpaginated, page 1 of 4.

96. Karl Heinz Pfeffer, *Die Angelsächsische Neue Welt und Europa*, Bd. I (Berlin: Junker & Dünnhaupt, 1941).

97. "Structure of the DAWI," from R4902–4800, 1112/0042–45, here at 0043.

98. Fassbender, "Stories," 493n57. Six, "Das Deutsche Auslandswissenschaftliche Institut im Jahre 1941," p. 4 of 4.

99. Undated report (1943) from R4902–4800///1112/0042–45.

100. REM/R4902, no. 9, p. 10ff.: Grewe, "Exposé für ein Handbuch der Politik: Grundlagen und Grundbegriffe deutscher Europapolitik," January 25, 1942. See Botsch, "Politische Wissenschaften," 150n175.

101. Botsch, "Politische Wissenschaften," 150.

102. R490111: DAWI Berichte der Zentrabteilungen, Archiv des DAWI-Berlin, December 6, 1943: "Volk und Staat," "Einführung in die Grundbegriffe der Rechtswissenschaft," "(*Staatswissenschaft*)," and "Völkerrechtliche Tagesfragen."

103. US Holocaust Memorial Museum Archive, RG 15.007, Reel 24, pp. 51–60. Cited in Botsch, "Politische Wissenschaften," 150.

104. In the questionnaire Grewe was required to fill out prior to assuming the position of ambassador to the United States, Grewe listed Gülich as a reference. Gülich (1895–1960), a DNVP party member from 1919–21, joined the SPD in 1945, and served in the Bundestag from 1949–1960. Levin (1909–1945), trained as a historian, obtained the rank of *Obersturmbannführer* in the SS. Mahnke (1913–1985), a SS *Hauptsturmführer* in the RSHA, was after WWII a leading editor at *Der Spiegel* and Springer Verlag. Both Mahnke and Levin had worked with Six in the RSHA Division VII, *Weltanschauliche Forschung*, and Mahnke had accompanied Six in the *Vorkommando* Moscow of the *Einsatzgruppe* B.

105. Letter, Franz Six to Hans Gülich (November 4, 1942), USHMMA, RG 15.007M, Reel 24, p. 57. The letter mentions Grewe's instructions for authors ("die Verfasservorschläge von Herrn Grewe").

106. Trevor Barnes and Christian Abrahamsson, "Tangled Complicities and Moral Struggles," *Journal of Historical Geography* 47 (2015): 72.

107. Memorandum from the acting dean of the DAWI to the Reichsministerium für Wissenschaft, Erziehung, und Bildung (November 11, 1943), R4901–1250a.

108. REM, R4901–1250a: WPWP 1162/44 (September 27, 1944).

109. REM, R1250a: WP 1162/44 (September 27, 1944), 26.

110. Anderson, *The Academy*, 464–65.

111. Fassbender, "Stories," 495. See A. Möhler, ed., *Carl Schmitt: Briefwechsel mit einem Schüler* (Berlin: Akademie Verlag, 1995), 125–27, at 126.

112. This is the argument of Helmut Quaritsch. See Quaritsch, "Eine sonderbare Beziehung: Carl Schmitt und Erich Kaufmann," 71–87, in *Bürgersinn und staatliche Macht in Antike und Gegenwart: Festschrift für Wolfgang Schuller zum 65. Geburtstag*, ed. M. Dreher (Konstanz: Universitätsverlag Konstanz, 2000).

113. Grewe, *Rückblenden*, 182–83.

114. Grewe, *Rückblenden*, 182.

115. Richard Evans, "The German Foreign Office and the Nazi Past," *Neue Politische Literatur* 56 (2011): 165–83. See also "Forum: The German Foreign Office and the Nazi Past," *Bulletin of the German Historical Institute* 49 (Fall 2011): 53–112.

116. Vagts, "International Law," 677.

117. "The other leading opportunist of our story is Friedrich Berber. Less vaultingly ambitious than Schmitt, he made fewer enemies during the Third Reich and did less drastically evil things." Vagts, "International Law," 680, 684.

Chapter 5

1. Neil Smith, *American Empire: Roosevelt's Geographer and the Prelude to Globalization* (Berkeley: University of California Press, 2004), 274ff. See, for example, "Germany's Brain Trust," *Life*, November 20, 1939, 60–66; Frederic Sondern, Jr., "The Thousand Scientists behind Hitler," *Reader's Digest*, June 1941, 23–27.

2. Gearóid Ó Tuathail, "'It's Smart to be Geopolitical': Narrating German Geopolitics in U.S. Political Discourse, 1939–43," in *Critical Geopolitics: The Politics of Writing Global Space* (Minneapolis: University of Minnesota Press, 1996), 111–40.

3. Derwent Whittlesey, *German Strategy of World Conquest* (New York: Farrar & Rinehart, 1942); Robert Strausz-Hupé, *Geopolitics: The Struggle for Space and Power* (New York: Putnam and Sons, 1942); Johannes Mattern, *Geopolitik: Doctrine of National Self-Sufficiency and Empire* (Baltimore: Johns Hopkins University Press, 1942); Andreas Dorpalen, *The World of General Haushofer: Geopolitics in Action* (New York: Farrar & Rinehart, 1942); Andrew Georgy,

Geopolitics: The New German Science (Berkeley: University of California Press, 1944).

4. Ó Tuathail, *Critical Geopolitics*, 121–35.

5. "Geopolitics in College," *Time*, January 19, 1942, 56.

6. Ó Tuathail makes a similar point: "Purified of its Nazism, [the study of German geopolitics] is also a powerful practice that Allies would do well to cultivate"; *Critical Geopolitics*, 123.

7. Renner was a prominent national figure. In addition to his teaching at Columbia Teacher's College, he consulted for the Civilian Aeronautics Administration and Rand McNally maps. See Susan Schulten, *The Geographical Imagination in America, 1880–1950* (Chicago: University of Chicago Press, 2002), 138–43.

8. Tuathail, *Critical Geopolitics*, 153n19.

9. Isaiah Bowman, "Geography vs. Geopolitics," *Geographical Review* 32, no. 4 (October 1942): 646–58, at 653.

10. Smith, *Roosevelt's Geographer*, 284.

11. In an exchange of letters with the editor of the *Geographic Review*, for example, Bowman admitted his oversimplifications, and the editor regretted that Bowman's invective was not consistent with the normal standards of the journal. See Smith, *Roosevelt's Geographer*, 289.

12. Maull described *Macht der Erde* as a "practical analysis of global power . . . culminating in a geopolitical overview of the earth . . . as a German counterweight to I. Bowman's New World." In Otto Maull, *Das Wesen der Geopolitik*, 2nd ed. (Leipzig: B.G. Taubner, 1936), 23. Quoted in Smith, *Roosevelt's Geographer*, 282.

13. Bowman, "Geography vs. Geopolitics," 657.

14. Council on Foreign Relations, "Studies of American Interests in the War and the Peace," (WPS), Territorial Series, memoranda of discussions, T-A1, 16 February 1940, cited in Smith, *Roosevelt's Geographer*, 516n6.

15. Smith, *Roosevelt's Geographer*, 319.

16. For Strausz-Hupé's racism, see Robert Vitalis, *White World Order, Black Power Politics: The Birth of American International Relations* (Ithaca, NY: Cornell University Press, 2015), 153–56.

17. Isaiah Bowman, "Political Geography of Power: Review of *America's Strategy in World Politics: The United States and the Balance of Power* by Nicholas J. Spykman," in *Geographical Review* 32, no. 2 (April 1942): 349–52, at 350.

18. Our understanding of turn-of-the-century American geopolitics is underdeveloped; research on Homer Lea and Morton Fullerton would be valuable.

19. Mattern, *Geopolitik*, 23.

20. The most comprehensive study of Spykman is that of Olivier Zajec, *Nicholas John Spykman, l'invention de la géopolitique americaine: un itineraire intellectuel aux origines paradoxales de la théorie realiste des relations internationales* (Paris: Maison de la Recherche, Université Paris-Sorbonne, 2016); see also the discussion of Bowman and Spykman in Or Rosenboim, *The Emergence of Globalism:*

Visions of World Order in Britain and the United States, 1939–1950 (Princeton, NJ: Princeton University Press, 2017).

21. Malcolm Cowley, "Geography's Fate," *Time*, April 20, 1942, 90–96.

22. Lippmann coined the term "Cold War" in his book, *The Cold War: A Study in US Foreign Policy* (New York: Harper, 1947).

23. "Geopolitics in College," *Time*, January 19, 1942, 56.

24. Grayson Kirk, *War and National Policy: A Syllabus*, foreword by Earle and others (New York: Farrar Straus, 1942). The preface reads: "Since 1938 scholars at the Institute for Advanced Study, working under the direction of Professor Edward Mead Earle, had been carrying on a program of research on the same general subject." The introduction gratefully acknowledges John Herz, Felix Gilbert, and Alfred Vagts.

25. "Geopolitics in College," 51.

26. Ó Tuathail, *Critical Geopolitics*, 127.

27. Weigert, "Workshop for Army Rule," *Harper's Magazine*, June 1, 1941, 586–97. Weigert was author of *Generals and Geographers: The Twilight of Geopolitics* (Oxford: Oxford University Press, 1942).

28. Dorpalen, *World of Haushofer*, 14. Dorpalen later became a successful historian with a distinguished career at Ohio State University, authoring a major study of Treitschke in 1957.

29. Herman Beukema, "Introduction," in Dorpalen, *World of Haushofer*, xvi.

30. Ó Tuathail, *Critical Geopolitics*, 128–29.

31. Derwent Whittlesey, "The Geopoliticians: Haushofer," in *Makers of Modern Strategy: Military Thought from Machiavelli to Hitler*, ed. Edward M. Earle, with the assistance of Gordon Craig and Felix Gilbert (Princeton, NJ: Princeton University Press, 1943).

32. Whittlesey, "The Geopoliticians: Haushofer," 389.

33. Folder "German Strategy of World Conquest—Stages in Preparation," Whittlesey Papers.

34. Colby to Hartshorne and Whittlesey, April 27, 1943, Folder "Beukema, Herman and corresp. re A.S.T. Geography," Whittlesey Papers.

35. Whittlesey to Beukema, August 16, 1944, Folder "Beukema, Herman and corresp. re A.S.T. Geography," Whittlesey Papers.

36. "Geopolitics in College," *Time*, January 19, 1942, 56.

37. The "Geopolitical Section" of the Military Intelligence Service was abolished in 1943; Ó Tuathail, *Critical Geopolitics*, 133n54.

38. Frank H. Simonds and Brooks Emeny, *The Great Powers in World Politics* (New York: American Book, 1935). Emeny wrote his doctorate with Spykman at Yale, and after years of directing the Cleveland, Ohio–based Council on World Affairs, took over direction of the New York City–based Foreign Policy Association from 1947 to 1952.

39. Whittlesey to Dunn, November 1, 1943, Folder "D-Unclassified," Whittlesey Papers.

40. Neil Smith writes that Bowman "despised" Whittlesey personally and actively conspired to undermine him at Harvard. This was on the eve of the Harvard geography department's dissolution by President Conant. See Smith, *Roosevelt's Geographer*, 441–44.

41. Bowman to Whittlesey, December 4, 1945, Whittlesey Papers.

42. Woolbert to Whittlesey, December 5, 1945, Whittlesey Papers.

43. Walsh, "The Mystery of Haushofer," *Life*, September 16, 1946, 107–20.

44. Patrick McNamara, *A Catholic Cold War: Edmund A. Walsh, S.J., and the Politics of American Anticommunism* (New York: Fordham University Press, 2005), 125–26.

45. Haushofer, "Defense of German Geopolitics" (1946), in Edmund A. Walsh, *Total Power: A Footnote to History* (New York: Doubleday, 1948), 348. Holdich (1834–1929) was a geographer who spent time in India and the Far East for the British government. He was superintendent of frontier surveys in India between 1892 and 1898, and the author of *Political Frontier and Boundary Making* (London: Macmillan, 1916).

46. Cited in Kearns, *Geopolitics and Empire*, 20.

47. Walsh, *Total Power*, 348.

48. The meetings took place September 25, 1945, and November 2, 1945; Karl Haushofer and his wife, Martha, committed suicide on March 11, 1946.

49. Homer Lea (1876–1912) was a soldier of fortune, geopolitical thinker, and adviser to Sun Yat-Sen during the 1911 revolution. He authored *The Valor of Ignorance* (New York: Harper and Bros., 1909) and *The Day of the Saxon* (New York: Harper and Bros., 1912).

50. See, for example, William McGovern, *From Luther to Hitler: The History of Fascist-Nazi Political Philosophy* (New York: Houghton-Mifflin, 1941).

51. Malcolm Cowley, "Review of Nicholas Spykman, *America's Strategy in World Politics: The US and the Balance of Power*," *The New Republic*, April 20, 1942.

52. Hans Speier, "Magic Geography," *Social Research* 8, no. 3 (September 1941): 313; for Speier's intellectual biography and political significance, see Daniel Bessner, *Democracy in Exile: Hans Speier and the Rise of the Defense Intellectual* (Ithaca, NY: Cornell University Press, 2018).

53. *The War in Maps, 1939/40*, ed. Giselher Wirsing, in collaboration with A. Haushofer et al. (New York: German Library of Information, 1941), in Hans Speier, "Magic Geography," *Social Research* 8, no. 3 (September 1941), 310–30.

54. Georgy, *New German Science*, 254n3. *Wehrgeopolitik* appears to be Georgy's neologism. Andrew Georgy (1917–1993) was a Hungarian-born political scientist who taught at Amherst College and Boston University.

55. Vagts's son was Detlev Vagts, a distinguished professor of international law, who taught at Harvard University until his death in 2013.

56. Alfred Vagts, "Geography in War and Geopolitics," *Military Affairs* 7, no. 2 (Summer 1943): 79–88, a review of Johannes Mattern, *Geopolitik: Doctrine*

of *National Self-Sufficiency and Empire* (Baltimore: Johns Hopkins University Press, 1942); Halford Mackinder, *Democratic Ideals and Realities: A Study in the Politics of Reconstruction* (London: Constable, 1919); Andreas Dorpalen, *The World of General Haushofer: Geopolitics in Action*, with an introduction by US Col. Herman Beukema (New York: Farrar & Rinehart, 1942).

57. Vagts, "Geography," 80.

58. Franz Neumann, *Behemoth: The Structure and Practice of National Socialism* (1942) (New York: Octagon, 1944).

59. For discussion of Neumann's intellectual development in Germany, and his relationship to Carl Schmitt and his thought, see William E. Scheuerman, *Between the Norm and the Exception: The Frankfurt School and the Rule of Law* (Cambridge, MA: MIT Press, 1997).

60. "The complete subjugation of political geography to the needs of German imperialism was the work chiefly of two men: Rudolf Kjellén and Haushofer . . . For all its 'empiricism' and supposed realism . . . Kjellén's theory remains basically a rehash of the organic theory of Ratzel," 137, 140.

61. On Wittfogel, see Ó Tuathail, *Critical Geopolitics,* 143–51.

62. See Ó Tuathail, *Critical Geopolitics,* 140: "At this time, geopolitics did not necessarily mean political realism. Weigert's call for a 'geopolitics of peace' was explicitly antirealist, while other instances of geopolitics, such as the clumsy effort by George Renner to draw new political maps of the world's continents, were far from that which could be described as 'realist'." Or Rosenboim points out that the regionally focused geopolitics of Owen Lattimore and Nicholas Spykman was marginalized after 1945, but that their thought nonetheless had a significant impact on "ideas of the 'global'" and "the categories of global order." See Rosenboim, *Globalism*, 98–99.

63. See Rosenboim, *Globalism*; Paolo Jorge Batista Ramos, "The Role of the Yale Institute for International Studies in the Construction of the United States National Security Ideology, 1935–1951" (PhD thesis, University of Manchester, 2003).

64. Beukema, "Introduction," *World of Haushofer*, xviii.

65. In his *New Republic* review of Spykman in 1942, Cowley dissented from the framing of geopolitics as art, too: "Geopolitics might be defined as an attempt to transform the art of international relations into a physical science by excluding everything qualitative; by excluding nothing that cannot be measured in terms of mass or energy." Cowley, "Geopolitik," 547.

Chapter 6

1. David Milne, *Worldmaking: The Art and Science of American Diplomacy* (New York: Farrar, Straus & Giroux, 2017).

2. John Lewis Gaddis, *The Long Peace: Inquiries into the History of the Cold War* (Oxford: Oxford University Press, 1987), 21–22; Melvyn Leffler, *A Preponderance of Power: National Security, the Truman Administration, and*

the Cold War (Stanford: Stanford University Press, 1992), 10–13, 191. Cited in John A. Thompson, "The Geopolitical Vision: The Myth of an Outmatched USA," 91–114, in *Uncertain Empire: American History and the Idea of the Cold War*, ed. Joel Isaac and Duncan Bell (Oxford: Oxford University Press, 2012).

3. Thompson, "Myth," in Isaac and Bell, *Uncertain Empire*, 92–93.

4. Beate Jahn, *Liberal Internationalism: Theory, History, Practice* (London: Palgrave Macmillan, 2013), 19.

5. A locus classicus is Alexander Wendt, "Anarchy Is What States Make of It: The Social Construction of Power Politics," *International Organization* 46, on. 2 (Spring 1992): 391–425.

6. Thompson, "Myth," 93, 94–95.

7. Nicolas Guilhot, "Politics between and beyond Nations: Hans J. Morgenthau's *Politics among Nations*," in *Classics of International Relations: Essays in Criticism and Appreciation*, ed. Henrik Blyddal, Casper Sylvest, and Peter Wilson (New York: Routledge, 2013), 69; Christoph Frei, *Hans Morgenthau: An Intellectual Biography* (Baton Rouge: LSU Press, 2001), 173.

8. Kissinger to Morgenthau, HM Papers, Box 14, Folder 14. There are about a hundred short pieces of correspondence, some very friendly, but bitter disagreements about the Vietnam War in 1968 caused a rift. Kissinger was invited to speak at Morgenthau's funeral in 1980.

9. The literature on Morgenthau is vast. One of the most important compilations is Michael C. Williams, *Realism Reconsidered: The Legacy of Hans Morgenthau in International Relations* (Oxford: Oxford University Press, 2007). His intellectual biography has been thoroughly traversed. An earlier wave of scholarship depicted Morgenthau as a conservative liberal (Stanley Hoffman, Christoph Frei), or a radical conservative (Alfons Söllner, Joachim Radkau, Martti Koskenniemi). Those who stress his reactionary conservatism, including prominently the link to Schmitt (Nicolas Guilhot), now appear outnumbered by the revisionists Udi Greenberg, William E. Scheuerman, Felix Rösch, Helmut Behr, and Oliver Jütersonke. The revisionists argue that the emphasis on Schmittian influence on Morgenthau is exaggerated or needs to be supplemented by numerous other influences, including Hans Kelsen, Hersch Lauterpacht, Hugo Sinzheimer, and Karl Mannheim. While Scheuerman initially emphasized the conservative influence of Carl Schmitt, his current position emphasizes the predominance of left-liberal German influences on Morgenthau's thought. See William E. Scheuerman, *Carl Schmitt: The End of Law* (Lanham, MD: Rowman and Littlefield, 1999), 225–52, and idem, *Morgenthau: Realism and Beyond* (London: Polity, 2009). Guilhot has updated the pioneering accounts by Söllner and Koskenniemi in his superb *After the Enlightenment: Political Realism and International Relations in the Mid-Twentieth Century* (Cambridge: Cambridge University Press, 2018) and his edited compilation of essays, *The Invention of International Relations Theory: Realism, the Rockefeller Foundation, and the 1954 Conference on Theory* (New York: Columbia University Press, 2011). The most important

guides to Morgenthau's relationship to German legal theory are Scheuerman, Oliver Jütersonke, and Peter M.R. Stirk. See Jütersonke, *Morgenthau, Law, Realism* (Cambridge: Cambridge University Press, 2012); Stirk, "International Law, Emigrés and the Foundation of International Relations," 61–80, in *Émigré Scholars and the Genesis of International Relations: A European Discipline in America?*, ed. Felix Rösch (London: Palgrave, 2014). For an important synthesis, see Christoph Rohde, *Hans J. Morgenthau und der Weltpolitische Realismus* (Wiesbaden: VS, 2004). See also Joachim Radkau, *Die deutsche Emigration in den USA: Ihr Einfluss auf die amerikanische Europapolitik, 1933–1945* (Düsseldorf: Bertelsmann, 1971); Christoph Frei, *Morgenthau: An Intellectual Biography* (Baton Rouge: LSU Press, 2001); Stanley Hoffmann, "International Relations: An American Social Science" (1977), in *Janus and Minerva: Essays in the Theory of International Politics* (New York: Westview, 1987), 3–22; idem, "The Limits of Realism," *Social Research* 49, no. 1 (Spring 1981): 653–59; Alfons Söllner, "Vom Völkerrecht zur science of international relations—Vier Typen der Internationalisierung," 134–45, in *Deutsche Politikwissenschaftler in der Emigration: Studien zu ihrer Akkulturation und Wirkungsgeschichte*, mit einer Bibliographie (Wiesbaden: VS, 1986); idem, "German Conservatism in America: Hans Morgenthau's Political Realism," *Telos* 72 (Summer 1987): 161–72; Martti Koskenniemi, *The Gentle Civilizer: Rise and Fall of International Law, 1870–1960* (Cambridge: Cambridge University Press, 2000), 413–509; Udi Greenberg, *The Weimar Century: German Emigres and the Ideological Foundations of the Cold War* (Princeton, NJ: Princeton University Press, 2014); Hartmut Behr and Felix Rösch, "Introduction," 1–82, in *Hans Morgenthau. The Concept of the Political*, ed. Behr and Rösch, trans. Maeva Vidal (London: Palgrave Macmillan, 2012). There are dozens of valuable articles on the relationship of Morgenthau and Max Weber, and Morgenthau and Carl Schmitt, which I have no space to adumbrate here. For a sensitive and enlightening analysis, see the essay by political theorist and former Morgenthau student Richard Ned Lebow, "German Jews and American Realism," 212–43. The works of Koskenniemi, Scheuerman, Guilhot, and Jütersonke have been the most important influences on the interpretation I develop here.

10. For "Pope of Realism" see Scheuerman," *Morgenthau*, 2. The title of the introduction is "Morgenthau's Uneasy Realism."

11. Greenberg, "From the League of Nations to Vietnam: Hans J. Morgenthau and Realist Reform of International Relations," 211–55, in *Weimar Century*, 227.

12. "The 'Realism' that German jurists such as Morgenthau, [John] Herz or Karl Deutsch inaugurated in IR academia espoused a Hobbesian anthropology, an obsession with the marginal situation, the pervading sense of a spiritual and political crisis in the West, and constant concern over political collapse . . . Political science departments at US universities received from the German refugees an image of international law as Weimar law writ large." Koskenniemi, *The Gentle Civilizer*, 467.

13. Guilhot, *After the Enlightenment*, 83.

14. See also Philip Mirowski's insightful "Realism and Neoliberalism: Reactionary Modernism to Postwar Conservatism," in Guilhot, *Invention*, 210–38.

15. See the essays in Felix Rösch, ed., *Émigré Scholars and the Genesis of International Relations: A European Discipline in America?* (London: Palgrave Macmillan, 2015).

16. See HJM Papers, Box 7 for the Barnet correspondence, and Box 49 for Raskin. Morgenthau's appointment to the board of trustees is recorded in a letter from Raskin to Morgenthau, March 5, 1963. His retirement from active board duty is requested and noted in Barnet to Morgenthau, November 10, 1971.

17. See the essays by Richard Barnet and Marcus Raskin in *Truth and Tragedy: A Tribute to Hans J. Morgenthau* (New York: Transaction Books, 1984).

18. They base their conclusions on a review of over twenty-five textbooks published from 1945–60. They note, however, that "[t]he centrality—if not the exclusivity—of power had already been stressed by wartime mainstream writers"(105). In William C. Olson and A.J.R. Groom, *International Relations Now and Then: Trends in Interpretation* (New York: Harper and Row, 1991), 111–12.

19. Christoph Frei, *Morgenthau: An Intellectual Biography* (Baton Rouge: LSU Press, 2001), 126.

20. For discussion, see Koskenniemi, *Gentle Civilizer*, 440–54; Scheuerman, *Morgenthau*, 18–24; Jütersonke, *Morgenthau*, 37–74; Greenberg, *Weimar Century*, 213–25.

21. Morgenthau, "Fragment of an Intellectual Autobiography: 1904–1932," in *Society* 15, no. 2 (January–February 1978): 68.

22. Jütersonke considers the story largely fanciful, and interpretations that build upon it misleading. See his *Morgenthau*, 28–68. There are but two pieces of correspondence with Schmitt in the Morgenthau papers, both dated 1929, and neither sheds light on the plagiarism episode or their relationship generally. See HJM Papers, Box 197, Folder 2.

23. See Scheuerman, *Morgenthau*, 11–39. Through Sinzheimer, Morgenthau met Paul Tillich, Martin Buber, Franz Neumann, Ernst Fraenkel, Otto Kahn-Freund, Max Horkheimer, and Herbert Marcuse (Frei, *An Intellectual Biography*, 38–39). See also Morgenthau, "Fragment of an Intellectual Autobiography," n. 20.

24. Morgenthau had contact with Mannheim in Frankfurt in the 1920s. Oliver Jütersonke, *Morgenthau, Law and Realism* (Cambridge: Cambridge University Press, 2010), 151, 168; Frei, *An Intellectual Biography*, 38–39.

25. Jütersonke, *Morgenthau*, 163.

26. Morgenthau, "Stresemann als Schöpfer der deutschen Völkerrechtspolitik," *Die Justiz* 5 (1929/30): 169–76.

27. Hugo Sinzheimer to Morgenthau, March 11, 1932, HJM Papers, Box 54.

28. HJM Papers, Box 197, Folder 1.

29. Behr and Rösch, *Concept of the Political*, Appendix 2, 155.

30. Karl Loewenstein to Morgenthau, March 28, 1935, HJM Papers, Box 196, Folder 23; Behr and Rösch, *Concept of the Political*, Annex 2.

31. Frei, *Intellectual Biography*, 61–66. The letter was written to Elener Balogh and is in HJM Papers, Box 208.

32. HJM Papers, Box 31, Folder 7.

33. Morgenthau, "Functionalism, Positivism and International Law," *American Journal of International Law* 34, no. 2 (April 1940): 260–84.

34. Oliver Jütersonke, *Morgenthau, Law and Realism* (Cambridge: Cambridge University Press, 2010), 147.

35. Morgenthau to Jessup, January 28, 1941, HJM Papers, Box 31, Folder 7.

36. Percy Corbett was the author, with Grayson Kirk, of *The Outlook for a Security Organization* (New Haven, CT: Yale University Press, 1944).

37. Morgenthau to Corbett, December 14, 1943, HJM Papers, Box 89. Morgenthau to Friedrich, September 7, 1943: "I finally accepted an offer from the University of Chicago, a visiting associate professorship to replace Quincy Wright for the first two quarters of the ensuing academic year. In March I shall join the Yale Institute for International Studies." HJM Papers, Box 22, Folder 8.

38. Jütersonke, *Morgenthau*, 25.

39. For a biographical sketch and insightful analysis of Wright (1890–1970), see Trygve Throntveit, "A Strange Fate: Quincy Wright and the Trans-War Trajectory of Wilsonian Internationalism," *White House Studies* 10, no. 4 (2011): 361–77.

40. See, for example, his review of Gerhart Niemeyer, *Law without Force* (1941), in *Iowa Law Review* 27 (1941–42): 350–55. Niemeyer had advised Morgenthau's dissertation in Frankfurt.

41. Quincy Wright was chairman; Morgenthau was president and honorary chairman.

42. Grayson Kirk, "Review of W.T.R. Fox, *The Super-Powers*," *American Journal of International Law* 29, no. 2 (April 1945): 369–70.

43. "The United Nations and the Organization of Peace and Security," July 9–13, 1945, in Norman Wait Harris Foundation, *Proceedings of the Twenty-First Institute under the Auspices of The Norman Wait Harris Foundation* (Chicago: University of Chicago Press, 1945), 5.

44. Morgenthau, "The Machiavellian Utopia," *Ethics* 55, no. 2 (January 1945): 147.

45. Morgenthau "Diplomacy," *Yale Law Journal* 55, no. 5 (1946): 1080.

46. In "About Cynicism, Perfectionism, and Realism in International Affairs" (1945), reprinted in Morgenthau, *The Decline of Democratic Politics* (Chicago: University of Chicago Press, 1962). Cited in Scheuerman, *Morgenthau*, 63.

47. Edward Hallett Carr, *The Twenty Years' Crisis: An Introduction to the Study of International Relations* (London: Macmillan, 1939); Morgenthau "The Political Science of E.H. Carr," *World Politics* 1, no. 1 (October 1948): 134. For good discussions of the Machiavelli question in Morgenthau, see Scheuerman, *Morgenthau*, 61–62, and Jütersonke, *Morgenthau*, 150–51, 162–65.

48. Many of its themes are revisited in his late work, *Science: Servant and Master* (New York: Norton, 1972). Five years before his death in 1980, Morgenthau described *Scientific Man* as his favorite book. See Frei, *Intellectual Biography*, 206.

49. It began as a lecture at the New School for Social Research in 1940 but was not published until 1946. The tenure he earned in 1945 protected him from the backlash he provoked. See Morgenthau, "Liberalism and Foreign Policy," HJM Papers, Box 168, Folder 5.

50. Jütersonke, *Morgenthau*, 135. "But . . . the fact that Morgenthau would increasingly turn his back on international law was not so much due to a change in his convictions, but rather due to an unwillingness to come to terms with the newer social scientific methodologies [being] developed to do precisely what he was calling for" (130). This seems only half-correct. It trivializes Morgenthau's shift in position and asks us to discount his polemical ferocity against legalism in favor of seeing him as very close to MacDougall: "It would not have taken Morgenthau long to discover that the functionalist research agenda he was advocating in International Law circles was already being followed by no other than Harold Lasswell (who had meanwhile resigned from his post as associate professor in Chicago and had moved to Washington D.C.), together with Myres MacDougal at Yale" (135). For MacDougall's part, Morgenthau was no ally: "In our contemporary disillusionment it is again becoming the fashion to minimize both the role that law presently plays in the world power process and the role that, with more effective organization, it could be made to play in maintaining the values of a free, peaceful, and abundant world society" (102). MacDougall, review of *In Defense of the National Interest: A Critical Examination of US Foreign Policy* (Knopf, 1951) and Kennan, *American Diplomacy 1900–1950* (Chicago, 1951), "Law and Power," in *American Journal of International Law* 46, no. 1 (January 1952): 102.

51. Harold Lasswell and Abraham Kaplan, *Power and Society: A Framework for Political Inquiry* (New Haven, CT: Yale University Press, 1950). *Power and Society* represented a "new scholasticism." Their "formalism" consisted of elaborating "self-sufficient abstraction" without demonstrating sufficient self-awareness of the values that guided their empirical inquiry. Morgenthau likened the abstractness of their political science to the abstractness of modern art: Both had a "common root in the disorders of our culture. Both retreat from empirical reality into a world of formal relations and abstract symbols." In "The State of Political Science" (1952) in *Dilemmas of Politics* (1958), 24. His claim that both forms of abstraction were decadent cultural forms is surprising given that he was, after all, a refugee from a regime that habitually characterized abstract ratiocination as decadent and Jewish.

52. See Jütersonke, *Morgenthau, Law and Realism*, 106–25. Jütersonke situates legal realism in a tradition stemming from Pound's writings advocating a "sociological" jurisprudence beginning around 1910. The systematic use of the term "realism" originated in 1930 in a brief exchange of views between a young

Llewelyn and Roscoe Pound, then dean of Harvard Law School and a Supreme Court justice. By the time Morgenthau arrived in the US, however, the legal realists were under attack as skeptics, nihilists, and moral relativists who were helping to destroy American civilization (119). The transatlantic link to Germany that had helped sustain legal realism became a liability after 1933. When in October 1934 Pound was awarded an honorary degree from the German ambassador to the US at Harvard University, Laski and Felix Frankfurter were extremely critical. Jütersonke argues that Morgenthau's timing could not have been worse: "With many US, law schools taking years to decide whether they should accept a single German legal scholar into their ranks . . . the situation was dismal" (123). For more of the context, see Katherine Graham, "The Refugee Jurist and American Law Schools, 1933–41," *American Journal of Comparative Law* 50 (2002): 777–818.

53. The primary discussion of international law is at 108–21; see also Scheuerman, *Morgenthau*, 31.

54. See Rohde, *Weltpolitische Realismus*, 193.

55. Morgenthau writes, "As Charles Beard put it: Foreign policy is a phase of domestic policy, an inseparable phase." He then adds that "it is the latter which determines the former" (Hans Morgenthau, *Scientific Man versus Power Politics*, 63). This alone is sufficient to be grouped with the "scientific" rationalists. He represents political scientist Paul Reinsch as belonging to a "school of thought [that] proceeds as though the political element did not exist or were, at best, an accidental element of it, bound to disappear in the near future" (45). See my discussion of Reinsch in chapter 1.

56. Guilhot, *After the Enlightenment*, 12–18. See also Morgenthau to Fox, June 2, 1956: "I am in agreement with the philosophic position of the paper [Butterfield's "Morality and Historical Process in International Affairs," also presented at the conference] as is obvious from *Scientific Man vs. Power Politics*." In HJM Papers, Box 22, Folder 6.

57. Morgenthau says the very point of the book is not to invent new solutions but rather to "lift the veil of oblivion from a truth once known," 10.

58. Morgenthau, *Scientific Man*, 68.

59. Scheuerman, *Morgenthau*, 71.

60. Guilhot, *Invention*, 16–17.

61. Morgenthau, *Scientific Man*, 92.

62. Frei, *Intellectual Biography*, 207.

63. Guilhot, *Invention*, 24. He is summarizing the argument of Brian Schmidt, "The Long Road to a Theory of International Politics." The essay is in *Invention*, 79–96.

64. After writing a dissertation at the University of Chicago on Arnold Toynbee, Thompson co-authored with Morgenthau, *Principles and Problems of International Politics: Selected Readings* (New York: Knopf, 1950).

65. For Morgenthau's hostility to behaviorism, see his "The State of Political Science" (1958) and "Commitments of Political Science" (1952), both in idem, *Dilemmas of Politics*.

66. Guilhot, *Invention*, Appendix 2, 265.

67. Morgenthau, "Realism in International Politics," lecture delivered at the Naval War College, October 2, 1957, in HJM Papers, Box 33, Folder 8, p. 5.

68. Behr and Rösch have made a valiant attempt to clarify Morgenthau's intentions and intellectual consistency in their introduction to Morgenthau's 1933 *Concept of the Political*. Morgenthau was "his worst popularizer" and therefore responsible for the misreadings. Moreover, some of his positions are not just confusing but seem fundamentally confused.

69. Greenberg, *Weimar Century*, 230–31.

70. Morgenthau, "The Twilight of International Morality," *Ethics: An International Journal of Social, Political and Legal Philosophy* 58, no. 2 (January 1948): 79–99; idem, "The Mainsprings of American Foreign Policy: The National Interest vs. Moral Abstractions," *American Political Science Review* 44, no. 4 (December 1950): 833–54; idem, "Power Politics," 36–51, in *The Atomic Era: Can It Bring Peace and Abundance?*, ed. Freda Kirchwey and Hans Morgenthau (New York: McBride, 1950); idem, "Another 'Great Debate': The National Interest of the US," *American Political Science Review* 46, no. 4 (December 1952): 961–88.

71. For an excellent analysis, see Brian Schmidt, "The National Interest Great Debate," in Schmidt, ed., *International Relations and the First Great Debate* (Oxford: Routledge, 2012), 94–117.

72. Greenberg, *Weimar Century*, 238.

73. Morgenthau, "The Problem of the National Interest," in *Dilemmas of Politics*, 80, 85.

74. MacDougall, "Law and Power," 102.

75. *The Economist*, June 7, 1951. Cited in John Bew, *Realpolitik: History of an Idea* (Oxford: Oxford University Press, 2018), 21.

76. Carl Friedrich, "How Enlightened Should Self-Interest Be?" in *Yale Review* (1952), cited in Bew, *Realpolitik*, 213.

77. A.J.P. Taylor, "No Illusions and No Ideas," *The Nation*, September 8, 1951, 196–97.

78. Morgenthau to Kirchwey, September 21, 1951, HJM Papers, Box 112, Folder 6.

79. Morgenthau to Kennan, March 7, 1952, HJM Papers, Box 33, Folder 7; "Realism in International Politics," a lecture delivered at the Naval War College, October 2, 1957, HJM Papers, Box 19, Folder 9.

80. Jessup to Morgenthau, January 6, 1954, HJM Papers, Box 31, Folder 5.

81. Morgenthau, "Mainsprings of American Foreign Policy," 836.

82. Morgenthau, "Mainsprings," 834. Compare: "As long as this [unchallengeable supremacy of the US in the Western Hemisphere] is secure, [it] can well afford to pursue a policy of the Good Neighbor. This is what the principle of the coordinate state amounts to in the Western Hemisphere." From "The Problem of the National Interest," in *Dilemmas of Politics*, 61.

83. Guilhot explains that "Rockefeller was an outspoken advocate of the relevance

of the Monroe Doctrine and its priority over any multilateral arrangements." In Guilhot, *Invention*, 20.

84. Morgenthau, "The Escape from Power" (1950), in Morgenthau, *Dilemmas*, 239–45.

85. Morgenthau, "The Evocation of the Past: Bertrand de Jouvenel" (1950), in Morgenthau, *Dilemmas, 358.*

86. Morgenthau, "Mainsprings," 850.

87. See Inderjeet Parmar, *Foundations of the American Century: The Ford, Carnegie, and Rockefeller Foundations and the Rise of American Power* (New Haven, CT: Yale University Press, 2015) on the emergence of globalism, and Stephen Wertheim on the turn from isolationism to the pursuit of global military primacy: Wertheim, *Tomorrow the World: The Birth of US Global Supremacy* (Cambridge, MA: Harvard University Press, 2020).

88. Ego-psychology, the Americanized version of psychoanalysis, which pursued the adjustment of ego to the reality principle, was part of the intellectual atmosphere of the day. See, for example, Russell Jacoby, *The Repression of Psychoanalysis: Otto Fenichel and the Political Freudians* (New York: Basic Books, 1983).

89. See Robert Schuett, "Freudian Roots of Political Realism: The Importance of Sigmund Freud to Hans J. Morgenthau's Theory of International Politics," *History of Human Sciences* 20, no. 4 (2007): 21–46. There are original library receipts for books he borrowed by Freud, Schmitt, and Rudolf Smend dated 1931, in HJM Papers, Box 152.

90. Morgenthau, "The Problem of the National Interest" (1954), in idem, *Dilemmas of Politics*, 62. Behr and Rösch try to make the case that Morgenthau's "standpoint epistemology" was highly sophisticated philosophically, and influenced by Karl Mannheim in particular, but phrases like this, which emphasize how easy it is to be *sachlich* (true to the facts), remain. See Behr and Rösch, *Concept of the Political*, 33–46.

91. See Daniel Bessner and Nicolas Guilhot, eds., *The Decisionist Imagination: Science and Sovereignty and Democracy in the Twentieth Century* (New York: Berghahn, 2018).

92. Hans Morgenthau, "The Theoretical and Practical Importance of a Theory of International Relations" (1954), Appendix II, in Guilhot, *Invention*, 265.

93. Fritz Ringer, *The Decline of the German Mandarins: The German Academic Community, 1890–1933* (Hanover, NH: University Press of New England, 1990).

94. Morgenthau, "Mainsprings," 833. Kennan also viewed Alexander Hamilton as the rare geopolitical thinker in US politics. See Milne, *Worldmaking*, 227.

95. Morgenthau, *Scientific Man*, 10.

96. Morgenthau, "The Military Displacement of Politics" (1952), in *Dilemmas of Politics, 266.*

97. Williams, "Aesthetic Realism," in Guilhot and Schmidt, *Historiographical Investigations in International Relations* (New York: Palgrave, 2018), 70, 73.

98. See Max Weber, "Politics as a Vocation," in *Weber, The Vocation Lectures,* edited with an Introduction by David Owen and Tracy B. Strong (Indianapolis: Hackett, 2004), 32–94, esp. 83–84 and 91–92.

99. Morgenthau, "Realism in International Politics," 1.

100. Morgenthau, "The Decline of Democratic Government" (1957), in idem, *Dilemmas,* 285.

101. Robbie Shilliam, *German Thought and International Relations: The Rise and Fall of a Liberal Project* (London: Palgrave, 2007), 316.

102. Jütersonke, *Morgenthau,* 142.

103. Morgenthau, "The State of Political Science" (1958), 23; and "The Commitments of Political Science" (1955), 31, both in Morgenthau, *Dilemmas.*

104. For the former view, see Scheuerman, *Morgenthau,* 101–34, and Scheuerman, *Realist Case for Global Reform,* 81–84, 90–91, 109–11. For the latter view, see Guilhot: "It is tempting to think that he refrained from developing a radical, principled critique of cosmopolitanism as a tactical concession, in order to harness its normative appeal to his own realist vision of diplomacy, which owed very little to cosmopolitan ideals"; in Guilhot, "Politics between and beyond Nations," in Sylvest and Wilson, *Classics of International Relations,* 75. For Scheuerman's earlier view, see Scheuerman, "Was Morgenthau a Realist?" *Constellations* 14, no. 4 (2007): 79: "Morgenthau was never able to think creatively enough about the possibility of a novel global order because he carried too much Schmittian intellectual baggage."

105. Stirk, "International Law," 73.

106. "For Machiavelli," Jütersonke explains, "*virtù* combines competence with energy . . . [it] represented all that was required of an individual and a people in order to fulfill the goal of the self-preservation and stability of a political community"; Jütersonke, *Morgenthau, Law and Realism* (Cambridge: Cambridge University Press, 2010), 164.

107. Stirk, "International Law," 75

108. Frei's account is unconvincing in this regard: "The potency of his own dismal experiences drives Morgenthau in a different direction: while he recognizes and acknowledges the reality of the 'political' and of 'politics', he does not affirm it. What is examined by the analyst is strongly condemned by the moralist: 'I do indeed believe that any exercise of power by one man over another is evil.'" Frei, *Intellectual Biography,* 173.

109. Morgenthau, "The Commitments of Political Science" (1955), 38.

110. Morgenthau, "The Escape from Power," 245.

111. John Herz, "Review of Kenneth W. Thompson, *Political Realism and the Crisis of World Politics," Political Science Quarterly* 75, no. 1 (March 1960): 290. Cited in Stirk, "International Law," 75.

112. Scheuerman, *Morgenthau,* 40.

113. See Bew, *Realpolitik.*

114. Morgenthau, *Scientific Man* at 169, cited in Scheuerman, *Morgenthau,* 62.

115. In a 1951 work, he described Hobbes ambivalently: "[There is a] profound and hidden truth in Hobbes' extreme dictum that the state creates morality as well as law." Cited in Stirk, "International Law," 76.

Chapter 7

1. According to the Paris treaty of 1954, the Allies maintained the right to station troops in West Germany, and while the state became formally sovereign, many important policy decisions required authorization by multinational forums dominated by the United States, e.g., the Atlantic Council and the Atlantic Policy Advisory Committee.

2. Hallstein was formulated in December 1955 at a conference of German ambassadors recalled to Bonn for discussion. The stakes of Hallstein concerned more than the question of dual vs. exclusive West German representation in the capitals of Eastern Europe. Grewe was also concerned that if Warsaw, Budapest, and Prague were permitted dual representation, "about thirty to fifty states of the neutral and nonaligned world" would seek the same. Grewe, *Deutsche Aussenpolitik der Nachkriegszeit* (Stuttgart: Deutsche Verlagsanstalt, 1960), 151. It was quite successful in limiting recognition of the GDR. For an excellent discussion, see William Glenn Gray, *Cold War Germany: The Global Campaign to Isolate East Germany, 1949–69* (Chapel Hill: University of North Carolina Press, 2003).

3. William C. Olson and A.J.R. Groom, *International Relations Then and Now: Origins and Trends in Interpretation* (London: Routledge, 1992).

4. Heuss to Steltzer, December 13, 1954, cited in Daniel Eisermann, *Aussenpolitik und Strategiediskussion: die Deutsche Gesellschaft für Auswärtige Politik 1955 bis 1972* (Berlin: De Gruyter, 1999), 71.

5. Eisermann, *Aussenpolitik*, 71. Scheuner was a student of Heinrich Triepel's in Berlin from 1933 to 1940. Scheuner taught at Jena, then at Göttingen (1940) and Strassburg (1941). From 1950 to 1972 he taught in Bonn.

6. On "cultural-sociological" and "synoptic" in Bergstraesser, see Eisermann, *Aussenpolitik und Strategiediskussion*, 103–17. Eisermann suggests that among Bergstraesser and his students, the concepts synthesis, integration, constellation-analysis, or, to some extent, interdependence were "similar, even used as synonyms."

7. Bergstraesser was thus an ambivalent figure whose terminology can be "interpreted as an attempt to not fully imitate the research methods of the English-speaking world," a "binding of empirical and normative methods" in a particularly German way; Eisermann, *Aussenpolitik und Strategiediskussion*, 117. See Bergstraesser, "Gemeinsame Ziele und Probleme der amerikanischen und deutschen Aussenpolitik" (1957), in *Weltpolitik als Wissenschaft: Geschichtliches Bewusstein und politische Entscheidung* (Köln/Opladen: Westdeutscher Verlag, 1965), 165–77.

8. Bergstraesser, "Auswärtige Politik," in *Weltpolitik*, 37–57; Hans Rothfels, "Vom Primat der Aussenpolitik," *Aussenpolitik* 6 (1955): 277–85.

9. Eisermann, *Aussenpolitik und Strategiediskussion*, 117. It was translated into German in 1959; the second edition would be issued with an introduction by Helmut Schmidt in 1974.

10. Founded by Wilhelm Cornides in July 1945, the *Europa Archiv (Europe Archive)* first appeared in July 1946 in a print run of 10,000. Its name was changed to *Internationale Politik (International Politics)* in 1995. In 1942, Cornides, a Wehrmacht sergeant, wrote an eyewitness account of the deportation of Jews to the Belzec concentration camp in Poland. Its content was published by historian, and fellow DGAP member, Hans Rothfels in a journal article in 1959.

11. "Arms Control," a special issue of *Daedalus* 89, no. 1 (Cambridge, MA: American Academy of Arts and Sciences, 1960).

12. Uwe Nerlich and Hans-Adolf Jacobsen provided the preface and afterword to *Strategie der Abrüstung: Achtundzwanzig Problemanalysen*, ed. Donald G Brennan and Uwe Nerlich (Gütersloh: Bertelsmann, 1962). Suttner and Philip Noel-Baker were both recipients of the Nobel Peace Prize.

13. Eisermann, *Aussenpolitik und Strategiediskussion*, 176.

14. See Kissinger, *The Troubled Partnership: A Reappraisal of the Atlantic Alliance* (New York: Doubleday, 1965); Jeffrey Boutwell, *The German Nuclear Dilemma* (Ithaca, NY: Cornell University Press, 1990).

15. Reyn, *De Gaulle*, 215.

16. The Harvard International Conference on Defense and Strategy was held from May 31 to June 9, 1963.

17. Eisermann, *Aussenpolitik und Strategiediskussion*, 162.

18. Morgenthau, "The Crisis of the Western Alliance," *Commentary* 35, no. 3 (March 1, 1963): 185–90.

19. Morgenthau to Acheson, March 30, 1963, Acheson Papers, Yale University, Box 23, Folder 289, Reel 15.

20. Grewe discussed the MLF in "Die Zukunft der Atlantischen Allianz," in *Internationale Rüstungslage und Bündnispolitik 1964* (Bonn: Bergisch-Gladbach, 1965), based on the conference held from October 29–November 1, 1964.

21. For the Kindermann-Bergstraesser relationship, see Horst Schmitt, "Die Freiburger Schule, 1954-70,"in *Schulen in der Deutschen Politikwissenschaft*, ed. Wilhelm Bleek (Opladen: Leske & Budrich, 1999), 213–43.

22. He completed his PhD thesis with Hans Morgenthau in 1956: "The Sino-Soviet Entente Policy of Sun Yat-Sen, 1923–1925." The details of his biography are in the correspondence.

23. Kindermann, "Philosophische Grundlagen und Methodik der Realistischen Schule von der Politik. Mit besonderer Berücksichtigung der Werke von Hans S. Morgenthau (*sic*) und Reinhold Niebuhr," 251–96, in Oberndörfer, *Wissenschaftliche Politik: Eine Einführung in Grundfragen ihrer Tradition und Theorie* (Freiburg im Breisau: Rombach, 1962).

24. Morgenthau to Kindermann, October 31, 1957, HJM Papers, Box 33, Folder 12.

25. "The national interest has indeed an objective character, as I tried to point out in *Politics among Nations*, and more particularly, *Dilemmas of Politics*. However incompletely contemporary actors and observers may be able to understand it, its objectivity becomes obvious in retrospective historic analysis. If it were otherwise, no historian could cast an objective judgment upon the actions of statesmen of the past." Morgenthau to Kindermann, April 18, 1961, HJM Box 33, Folder 12.

26. Morgenthau to Kindermann, April 5, 1961, HJM Papers, Box 33, Folder 12.

27. Morgenthau, *Macht und Frieden: Grundlegung einer Theorie der Internationalen Politik* (Gütersloh: Bertelsmann, 1963). It was part of a book series edited by Uwe Nerlich called *Krieg und Frieden: Beiträge zu Grundproblemen der Internationalen Politik*. Kindermann informed Morgenthau in 1957 that he was interested in pursuing such a translation and that Waldemar Gurian had intended to translate *Politics among Nations* before his death; Kindermann to Morgenthau, October 29, 1957, HJM Papers, Box 33, Folder 12.

28. "Hans J. Morgenthau und die theoretischen Grundlagen des politischen Realismus," 19–61, in *Macht und Frieden*. This reprises arguments made in his essay from two years before, "Philosophische Grundlagen und Methodik der Realitischen Schule von der Politik," published in *Wissenschaftliche Politik: Eine Einführung in Grundfragen ihrer Tradition und Theorie*, ed. Dieter Oberndörfer (Freiburg: Rombach, 1962).

29. Kindermann, "Introduction," *Macht und Frieden*, 19–47, at 36.

30. Morgenthau, *Macht und Frieden*, 33n42.

31. The foreword is dated August 1, 1963.

32. Kindermann to Morgenthau, May 24, 1965, HJM Papers, Box 33, Folder 12.

33. Kindermann to Morgenthau, June 1965 (exact date unknown), HJM Papers, Box 33, Folder 12.

34. Kindermann's neorealism is not to be confused with the one associated with Kenneth Waltz, and whose locus classicus is Waltz, *The Theory of International Politics* (1979).

35. Gottfried-Karl Kindermann, ed., *Grundelemente der Weltpolitik: Eine Einführung*. Mit einem Geleitwort von Hans J. Morgenthau (München/Zürich: R. Piper, 1976), 26. Osgood and Tsou were doctoral students of Morgenthau's at the University of Chicago.

36. Klaus Jürgen Gantzel and Gisela Gantzel-Kress, "The Development of International Relations Studies in West Germany," in *The Foreign Policy of West Germany: Formation and Contents*, ed. Volker Rittberger and Ekkehart Krippendorff (London: Sage, 1980), 234.

37. For a more generous assessment of the Munich School's impact in West Germany and its broader legacy, see Alexander Siedschlag, Gottfried-Karl Kindermann, eds., *Realistische Perspektiven internationaler Politik: Festschrift für Gottfried-Karl Kindermann zum 75. Geburtstag* (Opladen: Leske and Budrich, 2001).

38. Kaiser in Ernst Fraenkel and Karl-Dietrich Bracher, eds., *Internationale Beziehungen*, Fischer Lexicon, vol. 7 (Frankfurt: Fischer, 1969).

39. See Daniel Bessner, *Democracy in Exile: Hans Speier and the Rise of the Defense Intellectual* (Ithaca, NY: Cornell University Press, 2018); David Ekbladh, *The Great American Mission: Modernization and the Construction of an American World Order* (Princeton, NJ: Princeton University Press, 2010).

40. See Clay Clemens, *Reluctant Realists: The Christian Democrats and West German Ostpolitik* (Durham, NC: Duke University Press, 1989).

41. These included Volker Rittberger (1941–2011), Klaus Jürgen Gantzel (b. 1934), and Dieter Senghaas (b. 1940).

42. Oskar Schatz, ed., *Der Friede im nuklearen Zeitalter: Eine Kontroverse zwischen Realisten und Utopisten* (München: Manz, 1970).

43. See, for example, John Herz, *Staatenwelt und Weltpolitik: Aufsatze zur internationalen Politik im Nuklearzeitalter* (Hamburg: Hoffmann & Campe, 1974).

44. Eisernman, *Aussenpolitik und Strategiediskussion*, 205.

45. See the analysis in Daniel J. Sargent, *A Superpower Transformed: American Foreign Relations in the 1970s* (Oxford: Oxford University Press, 2015).

46. In Stanley Hoffmann, *Gulliver's Troubles oder die Zukunft des internationalen Systems* [1968] (Bielefeld: Bertelsmann, 1970), 393.

47. Hans Morgenthau, "The Intellectual and Political Functions of a Theory of International Relations," in *The Decline of Democratic Politics* (Chicago: University of Chicago Press, 1962), 77. See William E. Scheuerman, *Morgenthau: Realism and Beyond* (London: Polity, 2009), chap. 5: "Utopian Realism and the Bomb," 133–64, at 136. For comparable thinkers in the same context, see Campbell Craig, *Glimmer of a New Leviathan: Total War in the Realism of Niebuhr, Morgenthau and Waltz* (New York: Columbia University Press, 2003); Rens van Muster and Casper Sylvest, *Nuclear Realism. Global Political Thought during the Thermonuclear Revolution* (London: Routledge, 2016)

48. Scheuerman, *Morgenthau,* 137.

49. From his approving review of Jaspers in the *Saturday Review*, February 18, 1961, through to his 1972 book, *Science: Servant or Master*, Morgenthau remained convinced that the cataclysmic outcome of any use of nuclear weapons made them qualitatively distinct from conventional weapons. See Scheuerman, *Morgenthau*, chap. 5.

50. Erich Fromm, *May Man Prevail? An Inquiry into the Facts and Fictions of Foreign Policy* (New York: Doubleday, 1961); "The Case for Unilateral Disarmament," in *Arms Control, Disarmament, and National Security*, ed. Donald Brennan (New York: G. Brazilier, 1961), 187–97.

51. See Marcuse, "Die Friede als gesellschaftliche Lebensform," 85–93, in Schatz, *Kontroverse.*

52. Gert Krell, *Peace Research in Hesse: The History and Development of the Peace Research Institute Frankfurt* (PRIF/HSFK: Frankfurt am Main, 1988), 15.

53. Ernst-Otto Czempiel, ed., *Die Lehre von den Internationale Beziehungen* (Darmstadt: Wissenschaftliche Buchgesellschaft, 1969).

54. Krell, *Peace Research*, 16. Speech reported in the *Frankfurter Allgemeine Zeitung*, September 2, 1969, 3.

55. Karl Kaiser, *Friedensforschung in der Bundesrepublik. Gegenstand und Aufgabe der Friedensforschung* (Göttingen: Vandenhoek & Ruprecht, 1970).

56. Oskar Schatz, ed., *Der Friede im nuklearen Zeitalter: Eine Kontroverse zwischen Realisten und Utopisten*, 4. Salzburger Humanismusgesprach (München: Manz, 1970).

57. For more on Jungk and "futurology" see Jenny Andersson's article, "The Great Future Debate and the Future of the World," *American Historical Review* 117, no. 5 (2012): 1411–30.

58. Schatz, *Friede im nuklearen Zeitalter*, 10.

59. The best syntheses are by Udi Greenberg, *The Weimar Century: German Émigrés and the Ideological Origins of the Cold War* (Princeton, NJ: Princeton University Press, 2014), 237–46, and Lorenzo Zambernardi, "The Impotence of Power: Morgenthau's Critique of American Intervention in Vietnam," *Review of International Studies* 37, no. 3 (July 2011): 1335–56.

60. Greenberg, *Weimar Century*, 243

61. Morgenthau, "Johnson's Moral Crusade," in *The New Republic*, July 3, 1965.

62. Morgenthau to Martin Herz, August 15, 1967, General Correspondence, HJM Papers, Box 27, Folder 13.

63. Kindermann, "Schlusswort," *Kontroverse*, 274.

64. Eisermann, *Aussenpolitik und Strategiediskussion*, 292–23.

65. Gantzel, "International Relations," 224.

66. Ernst-Otto Czempiel, "Der Primat der Auswärtigen Politik—Kritische Würdigung der Staatsmaxime," and Ekkehart Krippendorff, "Ist Aussenpolitik AUSSENPOLITIK? Ein Beitrag zur Theorie und der Versuch, eine unhaltbare Unterscheidung aufzugeben," in *Politische Vierteljahresschrift* 4, no. 3 (September 1963): 243ff. See also Karl Dietrich Bracher's essay in *Faktoren der politischen Entscheidung: Festgabe für Ernst Fraenkel zum 65. Geburtstag*, ed. Gerhard Ritter et al. (Berlin: DeGruyter, 1963), 115–48.

67. See Hans-Ulrich Wehler, ed., *Eckart Kehr: Der Primat der Innenpolitik*, Veröffentlichungen der Historischen Kommission zu Berlin, vol. 19 (Berlin: DeGruyter, 1970).

68. See Paul Buhle and Edward Rice-Maximim, *William Appleman Williams: The Tragedy of Empire* (New York: Routledge, 1995).

69. Gantzel, "Rüstungswettlaufe und politische Entscheidungen," in Czempiel, *Die Anachronistische Souveranität*, 110–38.

70. Karl Kaiser completed his *Habilitation* thesis with Karl-Dietrich Bracher at Bonn, in 1969. He replaced Karl Carstens at the DGAP, who was at that time a skeptic of détente.

71. Karl Kaiser, "Interdependenz und Autonomie: Die Bundesrepublik und Großbritannien in ihrer Multinationalen Umwelt," 50–72, in *Strukturwandlungen der Aussenpolitik in Großbritannien und der Bundesrepublik*, ed. Karl Kaiser and Roger Pearce Morgan (München and Wien: Oldenbourg 1970).

72. Eisermann, *Aussenpolitik*, 292.

73. Hans-Peter Schwarz, "Die Rollen der Bundesrepublik in der Staatengesellschaft," 225–56, in Kaiser and Morgan, *Strukturwandlungen*.

74. Eisermann, *Aussenpolitik und Strategiediskussion*, 278. The language comes from an internal report dated December 5, 1966. A text representative of this discussion is Wolfgang Wagner, *Mittlere Mächte in der Weltpolitik* (Opladen, 1969): "Should not China, France and Great Britain be counted in the same breath as the 'great powers' [*Großmächte*] on account of their 'nuclear badges of rank' [*nukleare Rangabzeichen*]" (278). See also Daniel Frei, "Vom Mass der Macht: Überlegungen zum Grundproblem der internationalen Beziehungen," *Schweizer Monatshefte: Zeitschrift für Politik, Wirtschaft und Kultur* 49, no. 7 (1970): 642–54.

75. Grewe, *Spiel der Kräfte* (Düsseldorf/Wien: Econ Verlag, 1970).

76. Morgenthau, "Détente: Reality and Illusion," *Wall Street Journal*, July 18, 1974.

77. "Discussion" (October 26, 1974), in *Détente in Historical Perspective: The First CUNY Conference on History and Politics*, ed. George Schwab and Henry Friedlander (New York: Cyrco Press, 1975), 100.

78. Morgenthau, "The US and Europe in a Decade of Détente," 1–8, in *The US and Western Europe: Political, Economic and Strategic Perspectives*, ed. Wolfram F. Hanrieder (Cambridge, MA: Winthrop, 1974).

79. Morgenthau, "Détente: Reality and Illusion," 76.

80. Morgenthau, "The Pathology of American Power," *International Security* 1, no. 3 (Winter 1977): 3–20.

81. This is the thesis of Scheuerman's *Morgenthau* (2009).

82. Charles Yost, "World Order and American Responsibility," *Foreign Affairs* 47, no. 1 (October 1968): 1–14.

83. In 1976, Schwarz edited the first *Handbuch der deutschen Aussenpolitik*. From 1978–2012, he was co-editor of the important contemporary history journal, *Vierteljahrshefte für Zeitgeschichte*. He published a major biography of Konrad Adenauer in 1986.

84. Schwarz appreciates the theoretical modesty of Grewe's version of realism, which is at odds with the "often shrill tone" of some contemporary so-called Realists (124). Schwarz must have in mind the so-called "second debate" in postwar IR theory between the behaviorists and the traditionalists. Schwarz uses a quotation from a 1970 text of Morgenthau's to situate Grewe: in contrast to theorists who try "to rationalize the whole field with a coherent system of logical concepts," Grewe "is an introduction to the art (*Kunst*) of rational grappling with international relations" (126). Morgenthau, "International Relations:

Quantitative and Qualitative," in *A Design for International Relations Research: Scope, Theory, Methods, and Relevance*, ed. Norman D. Palmer (Philadelphia: American Academy of Political and Social Science, 1970).

85. Hans-Peter Schwarz, "Ein Lehrbuch Realpolitik?" *Politische Vierteljahresschrift* 14, no. 1 (1973): 122–27. Morgenthau's 1948 book was only translated into German in 1963; Schwarzenberger's 1941 book was translated into German in 1955. Carl Schmitt reviewed the Schwarzenberger book, calling it a "magnificent achievement." See Carl Schmitt, *Frieden oder Pazifismus? Arbeiten zum Völkerrecht und zur internationalen Politik, 1924–1978*, ed. Günter Maschke (Berlin: Duncker & Humblot, 2005), 883–84.

86. Compare Gottfried-Karl Kindermann, "Einleitung," in Morgenthau, *Macht und Frieden* (1963), 34ff.

87. Schwarz mentions here Albrecht Mendelssohn Bartholdy's *Europäische Gespräche*, the *Friedenswarte*, and the publications and activities of the Stresemann-Stiftung. The Morgenthau of 1929 would have disagreed with Schwarz's assessment that Stresemann lacked realism. See my chapter 6.

88. Eisermann, *Aussenpolitik und Strategiediskussion*, 270.

89. Sargent, *Superpower*, 155.

90. Eisermann, *Aussenpolitik und Strategiediskussion*, 277.

91. Hans-Peter Schwarz, "Die Politik der Westbindung oder die Staatsraison der Bundesrepublik," *Zeitschrift für Politik*, Neue Folge 22, no. 4 (1975): 336.

92. "Critical peace research might have remained a quirky, obscure utopia of little significance had Willy Brandt not remained a chairman of the [SPD] after 1974." Jeffrey Herf, "War, Peace and the German Intellectuals: The West German Peace Movement," *International Security* 10, no. 4 (Spring 1986): 200.

93. The DGFK in Bonn was the largest center. There were also institutes in Berlin, Hamburg, Frankfurt, Starnberg, and Heidelberg.

94. Herf, "War, Peace, German Intellectuals," 189. Herf says none. The data comes from a report written in 1980 by German political scientist Hans Joachim Arndt that was commissioned by the Bavarian state government. It was published one year after the state governments of Bavaria and Lower Saxony withdrew their support from the DGFK. According to Arndt only nine of 130 projects dealt at all with the Soviet Union, and none examined Soviet imperialism and/or Soviet control over Eastern Europe or East Germany. See Herf, 190–91.

95. I have confirmed with Dr. Kaiser that this is the correct interpretation of his resignation. Telephone conversation with Karl Kaiser, July 1, 2020.

96. Grewe, "Machtvergleich in der Weltpolitik: Kräfterelationen und Modelle der Konfliktvermeidung," 69–91, in *Der Neue Realismus*, ed. Helmut Kohl (Düsseldorf: Erb, 1980), orig. *Merkur* 5 (1980). It was based on a conference of the CDU held on March 4–5, 1980. Ten of the eleven authors were either American or West German.

97. Grewe, "Machtvergleich," 71.

98. Grewe, "Das Geteilte Deutschland und die Weltpolitische Lage," 7–20, in *Die aussenpolitische Lage Deutschlands am Beginn der achtziger Jahre* (Berlin: Duncker & Humblot, 1982).

99. Grewe, "Machtvergleich," 90.

100. Grewe, "Machiavelli und der Stil der gegenwärtigen Weltpolitik," in *Machtprojektionen und Rechtsschranken: Essays aus vier Jahrzehnten über Verfassungen, politische Systeme und internationale Strukturen* (Baden-Baden: Nomos Verlagsgesellschaft, 1991), 69. The original text was a radio address, "Machiavelli and After," aired on Hessischen Rundfunk on July 19, 1981.

101. Grewe *Nachlass*, file, undated.

102. Schwarz, *Die Gezähmten Deutschen*, 9.

Conclusion

1. See my article, "*Grossraum* and Geopolitics: Resituating Carl Schmitt in an Atlantic Context," *History and Theory* 56, no. 3 (2017): 398–406.

2. See John Bew's panoramic and brilliant discussion in his *Realpolitik: A History* (Oxford: Oxford University Press, 2018).

3. See J.A. Tickner, "Gendering a Discipline: Some Feminist Methodological Contributions to International Relations," *Signs* 30, no. 4 (Summer 2005): 173–88.

4. Peter Brooks, *Realist Vision* (New Haven, CT: Yale University Press, 2005), 3.

5. Gearóid Ó Tuathail, *Critical Geopolitics* (Minneapolis: University of Minnesota Press, 1996).

6. Morgenthau, "Escape from Power," in Morgenthau, *Dilemmas of Politics* (Chicago: University of Chicago Press, 1958).

7. Martti Koskenniemi, *The Gentle Civilizer: Rise and Fall of International Law, 1870–1960* (Cambridge: Cambridge University Press, 2000), 2.

8. For his use of "sensibility" with regard to realism, see Daniel Bessner, *Democracy in Exile: Hans Speier and the Rise of the Defense Intellectual* (Ithaca, NY: Cornell University Press, 2018), 74, 143, 158.

9. Pierre Bourdieu, *Outline of a Theory of Practice,* trans. Richard Nice (Cambridge: Cambridge University Press, 1977); Bourdieu, *The Logic of Practice*, trans. Richard Nice (Stanford: Stanford University Press), 1990.

10. Frank Costigliola and Michael J. Hogan, eds., *Explaining US Foreign Relations*, 3rd ed. (Cambridge: Cambridge University Press, 2016).

11. "Gender preoccupations shaped foreign policy discourse through the twentieth century, encouraging the confusion of physical courage with moral courage and promoting the personification of the nation as a (male) individual who could 'stand and fight' or 'cut and run.'" See T.J. Jackson Lears, "Pragmatic Realism vs. The American Century" 82–121, in *The Short American Century*, ed. Andrew Bacevich (Cambridge, MA: Harvard University Press, 2013), 84.

12. See my chapter 7.

13. Patricia Owens and Katharina Rietzler, *Women in International Thought: A New History* (Cambridge: Cambridge University Press, 2021).

14. For discussion of what I call the "high" realism of the 1950s, its limitations, contradictions, and exclusions, see my chapter 6.

15. Vincent Pouliot, *International Pecking Orders: The Politics and Practice of Multilateral Diplomacy* (Cambridge: Cambridge University Press, 2016).

16. Michael Zürn, *A Theory of Global Governance: Authority, Legitimacy and Contestation* (Oxford: Oxford University Press, 2018), vi.

17. See Hugo Drochon, *Nietzsche's Great Power Politics* (Princeton, NJ: Princeton University Press, 2016); Mark Gismondi, "Tragedy, Realism and *Kulturpessimismus* in the Theories of Max Weber, E.H. Carr, Hans J. Morgenthau, and Henry Kissinger," *Diplomacy and Statecraft* 15, no. 3 (2004): 435–64.

18. Ole Waever, "On the Sociology of a Not So International Discipline," *International Organization* 52, no. 4 (1998): 687–727; for the view that US dominance of International Relations has run its course, see Knud Erik Jørgensen, "After Hegemony in International Relations, or, the Persistent Myth of American Disciplinary Hegemony," *European Research in International Studies* 1, no. 1 (2014): 57–64.

19. See Matt Sleat, *Politics Recovered: Realism in Theory and Practice* (New York: Columbia University Press, 2018); Karuna Mantena, "Another Realism: The Politics of Gandhian Nonviolence," *American Political Science Review* 106, no. 2 (May 2012): 455–70.

20. See Daniel Bessner and Nicolas Guilhot, *The Decisionist Imagination: Sovereignty, Social Science, and Democracy in the Twentieth Century* (Oxford: Berghahn Books, 2018).

21. Richard Ned Lebow, *The Tragic Vision of Politics: Ethics, Interests and Orders* (Cambridge: Cambridge University Press, 2003), 258.

22. See Barry Posen, *Restraint: A New Foundation for US Grand Strategy* (Ithaca, NY: Cornell University Press, 2014).

23. In his 2012 edited collection, *The Short American Century: An American Postmortem*, Bacevich assembled a group of essays that he calls a "sort of dissenter's guide to the American Century" (14). In 2007, Bacevich wrote the preface to a reissue of classical realist Reinhold Niebuhr's 1949 work, *The Irony of American History*, calling it "the most important book ever written on US foreign policy." See Niebuhr, *The Irony of American History* (1952) (Chicago: University of Chicago Press, 2008), ix.

24. Stephen Walt, "Restraint Isn't Isolationism and It Won't Endanger America," *Foreign Policy*, July 22, 2019.

25. "In the tradition of classical realism, by stripping away euphemism, [this book] seeks less to transform than to reveal the hard-wired realities and constraints of an anarchic world, the hard trade-offs it imposes. If emancipation is impossible in this pessimistic tradition, if some hypocrisy and brutality is inevitable, if states and their rulers cannot be 'good,' they can at least be wiser and more self-aware. They can develop a prudential capacity to practice a more

restrained and self-aware power politics, to husband power more than waste it, to practice intrigue and competition without excess brutality, and to wage war without it destroying the state or in America's case, the republic." Patrick Porter, *The False Promise of Liberal Order: Nostalgia, Delusion and the Rise of Trump* (Cambridge: Polity, 2020), 26.

26. "The leading architects of Vietnam [did not] . . . conceive themselves as power brokers pure and simple . . . The policy makers of the nineteen-sixties combined what they took to be a hard-headed realism with Wilsonian idealism, ideological anticommunism and an intoxicatingly romantic notion of power to form one of the more extraordinary muddles of the modern age . . . Vietnam has brought many Americans to an awareness of the sham idealism of the 'responsibilities of power,' and of the inadequacies of the new 'realism' once it is stripped of its romantic façade." William J. Fulbright, *The Crippled Giant: American Foreign Policy and Its Domestic Consequences* (New York: Random House, 1972), 172–73.

Bibliography

Archives Consulted

Archives of the Reichsministerium für Wissenschaft, Erziehung und Volksbildung, Bundesarchiv Berlin

Dean Gooderham Acheson Papers, Yale University, Manuscripts and Archives

Derwent Stainthorpe Whittlesey Papers, Harvard University Archives

Grewe Nachlass, Legacy Archives, Max Planck Institute for Legal History and Legal Theory (formerly Max-Planck-Institut für Europäische Rechtsgeschichte)

Hans J. Morgenthau Papers, Library of Congress

Harold Dwight Lasswell Papers, Yale University, Manuscripts and Archives

Henry Harris Jessup Papers, Yale University, Divinity School Library

Institute of International Studies, Yale University Records, Manuscripts and Archives, Yale University

Das Politische Archiv, Auswärtiges Amt (Political Archive, Federal Foreign Office), Berlin, Germany

Records of the Deutsches Auslandswissenschaftliches Institut (DAWI), 1940–1945, Bundesarchiv Berlin

Records of Private Individuals (Captured German Records). Microfilm Publication T253. Dr. Karl Haushofer, rolls 46-R61, National Archives and Records Administration, College Park, Maryland

Select Bibliography

Adams, Ellen Elizabeth. "Ellen Churchill Semple and American Geography in an Era of American Imperialism." PhD diss., College of William and Mary, 2011.

Adcock, Robert. *Liberalism and the Emergence of American Political Science: A Transatlantic Tale.* Oxford: Oxford University Press, 2013.

Agnew, John A., Katharyne Mitchell, and Gerard Toal [Gearóid Ó Tuathail]. *A Companion to Political Geography.* Hoboken, NJ: Wiley-Blackwell, 2008.

Anderson, Dennis LeRoy. *The Academy for German Law, 1933–1944.* New York: Garland, 1987.

Anderson, Perry. "US Foreign Policy and Its Thinkers." *New Left Review* 83, special issue (September–October 2013).

Andersson, Jenny. "The Great Future Debate and the Struggle for the World." *American Historical Review* 117, no. 5 (December 1, 2012): 1411–30.

Anievas, Alexander. "International Relations between War and Revolution: Wilsonian Diplomacy and the Making of the Treaty of Versailles." *International Politics* 51, no. 5 (September 1, 2014): 619–47.

————, Nivi Manchanda, and Robbie Shilliam, eds. *Race and Racism in International Relations: Confronting the Global Colour Line*. London: Routledge, 2015.

Armitage, David. *Foundations of Modern International Thought*. Cambridge: Cambridge University Press, 2012.

————. "The Elephant and the Whale: Empires of Land and Sea." *Journal for Maritime Research* 9, no. 1 (2007): 23–36.

————. "The Fifty Years' Rift: Intellectual History and International Relations." *Modern Intellectual History* 1, no. 1 (April 2004): 97–109.

Ashley, Richard K. "The Poverty of Neorealism." *International Organization* 38, no. 2 (1984): 225–86.

Ashworth, Lucian M. "Did the Realist-Idealist Great Debate Really Happen? A Revisionist History of International Relations." *International Relations* 16, no. 1 (April 1, 2002): 33–51.

————. "Mapping a New World: Geography and the Interwar Study of International Relations." *International Studies Quarterly* 57, no. 1 (2013): 138–49.

————. *A History of International Thought: From the Origins of the Modern State to Academic International Relations*. London: Routledge, 2014.

Ayoob, Mohammed. "Inequality and Theorizing in International Relations: The Case for Subaltern Realism." *International Studies Review* 4, no. 3 (2002): 27–48.

Bacevich, A.J. "Charles Beard, Properly Understood." *The National Interest*, no. 35 (1994): 73–83.

————. "Introduction." *Reinhold Niebuhr: The Irony of American History* (1949), ix–xxii. Chicago: University of Chicago Press, 2008.

————, ed. *The Short American Century: A Postmortem*. Cambridge, MA: Harvard University Press, 2013.

Bagby, Laurie M. Johnson. "The Use and Abuse of Thucydides in International Relations." *International Organization* 48, no. 1 (1994): 131–53.

Barion, Hans, Ernst-Wolfgang Böckenförde, Ernst Forsthoff, Werner Weber, and Joseph Kaiser. "Europäisches Großraumdenken: die Steigerung geschichtlicher Größen als Rechtsproblem." In *Epirrhosis: Festgabe für Carl Schmitt zum 80. Geburtstag*. Berlin: Duncker & Humblot, 1968.

Barnes, Trevor J., and Christian Abrahamsson. "Tangled Complicities and Moral Struggles: The Haushofers, Father and Son, and the Spaces of Nazi Geopolitics." *Journal of Historical Geography* 47 (January 2015): 64–73.

Barnes, Trevor J., and Claudio Minca. "Nazi Spatial Theory: The Dark Geographies of Carl Schmitt and Walter Christaller." *Annals of the Association of American Geographers* 103, no. 3 (2013): 669–87.

Bassin, Mark. "Race contra Space: The Conflict between German Geopolitik and National Socialism." *Political Geography Quarterly* 6, no. 2 (April 1, 1987): 115–34.

————. "Imperialism and the Nation State in Friedrich Ratzel's Political Geography." *Progress in Human Geography* 11, no. 4 (September 1987): 473–95.

————. "Between Realism and the 'New Right': Geopolitics in Germany in the 1990s." *Transactions of the Institute of British Geographers* 28, no. 3 (2003): 350–66.

Beard, Charles. *The Idea of National Interest: An Analytical Study in American Foreign Policy.* New York: Macmillan, 1934.

Bell, Duncan S.A. "Anarchy, Power and Death: Contemporary Political Realism as Ideology." *Journal of Political Ideologies* 7, no. 2 (2002): 221–39.

————. "Political Theory and the Functions of Intellectual History: A Response to Emmanuel Navon." *Review of International Studies* 29, no. 1 (2003): 151–60.

————, ed. *Political Thought and International Relations: Variations on a Realist Theme.* Oxford: Oxford University Press, 2009.

Berber, Friedrich, ed. *Das Diktat von Versailles: Entstehung, Inhalt, Zerfall. Eine Darstellung in Dokumenten.* Veröffentlichungen des Deutschen Instituts für Aussenpolitische Forschung, 3. Essen: Essener Verlagsanstalt, 1939.

————. *Der Mythos der Monroe-Doktrin: von Friedrich Berber.* Probleme amerikanischer Aussenpolitik, Heft 6. 2nd edition. Essen: Essener Verlagsanstalt, 1943.

Berghahn, Volker R., ed. *Quest for Economic Empire: European Strategies of German Big Business in the Twentieth Century.* London: Berghahn Books, 1996.

Bergstraesser, Arnold. *Weltpolitik als Wissenschaft: Geschichtliches Bewußtsein und politische Entscheidung.* Köln: Westdeutscher Verlag, 1965.

Bessner, Daniel. *Democracy in Exile: Hans Speier and the Rise of the Defense Intellectual.* 1st edition. Ithaca, NY: Cornell University Press, 2018.

Bessner, Daniel, and Nicolas Guilhot. "How Realism Waltzed Off: Liberalism and Decisionmaking in Kenneth Waltz's Neorealism." *International Security* 40, no. 2 (October 1, 2015): 87–118.

————, eds. *The Decisionist Imagination: Sovereignty, Social Science, and Democracy in the 20th Century.* New York: Berghahn Books, 2019.

Best, Werner. "Nochmals: Völkische Großraumordnung statt 'Völkerrechtliche Großraumordnung'!" *Deutsches Recht: Zentralorgen des National-Sozialistischen rechtswahrerbundes.* Vol. 11 (1941): 1533-1534.

Bew, John. *Realpolitik: A History.* Oxford: Oxford University Press, 2018.

Blackbourn, David, and Geoff Eley. *The Peculiarities of German History: Bour-*

geois Society and Politics in Nineteenth-Century Germany. Oxford: Oxford University Press, 1984.

Bliddal, Henrik, ed. *Classics of International Relations: Essays in Criticism and Appreciation*. Abingdon: Routledge, 2013.

Bönker, Dirk. *Militarism in a Global Age: Naval Ambitions in Germany and the United States before World War I*. Ithaca, NY: Cornell University Press, 2012.

Botsch, Gideon. *"Politische Wissenschaft" im Zweiten Weltkrieg: Die "Deutschen Auslandswissenschaften" im Einsatz 1940–1945*. Paderborn: Schöningh, 2005.

Bourdieu, Pierre. *Outline of a Theory of Practice* (1972). Translated by Richard Nice. Cambridge: Cambridge University Press, 1993.

———. *The Logic of Practice* (1980). Translated by Richard Nice. Cambridge: Polity, 1990.

Bowring, Bill. *The Degradation of the International Legal Order? The Rehabilitation of Law and the Possibility of Politics*. New York: Routledge, 2008.

Bracher, Karl Dietrich. "Kritische Betrachtungen uber die Primat der Aussenpolitik." In *Faktoren der politischen Entscheidung: Festgabe für Ernst Fraenkel zum Geburtstag*, edited by Gerhard A. Ritter, Gilbert Ziebura, et. al., 115–48. Berlin: DeGruyter, 1963.

Bracher, Karl Dietrich, Ernst Fraenkel, and Karlheinz Niclauss, eds. *Internationale Beziehungen*. Fischer-Lexikon, Bd. 7. Frankfurt am Main: Fischer, 1974.

Brennan, Donald G. *Arms Control, Disarmament, and National Security*. New York: G. Braziller, 1961.

Brennan, Donald, and Uwe Nerlich, et. al. *Strategie der Abrüstung: Achtundzwanzig Problemanalysen*. Gütersloh: C. Bertelsmann, 1962.

Breuer, Stefan. *Carl Schmitt im Kontext: Intellektuellenpolitik in der Weimarer Republik*. Berlin: Akademie, 2012.

Brooks, Peter. *Realist Vision*. New Haven, CT: Yale University Press, 2008.

Brower, Charles N., Anne-Marie Slaughter, Anthony Carty, and Jonathan Zasloff. "Rereading Root." *Proceedings of the Annual Meeting—American Society of International Law*, 100 (2006): 203–16.

Brown, Chris, Terry Nardin, and Nicholas Rengger, eds. *International Relations in Political Thought: Texts from the Ancient Greeks to the First World War*. Cambridge: Cambridge University Press, 2012.

Bucklin, Steven J. *Realism and American Foreign Policy: Wilsonians and the Kennan-Morgenthau Thesis*. Westport, CT: Praeger, 2000.

Buhle, Paul, and Edward Francis Rice-Maximin. *William Appleman Williams: The Tragedy of Empire*. New York: Routledge, 1995.

Carr, Edward H. *The Twenty Years' Crisis, 1919–1939*. New York: HarperCollins, 1964.

Carvalho, Benjamin de, Halvard Leira, and John M. Hobson. "The Big Bangs of IR: The Myths That Your Teachers Still Tell You about 1648 and 1919." *Millennium* 39, no. 3 (May 1, 2011): 735–58.

Chandler, David. "The Revival of Carl Schmitt in International Relations: The Last Refuge of Critical Theorists?" *Millennium* 37, no. 1 (August 1, 2008): 27–48.

Clemens, Clay. *Reluctant Realists: The CDU/CSU and West German Ostpolitik.* Durham, NC: Duke University Press, 1989.

Collini, Stefan. "The Intellectual as Realist: The Puzzling Career of E. H. Carr." In *Common Reading: Critics, Historians, Publics.* Oxford: Oxford University Press, 2009.

Coolidge, Archibald Cary. *The United States as a World Power.* New York: Macmillan, 1919.

Costigliola, Frank. "'I React Intensely to Everything': Russia and the Frustrated Emotions of George F. Kennan, 1933–1958." *Journal of American History* 102, no. 4 (March 1, 2016): 1075–101.

Costigliola, Frank, and Michael J Hogan. *Explaining the History of American Foreign Relations.* Cambridge: Cambridge University Press, 2016.

Cowley, Malcolm. "Geography's Fate." *Time*, April 20, 1942, 90–96.

Craig, Campbell. *Glimmer of a New Leviathan: Total War in the Realism of Niebuhr, Morgenthau, and Waltz.* New York: Columbia University Press, 2003.

Czempiel, Ernst-Otto. "Der Primat der Auswärtigen Politik—Kritische Würdigung der Staatsmaxime." *Politische Vierteljahresschrift* 4, no. 3 (September 1963): 243ff.

———. "Die Entwicklung der Lehre von den Internationalen Beziehungen." *Politische Vierteljahresschrift* 6, no. 3 (1965): 270–90.

———. *Die anachronistische Souveränität: zum Verhältnis von Innen- und Außenpolitik.* Köln/Opladen: Westdeutscher Verlag, 1969.

———, ed. *Die Lehre von den internationalen Beziehungen.* Darmstadt: Wissenschaftliche Buchgesellschaft, 1969.

Devetak, Richard. *Critical International Theory: An Intellectual History.* Oxford: Oxford University Press, 2018.

Diekmann, Irene A., Peter Krüger, and Julius H. Schoeps. *Geopolitik: Grenzgänge im Zeitgeist.* 2 vols. Berlin: Verlag für Berlin-Brandenburg, 2000.

Diner, Dan. "'Grundbuch des Planeten': Zur Geopolitik Karl Haushofers." *Vierteljahresschrift für Zeitgeschichte* 32, no. 1 (January 1984): 1–28.

Dodds, Klaus, and David Atkinson, eds. *Geopolitical Traditions: A Century of Geopolitical Thought.* New York: Routledge, 2000.

Doll, Natascha. *Recht, Politik und 'Realpolitik' bei August Ludwig von Rochau (1810–1873): Ein wissenschaftsgeschichtlicher Beitrag zum Verhältnis von Politik und Recht im 19. Jahrhundert.* Frankfurt am Main: Klostermann, 2005.

Dorpalen, Andreas. *The World of General Haushofer: Geopolitics in Action.* New York: Farrar & Rinehart, 1942.

Dunn, Frederick S. *Peaceful Change: A Study of International Procedures.* Publications of the Council on Foreign Relations. New York: Council on Foreign Relations, 1937.

———. "The Present Course of International Relations Research." *World Politics* 2, no. 1 (October 1949): 80–95.

Dunne, Tim, Lene Hansen, and Colin Wight. "The End of International Relations Theory?" *European Journal of International Relations* 19, no. 3 (September 1, 2013): 405–25.

Earle, Edward Mead, Gordon A. Craig, and Felix Gilbert, eds. *Makers of Modern Strategy: Military Thought from Machiavelli to Hitler.* Princeton, NJ: Princeton University Press, 1943.

"Education: Geopolitics in College." *Time,* January 19, 1942.

Eich, Stefan, and Adam Tooze. "The Allure of Dark Times: Max Weber, Politics and the Crisis of Historicism." *History & Theory* 56, no. 2 (June 2017): 197–215.

Eisermann, Daniel. *Aussenpolitik und Strategiediskussion: Die Deutsche Gesellschaft für Auswärtige Politik 1955 bis 1972.* Schriften des Forschungsinstituts der Deutschen Gesellschaft für Auswärtige Politik, Bd. 66. München: Oldenbourg, 1999.

Eley, Geoff. "Commentary." In *Heimat, Region, and Empire: Spatial Identities under National Socialism,* edited by Claus-Christian W. Szejnmann and Maiken Umbach, 252–75. London: Palgrave Macmillan, 2012.

———. *Nazism as Fascism: Violence, Ideology, and the Ground of Consent in Germany 1930–1945.* New York: Routledge, 2013.

———. "Empire, Ideology and the East: Thoughts on Nazism's Spatial Imaginary." In *Nazism as Fascism: Violence, Ideology and the Ground of Consent in Germany, 1930–1945,* 131–55. New York: Routledge, 2013.

———. "Empire by Land or Sea? Germany's Imperial Imaginary, 1840–1945." In *German Colonialism in a Global Age,* edited by Bradley Naranch and Geoff Eley, 19–45. Durham, NC: Duke University Press, 2014.

Elman, Colin, and Michael Jensen, eds. *The Realism Reader.* New York: Routledge, 2014.

Epple, Angelika, Walter Erhart, and Johannes Grave, eds. *Practices of Comparing: Towards a New Understanding of a Fundamental Human Practice.* Bielefeld: Bielefeld University Press, 2020.

Evans, Richard. "The German Foreign Office and the Nazi Past." *Neue Politische Literatur* 56 (2011): 165–83.

Faber, K.G. "Die Vorgeschichte der Geopolitik: Staat, Nation und Lebensraum im Denken deutscher Geographen vor 1914." In *Weltpolitik, Europagedanke, Regionalismus. Festschrift für Heinz Gollwitzer zum 65 Geburtstag,* edited by Heinz Dollinger et al. Münster: Aschendorff, 1982.

Fairgrieve, James. *Geographie und Weltmacht. Eine Einführung in die Geopolitik.* Translated by Martha Haushofer with an introduction by Karl Haushofer. Berlin-Grunewald: K. Vowinckel, 1925.

Falk, Richard. "Casting the Spell: The New Haven School of International Law." *Yale Law Journal* 104, no. 7 (January 1, 1995).

Fassbender, Bardo. "Stories of War and Peace: On Writing the History of International Law in the 'Third Reich' and After." *European Journal of International Law* 13, no. 2 (April 2002): 479–512.

Fassbender, Bardo, and Ann Peters, eds. *The Oxford Handbook of the History of International Law.* Oxford: Oxford University Press, 2012.

Fergie, Dexter. "Geopolitics Turned Inwards: The Princeton Military Studies Group and the National Security Imagination." *Diplomatic History* 43, no. 4 (September 2019): 644–70.

Fitzpatrick, Matthew P. *Liberal Imperialism in Germany: Expansionism and Nationalism, 1848–1884.* New York: Berghahn Books, 2008.

Fox, William T.R. "Interwar International Relations Research: The American Experience." *World Politics* 2, no. 1 (October 1949): 67–79.

Frei, Christoph. *Hans J. Morgenthau: An Intellectual Biography.* Illustrated edition. Baton Rouge: LSU Press, 2001.

Frei, Daniel. "Vom Mass der Macht: Überlegungen zum Grundproblem der internationalen Beziehungen." *Schweizer Monatshefte: Zeitschrift für Politik, Wirtschaft und Kultur* 49, no. 7 (1969–70): 642–54.

Friedlander, Henry, and George Schwab. *Détente in Historical Perspective.* New York: Cyrco Press, 1974.

Fromm, Erich. *May Man Prevail? An Inquiry into the Facts and Fictions of Foreign Policy.* New York: Doubleday, 1964.

Fulbright, James William. *The Crippled Giant: American Foreign Policy and Its Domestic Consequences.* New York: Random House, 1972.

Furniss, Edgar S. "The Contribution of Nicholas John Spykman to the Study of International Politics." *World Politics* 4, no. 3 (1952): 382–401.

Gaddis, John Lewis. *Strategies of Containment: A Critical Appraisal of American National Security Policy during the Cold War.* Revised ed. New York: Oxford University Press, 2005.

Gantzel, Klaus Jürgen. *Wissenschaftliche Verantwortung und politische Macht: zum wissenschaftlichen Umgang mit der Kriegsschuldfrage 1914, mit der Versöhnungsdiplomatie und mit dem nationalsozialistischen Großmachtstreben; wissenschaftsgeschichtliche Untersuchungen zum Umfeld und zur Entwicklung des Instituts für Auswärtige Politik; Hamburg/Berlin 1923–1945.* Berlin: Reimer, 1986.

———. *Kolonialrechtswissenschaft, Kriegsursachenforschung, internationale Angelegenheiten: Materialien und Interpretationen zur Geschichte des Instituts für Internationale Angelegenheiten der Universität Hamburg 1923–1983 im Widerstreit der Interessen.* Veröffentlichungen aus dem Institut für

Internationale Angelegenheiten der Universität Hamburg, Bd. 12. Baden-Baden: Nomos, 1983.

"Germany's Brain Trust." *Life*, November 20, 1939.

Giaccaria, Paolo, and Claudio Minca, eds. *Hitler's Geographies: The Spatialities of the Third Reich*. Chicago: University of Chicago Press, 2016.

Gismondi, Mark. "Tragedy, Realism, and Postmodernity: *Kulturpessimismus* in the Theories of Max Weber, E.H. Carr, Hans J. Morgenthau, and Henry Kissinger." *Diplomacy & Statecraft* 15, no. 3 (September 2004): 435–64.

Göhler, Gerhard, and Bodo Zeuner, eds. *Kontinuitäten und Brüche in der deutschen Politikwissenschaft*. Baden-Baden: Nomos, 1991.

Grabowsky, Adolf. "Der Primat der Aussenpolitik: Ein Nachwort." *Zeitschrift für Politik* 17 (1928): 527–42.

Graham, Kyle. "The Refugee Jurist and American Law Schools, 1933–1941." *American Journal of Comparative Law* 50, no. 4 (2002): 777–818.

Gray, Colin S. "Nicholas John Spykman, the Balance of Power, and International Order." *Journal of Strategic Studies* 38, no. 6 (September 19, 2015): 873–97.

Greenberg, Udi. *The Weimar Century: German Émigrés and the Ideological Foundations of the Cold War*. Princeton, NJ: Princeton University Press, 2014.

Grell, Hugo. *Der Alldeutsche Verband, seine Geschichte, seine Bestrebungen und Erfolge*. München: Lehmann, 1898.

Grewe, Wilhelm G. "Der Begriff des Politischen-Politik und Moral." *Die Junge Mannschaft* 1, no. 6 (1931/32): 1–6.

———. "Die Umbildung der Republik." *Die Junge Mannschaft* 1 (July 1932): 1–6.

———. *Gnade und Recht*. Hamburg: Hamburg Hanseat, 1936.

———. "Zwischen Neutralität und Kollektivsicherheit: Zur Aussenpolitik der Vereinigten Staaten." *Monatshefte für Auswärtige Politik* 4 (October 1937): 628–29.

———. "Wehrbereitschaft und Verfassungsrecht." *Zeitschrift der Akademie für Deutsches Recht* 4 (1937): 110ff.

———. "Der Status der Nichtkriegsführung." *Zeitschrift der Akademie für Deutsches Recht* 7 (1940): 206ff.

———. "Die Bestimmung des Kriegszustandes." *Zeitschrift der Akademie für Deutsches Recht* 7 (1940): 355–56.

———. "Krieg und Frieden: Proudhons Theorie des Völkerrechts." *Zeitschrift für Politik* 30, no. 6/7 (1940): 233–45.

———. "Rechtsformen des Ökonomischen Imperialismus im Neunzehnten Jahrhundert." *Zeitschrift für Politik* 31, no. 4 (1941): 230–42.

———. "Stellungswechsel der Amerikanischen Völkerrechtspolitik." *Zeitschrift für Politik* 31, no. 5 (1941): 261–66.

————. "Die Neue Kriegsphase." *Monatshefte für Auswärtige Politik* 9 (September 1941): 748–51.

————. *Probleme des Luftkriegsrechts.* Königsberg/Berlin: Ost-Europa Verlag, 1942.

————. "Der Zweite Weltkrieg." *Monatshefte für Auswärtige Politik* 9, no. 1/2 (January–February 1942): 78–84.

————. "Das Bündnissystem der Alliierten." *Zeitschrift für Politik* 32, no. 7 (1942): 483–89.

————. "Das Schicksal der Neutralität im Europäischen Krieg und im Zweiten Weltkrieg." In *Jahrbuch der Weltpolitik*, special issue, 86–106. Sonderausgabe. Berlin: Junker & Dünnhaupt, 1942.

————. "Die Völkerrechtlichen Grundlagen der Stellung des Reiches in Europa." In *Jahrbuch der Weltpolitik*, 90–111.

————. "Die Epochen der Modernen Völkerrechtsgeschichte." *Zeitschrift für die Gesamte Staatswissenschaft / Journal of Institutional and Theoretical Economics* 103, no. 2 (1943): 260–94.

————. "Die Epochen der Völkerrechtsgeschichte." *Zeitschrift für die Gesamte Staatswissenschaft / Journal of Institutional and Theoretical Economics* 103, no. 1 (1943): 38–66.

————. "Von den 'Alliierten und Assoziierten Mächten' zu den 'Vereinigten Nationen'." *Zeitschrift für Politik* 33, no. 4/5 (1943): 262–66.

————. "Die Völkerbundspläne der Alliierten." *Zeitschrift für Politik* 34, no. 7/8 (1944): 265–86.

————. "Diplomatische Invasionsvorbereitungen." *Zeitschrift für Politik* 34, no. 5/6 (1944): 192–96.

————. *Deutsche Aussenpolitik der Nachkriegszeit.* Stuttgart: Deutsche Verlags-Anstalt, 1960.

————. *Spiel der Kräfte in der Weltpolitik. Theorie und Praxis der internationalen Beziehungen.* Dusseldörf/Wien: Econ-Verlag, 1970.

————. *Rückblenden, 1976/1951.* Frankfurt/Main/Berlin/Wien: Propyläen, 1979.

————. "Machtvergleich in der Weltpolitik: Kräfterelationen und Modelle der Konfliktvermeidung." In *Der Neue Realismus: Aussenpolitik nach Iran und Afghanistan*, edited by Helmut Kohl, 71–87. Düsseldorf: Erb, 1980.

————. *Die aussenpolitische Lage Deutschlands am Beginn der achtziger Jahre.* Studien der Deutschlandfrage, Bd. 5. Berlin: Duncker & Humblot, 1982.

————. *Epochen der Völkerrechtsgeschichte.* 1st ed. Baden-Baden: Nomos Verlag, 1984.

————. "Westbindung und Deutsche Frage: Wie weit reicht die Interessengemeinschaft mit den westlichen Partnern?" 89–97. In *Deutsche Frage und Westbindung*, edited by Dieter Blumenwitz and Klaus Weigelt. Melle: Knoth, 1986.

————. "Von der Besatzungsherrschaft zur Souveränitat der Bundesrepublik Deutschland." In *Entscheidung für den Westen: vom Besatzungstatut zur Souveränitat der Bundesrepublik 1949–1955*, edited by Manfred Franke. Bonn: Bouvier, 1988.

————. *Machtprojektionen und Rechtsschranken: Essays aus vier Jahrzehnten über Verfassungen, politische Systeme und internationale Strukturen*. Baden-Baden: Nomos-Verlag, 1991.

————. "Ein Leben mit Staats- und Völkerrecht im 20. Jahrhundert." *Freiburger Universitätsblätter* Jg. 31, H. 118 (December 1992): 25–40.

————. "Aussenpolitik und Völkerrecht in der Praxis" (1989). *Archiv des Völkerrechts* 36, Bd. I (March 1998): 1–18.

————. "The Role of International Law in Diplomatic Practice." *Journal of the History of International Law* 1 (1999): 22–37.

————. *The Epochs of International Law*. Translated and revised by Michael Byers. Berlin: DeGruyter, 2000.

Grimmer-Solem, Erik. *Learning Empire: Globalization and the German Quest for World Status, 1875–1919*. Cambridge: Cambridge University Press, 2019.

Groom, A.J.R., and William C. Olson. *International Relations Then and Now: Origins and Trends in Interpretation*. London: Routledge, 1992.

Gross, Raphael. *Carl Schmitt and the Jews: The "Jewish Question," the Holocaust, and German Legal Theory*. Translated by Joel Golb. Madison: University of Wisconsin Press, 2007.

Guettel, Jens-Uwe. *German Expansionism, Imperial Liberalism and the United States, 1776–1945*. Cambridge: Cambridge University Press, 2012.

Guilhot, Nicolas, ed. *The Invention of International Relations Theory: Realism, the Rockefeller Foundation, and the 1954 Conference on Theory*. New York: Columbia University Press, 2011.

————. "Imperial Realism: Post-War IR Theory and Decolonisation." *International History Review* 36, no. 4 (August 8, 2014): 698–720.

————. *After the Enlightenment: Political Realism and International Relations in the Mid-Twentieth Century*. New York: Cambridge University Press, 2018.

Guzzini, Stefano. *Realism in International Relations and International Political Economy: The Continuing Story of a Death Foretold*. London: Routledge, 1996.

Gyorgy, Andrew. *Geopolitics, the New German Science* (1944). Berkeley: University of California Press, 1971.

Habermas, Jurgen. *The Divided West*. Edited and translated by Ciaran Cronin. Cambridge: Polity, 2006.

Hacke, Christian. *Weltmacht wider Willen: die Aussenpolitik der Bundesrepublik Deutschland*. Frankfurt/Main: Ullstein, 1993.

Hacke, Christian, and Jana Puglierin. "John H. Herz: Balancing Utopia and Reality." *International Relations* 21, no. 3 (September 2007): 367–82.

Hachmeister, Lutz. *Der Gegnerforscher: die Karriere des SS-Führers Franz Six* (München: Beck, 1998)

Hanrieder, Wolfram F. *The United States and Western Europe: Political, Economic, and Strategic Perspectives.* Cambridge, MA: Winthrop, 1974.

Haushofer, Karl. *Dai Nihon: Betrachtungen über Groß-Japans Wehrkraft, Weltstellung zur Zukunft.* Berlin: E.S. Mittler und Sohn, 1913.

———, Erich Obst, Hermann Lautensach, and Otto Maull. *Bausteine zur Geopolitik.* Berlin-Grunewald: Kurt Vowinckel, 1928.

———. *Macht und Erde.* Leipzig and Berlin: B.G. Teubner, 1930.

———, and Friedrich Ratzel. "Friedrich Ratzel als raum- und volkspolitischer Gestalter." In *Erdenmacht und Völkerschicksal: Eine Auswahl aus seinen Werken,* 2nd ed. Stuttgart: A. Kröner Verlag, 1941.

———. "Last Will and Testament of German Geopolitics." In *Total Power: A Footnote to History,* by Edmund J. Walsh, 35–51. New York: Doubleday, 1948.

Hawkins, Mike. *Social Darwinism in European and American Thought, 1860–1945: Nature as Model and Nature as Threat.* Cambridge: Cambridge University Press, 1997.

Heffernan, Michael. "The Origins of European Geopolitics, 1890–1920." In *Geopolitical Traditions: Critical Histories of a Century of Geopolitical Thought,* edited by David Atkinson and Klaus Dodds, 51–70. London: Routledge, 2000.

Herbert, Ulrich. *Best: Biographische Studien über Radikalismus, Weltanschauung und Vernunft, 1903–1989.* München: C.H. Beck, 1996.

Herf, Jeffrey. "War, Peace, and the Intellectuals: The West German Peace Movement." *International Security* 10, no. 4 (1986): 172–200.

Herz, John H. *Political Realism and Political Idealism: A Study in Theories and Realities.* Chicago: University of Chicago Press, 1951.

———. "Gedanken über Legitimität, Gewalt, und die Zukunft des Staates." In *Staatenwelt und Weltpolitik: Aufsätze zur internationalen Politik im Nuklearzeitalter,* 183–98. Hamburg: Hoffmann und Campe, 1974.

Herpolsheimer, Ralf and Regina Urban. "Franz Alfred Six." In *Zeitungswissenschaftler im Dritten Reich: Sieben biographische Studien,* edited by Arnulf Kutsch, et. al., 169–214. Köln: Studienverlag Hayit, 1984.

Herwig, Holger H. *The Demon of Geopolitics: How Karl Haushofer "Educated" Hitler and Hess.* Lanham, MD: Rowman & Littlefield, 2016.

Hobson, John M. *The Eurocentric Conception of World Politics: Western International Theory, 1760–2010.* Cambridge: Cambridge University Press, 2012.

Hobson, John M., and J.C. Sharman. "The Enduring Place of Hierarchy in World Politics: Tracing the Social Logics of Hierarchy and Political Change." *European Journal of International Relations* 11, no. 1 (March 1, 2005): 63–98.

Hoffmann, Stanley. *Gulliver's Troubles: Or the Setting of American Foreign Policy*. New York: McGraw-Hill, 1968.

———. "An American Social Science: International Relations." *Daedalus* 106, no. 3 (1977): 41–60.

———. "Notes on the Limits of 'Realism.'" *Social Research* 48, no. 4 (1981): 653–59.

Höhn, Reinhard. "Großraumordnung und völkisches Rechtsdenken." In *Reich, Volksordnung, Lebensraum: Zeitschrift für Völkische Verfassung und Verwaltung*, 1: 256–313. Darmstadt: L.C. Wittich Verlag, 1943.

Holborn, Hajo. "Bismarck's Realpolitik." *Journal of the History of Ideas* 21, no. 1 (1960): 84–98.

Holdar, S. "The Ideal State and the Power of Geography: The Life and Work of Rudolf Kjellén." *Political Geography* 11 (1992): 307–23.

Hooker, William. *Carl Schmitt's International Thought: Order and Orientation*. Cambridge: Cambridge University Press, 2009.

Hughes, Charles Evans. "The Centenary of the Monroe Doctrine." *Advocate of Peace through Justice* 86, no. 2 (February 1924): 100–109.

Immerwahr, Daniel. *How to Hide an Empire: A History of the Greater United States*. New York: Farrar, Straus and Giroux, 2019.

Ingrao, Christian. *Believe and Destroy: Intellectuals in the SS War Machine*. Translated by Andrew Brown. New York: Polity, 2013.

Jacobsen, Hans-Adolf, ed. *Karl Haushofer, Leben und Werk, Bd. 1: Lebensweg 1869–1946 und ausgewählte Texte zur Geopolitik; Bd. 2: Ausgewählter Schriftwechsel 1917–1946*. 1st ed. Boppard am Rhein: Bolt, 1979.

Jahn, Beate. *Classical Theory in International Relations*. Cambridge: Cambridge University Press, 2006.

———. *Liberal Internationalism: Theory, History, Practice*. London: Palgrave Macmillan, 2013.

———. "Liberal Internationalism: Historical Trajectory and Current Prospects." *International Affairs* 94, no. 1 (January 1, 2018): 43–61.

Jahrreiss, Hermann. "Wandel der Weltordnung." *Zeitschrift für öffentliches Recht* 21 (1941): 513–36.

Jørgensen, Knud Erik. "After Hegemony in International Relations, or, the Persistent Myth of American Disciplinary Hegemony." *European Review of International Studies* 1, no. 1 (2014): 57–64.

———, Audrey Alejandro, Alexander Reichwein, Felix Rösch, and Helen Turton. *Reappraising European IR Theoretical Traditions*. London: Palgrave, 2017.

Jureit, Ulrike. *Das Orden von Räumen: Territorium und Lebensraum im 19. und 20. Jahrhundert*. Hamburg: Hamburger Edition, 2012.

———. "Mastering Space: Laws of Movement and the Grip on the Soil." *Journal of Historical Geography* 61 (July 1, 2018): 81–85.

Jütersonke, Oliver. *Morgenthau, Law and Realism*. Cambridge: Cambridge University Press, 2012.

Kaiser, Karl. *Friedensforschung in der Bundesrepublik. Gegenstand und Aufgabe der Friedensforschung.* Göttingen: Vandenhoeck u. Ruprecht, 1970.

———. *Strukturwandlungen der Aussenpolitik in Grossbritannien und der Bundesrepublik.* München/Wien: R. Oldenbourg, 1970.

———, and Roger Morgan, eds. *Britain and West Germany: Changing Societies and the Future of Foreign Policy;* London: Oxford University Press for the Royal Institute of International Affairs, 1971.

Kearns, Gerry. "Closed Space and Political Practice: Frederick Jackson Turner and Halford Mackinder." *Environment and Planning: Society and Space* 2, no. 1 (March 1, 1984): 23–34.

———. *Geopolitics and Empire: The Legacy of Halford Mackinder.* Oxford: Oxford University Press, 2009.

Kehr, Eckart. "Englandhaß und Weltpolitik." *Zeitschrift für Politik* 17 (1928): 500–526.

Keighren, Innes M. *Bringing Geography to Book: Ellen Semple and the Reception of Geographical Knowledge.* London: I.B. Tauris, 2010.

Kelly, Duncan. "August Ludwig von Rochau and Realpolitik as Historical Political Theory." *Global Intellectual History* 3, no. 3 (September 2, 2018): 301–30.

Kennan, George F. *American Diplomacy 1900–1950.* New York: New American Library, 1955.

Keohane, Robert. *Neorealism and Its Critics.* New York: Columbia University Press, 1986.

Kindermann, Gottfried-Karl, and Hans J. Morgenthau. *Grundelemente der Weltpolitik: Eine Einführung.* 2nd ed. München: Piper, 1981 [1976].

Kirk, Grayson. *The Study of International Relations in Colleges and Universities.* New York: Council on Foreign Relations, 1947.

Kissinger, Henry A. *Nuclear Weapons and Foreign Policy.* New York: Council on Foreign Relations, 1957.

———. *The Troubled Partnership: A Re-Appraisal of the Atlantic Alliance.* New York: McGraw Hill, 1965.

———. "The White Revolutionary: Reflections on Bismarck." *Daedalus* 97, no. 3 (1968): 888–924.

———. "Hans Morgenthau." *New Republic* 183, no. 5/6 (1980): 12–14.

Koelsch, William A. "Miss Semple Meets the Historians: The Failed AHA 1907 Conference on Geography and History and What Happened Afterwards." *Journal of Historical Geography* 45 (July 1, 2014): 50–58.

Kohl, Helmut, ed. *Der Neue Realismus: Aussenpolitik nach Iran und Afghanistan.* Düsseldorf: Erb, 1980.

Kohn, Hans. "Book Review of *German Geopolitics*, by Robert Strausz-Hupé and Hans W. Weigert." *Annals of the American Academy of Political and Social Science* 223 (1942): 207–8.

Koskenniemi, Martti. *The Gentle Civilizer of Nations: The Rise and Fall of*

International Law, 1870–1960. Cambridge: Cambridge University Press, 2001.

———. "Review of *The Epochs of International Law* by Wilhelm Grewe." *International and Comparative Law Quarterly* 51, no. 3 (July 2002): 746–51.

———. "A History of International Law Histories." In *The Oxford Handbook of the History of International Law*, edited by Bardo Fassbender and Anne Peters, 943–71. Oxford: Oxford University Press, 2012.

Krell, Gert. *Peace Research in Hesse: The History and Development of the Peace Research Institute Frankfurt*. Frankfurt am Main: PRIF/HSFK, 1988.

Krippendorff, Ekkehart. "Ist Aussenpolitik AUSSENPOLITIK? Ein Beitrag zur Theorie und der Versuch, eine unhaltbare Unterscheidung aufzugeben." *Politische Vierteljahresschrift* 4, no. 3 (September 1963): 222–40.

Krippendorff, Ekkehart, and Volker Rittberger, eds. *The Foreign Policy of West Germany: Formation and Contents*. London: Sage, 1980

Kuklick, Bruce. *Blind Oracles: Intellectuals and War from Kennan to Kissinger*. Princeton, NJ: Princeton University Press, 2007.

Laak, Dirk von. "Von Alfred T. Mahan zu Carl Schmitt: Das Verhältnis von Land und Seemacht." In *Geopolitik: Grenzgänge im Zeitgeist*, Bd.1, edited by Irene Diekmann, 257–82. Berlin: Verlag für Berlin-Brandenburg, 2000.

Lake, David A. "White Man's IR: An Intellectual Confession." *Perspectives on Politics* 14, no. 4 (December 2016): 1112–22.

Landauer, Carl. "Review of Wilhelm Grewe, *The Epochs of International Law*." *Leiden Journal of International Law* 16, no. 1 (March 2003): 191–204.

———. "The Ambivalences of Power: Launching the American Journal of International Law in an Era of Empire and Globalization." *Leiden Journal of International Law* 20, no. 2 (June 2007): 325–58.

Lange, Karl. "Der Terminus 'Lebensraum' in Hitlers 'Mein Kampf.'" *Vierteljahresschrift für Zeitgeschichte* 13, no. 4 (1965): 430–31.

Lea, Homer. *The Valor of Ignorance*. New York: Harper & Bros., 1942.

Lebow, Richard Ned. *The Tragic Vision of Politics: Ethics, Interests and Orders*. Cambridge: Cambridge University Press, 2003.

———. "German Jews and American Realism." *Constellations* 18, no. 4 (2011): 545–66.

Levine, Emily J. *Allies and Rivals: German American Exchange and the Rise of the Modern Research University*. Chicago: University of Chicago Press, 2021.

Lippmann, Walter. *The Cold War: A Study in US Foreign Policy*. New York: Harper & Row, 1947.

Long, David, and Brian C. Schmidt, eds. *Imperialism and Internationalism in the Discipline of International Relations*. Albany: State University of New York Press, 2006.

Long, David, and Peter Wilson, eds. *Thinkers of the Twenty Years' Crisis: Inter-War Idealism Reassessed*. Oxford: Clarendon Press, 1996.

Longerich, Peter. *Propagandisten im Krieg: Die Presseabteilung des Auswärtigen Amtes unter Ribbentrop*. Berlin/Boston: De Gruyter Oldenbourg, 1987.

Mackinder, Halford John. "The Scope and Methods of Geography, and the Geographical Pivot of History, Being Papers Read to the Royal Geographical Society on 31 January 1887 and on 25 January 1904." *Geographic Journal* 23 (1904): 421–37.

————. *Democratic Ideals and Reality: A Study in the Politics of Reconstruction*. New York: H. Holt, 1942.

Maier, Charles S. *Among Empires: American Ascendancy and Its Predecessors*. Cambridge, MA: Harvard University Press, 2009.

————. *Leviathan 2.0: Inventing Modern Statehood*. Cambridge, MA: Harvard University Press, 2012.

————. *Once within Borders: Territories of Power, Wealth and Belonging since 1500*. Cambridge, MA: Harvard University Press, 2016.

Mahan, Alfred Thayer. "The United States Looking Outward" (1890). In *The Interest of America in Sea Power, Present and Future*. Boston: Little, Brown, 1917.

————. "Possibilities of an Anglo-American Reunion" (1894). In *The Interest of America in Sea Power, Present and Future*.

————. "The Future in Relation to American Naval Power" (1895). In *The Interest of America in Sea Power, Present and Future*.

————. "The Peace Conference and the Moral Aspect of War." *North American Review* 169, no. 515 (1899): 433–47.

————. "The Persian Gulf and International Relations" (1902). In *Retrospect and Prospect: Studies in International Relations, Naval and Political*, 209–54. New York: Kenniket Press, 1968.

————. "The Monroe Doctrine" (1902). In *Naval Administration and Warfare: Some General Principles, with Other Essays*, 355–409. New York: Little, Brown, 1908.

————. "The Deficiencies of Law as an Instrument of International Adjustments" (1911). In *Armaments and Arbitration, Or, The Place of Force in the International Relations of States*, 78–99. New York: Harper and Bros., 1912.

————. "The Place of Force in International Relations" (1911). In *Armaments and Arbitration, Or, The Place of Force in the International Relations of States*, 100–120.

————. "The Great Illusion" (1912). In *Armaments and Arbitration, Or, The Place of Force in the International Relations of States*, 121–54.

————. "The Naval War College" (1912). In *Armaments and Arbitration, Or, The Place of Force in the International Relations of States*, 196–217.

Maltzahn, Curt von. "Friedrich Ratzel: Ein Gedenkwort." *Marine Rundschau* 16 (1905): 217–20.

Mantena, Karuna. "Another Realism: The Politics of Gandhian Nonviolence." *American Political Science Review* 106, no. 2 (2012): 455–70.

Marks, Susan, ed. *International Law on the Left: Re-Examining Marxist Legacies*. Cambridge: Cambridge University Press, 2008.

Mattern, Johannes. *Geopolitik: Doctrine of National Self-Sufficiency and Empire*. Baltimore: Johns Hopkins University Press, 1942.

Maull, Otto. *Das Wesen der Geopolitik*. Leipzig: B.G. Teubner, 1936.

Maull, Otto, Walther Vogel, and Rudolf Reinhard, eds. "Some German Works on Political Geography." *Geographical Review* 17, no. 3 (1927): 511–13.

McDougal, Myres S. "Law and Power." *American Journal of International Law* 46, no. 1 (January 1952): 102–14.

McNamara, Patrick J. *A Catholic Cold War: Edmund A. Walsh, S.J., and the Politics of American Anticommunism*. New York: Fordham University Press, 2005.

McQueen, Alison. *Political Realism in Apocalyptic Times*. Cambridge: Cambridge University Press, 2017.

Mearsheimer, John J. *The Tragedy of Great Power Politics*. Updated ed. New York: W.W. Norton, [2001] 2014.

———. "Hans Morgenthau and the Iraq War: Realism versus Neoconservatism." May 18, 2005. Accessed March 21, 2021. www.opendemocracy.net/en/morgenthau_2522jsp/.

Mehring, Reinhard. *Carl Schmitt: A Biography*. Translated by Daniel Steuer. Cambridge: Polity, 2014.

Meyer, Karl E. "Weighing Iraq on Morgenthau's Scale." *World Policy Journal* 20, no. 3 (2003): 89–92.

Mills, Charles Wright. *The Causes of World War Three*. London: Secker and Warburg, 1959.

Milne, David. *Worldmaking: The Art and Science of American Diplomacy*. New York: Farrar, Straus and Giroux, 2015.

Minca, Claudio, and Rory Rowan. *On Schmitt and Space*. New York: Routledge, 2016.

———. "The Question of Space in Carl Schmitt." *Progress in Human Geography* 39, no. 3 (Fall 2015): 268–89.

Mitchell, Nancy. *The Danger of Dreams: German and American Imperialism in Latin America*. 1st ed. Chapel Hill: University of North Carolina Press, 1999.

Molloy, Sean. *The Hidden History of Realism: A Genealogy of Power Politics*. Palgrave Macmillan History of International Thought. New York: Palgrave Macmillan US, 2006.

Mommsen, Wolfgang J. *Max Weber and German Politics, 1890–1920*. Chicago: University of Chicago Press, 1990.

Morefield, Jeanne. *Covenants without Swords: Idealist Liberalism and the Spirit of Empire*. Princeton, NJ: Princeton University Press, 2005.

Morgan, Roger. "Transnational Relations and World Politics and Regional Integration: Theory and Research." *International Affairs* 49, no. 4 (October 10, 1973): 626–27.

Morgenthau, Hans. "Positivism, Functionalism, and International Law." *American Journal of International Law* 34, no. 2 (April 1940): 260–84.

———. "The Machiavellian Utopia." *Ethics* 55, no. 2 (January 1, 1945): 145–47.

———. "About Cynicism, Perfectionism and Realism in International Affairs" (1945). In *The Decline of Democratic Politics*. Chicago: University of Chicago Press, 1962.

———. "Diplomacy." *Yale Law Journal* 55, no. 5 (January 1, 1946).

———. "The Political Science of E.H. Carr." *World Politics* 1, no. 1 (1948): 127–34.

———. "National Interest and Moral Principles in Foreign Policy: The Primacy of National Interest." *American Scholar* 18 (1949): 207–12.

———. *Principles & Problems of International Politics; Selected Readings.* Edited with Kenneth W. Thompson. New York: Alfred A. Knopf, 1950.

———. "The Mainsprings of American Foreign Policy: The National Interest vs. Moral Abstractions." *American Political Science Review* 44, no. 4 (December 1950): 833–54.

———. *In Defense of the National Interest: A Critical Examination of American Foreign Policy.* New York: Alfred A. Knopf, 1951.

———. "Review of Power and Society; A Framework for Political Inquiry." *American Political Science Review* 46, no. 1 (1952): 230–34.

———. "What Is the National Interest of the United States?" *Annals of the American Academy of Political and Social Science* 282, no. 1 (July 1, 1952): 1–7.

———. "The Yardstick of National Interest." *Annals of the American Academy of Political and Social Science* 296, no. 1 (January 1, 1954): 77–84.

———. *Dilemmas of Politics.* Chicago: University of Chicago Press, 1958.

———. *The Decline of Democratic Politics.* Chicago: University of Chicago Press, 1962.

———. *Macht und Frieden; Grundlegung einer Theorie der internationalen Politik.* Translated by Odette Jankowitsch and Dieter G.Wilke. Introduction by Gottfried-Karl Kindermann. Gütersloh: C. Bertelsmann, 1963.

———. "The Crisis in the Western Alliance." *Commentary* 35, no. 3 (March 1, 1963): 185–90.

———. *Science: Servant or Master?* New York: New American Library, 1972.

———. "Détente: Reality and Illusion." *Wall Street Journal* 184 (July 18, 1974): 16.

———. "The Pathology of American Power." *International Security* 1, no. 3 (1977): 3–20.

———. *The Concept of the Political.* Edited by Hartmut Behr and Felix Rösch. Translated by Maeva Vidal. New York: Palgrave, 2012.

————. William Lee Bradley, and Council on Religion and International Affairs. *Human Rights & Foreign Policy*. New York: Council on Religion & International Affairs, 1979.

————, and Wolfram F. Hanrieder. "The US and Europe in a Decade of Détente." In *The United States and Western Europe: Political, Economic, and Strategic Perspectives*. Cambridge, MA: Winthrop, 1974.

————, Kenneth Thompson, and David Clinton. *Politics among Nations*. 7th ed. Boston: McGraw-Hill Education, 2005.

Mouffe, Chantal. "Schmitt's Vision of a Multipolar World Order." *South Atlantic Quarterly* 104, no. 2 (April 1, 2005): 245–51.

Munster, Rens van, and Casper Sylvest. *Nuclear Realism: Global Political Thought during the Thermonuclear Revolution*. New York: Routledge, 2016.

Murphy, David T. *The Heroic Earth: Geopolitical Thought in Weimar Germany, 1918–1933*. Kent, OH: Kent State University Press, 1997.

Naranch, Bradley, and Geoff Eley, eds. *German Colonialism in a Global Age*. Durham, NC: Duke University Press, 2015.

Natter, Wolfgang. "Geopolitics in Germany, 1919–45: Karl Haushofer and the *Zeitschrift für Geopolitik*." In *A Companion to Political Geography*, edited by John A. Agnew, Katharyne Mitchell, and Gerard Toal, 186–203. Oxford: Wiley-Blackwell, 2003.

Navari, Cornelia. *Hans J. Morgenthau and the American Experience*. London: Palgrave, 2018.

Neitzel, Sönke. *Weltmacht oder Untergang: die Weltreichslehre im Zeitalter des Imperialismus*. Paderborn: Schöningh, 2000.

Nelson, Robert L., ed. *Germans, Poland and Colonial Expansion to the East: 1850 through the Present*. London: New York: Palgrave, 2009.

Nerlich, Uwe. *Beiträge der Sozialwissenschaft. Bd. I: Krieg und Frieden in der modernen Staatenwelt*. Gütersloh: C. Bertelsmann, 1966.

Neumann, Franz L. *Behemoth: The Structure and Practice of National Socialism, 1933–1944*. Chicago: Ivan R. Dee, 2009.

Niebuhr, Reinhold. *The Irony of American History*. Chicago: University of Chicago Press, 1952.

Nunan, Timothy, ed. *Carl Schmitt: Writings on War*. Cambridge: Polity, 2011.

Odysseos, Louiza, and Fabio Petito, eds. *The International Political Thought of Carl Schmitt: Terror, Liberal War and the Crisis of Global Order*. London: Routledge, 2007.

Olson, William, and A.J.R. Groom. *International Relations Then and Now: Origins and Trends in Interpretation*. London: HarperCollins, 1991.

Osiander, Andreas. "Rereading Early Twentieth-Century IR Theory: Idealism Revisited." *International Studies Quarterly* 42, no. 3 (1998): 409–32.

Ó Tuathail, Gearóid. *Critical Geopolitics: The Politics of Writing Global Space*. Minneapolis: University of Minnesota Press, 1996.

Owens, Patricia, and Katharina Rietzler, eds. *Women's International Thought: A New History.* Cambridge: Cambridge University Press, 2021.

Palmer, Norman. *A Design for International Relations Research: Scope, Theory, Methods, and Relevance.* Philadelphia: American Academy of Political and Social Science, 1970.

Parmar, Inderjeet. *Foundations of the American Century: The Ford, Carnegie, and Rockefeller Foundations in the Rise of American Power.* New York: Columbia University Press, 2015.

Pashakhanlou, Arash Heydarian. *Realism and Fear in International Relations: Morgenthau, Waltz and Mearsheimer Reconsidered.* London: Palgrave Macmillan, 2017.

Pero, Mario Del. *The Eccentric Realist: Henry Kissinger and the Shaping of American Foreign Policy.* Ithaca, NY: Cornell University Press, 2009.

Pfeffer, Karl Heinz. *Die angelsächsische Neue Welt und Europa.* Vol. 1. Berlin: Junker & Dünnhaupt, 1941.

Porter, Patrick. *The False Promise of Liberal Order: Nostalgia, Delusion and the Rise of Trump.* Cambridge, MA: Polity, 2020.

Posen, Barry R. *Restraint: A New Foundation for US Grand Strategy.* Ithaca, NY: Cornell University Press, 2015.

Pouliot, Vincent. *International Pecking Orders: The Politics and Practice of Multilateral Diplomacy.* Cambridge: Cambridge University Press, 2016.

Pugach, Noel H. *Paul S. Reinsch, Open Door Diplomat in Action.* Millwood, NY: KTO Press, 1979.

Puglierin, Jana. *John H. Herz: Leben und Denken zwischen Idealismus und Realismus, Deutschland und Amerika.* Zeitgeschichtliche Forschungen, Bd. 42. Berlin: Duncker & Humblot, 2015.

Quaritsch, Helmut. "Eine sonderbare Beziehung: Carl Schmitt und Erich Kaufmann." In *Bürgersinn und staatliche Macht in Antike und Gegenwart: Festschrift für Wolfgang Schuller zum 65. Geburtstag,* edited by M. Dreher. Konstanz: Universitätsverlag Konstanz, 2000.

Quirk, Joel, and Darshan Vigneswaran. "The Construction of an Edifice: The Story of a First Great Debate." *Review of International Studies* 31, no. 1 (2005): 89–107.

Radkau, Joachim. *Die deutsche Emigration in den USA: Ihr Einfluss auf die amerikanische Europapolitik, 1933–1945.* Düsseldorf: Bertelsmann, 1971.

Ramos, Paulo Jorge Batista. "Role of the Yale Institute of International Studies in the Construction of the United States National Security Ideology, 1935–1951." PhD thesis, University of Manchester, 2003.

Rasch, William. "Human Rights as Geopolitics: Carl Schmitt and the Legal Form of American Supremacy." *Cultural Critique,* no. 54 (2003): 120–47.

Ratzel, Friedrich. *Wider die Reichsnörgler: ein Wort zur Kolonialfrage aus Wählerkreisen* (München: R. Oldenbourg, 1884).

————. *Die Vereinigten Staaten von Amerika.* 2nd ed. München: R. Oldenbourg, 1893 [1879–80].

————. *Politische Geographie.* München: R. Oldenbourg, 1897.

————. *Das Meer als Quelle der Völkergrösse: Eine politisch-geographische Studie.* München: R. Oldenbourg, 1900.

————. *Der Lebensraum: eine biogeographische Studie.* Tübingen: H. Laupp, 1901.

————. *Die Erde und das Leben: eine vergleichende Erdkunde*, 2 vols. Ann Arbor: University of Michigan Library, 1901.

————. "Die Nordatlantischen Mächte." *Marine Rundschau* 14 (1903): 911–39, 1047–62.

————. "Geschichte, Völkerkunde und Historische Perspektive." *Historische Zeitschrift* 93, no. 1 (1904): 1–46.

————. *Glücksinseln und Träume: gesammelte Aufsätze aus den Grenzboten.* Leipzig: Grunow, 1905.

————. *Kleine Schriften II.* München: R. Oldenbourg, 1906.

————. *Erdenmacht und Völkerschicksal: eine Auswahl aus seinen Werken.* Hrsg. Karl Haushofer. Stuttgart: A. Kröner, 1940.

Reinsch, Paul Samuel. *World Politics at the End of the Nineteenth Century: As Influenced by the Oriental Situation.* London: Macmillan, 1900.

Rice, Daniel. "Reinhold Niebuhr and Hans Morgenthau: A Friendship with Contrasting Shades of Realism." *Journal of American Studies* 42, no. 2 (2008): 255–91.

Rietzler, Katharina. "Counter-Imperial Orientalism: Friedrich Berber and the Politics of International Law in Germany and India, 1920s–1960s." *Journal of Global History* 11, no. 1 (March 2016): 113–34.

Ringer, Fritz K. *The Decline of the German Mandarins: The German Academic Community, 1890–1933.* Hanover, NH: Wesleyan University Press, 1990.

Rochau, Ludwig August von. *Grundsätze der Realpolitik angewendet auf die staatlichen Zustände Deutschlands.* Frankfurt/Main: Ullstein, 1972.

————. *Grundsätze der Realpolitik angewendet auf die staatlichen Zustände Deutschlands.* 2 vols. Stuttgart: K. Göpel, 1853–69.

Roelofsen, C. "The Epochs of International Law." *American Journal of International Law* 98 (October 1, 2004).

Rohde, Christoph. *Hans J. Morgenthau und der weltpolitische Realismus.* Wiesbaden: VS, 2004.

Rösch, Felix, ed. *Émigré Scholars and the Genesis of International Relations: A European Discipline in America?* London: Palgrave Macmillan, 2015.

Rosenboim, Or. *The Emergence of Globalism: Visions of World Order in Britain and the United States, 1939–1950.* Princeton, NJ: Princeton University Press, 2017.

Sargent, Daniel J. *A Superpower Transformed: The Remaking of American Foreign Relations in the 1970s.* Oxford: Oxford University Press, 2015.

Sassen, Saskia. *Losing Control? Sovereignty in an Age of Globalization*. New York: Columbia University Press, 1996.

Sauer, C.O. "The Formative Years of Ratzel in the United States." *Annals of the Association of American Geographers* 61, no. 2 (1971): 245–54.

Scarfi, Juan Pablo. *The Hidden History of International Law in the Americas: Empire and Legal Networks*. Oxford: Oxford University Press, 2017.

Schatz, Oskar, ed. *Der Friede im nuklearen Zeitalter: Eine Kontroverse zwischen Realisten und Utopisten*. München: Manz Verlag, 1970.

Scheuerman, William E. "Was Morgenthau a Realist? Revisiting Scientific Man vs. Power Politics." *Constellations* 14, no. 4 (2007): 506–30.

———. *Morgenthau*. Cambridge, MA: Polity, 2009.

———. *The Realist Case for Global Reform*. Cambridge, MA: Polity, 2011.

———. *The End of Law: Carl Schmitt in the Twenty-First Century* (1999). Lanham, MD: Rowman & Littlefield, 2019.

Schmidt, Brian. *The Political Discourse of Anarchy: A Disciplinary History of International Relations*. Albany: State University of New York Press, 1997.

———, ed. *International Relations and the First Great Debate*. London: Routledge, 2012.

Schmidt, Brian C., and Tim Dunne. "Realism." In *Globalization of World Politics: An Introduction to International Relations*, 7th ed., 99–112. Oxford: Oxford University Press, 2017.

Schmidt, Brian C., and Nicolas Guilhot, eds. *Historiographical Investigations in International Relations*. London: Palgrave, 2019.

Schmitt, Carl. *Der Nomos der Erde im Völkerrecht des Jus Publicum Europaeum*. Berlin: Duncker & Humblot, 1950.

———. "Interrogation of Carl Schmitt by Robert Kempner (I)." *Telos*, no. 72 (July 1987): 97–129.

———. *Glossarium: Aufzeichnungen der Jahre 1947–1951*. Edited by Eberhard Freiherr von Medem. Berlin: Duncker & Humblot, 1991.

———. *Staat, Großraum, Nomos: Arbeiten aus den Jahren 1916–1969*. Edited by Günter Maschke. Berlin: Duncker & Humblot, 1995.

———. *The Concept of the Political* (1932). Translated by George Schwab. Chicago: University of Chicago Press, 1996.

———. *Frieden oder Pazifismus: Arbeiten zum Völkerrecht und zur internationalen Politik, 1924–78*. Edited by Günter Maschke. Berlin: Duncker & Humblot, 2005.

———. *Völkerrechtliche Großraumordnung mit Interventionsverbot für raumfremde Mächte: Ein Beitrag zum Reichsbegriff im Völkerrecht*. 3, Unveränd. Aufl. der Ausg. von 1941. Berlin: Duncker & Humblot, 2009.

———. *Land and Sea: A World-Historical Meditation* (1942). Edited by Samuel Garrett Zeitlin and Russell A. Berman. Candor, NY: Telos Press, 2015.

———. *Land und Meer: Eine weltgeschichtliche Betrachtung*. Neuauflage. Stuttgart: Klett-Cotta Verlag, 2016.

Schmitt, Carl, and Helmut Quaritsch. *Antworten in Nürnberg*. Berlin: Duncker & Humblot, 2000.

Schmitt, Horst. "Die Freiburger Schule 1954–1970." In *Schulen der deutschen Politikwissenschaft*, edited by Wilhelm Bleek and Hans J. Lietzmann, 213–43. Wiesbaden: VS Verlag für Sozialwissenschaften, 1999.

Schulten, Susan. *The Geographical Imagination in America, 1880–1950*. Chicago: University of Chicago Press, 2004.

Schwab, George, and Henry Friedlander. *Detente in Historical Perspective: The First CUNY Conference on History and Politics*. 1st ed. New York: Cyrco Press, 1975.

Schwarz, Hans-Peter. "Die Rolle der Bundesrepublik in der Staatengesellschaft." In *Strukturwandlungen der Aussenpolitik in Grossbritannien und der Bundesrepublik*, edited by Karl Kaiser and Roger Morgan, 243–66. München: Oldenbourg, 1970.

———. "Ein Lehrbuch der Realpolitik." *Politische Vierteljahresschrift* 14, no. 1 (1973): 122–27.

———. "Die Politik der Westbindung oder die Staatsraison der Bundesrepublik." *Zeitschrift Für Politik* 22, no. 4 (1975): 307–37.

———. *Die Gezähmten Deutschen: von der Machtbesessenheit zur Machtvergessenheit*. Stuttgart: Deutsche Verlags-Anstalt, 1985.

Schwarz, Hans-Peter, and Karl Kaiser, eds. *America and Western Europe: Problems and Prospects*. Lexington, MA: Lexington Books, 1978.

See, Jennifer W. "A Prophet without Honor: Hans Morgenthau and the War in Vietnam, 1955–1965." *Pacific Historical Review* 70, no. 3 (August 2001): 419–48.

Semple, Ellen C. *American History and Its Geographic Conditions*. New York: Houghton, Mifflin, 1903.

———. "Review of *Der Staat und Sein Boden* by Friedrich Ratzel." *Annals of the American Academy of Political and Social Science* 9, no. 2 (1908): 102–4.

———. *Influences of Geographic Environment: On the Basis of Ratzel's System of Anthropo-Geography*. New York: Henry Holt, 1911.

———. "Review of *Anthropogeographie* by Friedrich Ratzel." *Annals of the American Academy of Political and Social Science* 16 (1915): 137–39.

———. "Two Works on Political Geography." Edited by Alexander Supan, Erich Obst, and Friedrich Ratzel. *Geographical Review* 14, no. 4 (1924): 665–67.

Sexton, Jay. *The Monroe Doctrine: Empire and Nation in Nineteenth-Century America*. New York: Hill and Wang, 2012.

Shaler, Nathaniel Southgate. *Nature and Man in America*. New York: C. Scribner & Sons, 1902.

Siedschlag, Alexander and Gottfried-Karl Kindermann, eds. *Realistische Per-*

spektiven internationaler Politik: Festschrift für Gottfried-Karl Kindermann zum 75. Geburtstag. Opladen: Leske & Budrich, 2001.

Simonds, Frank Herbert, and Brooks Emeny. *The Great Powers in World Politics: International Relations and Economic Nationalism*. New York: American Book, 1935.

Six, Frank Alfred. "Das Deutsche Auslandswissenschaftliche Institut im Jahre 1941." *Zeitschrift für Politik* 31, no. 12 (1941): 733–39.

———. *Jahrbuch der Weltpolitik 1942*. Berlin: Junker & Dünnhaupt, 1942.

Skop, Arthur Lloyd. "The Primacy of Domestic Politics: Eckart Kehr and the Intellectual Development of Charles A. Beard." *History and Theory* 13, no. 2 (1974): 119–31.

Sleat, Matt, ed. *Politics Recovered: Realist Thought in Theory and Practice*. New York: Columbia University Press, 2018.

Smith, Neil. *American Empire: Roosevelt's Geographer and the Prelude to Globalization*. Berkeley: University of California Press, 2004.

Smith, Tony. *Why Wilson Matters: The Origin of American Liberal Internationalism and Its Crisis Today*. Princeton, NJ: Princeton University Press, 2017.

Smith, Woodruff D. "Friedrich Ratzel and the Origins of Lebensraum." *German Studies Review* 3, no. 1 (1980): 51–68.

———. *The Ideological Origins of Nazi Imperialism*. Oxford: Oxford University Press, 1986.

Söllner, Alfons. "German Conservatism in America: Morgenthau's Political Realism." *Telos*, no. 72 (July 1987): 161–72.

———. *Deutsche Politikwissenschaftler in der Emigration: Studien zu ihrer Akkulturation und Wirkungsgeschichte*. Wiesbaden: VS Verlag für Sozialwissenschaften, 1996.

———. "From Public Law to Political Science? The Emigration of German Scholars after 1933 and Their Influence on the Transformation of a Discipline." In *Forced Migration and Scientific Change: Émigré German-Speaking Scientists and Scholars after 1933*, edited by Mitchell Ash and Alfons Söllner. Cambridge: Cambridge University Press, 1996.

Spang, Christian W. *Karl Haushofer und Japan: die Rezeption seiner geopolitischen Theorien in der deutschen und japanischen Politik*. München: Iudicium Verlag, 2013.

———. *Karl Haushofer und die OAG: deutsch-japanische Netzwerke in der ersten Hälfte des 20. Jahrhunderts*. München: Iudicium Verlag, 2018.

Spang, Christian W., and Rolf-Harald Wippich, eds. *Japanese-German Relations, 1895–1945: War, Diplomacy and Public Opinion*. New York: Routledge, 2006.

Sparrow, James T. "Morgenthau's Dilemma: Rethinking the Democratic Leviathan in the Atomic Age." In "Beyond Stateless Democracy," edited by James Novak, Stephen Sawyer, and James T. Sparrow, special issue, *Tocqueville Review* 36, no. 1 (2015): 93–133.

Specter, Matthew G. "What's Left in Schmitt? From Aversion to Appropria-
    tion in Contemporary Political Theory." In *The Oxford Handbook of Carl
    Schmitt*, edited by Jens Meierhenrich and Oliver Simons, 426–46. Oxford:
    Oxford University Press, 2016.
————. "Geopolitics and *Grossraum*: Resituating Carl Schmitt in an Atlantic
    Context." *History and Theory* 56, no. 3 (September 2017): 398–406.
————. "Second Nature: Realism's Transatlantic Origins, 1880–1910." *Duke
    Global Working Papers*, no. 13 (September 2019).
Speier, Hans. "Magic Geography." *Social Research* 8, no. 3 (1941): 310–30.
Spykman, Nicholas J. *America's Strategy in World Politics: The United States
    and the Balance of Power*. New York: Harcourt & Brace, 1942.
Spykman, Nicholas John, and Helen R. Nicholl. *The Geography of the Peace*.
    New York: Harcourt & Brace, 1944.
Stebbins, Richard Poate, and Grayson L. Kirk, eds. *War and National Policy: A
    Syllabus*. New York: Farrar & Rinehart, 1942.
Steinmetz, Willibald, ed. *The Force of Comparison: A New Perspective on
    Modern European History and the Contemporary World*. New German
    Historical Perspectives, vol. 11. New York: Berghahn Books, 2019.
Stephanson, Anders. *Kennan and the Art of Foreign Policy*. Cambridge, MA:
    Harvard University Press, 1989.
————. *Manifest Destiny: American Expansion and the Empire of Right*. New
    York: Hill and Wang, 1995.
Stirk, Peter. "Carl Schmitt's *Völkerrechtliche Grossraumordnung*." *History of
    Political Thought* 20, no. 2 (1999): 357–74.
Stoddard, Lothrop. *The Rising Tide of Color against White World-Supremacy*.
    With an introduction by Madison Grant. New York: Scribner, 1920.
Stolleis, Michael. *Geschichte des öffentlichen Rechts in Deutschland*. Bd. IV:
    Staats und Verwaltungsrechts in West und Ost 1945–1990. München: C.H.
    Beck, 2012.
————. *A History of Public Law in Germany, 1914–1945*. Translated by
    Thomas Dunlap. Oxford: Oxford University Press, 2004.
Strausz-Hupé, Robert. *Geopolitics: The Struggle for Space and Power*. New
    York: Putnam & Sons, 1942.
Suri, Jeremy. *Henry Kissinger and the American Century*. Cambridge, MA:
    Harvard University Press, 2009.
Sylvest, Casper. *British Liberal Internationalism, 1880–1930: Making Progress?*
    Manchester: Manchester University Press, 2010.
Taylor, A.J.P. "No Illusions and No Ideas." *The Nation*, September 8/15, 1951,
    96–97.
Teschke, Benno. "IR Theory, Historical Materialism and the False Promise of
    International Historical Sociology." *Spectrum Journal of Global Studies* 6,
    no. 1 (2014): 1–66.
————. "Decisions and Indecisions: Political and Intellectual Reception of
    Carl Schmitt." *New Left Review*, no. 67 (January–February 2011): 61–95.

————. "Fetish of Geopolitics: Reply to Balakrishnan." *New Left Review*, no. 69 (May–June 2011): 81–100.

Thakur, Vineet, Alexander E. Davis, and Peter Vale. "Imperial Mission, 'Scientific' Method: An Alternative Account of the Origins of IR." *Millennium* 46, no. 1 (September 1, 2017): 3–23.

Thompson, John A. "Woodrow Wilson and a World Governed by Evolving Law." *Journal of Policy History* 20, no. 1 (2008): 113–25.

————. *A Sense of Power: The Roots of America's Global Role.* 1st ed. Ithaca, NY: Cornell University Press, 2015.

Thompson, Kenneth. *Truth and Tragedy: Tribute to Hans J. Morgenthau.* New Brunswick, NJ: Routledge, 1984.

Tickner, J. Ann. "Gendering a Discipline: Some Feminist Methodological Contributions to International Relations." *Signs: Journal of Women in Culture and Society* 30, no. 4 (June 1, 2005): 2173–88.

————. "Retelling IR's Foundational Stories: Some Feminist and Postcolonial Perspectives." *Global Change, Peace & Security* 23, no. 1 (February 1, 2011): 5–13.

Tooze, Adam. *The Deluge: The Great War, America and the Remaking of Global Order, 1916–1931.* New York: Viking, 2014.

Triepel, Heinrich. *Die Hegemonie: Ein Buch von führenden Staaten.* Stuttgart: W. Kohlhammer, 1938.

Troll, C. "Die Geographische Wissenschaft in Deutschland in den Jahren 1933 bis 1945." *Erdkunde* 1, no. 1/3 (1947): 3–48.

Vagts, Alfred. "Geography in War and Geopolitics." *Military Affairs* 7, no. 2 (1943): 79–88.

————, and William Beard, eds. *Charles A. Beard: The National Interest—An Analytical Study in American Foreign Policy.* Chicago: Quadrangle Books, 1966.

Vagts, Alfred, and Detlev F. Vagts. "The Balance of Power in International Law: A History of an Idea." *American Journal of International Law* 73, no. 4 (1979): 555–80.

Vagts, Detlev F. "International Law in the Third Reich." *American Journal of International Law* 84, no. 3 (July 1990): 661–704.

————. "Hegemonic International Law." *American Journal of International Law* 95, no. 4 (2001): 843–48.

Vitalis, Robert. *White World Order, Black Power Politics: The Birth of American International Relations.* Ithaca, NY: Cornell University Press, 2017.

Von, Maltzahn Curt Freiherr. *Der Seekrieg; Seine geschichtliche Entwickelung vom Zeitalter der Entdeckungen bis zur Gegenwart.* Aus Natur und Geisteswelt, 99. Leipzig: G. Teubner, 1906.

Waever, Ole. "The Sociology of a Not So International Discipline: American and European Developments in International Relations." *International Organization* 52, no. 4 (1998): 687–727.

Wagner, Wolfgang. *Mittlere Mächte in der Weltpolitik*. Opladen: Leske, 1969.

Walsh, Edmund A. *Total Power: A Footnote to History*. New York: Doubleday, 1948.

———. "The Mystery of Haushofer." *Life* 21, no. 12 (September 16, 1946): 106–20.

Walt, Stephen M. "Restraint Isn't Isolationism—and It Won't Endanger America." *Foreign Policy* (blog). Accessed March 16, 2021. https://foreignpolicy.com/2019/07/22/restraint-isnt-isolationism-and-it-wont-endanger-america-offshore-balancing-quincy-institute/.

Waltz, Kenneth N. *The Theory of International Politics*. New York: McGraw-Hill, 1979.

Weber, Hermann. "Rechtswissenschaft im Dienst der NS-Propaganda: Das Institut für Auswärtige Politik und die Deutsche Völkerrechtsdoktrin in den Jahren 1933 bis 1945." In *Wissenschaftliche Verantwortung und politische Macht: zum wissenschaftlichen Umgang mit der Kriegsschuldfrage 1914, mit Versöhnungsdiplomatie und mit dem nationalsozialistischen Großmachtstreben; wissenschaftsgeschichtliche Untersuchungen zum Umfeld und zur Entwicklung des Instituts für Auswärtige Politik, Hamburg/Berlin 1923–1945*. Edited by Klaus Jürgen Gantzel. Berlin: Reimer, 1986.

Weber, Max. *Weber: Political Writings*. Edited by Peter Lassman. Translated by Ronald Speirs. Cambridge: Cambridge University Press, 1994.

———. *The Vocation Lectures*. Edited by David Owen and Tracy B. Strong. Translated by Rodney Livingstone. Indianapolis: Hackett, 2004.

Wehler, Hans-Ulrich, ed. *Eckart Kehr: Der Primat der Innenpolitik*. Veröffentlichungen der Historischen Kommission zu Berlin, vol. 19. Berlin: DeGruyter, 1970.

Weigert, H.W. "German Geopolitics." *Harper's Magazine*, November 1941.

———. "Haushofer and the Pacific." *Foreign Affairs*, July 1, 1942.

Weinberg, Gerhard L. "Hitler's Image of the United States." *American Historical Review* 69, no. 4 (1964): 1006–21.

Wendt, Alexander. "Anarchy Is What States Make of It: The Social Construction of Power Politics." *International Organization* 46, no. 2 (1992): 391–425.

Wertheim, Stephen. *Tomorrow, the World: The Birth of US Global Supremacy*. Cambridge, MA: Harvard University Press, 2020.

Westad, Odd Arne. *The Global Cold War: Third World Interventions and the Making of Our Times*. New ed. Cambridge: Cambridge University Press, 2011.

Whitman, James Q. *Hitler's American Model: The United States and the Making of Nazi Race Law*. Princeton, NJ: Princeton University Press, 2018.

Whittlesey, Derwent. "The Geopoliticians: Haushofer." In *Makers of Modern Strategy: Military Thought from Machiavelli to Hitler*, edited by Edward

Mead Earle, Gordon A. Craig, and Felix Gilbert, 1st ed., 388–414. Princeton, NJ: Princeton University Press, 1943.

Whittlesey, Derwent Stainthorpe. *German Strategy of World Conquest.* New York: Farrar & Rinehart, 1942.

Williams, Michael. ed. *Realism Reconsidered: The Legacy of Hans Morgenthau.* Oxford: Oxford University Press, 2008.

———. *The Realist Tradition and the Limits of International Relations.* Cambridge: Cambridge University Press, 2009.

Winzen, Peter. "Treitschke's Influence on the Rise of Imperialist and Anti-British Nationalism in Germany," In *Nationalist and Racialist Movements in Britain and Germany before 1914,* edited by Paul M. Kennedy and Anthony James Nicholls, 154–70. New York: Palgrave Macmillan, 1981.

Wirsing, Giselher, Horst Michael, Ulrich Link, Wolfgang Höpker, Albrecht Haushofer, and New York German Library of Information. *The War in Maps, 1939/40.* New York: German Library of Information, 1941.

Wolfers, Arnold, and Laurence W. Martin. *The Anglo-American Tradition in Foreign Affairs: Readings from Thomas More to Woodrow Wilson.* New Haven, CT: Yale University Press, 1956.

Wright, Quincy. *Human Rights and the World Order.* New York: Commission to Study the Organization of Peace, 1943.

———. *The Study of International Relations.* New York: Appleton-Century-Crofts, 1955.

Yan, Xuetong. *Leadership and the Rise of Great Powers.* Princeton, NJ: Princeton University Press, 2019.

Yost, Charles W. "World Order and American Responsibility." *Foreign Affairs* 47, no. 1 (1968): 1–14.

Zajec, Olivier. *Nicholas John Spykman. L'invention de la géopolitique americaine: Un itineraire intellectual aux origines paradoxales de la théorie realiste des relations internationales.* Paris: Maison de la Recherche, Université Paris-Sorbonne, 2016.

Zambernardi, Lorenzo. "The Impotence of Power: Morgenthau's Critique of American Intervention in Vietnam." *Review of International Studies* 37, no. 3 (July 2011): 1335–56.

Zimmerman, Andrew. *Alabama in Africa: Booker T. Washington, the German Empire, and the Globalization of the New South.* Princeton, NJ: Princeton University Press, 2012.

Zürn, Michael. *A Theory of Global Governance: Authority, Legitimacy, and Contestation.* Oxford: Oxford University Press, 2018.

Index

CPSIA information can be obtained
at www.ICGtesting.com
Printed in the USA
LVHW031918091221
705691LV00002B/7